Heidegger on Death and E

Johannes Achill Niederhauser

Heidegger on Death and Being

An Answer to the Seinsfrage

 Springer

Johannes Achill Niederhauser
Department of Philosophy
Birkbeck College
University of London
London, UK

ISBN 978-3-030-51377-1   ISBN 978-3-030-51375-7   (eBook)
https://doi.org/10.1007/978-3-030-51375-7

This Springer imprint is published by the registered company Springer Nature Switzerland AG
The registered company address is: Gewerbestrasse 11, 6330 Cham, Switzerland

To my parents. Whose ways of being have released and sheltered mine.

Acknowledgements

The present book is the result of a journey that began—if a date can be given—during my days as a degree student of Philosophy, Politics, and Economics in Bolzano. There I came in touch with the thought of Martin Heidegger thanks to Ivo De Gennaro who teaches philosophy at the Free University of Bolzano. But it was not Heidegger the man I was interested in. I was struck by the question of existence, the question of being, the problem of death, and the problem of nihilism. It just so happened that Heidegger is a philosopher who thinks after those questions in a most profound way. I remain grateful to Ivo De Gennaro's sustained support and inspiration to think that he has given me for the better of 10 years now.

While at Bolzano, I took a detour and studied for some time at the University of Washington in Seattle. Thanks to a generous scholarship from the University of Washington and the Italian Government, I was able to spend some time in the Pacific Northwest. In Seattle, I took a course on Kierkegaard taught by Jan Sjavik. I am grateful to him for having introduced me to the thoughts of Kierkegaard, his critique of modernity.

Before I began my PhD studies on the thoughts of Heidegger, I read philosophy at King's College London. During my time in London, I met Ken Gemes whose classes on Nietzsche have helped me gain a sharper understanding of what nihilism means for modernity. I am also grateful to Andrew Huddleston and Simony May, both at Birkbeck, for their sustained support for my work. I would also like to thank my other colleagues at the Birkbeck Philosophy Department for making it such a unique and collegiate environment of learning and teaching.

At Warwick, I was supervised by Miguel de Beistegui who has been a tremendous support and source of inspiration throughout—and beyond—my doctoral studies. I could not have had a better *Doktorvater*, and I am deeply grateful for his philosophical guidance. At Warwick I am also very grateful to Stephen Houlgate and Peter Poellner for their valuable guidance throughout this project.

The thesis, the findings of which are the foundation of this book, was researched and written with the support of a Centre for Arts Doctoral Research Excellence (CADRE) scholarship at Warwick (2015–2018). Part of the research for my thesis was conducted as a doctorate fellow of the "CRC 1015 Otium. Boundaries,

Chronotopes, Practices" at the Albert-Ludwigs-Universität Freiburg (2015), funded by the DFG.

Besides my stay in Freiburg, I am grateful for having been able to attend the *Collegium Phaenomenologicum* in 2017, which has greatly benefited my research on the Heidegger later. Furthermore, I would like to thank the City of Meßkirch and Alfred Denker for having allowed me to stay and work at the Heidegger archives in March 2018.

I would especially like to thank my friend David Ashton for reading the book with me over several months. David's questions have helped me articulate the argument of the book more clearly than I could have been capable of on my own.

I would also like to thank Christopher Coughlin and his editorial team at Springer for their support and guidance during the process of finishing this book.

I am also very grateful for the philosophical friendships and acquaintances I have been allowed to enjoy over the years. In alphabetical order I would like to thank Shaun Berke, Alastair Brook, Kubilai Iksel, Chris Ivins, Bogdan Minca, Justin Murphy, Filip Niklas, Guy Sengstock, Chris Sykes, and Benjamin Varas. Leo Harrington has a special place in my heart for showing me another, most beautiful way of hearing saying thinking.

I am especially thankful to Max Gottschlich for his philosophical support and friendship beyond Academia. Dietmar Koch in Tübingen has also been a great source of inspiration for this book. I am grateful for his support for my work and for his guidance for *die Sache des Denkens*.

My sister, Tina Niederhauser, herself a philosopher, has since her birth been a constant source of joy and support.

Without Birgit's love and faith in me, I could not have finished this project. My deepest thanks to you for guiding me through these—sometimes uncanny—paths.

Abbreviation

References to Heidegger have the following form: GA [volume number]: [page number German version/if available, page number English translation]. If I do not provide a reference to an English translation, I have translated the passage in question myself. Quotes from *Sein und Zeit* have the following form: SZ [page number German Version, Niemeyer Verlag/page number Stambaugh translation.]

Other Abbreviations:

ta: Translation amended
me: My emphasis
n: Footnote

Cited Works from Heidegger

Heidegger, Martin. 1967. *Sein und Zeit*. elfte unveränderte Auflage ed. Tübingen: Max Niemeyer Verlag.
———. 1989. *Überlieferte Sprache und Technische Sprache*. St. Gallen: Erker Verlag.

From the Gesamtausgabe

GA 3 Gesamtausgabe, Vol. 3: *Kant und das Problem der Metaphysik*. F.-W. von Herrmann, ed. Frankfurt am Main: Vittorio Klostermann, 1991.
GA 4 *Gesamtausgabe*, Vol. 4: *Erläuterungen zu Hölderlins Dichtung*. F.-W. von Herrmann, ed. Frankfurt am Main: Vittorio Klostermann, 1981.
GA 5 *Gesamtausgabe*, Vol. 5: *Holzwege*. F.-W. von Herrmann, ed. Frankfurt am Main: Vittorio Klostermann, 1977.
GA 6.1 *Gesamtausgabe*, Vol. 6.1: *Nietzsche I (1936 - 1939)*. B. Schillbach, ed. Frankfurt am Main: Vittorio Klostermann, 1996.
GA 7 *Gesamtausgabe*, Vol. 7: *Vorträge und Aufsätze*. F.-W. von Herrmann, ed. Frankfurt am Main: Vittorio Klostermann, 2000.
GA 8 *Gesamtausgabe*, Vol. 8: *Was heißt Denken?* P.-L. Coriando, ed. Frankfurt am Main: Vittorio Klostermann, 2002.
GA 9 *Gesamtausgabe*, Vol. 9: *Wegmarken*. F.-W. von Herrmann, ed. Frankfurt am Main: Vittorio Klostermann, 1976.

GA 10 *Gesamtausgabe*, Vol. 10: *Der Satz vom Grund*. P. Jaeger, ed. Frankfurt am Main: Vittorio Klostermann, 1997.

GA 11 *Gesamtausgabe*, Vol. 11: *Identität und Differenz*. F.-W. von Herrmann, ed. Frankfurt am Main: Vittorio Klostermann, 2006.

GA 12 *Gesamtausgabe*, Vol. 12: *Unterwegs zur Sprache*. F.-W. von Herrmann, ed. Frankfurt am Main: Vittorio Klostermann, 1985.

GA 13 *Gesamtausgabe*, Vol. 13: *Aus der Erfahrung des Denkens*. H. Heidegger, ed. Frankfurt am Main: Vittorio Klostermann, 1983.

GA 14 *Gesamtausgabe*, Vol. 14: *Zur Sache des Denkens*. F.-W. von Herrmann, ed. Frankfurt am Main: Vittorio Klostermann, 2007.

GA 15 *Gesamtausgabe*, Vol. 15: *Seminare*. C. Ochwadt, ed. Frankfurt am Main: Vittorio Klostermann, 1986.

GA 16 *Gesamtausgabe*, Vol. 16: *Reden und andere Zeugnisse eines Lebensweges*. H. Heidegger, ed. Frankfurt am Main: Vittorio Klostermann, 2000.

GA 20 *Gesamtausgabe*, Vol. 20: *Prolegomena zur Geschichte des Zeitbegriffs*. P. Jaeger, ed. Frankfurt am Main: Vittorio Klostermann, 1979.

GA 22 *Gesamtausgabe*, Vol. 22: *Die Grundbegriffe der antiken Philosophie*. Blust, F.-K., ed. Frankfurt am Main: Vittorio Klostermann, 2004.

GA 25 *Gesamtausgabe*, Vol. 25: *Phänomenologische Interpretation von Kants Kritik der reinen Vernunft*. I. Görland, Frankfurt am Main: Vittorio Klostermann, 1995.

GA 26 *Gesamtausgabe*, Vol. 26: *Metaphysische Anfangsgründe der Logik im Ausgang von Leibniz*. K. Held, ed. Frankfurt am Main: Vittorio Klostermann, 2007.

GA 29/30 *Gesamtausgabe*, Vol. 29-30: *Die Grundbegriffe der Metaphysik: Welt - Endlichkeit - Einsamkeit*. F.-W. von Herrmann, ed. Frankfurt am Main: Vittorio Klostermann, 1983.

GA 32 *Gesamtausgabe*, Vol. 32: *Hegels Phänomenologie des Geistes*. I. Görland, ed. Frankfurt am Main: Vittorio Klostermann, 1997.

GA 33 *Gesamtausgabe*, Vol. 33: *Aristoteles: Metaphysik IX, 1-3*. H. Hüni, ed. Frankfurt am Main: Vittorio Klostermann, 2006.

GA 34 *Gesamtausgabe*, Vol. 34: *Vom Wesen der Wahrheit: Zu Platons Höhlengleichnis und Theätet*. H. Mörchen, ed. Frankfurt am Main: Vittorio Klostermann, 1988.

GA 40 *Gesamtausgabe*, Vol. 40: *Einführung in die Metaphysik*. P. Jaeger, ed. Frankfurt am Main: Vittorio Klostermann, 1983.

GA 45 *Gesamtausgabe*, Vol. 45: *Grundfragen der Philosophie: Ausgewählte "Probleme" der "Logik."* F.-W. von Herrmann, ed. Frankfurt am Main: Vittorio Klostermann, 1984.

GA 54 *Gesamtausgabe*, Vol. 54: *Parmenides*. M. Frings, ed. Frankfurt am Main: Vittorio Klostermann, 1992.

GA 58 *Gesamtausgabe*, Vol. 58: *Grundprobleme der Phänomenologie*. H.-H. Gander, ed. Frankfurt am Main: Vittorio Klostermann, 1993.

GA 65 *Gesamtausgabe*, Vol. 65: *Beiträge zur Philosophie (Vom Ereignis)*. F.-W. von Herrmann, ed. Frankfurt am Main: Vittorio Klostermann, 1989.

GA 67 *Gesamtausgabe*, Vol. 67: *Metaphysik und Nihilismus*. H.-J. Friedrich, ed. Frankfurt am Main: Vittorio Klostermann, 1999.
GA 68 *Gesamtausgabe*, Vol. 68: *Hegel*. I. Schüssler, ed. Frankfurt am Main: Vittorio Klostermann, 1993.
GA 70 *Gesamtausgabe*, Vol. 70: *Über den Anfang*. P.-L. Coriando, ed. Frankfurt am Main: Vittorio Klostermann, 2005.
GA 71 *Gesamtausgabe*, Vol. 71: *Das Ereignis*. F.-W. von Herrmann, ed. Frankfurt am Main: Vittorio Klostermann, 2009.
GA 76 *Gesamtausgabe*, Vol. 76: *Leitgedanken zur Entstehung der Metaphysik, der neuzeitlichen Wissenschaft und der modernen Technik*. C. Strube, ed. Frankfurt am Main: Vittorio Klostermann, 2009.
GA 79 *Gesamtausgabe*, Vol. 79: *Bremer und Freiburger Vorträge*. P. Jaeger, ed. Frankfurt am Main: Vittorio Klostermann, 1994.
GA 81 *Gesamtausgabe*, Vol. 81: *Gedachtes*. P.-L. Coriando, ed. Frankfurt am Main: Vittorio Klostermann, 2007.
GA 89 *Gesamtausgabe*, Vol. 89: *Zollikoner Seminare*. P. Trawny, ed. Frankfurt am Main: Vittorio Klostermann, 2017.
GA 90 *Gesamtausgabe*, Vol. 90: *Zu Ernst Jünger*. P. Trawny, ed. Frankfurt am Main: Vittorio Klostermann, 2004.
GA 97 *Gesamtausgabe*, Vol. 97: *Anmerkungen I-V (Schwarze Hefte 1942-1948)*. Peter Trawny, ed. Frankfurt am Main: Vittorio Klostermann, 2015.
Heidegger, Martin. 1999. Das Sein (Ereignis). In *Heidegger Studies, Vol. 15, Renewal of Philosophy, Questions of Theology, and Being-Historical Thinking*, 9–15. Berlin: Duncker & Humblot GmbH.

Translations of Heidegger

Heidegger, Martin. 1968. *What Is Called Thinking?* Trans. F. D. Wieck and J. Glenn Gray. New York: Harper & Row.
———. 1971a. *On the Way to Language*. Trans. Peter D. Hertz. New York: Harper & Row.
———. 1971b. *Poetry, Language, Thought*. Trans. Albert Hofstadter. New York: Harper & Row.
———. 1974. *Identity and Difference*. Trans. Joan Stambaugh. New York: Harper Torchbooks.
———. 1975. *Early Greek Thinking*. Trans. D. F. Krell and F. A. Capuzzi. New York: Harper & Row.
———. 1977. *The Question Concerning Technology and Other Essays*. Trans. William Lovitt. New York: Harper & Row.
———. 1985. *History of the Concept of Time: Prolegomena*. Trans. Theodore Kisiel. Bloomington: Indiana University Press.
———. 1988. *Hegel's Phenomenology of Spirit*. Trans. P. Emad and K. May. Bloomington: Indiana University Press.
———. 1990. *Kant and the Problem of Metaphysics*. Trans. Richard Taft. Bloomington: Indiana University Press.

————. 1991. *Nietzsche, Volume I: The Will to Power and Art*. Trans. D. F. Krell. New York: Harper & Row.

————. 1992. *Parmenides*. Trans. A. Schuwer and R. Rojcewicz. Bloomington and Indianapolis: Indiana University Press.

————. 1995a. *Aristotle's Metaphysics Θ 1-3: On the Essence and Actuality of Force*. Trans. W. Brogan and P. Warnek. Bloomington: Indiana University Press.

————. 1995b. *The Fundamental Concepts of Metaphysics: World, Finitude, Solitude*. Trans. W. McNeill and N. Walke. Bloomington: Indiana University Press.

————. 1996a. *Being and Time*. Trans. Joan Stambaugh. Albany: New York State University Press.

————. 1996b. *The Principle of Reason*. Trans. Reginald Lilly. Bloomington: Indiana University Press.

————. 1998. In *Pathmarks*, ed. William McNeill. Cambridge: Cambridge University Press.

————. 2000a. *Elucidations of Hölderlin's Poetry*. Trans. Keith Hoeller. New York: Humanity Books.

————. 2000b. *Introduction to Metaphysics*. Trans. G. Fried and R. Polt. New Haven: Yale University Press.

————. 2001. *Zollikon Seminars: Protocols – Conversations – Letters*. Trans. Franz Mayr and Richard Askay. Evanston: Northwestern University Press.

————. 2002a. *Off the Beaten Track*. Trans. J. Young and K. Haynes. Cambridge: Cambridge University Press.

————. 2002b. *The Essence of Truth: On Plato's Cave Allegory and Theaetetus*. Trans. Ted Sadler. London: Continuum.

————. 2009a. *The Event*. Trans. Richard Rojcewicz. Bloomington and Indianapolis: Indiana University Press.

————. 2009b. *The Heidegger Reader*. Trans. J. Veith. Bloomington: Indiana University Press.

————. 2012a. *Bremen and Freiburg Lectures: Insight into That Which Is and Basic Principles of Thinking*. Trans. A. J. Mitchell. Bloomington: Indiana University Press.

————. 2012b. *Contributions to Philosophy*. Trans. Richard Rojcewicz and Daniela Vallega-Neu. Bloomington: Indiana University Press.

————. 2015. *Hegel*. Trans. J. Arel and N. Feuerhahn. Bloomington: Indiana University Press.

Introduction

ταὐτό τ᾽ ἔνι ζῶν καὶ τεθνηκὸς καὶ [τὸ] ἐγρηγορὸς καὶ καθεῦδον καὶ νέον καὶ γηραιόν·
τάδε γὰρ μεταπεσόντα ἐκεῖνά ἐστι κἀκεῖνα πάλιν μεταπεσόντα ταῦτα
    – Heraclitus DK B88

Exposition of the Question

What, today, of death? Are we at all perplexed by the fact that we die, that we are mortal? Or are we rather rushing away from our mortality? Our mortality seems to be the most obvious fact of all. After all, logic has long since been using the proposition "all men are mortal" as a standard example of the syllogism: all men are mortal, Socrates is a man, therefore Socrates is mortal (cf. Demske 1970: 1). The concept of "man" always already contains the predicate "mortal". *That* man is mortal is obvious. But do we encounter death as something obvious, something almost benign as the syllogism example seems to suggest? Or do we rather encounter death as something uncanny and unknown? The obviousness with which death is encountered here might hence cover over something crucial. The abstraction of mortality, which serves to prove the validity of the logic of the syllogism, abstracts away from death—from our death that we each have to die. Perhaps this indicates that death has become an abstract problem for us, which as such can and must be solved. Consequently, Harari and Kahnemann confirm in a conversation that "death is optional" (Harari and Kahnemann 2015, published online). In the same conversation, Harari points out that "[d]eath has been relocated from the metaphysical realm to the technical realm". For transhumanism death has become but a technical problem to be resolved by instrumental rationality. Here death is no longer, to borrow Goethe's expression, threefold separation "not hoping ever to meet again" (Goethe 1874: 165), which speaks to the pain and helplessness humans confront when a loved one dies. Here death is simply something to choose or not choose from a catalogue. Is such a technical response a humane response or do they already echo another non-human dimension? Are they not already signs of the replacement of the human-ethical with the epistemic-rational?

What are the "solutions" posthumanism offers? Biohacking and bio-enhancement want to lure us into believing that the limitations of the human body can be eradicated at will. The human body can be enhanced by machine parts. Some suggest that it is possible to dispose of the body *qua* prison of the flesh entirely by uploading copies of selves to the cloud. The aim here is digital immortality. In the cloud, the laws of physics and biology no longer apply. The mind is perfectly free to choose at any time any virtual body it desires. If anything, death is but a necessary evil, a passageway to a better, fuller life without limitations, a life of absolute negative freedom in the digital sphere. Here death is not something that pushes us back into our existence and our possibilities. Instead, death is but something to be overcome and something that does not concern us, at best death here only concerns us insofar as it serves as a passageway towards a better "life", some enlightened and liberated state. Of course, it remains questionable whether notions such as "liberation" and "freedom" even make sense in such a world.

And still, we are mortal. Still human beings die every day and if we follow Heraclitus, then new death is born every day. Why this shying away from death? Whence this groundless abstraction and even failure to face up to this "problem" that death is for our existence and being? What is the concealed history which motivates some to dream up transhumanist techno-fantasies of digital immortality in this particular epoch—the epoch we call modernity, the epoch of technology? Is it not death itself that drives all of these endeavours? Those who wish to eradicate death, who already call death "optional", are still bound and driven by the horizon death constitutes. The meaning of their projects originates precisely from what they want to control. They want to be "im-mortal", yet is there im-mortality without mortality? Put differently, even if some version of fantasised im-mortality were technologically achievable, would it not rest on being mortal and eternally be in opposition to mortality? Our mortality, then, is not a source of meaninglessness, but a source of meaning. Yet, how we respond to death and to our mortality and finitude seems to be pivotal. The assumed technical controllability of death amounts to little more than the fantasies of subjectivity at its utmost extreme trying to cling on to absolute certainty. Is not transhumanism collectively the fantasies of the inflated (post-) modern[1] subject that assumes to be capable to posit itself as the ultimate foundation of beings. Do we not resort to various fantasies regarding our desired subjective immortality, for we are utterly unwilling to face our death? These escapist fantasies, however, indicate and at once cover over a certain need. In fact, they indicate the need to consider more profoundly the question of death in a way that does not escape death, but rather in a way that confronts death and in a way that is thus neither technological nor purely metaphysical. It is striking that the technological responses to death are rather similar to some of metaphysics' responses, if by "metaphysics" we mean some sort of supersensual world. Transhumanism tries to

---

[1] For Heidegger the *modern* subject makes itself the ground of all beings *qua* objectivity. This revolt against being is concluded by the post-modern subject, I would argue, which not only makes itself the ground of all beings but also considers itself to be perfectly transmutable at will.

justify and overcome the cosmic "evil" of death, the perceived "screaming injustice" that such a noble creature as man is bound to die and thus ultimately utterly powerless. Death is here but a passageway and both "solutions" speculate or even calculate what comes after death.

If there is one philosopher, not just of the twentieth century, but of the whole of the history of Western philosophy, who substantially devoted his thinking to death, then this philosopher is Martin Heidegger. In fact, we find in Heidegger one of the most profound and most enduring engagements with questions concerning mortality, finitude, and death. In *Das Ereignis* (*The Event*), a text written from the perspective of the history of being, Heidegger writes that "[w]e devastate the abyssal … event-related essence of death if we seek to calculate what might be 'after' it. Thereby we degrade death to a null passageway" (Heidegger GA 71: 194/165).[2] The technological fantasies of transhumanism essentially see death as a passageway. Moreover, religious responses to mortality and death see death as a passageway. Heidegger's thought, however, is devoted to a thinking of death that is neither metaphysical nor technological. Death is central to Heidegger's thought precisely because death here comes into focus in a radically different way. One could say that death comes into focus in its own right.

The core argument of this book is thus twofold. First, death is central to Heidegger's thinking path. I argue that the question of being can only be asked in light of death. We might expect death to be significant in Heidegger's seemingly more existential endeavours in *Being and Time*. Nevertheless, I attempt to show that death remains of key importance far beyond the analytic of Dasein. I shall hence argue that death is pivotal for Heidegger's entire thinking path. Second, this means that one can articulate a response to the question of being, Heidegger's "unique question" (GA 65: 10/11)[3]—as manifold as this question is along the thinking path—if one takes death into consideration at every major step of the thinking path. In the *Contributions to Philosophy*, Heidegger hence even goes as far as calling death the "highest testimony to beyng" (GA 65: 230/181). I take this to be definitive for his philosophy as a whole. By explicating death's fundamental role, I thus attempt to formulate a response to the question of being and that also means to the historical situation we are in and how the history of being moves. As any access to being is temporally structured, my attempt at a response to the *Seinsfrage*, of course, "cannot lie in an isolated and blind proposition", as Heidegger puts it in *Being and Time* (SZ: 19/18).[4] Thus, the response to the question of being here emerges as the argument develops. For the sake of clarity, I should now point out that my response shows death to be a primary entry point into Heidegger's manifold ways of approaching the question of being. This is why this book follows the development of the thinking path. This book should thus also be helpful for those interested in the unity of Heidegger's thought.

---

[2] Translation by Richard Rojcewicz.

[3] Translation by Richard Rojcewicz and Daniela Vallega-Neu.

[4] *Sein und Zeit* abbreviated as SZ. Translated by Joan Stambaugh.

The Structure

In my view there are four major themes in Heidegger's thinking path. These are not random but display four interrelated approaches to the question of being: (1) the existential-ontological and transcendental analytic of Dasein; (2) the thinking of *Ereignis*; (3) the question concerning technology and the world as fourfold; (4) language and more specifically poetry.

Following the thinking path, the structure of the book is as follows. Part I engages with the phenomenon of death in the context of Dasein's fundamental ontology. *Being and Time* is the main focus here, but I also consult surrounding texts from Heidegger's time in Marburg and from his early years in Freiburg. Part I argues that death brings Dasein before being. On the one hand, being is here the understandable disclosedness and presence of beings, a presence which, however, withdraws from focus. On the other hand, being is the being of Dasein insofar as being cares for its own being in its everyday existence. In the analytic of Dasein, Death is Dasein's utmost limit and as such death co-constitutes Dasein's horizon of understanding. Thus, Dasein can at all project possibilities of existence and can at all take issue with its own being and understand what it means to be because it is mortally finite. Moreover, Dasein is closest to being, which is an issue for Dasein, when Dasein authentically takes over its ownmost possibility, death. By facing death, Dasein realises the withdrawal of its own being, for death means the impossibility of Dasein's being. This pushes Heidegger to think being itself as abeyant possibility.

Part II begins with the reconstruction of the so-called *Kehre*, "the turn" in Heidegger's thinking. Simply put, the turn means Heidegger moves away from *Being and Time*'s indirect, transcendental approach to being towards an attempt to think being directly *as Ereignis*, where the "as" indicates the realm out of which being is thought. I develop my reconstruction by focussing on Heidegger's radicalisation of the movement of truth as ἀλήθεια, which he presents in a lecture course on Plato's Cave Analogy. The main body of Part II then explicates the role death plays in the thinking of *Ereignis*. The main texts of interest here are the *Contributions to Philosophy* and *The Event*, both published posthumously. Parts I and II serve as the foundation for the rest of the book since they reconstruct the transition from *Being and Time* as a text steeped in metaphysics to Heidegger's unique being-historical (*seinsgeschichtlich*) approach to being. The tension between metaphysics and history of being, I claim, does not leave Heidegger's thought after the turn, but rather continues to drive it. I shall argue here that death is central to a proper and sound understanding of both the *Ereignis* as the realm where being and human beings encounter each other. Hence a sound understanding of the role of death in the texts on *Ereignis* is also crucial for a sound understanding of the movement of the history of being—the history of simultaneous withdrawal and coming-into-presence. Death, I shall show, is the locus of being's withdrawal.

Part III investigates Heidegger's writings on technology and looks at the relation between death and technology. In this part, I aim to show that death harbours the distinct possibility to overcome *Gestell*. Heidegger refers to death as the *Gebirg* of being by the time he engages with questions concerning technology. As the *Gebirg* of being death is the gathering of all *bergen* (sheltering, recovering, concealing) and also of ἀλήθεια as *Ent-bergung* (un-concealment). The mode of *bergen* is aware that any disclosing is simultaneously a covering over. *Stellen*, in turn, is the prevalent mode of technology, and *stellen*, positioning, forgets that all disclosure means simultaneous concealment. *Gestell* wants to position everything everywhere at any time in perfect presence and availability. In technology, positioning takes the upper hand. Nevertheless, the sheltering mode of disclosure, *bergen*, is still possible precisely because death utterly defies control and positioning. Hence, Part III in a nutshell argues that Heidegger sees in death a prime possibility to dismantle the power of technology. In the light of his critique of technology, Heidegger begins to develop the fourfold as a possibility to overcome technology. In the writings on the fourfold (*Geviert*) Heidegger begins to call human beings "mortals", for they need to face death in order to provide a way out of *Gestell*.

In Part IV, I further develop the possibility of overcoming technology in the light of poetry. Poetic language provides a path towards the fourfold, a world where technology does not rule over us, because, as Heidegger claims, there is an "essential relation [*Wesensverhältnis*] between death and language … [which] remains still unthought" (GA 12: 203/107).[5] Part IV develops this "unthought" relation from within the thinking path.

Memento Mori

Before I begin to explicate the role of death, I would like to address claims that Heidegger's philosophy of death amounts to little more than antihuman pessimism. Givsan, for example, claims Heidegger is an inhumane philosopher because of the importance Heidegger places on death in *Being and Time* (cf. Givsan 2011). To be sure, Givsan maintains that Heidegger's is a "*Denken der Inhumanität*—thinking of inhumanity", as though what Heidegger is after with the focus on death is really a project of dehumanisation. With death as a constitutive trait of Dasein, maintains Givsan, Dasein must of necessity be *supposed to* die. The sooner Dasein dies the better, Givsan claims. Givsan admits that Heidegger rules out suicide (cf. Givsan 2011: 103, 170). Yet, Givsan does not buy that Heidegger's analysis of Dasein's death is purely ontological, thus only related to the question, *what it is to be*, but not a moral or ethical endeavour.

Of course, one could point out against Givsan that human beings are mortal beings and that human beings—throughout the ages and across various cultures and civilisations—have thought of themselves as mortal beings, often in opposition to gods. Heidegger's appreciation of death is a reformulation of *memento mori* for modern times. He warns us against being blinded by hubris and assuming that finite human beings have now reached absolute power and the end of history, where

---

[5] Translation by Peter D. Hertz.

everything that is can be manipulated and dominated at will. This is not a moral, but an ontological warning. What is at stake is the being of beings. The question is whether all beings are just manipulable objects of use for the all-controlling and all-consuming subject deluding itself to be the centre of history or whether beings are allowed to be on their own accord. Instead of a crude, misanthropic pessimism, Luther's and Kierkegaard's formulation of the *memento mori* is in the background of Heidegger's analysis of death, as George Pattison stresses in his recent study of death in Heidegger (cf. Pattison 2016: 83). Death brings us before the simplicity of existence, which we participate in but which we certainly do not control. Heidegger's focus on death and mortality is not at all "inhumane", except, of course, if our mortality is inhumane. Heidegger stands in the tradition of, among others, Socrates, Augustine, Luther, Hegel, and Kierkegaard. For them, our mortality is so fundamentally human that one has to wonder whether our current ignorance of our mortality, the attempts to eradicate mortality scientifically, might not itself be of a great inhumaneness. Is human hubris not rampant in an epoch that assumes that everything can at will be controlled at any time and place? Heidegger wishes to confront this hubris of modern man by his sustained focus on mortality. Heidegger's *memento mori* aims to show us once more how fragile we are in the face of one of the oldest questions: the question of being. By regarding death as integral to our existence, we begin to appreciate our existence. "*Dasein* never [merely] perishes" (SZ: 247/238), as Heidegger writes in *Being and Time*, because death is at Dasein's core. Instead, human beings *die*, and they die, for they are mortal and finite beings, dwelling on the earth and bound by the earth. In an age rampant with human self-aggrandisement, death reminds us of our place in the world. We are neither the centre of history nor the measure of all things. Rather, we are in the midst of beings.

Heidegger's teacher, Husserl, on the other hand, levels the exact opposite accusation against Heidegger's analysis of death in *Being and Time*. While Givsan sees Heidegger's interpretation of death at the heart of Heidegger's "inhumaneness", Husserl does not accuse Heidegger of reducing human beings to mortality. Instead, Husserl argues that Heidegger reduces the peril of death: "The dazzling, profound ways in which Heidegger tackles death will hardly prove acceptable to death" (Husserl 1985: 332).[6] In my view, Husserl's interpretation fails to see the true meaning of death for Heidegger's thought. Neither does Heidegger reduce existence to death, nor does he try to tackle or domesticate death. Rather, death is welcomed into existence, not as domesticated and tamed, but as a mystery of our existence.

Other Studies of Death in Heidegger

If I am right to assume that the problem of death is central to Heidegger's thinking path, then it should be fair to assume that there is an abundant amount of commentary on the subject. There have been several studies of death in Heidegger in recent

---

[6] As quoted by Tanja Staehler (2016: 207).

years. Yet, these studies mostly deal with *Being and Time* or are comparative studies.[7] A welcome exception is Raj Singh's book on *Heidegger, World, and Death* (cf. Singh 2013). Singh argues that world and death are intimately related in Heidegger's thought, that there is world only because of death as utmost limit that gives rise to a meaningful horizon. I shall argue along similar lines in Part I and to some degree also in Part IV in regard to the fourfold. Singh's book looks at some of the most important texts of Heidegger's thought and finds death to be key precisely because death co-constitutes the world of human beings. However, Singh's interpretation suffers from his neglecting the full impact of the "turning" of concealment-unconcealment in Heidegger's later thought and which role plays here. Singh does not properly address the thinking of *Ereignis* without which Heidegger's diagnosis of technology and his writings on the fourfold and language are not fully appreciated. Thus, Singh does not regard core texts concerned with the thinking of *Ereignis* and the crucial role death plays there. Hence, Singh's analysis regards all of the later texts from the perspective of Dasein but not in terms of the *Ereignis*. Singh's argument is diametrically opposed to the Dreyfusian reading of Heidegger on death. From slightly different angles, Blattner (1994) and more recently Thomson (2013) have argued that death means something like world collapse. According to their readings, death is not constitutive of Dasein's world. Their interpretations of death also focus exclusively on *Being and Time*. Regarding Heidegger's later philosophy, both Oberst and Agamben have each in their own way devoted an entire study to Heidegger's claim that there is an "essential relation between death and language". I shall address their studies in Part IV. Pattison's (2016) recent theological essay on Heidegger also focuses on both Being and Time and the later works by Heidegger. Pattison here attempts to show the roots of Heidegger's philosophy of death in the theological thought of Kierkegaard and Luther. Pattison's study also tends to recur to *Being and Time* as a main reference for the later texts.

To this date, there has been only one major study on the phenomenon of death that considers the whole of Heidegger's philosophy and respects the turn: James Demske's *Being, Man, and Death: A Key to Heidegger* published in 1970. Even though Demske did not have access to texts like *Contributions* and *The Event*, he is able to show that death plays a key role for the whole of Heidegger's philosophy. Demske's remarkable study looks at the same major issues of the thinking path as do I. Demske's crucial insight is that from the beginning the question of being is intimately related with death: "Death plays a subsidiary, yet necessary, role in the work of Heidegger" (Demske 1970: 2). He also argues that "[d]eath is the key to Heidegger's turning" (Demske 1970: 190). As outlined above, I shall critically qualify Demske's first claim. Death is not subsidiary to the question of being. Death is at the heart of Heidegger's formulation of the question of being. Thus, death is central to the question of being, and we can only ask the question because we are

---

[7] Comparative studies of the phenomenon of death in Heidegger include: Havi Carel, *Life and Death in Freud and Heidegger* (2006); Tina Chanter, *Time, Death, and the Feminine: Levinas with Heidegger* (2002); Brent Adkins, *Death and Desire in Hegel, Heidegger and Deleuze* (2007); Françoise Dastur, *Death: An Essay on Finitude* (1996).

mortal. How we understand death in Heidegger fundamentally determines our understanding of the question of being.

For all its merits Demske's study shows a profound misunderstanding of the implications of the turn. Demske rightly stresses that after the turn Heidegger tries to think being directly. To my mind, however, Demske fundamentally misreads the turn when he asserts that "[t]he turning in Heidegger's thought is *(a)* a change of perspective, in which the focus moves from the transcendence of Dasein to being as the horizon of this transcendence, and *(b)* a change in the relation between being and Dasein, in which being assumes the role of ontological primacy in the process of transcendence" (Demske 1970: 91). Being is precisely not a horizon after the turn. One should also point out that being is not a horizon even in the analytic of Dasein. The very term horizon only makes sense for a projecting subject. Heidegger's attempt to think being directly means something else, and Part II of this book attempts a reconstruction of this thinking. As a consequence of this, what I take to be a misreading of the turn, Demske tends to fall back on *Being and Time* when he discusses *Gestell*, the fourfold, and the relation between death and language. Demske does consider, what he refers to as "the event (*Ereignis*) of being" (Demske 1970: 145). Yet, he does not explicate in enough detail the thinking of the event in its own right. In his later thought, Heidegger, however, finds genuine new ways of thinking being, language, and death, which we fail to notice, if we misread the meaning of the turn. I shall argue in Parts I and II that the "turn", or rather the "turning", in Heidegger's thinking begins precisely with the problem that horizonal transcendence poses to thinking being directly: transcendence introduces an element of subjectivity. But this is precisely what Heidegger wishes to get away from in order to think being and its history directly.

Contents

Part I
Sum Moribundus Death as Possibility

Abstract The first part introduces Heidegger's question of being as a question that is possible for Dasein to ask because of Dasein's relationship with death. The focus of the first part are Heidegger's early writings. By early writings I mean Heidegger's endeavours of an analytic of Dasein, which was supposed to bring about a funda-mental ontology for all sciences. Hence *Being and Time* is here the central text, but I also work in other relevant texts of this period of the 1920s in which Heidegger's focus was on Dasein. These texts include the *History of the Concept of Time*, *Fundamental Concepts of Metaphysics*, and *What is Metaphysics?* On the existential-ontological level I argue that it is for Dasein's directedness towards its death as its utmost limit that the world of Dasein arises. For world is the horizon against which beings appear as meaningful for Dasein. On the ecstatic-temporal level I argue that it is again Dasein's directedness towards its death that gives rise to the primacy of the future. However, the core argument of this part is that it is in the analytic of death where Heidegger makes the experience that being is always already withdrawing, that there is withdrawal in all presence.

Keywords *Seinsfrage* · Question of being · Heidegger · *Being and Time* · Sein und Zeit · Phenomenology · Mortality · Dasein · Existential ontology · Ecstatic temporality

Introduction

As is well known the prologue of *Being and Time* begins with a quote from Plato's *Sophist*. The quote reads: "We … who used to think we understood [the expression being], have now become perplexed." (SZ: 1/xxix) Heidegger maintains that we, *today*, are in a similar situation as Plato and his contemporaries. We are not, says Heidegger, in any way thematically wiser when it comes to our understanding of the meaning of being. This short note is decisive not just for *Being and Time*, but also for Heidegger's thought beyond this foundational text. Yet, Heidegger here also points out that we are in a much more precarious situation today than Plato because at least the Ancient Greeks were perplexed by the question of being. We today do not even seem to be bothered by this question. Being has been forgotten is the grand claim. The task Heidegger hence sets for *Being and Time* is to "reawaken an understanding for the meaning of this question." (ibid.)

This is necessary because of modernity's reductive understanding of being that is, according to Heidegger, to a large degree formed by the Cartesian dictum *cogito sum*. This dictum is one of the defining moments of modernity because Descartes here places the self-referential subject at the centre of the world, the ground of beings *qua* objects and in opposition to its world. In simplified terms, the Cartesian dictum encloses the subject and disconnects it from its world. To Heidegger all of modern philosophy is incapable of overcoming Cartesianism, which is what he shall attempt with the analytic of Dasein. Descartes's dictum presupposes the meaning of the little word "*sum*" as given The meaning of being is not questioned any further. Thus, the dictum fails to address the question of being (cf. SZ: 24/23) and hence the responses to his dictum also fail to address the meaning of being. Heidegger does not presuppose the meaning of being as given, as Descartes appears to do. Instead, Heidegger specifically asks for the meaning of being for Dasein and from early on he does so in view of death.

Thus, we find in Heidegger's lecture course on *The History of the Concept of Time: Prolegomena* from 1925, a response to the Cartesian *cogito sum* that is decisive not only for the project of *Being and Time*, but also for Heidegger's entire thinking path. Heidegger's response to Descartes reads as follows:

> If such pointed formulations mean anything at all, then the appropriate statement pertaining to Dasein in its being would have to be *sum moribundus* ["I am in dying"], *moribundus* not as someone gravely ill or wounded, but insofar as I am, I am *moribundus*. *The* MORIBUNDUS *first gives the* SUM *its sense [Sinn].* (GA 20: 437f/317)[1]

It is crucial to see that Heidegger here does not wish to exaggerate. Where Descartes had simply assumed the meaning of being and even presupposed being (and its ramifications), Heidegger clearly states that the *Sinn*, meaning and sense, of being originates from Dasein's ontological relationship with its death. For Heidegger this relationship is the only true certainty of Dasein's existence. More precisely, the "certainty" which Heidegger has in mind is only the certainty of the possibility of a total and sudden withdrawal. The ego does not posit the "sum", the ego's being, by thinking of itself, as Descartes suggests. Rather, death posits the ego's being. The "*cogito sum* is only the semblance [of a genuine statement of Dasein]." (ibid.) *Sinn*, then, as will be shown in this part, arises for Dasein from a limit situation that at once encircles and frees Dasein. This limit situation is Dasein and it is *thanks to* this very limit that the question for the *sense* of being can at all be asked.

Hence, I shall argue that from early on Heidegger sees a profound connection between being—which in *Being and Time* primarily means Dasein's *understanding* of being—and death. Moreover, I shall show that Dasein's very possibility to ask the

---

[1] <Footnote ID="Fn1"><Para ID="Par8">Translated by Theodore Kisiel.</Para></Footnote>

question of being arises directly from Dasein's ontological relationship with its death. Dasein can ask the question of being and Dasein's being is an issue for it because Dasein is fundamentally directed towards its death. This is why Heidegger calls death Dasein's "*ownmost* possibility" (SZ: 263/252) in *Being and Time*.

The short passage from the *Prolegomena* epitomises Heidegger's early philosophical project. He specifically addresses the question of being in existential terms because the Cartesian dictum reduces *being* to the existential dimension of the subject. In order to free being *as such*, the being of the human being needs to be freed from the narrow subjective perspective. As long as modernity does not get over the Cartesian dictum, the question of being cannot be asked meaningfully and directly. This is why the first articulation of the *Seinsfrage* needs to be asked in relation to a being (*ein Seiendes*) called Dasein, for whom its being is an issue. The being called Dasein is, in turn, not primarily a self-referential cognising entity, not a *res cogitans*. Instead, Dasein is an attuned structure that is as such always already in the world. Dasein derives its meaning not from self-reflection, from thinking of and about itself, but from its death insofar as death lets Dasein *transcend* and move out there into the world in the first place. For Dasein *is directed towards death as its utmost— äußerst, most out there—limit* whence Dasein receives its meaning. For it is at the outermost where Dasein begins. From this very directedness and from Dasein's transcending movement world arises, for world is, as Max Müller puts it, "[o]ntologically seen … always the emergence [*Aufgang*] of being." (Müller 1964: 109).[2] Thus, death *qua* Dasein's limit co-constitutes Dasein's world and as such brings Dasein most radically before Dasein's authentic understanding of being.

This is of direct import for the most profound claim of Heidegger's philosophy, a project that sustains his thought until the end: the transformation of the human being. By transformation Heidegger means the possibility of overcoming the subject-object-dichotomy prevalent today in form of a crude subjectivism that lets the subject assume it has the power to create both itself and the world according to its desires. The analytic of Dasein, and especially the chapters on death, form Heidegger's response to that challenge of modernity. His approach is to show that Dasein is always already *in* the world and thrown *into* it. Thus, Dasein does not make itself but has to accept itself and its finite ways of being. In the early philosophy Heidegger shows that the subject is an ontological narrowing and reduction of Dasein, of existence itself. In his post-war philosophy Heidegger begins to call human beings simply "mortals." Thus, the early transformation is meant to push the subject back into its world, into its authentic possibilities, and back into its relationship with others. In the post-war texts on technology, the fourfold and dwelling, which I shall consider in Parts III and IV of this book, Heidegger speaks of communities of mortals. Thus, the ultimate transformation, or liberation, of the human being, which Heidegger appears to have in mind, is to become properly mortal.

The purpose of the first part of this book then is to explicate Heidegger's early attempt at the question of being and its relation to death. Therefore, I analyse

---

[2] <Footnote ID="Fn2"><Para ID="Par12">My translation.</Para></Footnote>

Dasein's understanding of being in light of Dasein's ownmost possibility, death. I read *Being and Time* as Dasein's transcendental self-investigation and self-foundation. I draw inspiration for this approach from Karl Cardinal Lehmann's PhD thesis on Heidegger, which was written in the 1960s, but published only in 2003. Lehmann argues that in *Being and Time* Dasein assumes itself as its own hypothesis and begins to investigate itself *fundamentally*. The text aims to establish a proper and full fundamental ontology of existence, rather than the curtailed ontology of modernity. Fundamental ontology then serves as the foundation for more specific ontologies such as anthropology, biology, and psychology. In order to do so Dasein must ask what it *authentically* is: "Dasein wants to get to know itself in its being in order to "ground" itself." (Lehmann 2003: 237) As Dasein gets to know its structures, its relationships with others, beings, and being and world the transformation of the human being is initiated. This transformation is to guide the human being out of subjectivism, and this means that Dasein becomes itself: "Dasein, as itself, has to *become*, that is, *be*, what it is not yet." (SZ: 243/234) The investigation is transcendental insofar as Dasein always already *is* and knows *that* it is. Dasein cannot get beyond this "that" (cf. SZ: 42/41f). Nevertheless, *Being and Time* scrutinises and explicates the "that" of Dasein's being by investigating Dasein's understanding of being precisely because Dasein is not something present-at-hand. That Dasein has to explicate its "that" also emphasises the performativity of being. This is possible, first, because of Dasein's ecstatic ways of being, i.e., because Dasein *stands out* into the world. Second, this is possible because Dasein's being is an issue for it, i.e., Dasein can begin to investigate "that" it exists. The expression that Dasein "*transcends*" means that it can separate itself from its ordinary modes of being. The ontic is the foundation for the ontological, insofar as the investigation begins not in the abstract but with where and how Dasein finds itself in its world, while doing something as seemingly benign as using a hammer. The question could arise, why Heidegger attempts a response to the question of being by the apparent detour around some entity called Dasein. Yet, this detour is necessary precisely because of the Cartesian dictum that to a certain degree narrowed being down to the being of the subject. Before properly and directly approaching being as such, a peculiar being, *Seiendes*, called Dasein, has to be reconnected with its world and being, *Sein*, as a question. This initial investigation is transcendental because Dasein gets to know its *a priori* necessary conditions for the possibility of experience. These conditions are not abstract but emerge from Dasein's structures. Heidegger's transcendental approach specifically asks for the being of beings, more precisely, Heidegger asks for the way in which beings are disclosed and hence become meaningful phenomena. This transcendental philosophy can ask for being, *Sein*, precisely because its presupposition is a peculiar being, *Seiendes*, Dasein, which as the "there" of being can ask what and how beings *are*. In order for Dasein to get to know itself and its being, the ontic-ontological difference must be presupposed. In a nutshell, this transcendental philosophy not only includes the conditions of the possibility of experience, but also the condition of these conditions: Dasein. Yet, in contrast to, say, Fichte's subject, Dasein does not posit itself. Rather, Dasein is "posited" by being, put differently, Dasein is thrown. In sum, *Being and Time* thus aims at a transcendental unity of ontology and *existence*.

The structure of this part is as follows: The first chapter briefly summarises what I take to be misunderstandings of the meaning of death in Heidegger's existential philosophy. The second chapter addresses the necessity of the question of being. The third chapter analyses Dasein's temporality. The fourth chapter develops Heidegger's problematic notion of possibility in light of death and in view of his later interpretation of being itself as possibility. I will show that Heidegger's initial analysis of death as Dasein's ownmost possibility is what leads him to conceptualise being as pure possibility outside the Aristotelian schema of *potentiality* and *actuality*. The fifth chapter addresses birth and Dasein's historicity and points out the trajectory of the history of being that begins here. Part II will further develop the history of being. The sixth and final chapter of this part summarises early signs of the so-called "turn" in Heidegger's philosophy and what role death plays there.

It may also be helpful to point out which critical hermeneutical principle, as it were, I here adhere to. The ordinary story is that there are two possibilities to read Heidegger. On the one hand, one could engage in a backward reading of *Being and Time* showing how Heidegger's late works can help us reach a better understanding of Being and Time. On the other hand, a forward reading of the thinking path where *Being and Time* initiates (of course, not in linear or causal sense) many of the ideas of Heidegger's later philosophy. Those would be two standard assumptions of how one is to read Heidegger, following the narrow understanding of the so-called "turning" (I shall say more on this in Part II). What I suggest is something in-between. In fact, *Being and Time* does of course serve as an initiation, as the ignition of Heidegger's thinking path—by which I also mean that Heidegger here begins to see structures of being and of the forgetting of being which he cannot respond to continuing on the trajectory he had been on since his time in Marburg. But of course, this does not mean that we need to read Heidegger in a linear fashion. In fact, it would be rather ironic and myopic to read Heidegger in a linear fashion so with the thinker who saw the possibility of *Seinsgeschichte* and the simultaneity of Dasein's temporal ecstasies. So, of course, and this is in line with the hermeneutic circle and the ecstatic temporality of Dasein, reading later texts of Heidegger (again without the understanding of "history" as a mere linear process) discloses dimensions in the gist of *Being and Time* which would have remained concealed without the later texts. Just as Heidegger himself reads the "history" of philosophy *anew* and searches in these texts another beginning. None of this is to suggest that Heidegger simply continues the project of *Being and Time*. He fundamentally does not. Yet, the *later* Heidegger of the *Ereignis* and of *Seinsgeschichte* is born with *Being and Time* and the possibilities and impossibilities, the paths and impasses this text opens up. None of this is to suggest that there are not critical developments after *Being and Time*. In fact, I hold to the view that the later Heidegger is a radically different thinker than the early Heidegger. Nonetheless, *both* the earlier and the later Heidegger are obviously not possible without each other.

Overall the first part argues that it is in fact by way of ontological death that the openness of being comes is disclosed. In Davos Heidegger explicitly states that death is introduced in *Being and Time* as a marker for the radical *futurity*, toward-structure of Dasein (cf. GA 3: 283/177).[3] I will return to this in further detail below in my account of Dasein's ecstatic temporality. But note for now that Heidegger explicitly connects Dasein's ontological death with ecstatic temporality and the ecstasy of the future, which is in fact that which opens up being in its openness. If the *future* (as that which is to come) is where we find being in its openness, then death as that *towards* which Dasein is as soon as Dasein is, is in fact a necessary condition for disclosing being in its very openness. A necessary condition that cannot be ignored. At the heart of the text is, in my view, the analysis of death precisely because Dasein here comes into closest contact with its most authentic understanding of being and hence it is here that being most authentically opens up—and this is not meant on some individual level but on the level of Dasein as the *being* of the human being, the horizon in which all humans participate. Hence, I will also later in the book argue that there is a deep connection between death and ἀλήθεια, which Heidegger articulates in later texts.[4] Of course, in *Being and Time* Heidegger does not do this yet. In fact, his later thinking is even more open to death and death becomes even more important precisely because later on he explicitly focusses on that which has been concealed in traditional ontology. In *Being and Time* death is nonetheless central for death brings Dasein most radically before itself and before its understanding of being and hence it is through this being-pushed against death that Dasein is opened to the possibility of unearthing what traditional ontology has ignored. In fact, Heidegger will only later radicalise the importance of concealment even further. In *Being and Time* "openness", "disclosing" etc. still factor ore importantly than concealment. This is what Heidegger will radicalise in his lecture course on Plato's *Cave*, to which I will turn in more detail at the beginning of Part II.

On another level one could certainly raise the objection why death is, in fact, taken as so central. Is not *Destruktion* the way in which Heidegger aims to get to that which has been forgotten? The never written second volume of *Being and Time* should have officially been a destruction of traditional ontology. But note that also *Being and Time* treats Descartes' ontology as a prime example of the modern understanding of being as presence-at-hand what this means for Dasein's understanding of being. I understand *Destruktion* not as a literal destruction, nor as a "deconstruction". Rather, *destruction* in the Heideggerian sense is the method of fundamental ontology by which the original source of experience is laid bare. The prime example of this is ἀλήθεια, which Heidegger discloses as meaning the unconcealment *from* concealment rather than "truth" as correspondence truth. The project of fundamental ontology is to return to the sources of concepts and phenomena. My claim is

---

[3] Translated by Richard Taft.

[4] Heidegger will later call the *Ge-Birg* des Seins, i.e., the concentration of all modes of *bergen*, which unfolds as concealing and unconcealing (*ver-bergen* and *ent-bergen*).

now—to try and articulate this even more precisely—that in order to reach into those sources Dasein first needs to get in touch with its original understanding of being. Hence, and I will explicate this in great detail at the end of this part, Heidegger explicitly begins the analytic of Dasein's historicity in light of the tension between birth *and* death. And without genuine historicity there can be no genuine destruction, i.e., no genuine return to the question of being. Still, the approach of *Being and Time*, Dasein's fundamental ontology, will prove to be futile for the project of radicalising the thought of concealment further. It is here though that death, in a different form, remains crucial because death as utter non-availability is the "passageway" to understand the fundamental "withdrawal" of being. More on this in Part II.

Chapter 1
Death in *Being and Time*: Preliminary Remarks

Before delving into the analytic of Dasein it is helpful to point out how not to understand death in *Being and Time*. First of all, death is not to be taken in the ordinary sense of the end of someone's life, or more technically, death is not demise. Thus, the ontological phenomenon of death Heidegger is after has nothing to do with the measurable end of someone's life, or with dying in the ordinary sense of the word. Yet, death, and this is the crux, is neither of merely metaphorical meaning nor does death have nothing to with mortality, as, for example, Blattner maintains in his paper on "The Concept of Death in *Being and Time*" (Blattner 1994). Blattner there defines death as an episode of psychiatric depression that Dasein has to experience in order to become fully authentic. For Blattner "death" in *Being and Time* has nothing to do with mortality. Instead, death just signifies an episode where meaning collapses globally. Put differently, death is an episode of someone's life where the world, simply defined as a set of meaningful relationships with others and things, collapses. In a recent paper on the distinction between death and demise in *Being and Time* Thomson has attempted to synthesise claims that "death" is but a marker for global world collapse with the fact that Heidegger does not appear to speak of death in purely metaphorical terms. In a nutshell, Thomson follows Blattner and argues that death means momentary *"global collapse of significance."* (Thomson 2013: 263) Furthermore, and this is how Thomson wants to retain some sense of mortality attached to "death" in *Being and Time*, Thomson argues that we each have to live through such an episode of utter meaninglessness in order to make peace with the fact that we demise at some point in time. I strongly disagree with such readings. Not only does Heidegger clearly state that "edification" or "rules of behavior toward death" (SZ: 248/238) are not at all at stake in the analytic of death. Additionally, such a reading entirely ignores Dasein's ecstatic temporality and distorts that death in *Being and Time* does something else entirely. I shall show that death as the utmost limit of Dasein's existence is precisely the *condition* for world to arise and not the cause of its collapse!

© Springer Nature Switzerland AG 2021
J. A. Niederhauser, *Heidegger on Death and Being*,
https://doi.org/10.1007/978-3-030-51375-7_1

I have elsewhere provided an in-depth critique of Iain Thomson's interpretation of death in *Being and Time* (cf. Niederhauser 2017a). Still, I would like to point out here as well that Thomson maintains that Heidegger's understanding of death is ultimately informed by Jakob Böhme. Thomson claims that Heidegger quotes Jakob Böhme, when in fact, and I want to point this out here as well, Heidegger actually quotes from the *Ackermann aus Böhmen* written by Johannes von Tepl and nowhere refers to Jakob Böhme in *Being and Time*. The *Ackermann aus Böhmen* is a dialogue between a farmer who just his wife and the Grim Reaper himself, who tells the farmer that "As soon as a human being is being born, he is old enough to die right away." (SZ: 245/228) It is crucial to see that there is nothing mystic or theosophic about this quote, as Thomson's misreading suggests by wrongly attributing this quote to Jakob Böhme. Instead, Heidegger refers to what death tells the *Ackermann aus Böhmen* in order to show that his own understanding of death as a way of being that Dasein takes over as soon as it is, is not so far-fetched as it may seem. Heidegger refers to Tepl's text for historical reference, to show that it is an old wisdom and that death is invariably structurally co-constitutive of Dasein. Heidegger's reference to Tepl to me is indicative that one can also read parts of *Being and Time* as a meditation on human mortality, a retelling of the *memento mori* for our age.

Heidegger's distinction between demise and death intends to make clear that the ontic scientific assumptions about death in the ordinary sense are not the primary concern and do not directly influence his ontological investigation. What we usually call death is what Heidegger calls demise in *Being and Time*. Yet, we can only make sense of demise, ontic death, as it were, because of ontological death. Heidegger wishes to disclose the phenomenon of death fully in order to show thereby that we can at all relate to death the way we do only because we are always already directed toward it and, more precisely, our very being is structured by it. This is what he calls being-toward-death and this very structure is care itself. (SZ: 329/315) I shall discuss this in further detail below. Dastur puts our relationship with ontological death as follows: "If Dasein as such did not already have an inherent relation to death, it could never be put in such relation by any event in the world." (Dastur 1996: 51) That is to say, we could not relate to the demise of others in the way we, if we were not always already inherently directed toward it. Nevertheless, this relationship must be fully and properly disclosed because, like any other phenomenon, death is not simply given but concealed. The investigation of death, then, that *Being and Time* comes "prior to the questions of a biology, psychology, theodicy or theology of death." (SZ: 248/239) The text provides an ontology of death. Readings that define death as some sort of a psychological "state" that Dasein at times is in, I think, fail to account for the depth of the phenomenon of death and its meaning for the course of the thinking path.[1] Heidegger's analysis of death is, moreover, not a

---

[1] Sacha Golob's reading of death as a "state" is symptomatic of that (cf. Golob 2014: 151). Golob maintains that ordinary relations break down in the "states" which Heidegger calls death and angst. If Golob understands "death" in biological terms, then death is, of course, the collapse of all ordinary relations. But this would be a rather trivial existential truism. If he understands death like

"metaphysics of death" (SZ: 248/239) Questions regarding its origin, whether death is a transition to another life or whether death is an evil and other such moral concerns are outside the scope of the question. Heidegger consequently calls the "dying of others" a "substitute theme" (SZ: 238/231) because it is an ontic event. Heidegger rather wishes to arrive at the ground for why such ontic occurrences can be meaningful to us. His question is thus, how we can at all relate to the dying of others and our own death.

Thus, ontological death does have to do with mortal finitude. Still, death is not simply the end of someone's "life." For Heidegger in *Being and Time* death is not external to us, not some event in the future that occurs at some point or other. Rather, death is inherent in Dasein. Death is as soon as Dasein is. I will develop this further in this part and also in Part IV on language.[2] Death is not nothing to us. It has, nevertheless, become a common trope in Heidegger scholarship to compare Heidegger's analytic of ontological death with Epicurus' musings about mortality. In his letter to Menoeceus, Epicurus argues that death is nothing to us: "When I am, death is not, and when death is, I am not." We should not worry about death because when death is, we are not, and when we are, death is not. In German Heidegger reception among others[3] Figal has compared Heidegger with Epicurus and have attributed at least a mild form of Epicureanism to him (cf. Figal 2013: 190ff). Figal's interpretation of the analytic of death in *Being and Time* seems to be quite limited, since he understands death as the cessation of all perception and knowledge Moreover, as his approach is rather epistemological, death is for him only really meaningful as an occurrence in the world, as something we experience with others. Hence, Figal does not buy Heidegger's ontological analytic of the phenomenon of death, but instead alleges that Heidegger does not fully overcome Epicurus, as all perception and knowledge cease in death, Figal argues. For Heidegger, it is the other way around, however, as I have argued above. The ontological comes first, as it were. As soon as Dasein is, Dasein is in an inherent relationship with its death, which is not the cessation of Dasein's "life", but the limit where Dasein begins. It is for this very relationship with death that why we can make sense of and are touched by the dying of others in the first place. Dasein is as soon as death is also means that death is as soon as Dasein is. In recent Anglophone Heidegger reception Thomson has argued that Heidegger incorporates Epicurus' notorious remarks insofar as we cannot experi-

---

Thomson does, then there is virtually no difference between death and angst understood in psychological terms. Why, then, should Heidegger call death the "ownmost possibility" of Dasein, if there were not something peculiar about death? Death is a limit concept, angst is not. Both are, however, not psychological states.

[2] Note that this is where Heidegger is closest to Rilke. For Rilke, and I shall explore this further in Part IV and in the Epilogue, death is something that grows within us. We are to nourish and cherish death in order to become proper adults and grow to our full potential.

[3] Another reading of death in *Being and Time* as Epicurean is Inga Römer's interpretation of the matter (cf. Römer 2010: 146f). Even if just to point out that her reading lacks from a proper understanding of what *Möglichkeit*, possibility, means in Heidegger's philosophy. For Römer "*Möglichkeit*" in Heidegger seems to be something that requires actualisation. But the "possibility" that is death is and cannot be actualised. This will be a crucial issue at the end of this part.

ence our own full demise, come back from it and talk about it. In a similar fashion as Figal, Thomson also disregards the importance and prevalence of ontology over epistemology. Put differently, the experience Heidegger is after in context of death, is an experience in thinking, an experience of being, not an experience of the empirical realm.

Therefore, I argue that just the opposite is the case. Heidegger's analysis of death has nothing in common with Epicurus. If anything, the proper ontologically determined phenomenon of death in *Being and Time* is a complete rejection of the Epicurean dictum. To say that death is nothing to us would be a meaningless claim for Heidegger. For him, death always already determines Dasein's possibilities since Dasein is, as soon as it is, directed towards its ownmost possibility, it is death that co-constitutes Dasein's horizons of understanding. It is from that very directedness that Dasein receives its meaning in the sense that this directedness-towards… lets disclose beings and its world. If anything, then "the they" is stuck in an Epicurean understanding of death, because "[t]he they never dies." (SZ: 424/403) Moreover, the Epicurean stance serves as a tranquiliser against the fear of demise. Heidegger wants the exact opposite, and that is, to bring us closer to death, to show us that we are in an inherent relationship with our death and that death is what pushes us outside and into the world. Being-in-the-world, as I show in further detail below, is authentically performed by Dasein only in authentic being-towards-death. In Heideggerian terms the Epicurean position on death is worldless because death here does not give rise to a horizon against which Dasein can meaningfully disclose and understand itself and the world. It is important to note that such a worldlessness is, if not identical with, still close to the forgetting of being. The lack of being-in-the-world, which is the story of modernity epitomised in the subject-object-dichotomy, is, if not identical with, still at the heart of the forgetting of being. Thus, to read into Heidegger some form of Epicureanism would mean to jeopardise the entire Heideggerian project and to impede oneself from grasping its full scope.

Lastly, it is crucial to note that even though death is central to Heidegger's entire philosophical project, he does not advocate for suicide. Precisely the opposite is the case. Suicide does not play a role in *Being and Time* at all and is barely mentioned in the later philosophy either. But in the *Prolegomena* Heidegger points out very clearly that suicide perverts death, because suicide turns death into something present-at-hand, into an actuality. As Heidegger points out, this turns also being into an actuality and no longer understands our existence as possibility, but as something present-at-hand over which we believe to exercise full control (GA 20: 439/317f). Note that Heidegger here also explicitly makes the connection of death and being and that the possibility-character of death is crucial to understand the possibility-character of being. Furthermore, this means that by maintaining and living up to the possibility-character of death, its hovering in a way, Dasein gets to understand that being itself is possibility. This early insight will be crucial for the rest of the thinking path.

Chapter 2
The Necessity of the *Seinsfrage*

1 The Forgetting of Being

For Heidegger the necessity of the question of being is intimately related to the forgetting of being. Yet, how is that forgetting characterised? The forgetting of being is not a result of the utter failure of philosophy to address being. Has philosophy not addressed being, time and time again? Does not Schelling speak of will as "Urseyn"? Does not Hegel's *Science of Logic* begin with pure being? Is not being identical with thinking for Parmenides? How, then, can Heidegger make the grandiose claim that being has been forgotten?[1] In what follows, I shall explicate this claim further. As pointed out in the introduction to this part, for Heidegger modernity begins with an explicit leap over the "that" of the subject's being because of Descartes' dictum. But for Heidegger, the forgottenness begins even earlier with Greek ontology and its neglect of time with regards to being as presence, *Anwesen*. I thus see three decisive moments as constitutive of the forgetting of being. First, there are three encrusted prejudices about being, which both philosophy *and* the everyday operate with—without specifically asking for the meaning of being. Second, metaphysics' forgetting of the origin of the ontological difference. Third, the forgottoness of being is intimately related to what could be called the forgetting of time.[2] In what follows, I explicate these intertwined moments of the forgetting of being.

---

[1] It is crucial to note that Heidegger later clarifies in several texts, talks and conversations that what he means by being is presence, *An-wesen*, in the Greek sense of οὐσία. The latter also means estate, a place for dwelling, and *Eigentum*, property, and this is how Heidegger understands being already in *Being and Time*. Heidegger emphasises this, for example, in a conversation with a Japanese scholar.

[2] In anticipation of the turn please note that the forgetting of being pushes back into being as historical. What is forgotten, is not *per se* lost. Instead, forgetting and concealment are what move the history of being. Time plays a pivotal role in this, but in *Being and Time* we are not quite there yet. It will become clearer, however, that Heidegger sees the possibility of total abandonment and total loss, which he calls *Seinsverlassenheit*. Hence there can be total loss and that means that there is

© Springer Nature Switzerland AG 2021
J. A. Niederhauser, *Heidegger on Death and Being*,
https://doi.org/10.1007/978-3-030-51375-7_2

The first prejudice is that ""being" is the most "universal" concept." (SZ: 3/2) All judgments about beings include an understanding of being but being itself is neither category nor genus. Being rather *transcends* them. This hints at the ontological difference. As the most universal concept being is unitary. In this way being relates to the manifoldness of beings. Aristotle calls this the "unity of analogy." Beings are analogous to being. However, and without going into too much detail, how being and beings are connected has remained concealed throughout history, maintains Heidegger. Before Heidegger the last grand attempt to explicate being was Hegel's *Science of Logic*. For Heidegger Hegel's *Logic* is the culmination of Greek ontology. Its determination of being as "indeterminate immediate," however, means that Hegel gives up on the unity of analogy. Indeterminate being forms the basis of the *Logic's* categories. But how are beings to be analogous to being, if being is utterly indeterminate? Heidegger here indicates that he understands being as analogous to beings and that he looks for a determinate understanding of being. In his lectures on Aristotle's metaphysics from 1931 Heidegger argues: "Oneness belongs to the essence of being in general and being is always already implied in oneness." (GA 33: 30/24)[3] Therefore, Friedrich-Wilhelm von Herrmann points out that Heidegger in principle agrees with this (cf. von Herrmann 1987: 41). Being denotes the *way* beings *are*. The notion of analogy will thus also be significant for the thinking of the history of being.[4] Heidegger thus takes two things from the first prejudice. First, that there is something to analogy and that this needs to be investigated further. Second, and intimately related to the first, that even though the traditional assumption of being as the most universal and apparently most available concept seems to imply that being is the most obvious concept, ""being" is rather the most obscure [concept] of all." (SZ: 3/2) Obscure it is, not least because its relationship with beings is unclear. The missing connection between being and beings will turn out to be Dasein as the place of being's temporal disclosure. This relation between being and beings also already indicates the ontological difference.

This is of direct import to the second prejudice about being which states that being cannot be defined. This prejudice also has its origins in Greek ontology. Being cannot be defined because it is not something, not *a* being, and thus no genus and no differentiating specification applies to being. This also points to being's *transcendence*. What matters most for our purposes here, is that we can see here that already in *Being and Time* Heidegger approaches being and our understanding of being as *historical*. This is not to suggest that Heidegger in *Being and Time* is already anywhere near to what he will later call "*Seinsgeschichte*". Rather, this is to stress that

---

not a perfectly positive feedback loop, as it were, in the history of being, where any negativity is immediately consumed by the direction of the history of being.

[3] Translated by W. Brogan and P. Warnek.

[4] In Heidegger's later philosophy the notion of analogy will play a pivotal role. Take, for example, the workings of *Gestell*. In the age of the *Gestell* beings are *according to* or analogue to the workings or demands of *Gestell*. Thus, Heidegger does not do disperse with analogy. Instead, he later attempts a justification of how being and beings are analogous *historically*. More on this Part III.

the ways in which both the everyday and philosophy understand being are histori-cally conditioned. There is, then, for the early Heidegger a quasi-identity of being and the understanding of being.

This is of direct import for the third prejudice about being which states that being is self-evident. There is seeminly a givenness of being and that means that Dasein is always already in a pre-ontological, vague, oftentimes even indifferent understand-ing of being. An understanding of being is apparently immediately available to Dasein in any encounter of its world, but also in Dasein's self-relationality. Heidegger illustrates this by simple propositions such as "the sky *is* blue" and "I *am* happy". (SZ: 4/3) Heidegger's seemingly trivial claim is that there is always already a meaning of being at work when we speak even though we do not question it any further. There is *always already* a vague understanding at work, which is, however, concealed: "But this average comprehensibility only demonstrates the incompre-hensibility." (ibid.) Note that the "always already" indicates a sense of pastness, of thrownness. Yet, why is "being" concealed in such statements? Being is concealed precisely because our very seemingly immediate understanding of such simple propositions that works *without* having to ask for the meaning of the word "to be" covers over that very understanding. There is a givenness at work that conceals being. Hence, we must disclose or uncover the workings of that understanding in order to achieve an original and genuine understanding of being. Thus, for Heidegger it holds true that if we simply assume a givenness of being, then that only increases being's concealment. Put differently, the apparent positivity of our understanding of being, if not further questioned, turns into negativity, a loss and forgetting of the meaning of being. Our being-in-the-world is diminished, reduced to an instrumen-tal, operational, calculative access to beings. Dasein's initial and only vague under-standing must hence be radicalised. That is to say, the understanding of being must be developed and disclosed through a phenomenological investigation, for it is phe-nomenology that lets beings appear as they are and disclose their meaning. Such is the task of *Being and Time*.

The prejudices Heidegger identifies lead him to appreciate that being moves tem-porally *and* historically. On the one hand, there is always a sense of presence at work when I say, "the sky is blue," or "the cat is black." On the other hand, by bring-ing in Plato, Aristotle, Greek ontology in general, the Scholastics and Hegel Heidegger points out that our understanding of being is historically conditioned. From the latter insight Heidegger takes that there are moments of forgetting in that history that co-structure our understanding of being. From the former Heidegger takes that the very presence of being in such everyday propositions does not neces-sarily mean that its sense is perfectly clear to us. There is a concealedness in that presence. Based on this Heidegger then establishes on the first pages of *Being and Time* that there is "an enigma" that "*a priori*" (SZ: 4/3) structures Dasein's under-standing of being. Being does so by denying immediate access to its meaning. The meaning of being is concealed precisely because its meaning appears obvious. Put differently, what simply appears to be given and available, is of such a sheer availability that it self-conceals. Yet, this also means that the forgetfulness of being is inscribed in being as such. Being is necessarily "forgotten." This is an important first hint at truth as ἀλήθεια and the simultaneity of concealment and unconcealment, which moves Heidegger's thought. I shall further explicate ἀλήθεια in Part II. Note for now that concealment is at the heart of being already in *Being and Time*. Heidegger later thinks of being itself in terms of *bergen*, the root of *ver-* and *ent-bergen*, concealing and unconcealing—and of death as the concentration of concealment (*Ge-birg*). For Heidegger the seeming obviousness with which both philosophy and everyday language approach being indicates being's concealment. Dasein is always already in a pre-ontological understanding of being, yet being's ontological content must be specifically disclosed and determined.

The second important aspect of the forgetting of being is the ontological difference between being and beings, for the way in which they relate is obscure. Of course, traditional metaphysics knows of the difference between essence and something in question, but whence that difference comes, remains unquestioned. The ontological difference between being and beings is manifest in the fact that being is for the tradition the *transcendens* and the absolutely undefinable, while beings are definable. The ontological difference is not an unproblematic situation, as Heidegger points out, but rather invites us to think after the meaning of being. Heidegger retains the notion that being is the *transcendens* and makes this a thematic focus. I explicate being as *transcendens* further in Chap. 3. That being is forgotten hence also means having forgotten the origin of that difference. The question of being must hence explicitly ask for the difference between being and beings. In 1949 Heidegger added an important foreword to *On the Essence of Ground*. There Heidegger points out that "[t]he ontological difference is the "not" between beings and being." (GA 9: 123/97)[5] This is the case because being is *not* a being. In context of *Being and Time* I aim to show that the "not" between being and beings—which is neither privative nor negative, but rather gives rise to…, lets appear something as something, for there can be a presence where beings appear, only when that presence itself withdraws itself—can at all be experienced because of Dasein's relation to death. Dasein's fundamental relation to death means that Dasein ontologically always already exists as its "not-yet," that Dasein is always already not yet something. But this also means that a "not" is instantiated in Dasein insofar as Dasein, as soon as it is, is always already threatened by the possibility of not-being. Dasein is structured by a "not," for it is towards its possibility of not-being: death. Of course, the "not" of the ontological difference and the "not" of Dasein's structure are not identical. Nonetheless, the "not" that is introduced into Dasein's existence by death opens a window toward the "not" between being and beings. I will further develop these claims below. As we shall see, this "not" is related to *care* as Dasein's being.[6] That is to say death lets us experience the difference between beings and that which

---

[5] Translated by William McNeill.

[6] On this point see also (GA 97: 289ff) where Heidegger notes that the human being can differentiate between presence, *Anwesen*, i.e., being, and that which is present, *Anwesendem*, i.e., beings, because of death. In the *Zollikon Seminars*. There Heidegger says that "death is the leave-taking

is not a being. In this sense Dasein is "the placeholder of the nothing" (GA 9: 118) as Heidegger later calls Dasein in *What is Metaphysics?* There is an open wound in Dasein already in *Being and Time* insofar as Dasein is always already not-yet, always already towards some possibility or other, and it is that very openness, a result of the active nothingness, that lets Dasein enter its world and into a meaningful relationship with it.

The talk of the forgetting of being also indicates an at best impoverished understanding of what it means to be. At worst, "today" a proto-nihilism rules. This is a further indication that already in *Being and Time* our historical situation is crucial. Although being itself is not yet properly addressed as historical, Dasein's finite understanding of being is historical. As a consequence, *Being and Time* ends with an analysis of Dasein's historicity and its last question asks whether the proper horizon—and horizon, of course, also means limit—of the understanding of being is time. The finitude of Dasein's understanding of being is conditional on Dasein's mortality. As Müller puts it, *Being and Time* primarily "tries to make room [for Dasein] to be able to bear the infinite question of being with the finite strength of the human being." (Müller 1964: 48) Thus, I argue that the analysis of death intends to take us out of our impoverished and towards a proper understanding of the question of being.

Being and Time's final question, whether time is the proper horizon of the understanding of being, reflects back on the project as a whole. In fact, when Heidegger addresses the forgetting of being, he could just as well speak of the oblivion of time. More precisely of time as the ecstatic temporality of Dasein. I will return to this in more detail in Chap. 2 where I explicate Heidegger's radically new conception of time in light of death. Traditionally, being is understood as transtemporal and eternal. Beings, on the other hand, are temporal, i.e. *in* time. Beings are prone to fall prey to the flow of time.[7] Yet, Heidegger points to the crucial role of time for this traditional ontological difference between timeless being and temporal beings. Time itself, Heidegger argues, is what here brings about "regions of being." (SZ: 18/18) That is to say, time is the origin of the ontological difference in the tradition, but tradition, maintains Heidegger, has failed to account for the role of time. Heidegger here critiques the medieval conception of being as timeless order. Whereas being is timeless, beings are placed in the sphere of becoming and ephemerality. Being as order signifies a non-historical and non-temporal understanding of being. Instead of following that tradition Heidegger, post-Hegel, aims to show that "*in the phenomenon of time correctly viewed and correctly* [i.e. non-linearly, but ecstatically] *explained*" "*the central range of problems of all ontology is rooted*". (ibid.) For Heidegger the assumption of being's timelessness is only possible *because of* time. Even for "time-less" being time has an ordering function because being is understood as what is not temporal. There can be no timelessness without

---

from [*Abschied*] beings." (GA 89: 230/184; translated by Franz Mayr and Richard Askay). That is to say death lets us experience the difference between beings and that which is not a being.

[7] Heidegger returns to his early critique of the ordinary understanding of time in *What Calls for Thinking?* This will be a topic of Part III.

time, but time must be understood ecstatically in order to understand how it structures the very presence—and continuation of that presence—of beings.

As mentioned, according to Heidegger the oblivion of time begins already with
Greek ontology. In Greek ontology something is considered "to be" only when it is
present. Beings in their *being* are disclosed as what they are thanks to presence.
Heidegger hence translates the Greek word for being, οὐσία, as presence, *Anwesen*.
For Plato, only the permanently present has true ontological status is. Ergo, the
being of beings is understood in terms of time. The same holds true for the modern
Cartesian understanding of nature and world as presence-at-hand and availability.
(SZ: 25f/24f) However, Greek ontology and subsequently modern ontology forget
time insofar as, firstly, time does not become the specific thematic focus of the
investigation of being. Secondly, these ontologies have reduced time to the flow of
homogenous now-states. The sphere of beings is characterised by *nunc* after *nunc*
after *nunc* and the timeless sphere of being, eternity, is characterised by a standing
now, the *nunc stans*. Hence the oblivion of time is the linear understanding of time
that is ultimately sublated only by the permanent presence of a standing now.
Furthermore, the prevalence of presence means that metaphysics operates with a
sense of being that forgets withdrawal and concealment. This history ended in the
nineteenth century with Hegel's finalising response to the question of metaphysics.

In his 1930/1931 lectures on the *Phenomenology of Spirit*, Heidegger points out
that Hegel's system answers and finalises the guiding question of Greek ontology,
τί τὸ ὄν; (*what are beings?*), which means that beings have been corroborated in
their beingness once and for all and with certainty. This finds expression in the
claim to absolute and infinite knowledge (GA 32: 16ff/11ff)[8] The *Science of Logic*
is of timeless truth. The final response to the guiding question claims to be timeless.
Beings as such *are* insofar as they are "the actual in its genuine and whole reality
[*Wirklichkeit*], or the idea, the *concept*." (ibid.: 17/12) Yet, argues Heidegger, and
this is crucial, "*the pure concept annuls time*." (ibid.: 17/12) Thus with Hegel "*time
is made to disappear*." (ibid.: 17/12) Time disappears behind the dominant presence
of the actual. The disappearance of time in Hegel's system, as Heidegger explicitly
states, leads to the necessity of the question of being as explicated in *Being and
Time*! It is crucial to note that Heidegger here explicitly also says that *Being and
Time* is not "existentia philosophy," but that *Being and Time* rather aims to reconnect with the fundamental problem of occidental ontology and that simply is the
question of being, which has the λόγος as its content (ibid.: 18/13). With Hegel the
actuality of beings is secured and fully explicated, but time is obscured, precisely by
this utter actuality of Hegel's response. Hegel's finalising response to the guiding
question represents an encrustation and closure. Heidegger wishes to counter this
development with a radical openness of the future. This is also why Heidegger
begins to regard possibility as higher than actuality. This allows him to pave the way
for a radical openness and to break free from the encrustation of the metaphysics of
presence: "Higher than actuality stands *possibility*." (SZ: 38/36) Heidegger says this
in relation to phenomenology. I shall explicate Heidegger's notion of possibility in

---

[8] Translated by Parvis Emad and Kenneth May.

relation to death in Chap. 4. It may for now suffice to say that death as Dasein's *ownmost possibility* plays a pivotal role in this context. Heidegger's critique of Hegel also already points to the history of being. The history of being breaks open the closure of metaphysics and grants the possibility of an open future.

In *Being and Time* Dasein's ecstatic temporality is the thematic focus of the analysis of the importance of time for being. It is my goal here to show that Dasein's temporality, which is fundamental to time, is conditional on death as ownmost possibility. At the beginning of the thinking path Heidegger's thought is horizonal. It is a thinking *towards* being. Dasein is fundamentally structured in futural terms, for example, as "being-*toward*-death" and "in-order-*to…*", and Dasein is always already "*ahead*-of-itself." Thus, the future apparently has priority. As noted above, Heidegger explicitly stated at Davos that death is brought into play to account for the primacy of the horizon of the future: "the analysis of death [in *Being and Time*] has the function of bringing out the radical futurity of Dasein." (GA 3: 283/177)[9] It is important to note that this is not primarily of "existential" or even personal import, but of ontological and philosophical significance. This claim is of philosophical significance insofar as Heidegger's privileging of the future implies that Heidegger sees the question of being as *the* question of a philosophy concerned with what is to come. In this future we are to face our mortality more radically than before. Heidegger's remarks at Davos are also of ontological import insofar as Dasein is always already directed towards the future and this very directedness is where meaning arises. More to the point, meaning arises *ex negativo*. Thus, in the context of *Being and Time*, where the understanding of being is the focus, the question of being turns out to be the following: *How does Dasein's futural-horizonal temporality determine Dasein's understanding of being?* In the context of my argument the question of being can be reformulated as follows: If Dasein's directedness towards death allows for Dasein's radical futural temporality, then how does death enable Dasein's understanding of being?

As we shall see, based on this radical futurity Heidegger will later begin to conceptualise being itself as possibility. Death as ownmost possibility, towards which Dasein is, brings Dasein before being as possibility. More precisely, the analysis of death in *Being and Time* opens the path to think being itself as possibility. Note exactly what I am trying to say here. I am explicitly not saying that in *Being and Time* already thinks *being itself* as possibility. I am instead claiming that to us as readers of Heidegger we can see how and why Heidegger ends up understanding being itself as the possible because of his early analysis of death as Dasein's *being*-towards its ownmost possibility, death. This will show itself fully in the "turn." Müller articulates the fact that for Heidegger being is the possible as follows:

> Being is not actual *in itself*, it is not "*actus purus.*" Instead, being is reality as the possibility that enables everything. As such being is even "*realitas realitatum et omnitudo realitatum,*" i.e., the primary reality in which and through which everything is. (Müller 1964: 67)

---

[9] Translated by Richard Taft.

Müller here already speaks from the perspective of the history of being. Müller's remark is nonetheless rather important, if we want to gain a clearer understanding of *Being and Time*. This also already hints at the reason why Heidegger must ultimately move away from the project of *Being and Time*. He must do so because the centrality of Dasein's *understanding* impedes the path to being as such. This is why Heidegger writes in the last paragraph of *Being and Time* that only "something like "being" ["*Sein*"] has been disclosed in the understanding of being that belongs to existing Dasein as a way in which it understands." (SZ: 437/414)

This account of the forgetting of being is, of course, too brief and neglects, for example, the impact of *Wesensphilosophie*.[10] Nevertheless, my account sheds light on three moments of the forgetting of being that are pivotal for this project. First of all, being itself is always already concealed. Being forgets itself as much as Dasein forgets being, while Dasein still operates with a vague sense of what being means. Therefore, it is the task of philosophy to bring being to light again and again. This means that being remains a *question*. Second, the forgetting of being is intimately related to the oblivion of time as that which grants and structures presence. Following from this, Dasein must overcome the oblivion of its ecstatic temporality in order to overcome the forgetting of being. Dasein does so in that it investigates itself as radically directed towards its death since death is what constitutes the primary temporal horizon, called future. As we can see, in *Being and Time* the forgetfulness of being already appears to be integral to being. This is articulated in one word with ἀλήθεια. The play between concealed and unconcealed, dark and light that will prove to be the fundamental tension driving Heidegger's thought. However, in *Being and Time* the focus is much more still on dis-closure, on presence and un-concealing rather than concealing. This finds expression in the notion of *fundamental ontology* which aims to provide the foundation for all future ontologies. Thus, the initial project of Heidegger's philosophy favours disclosure. Yet, the thought of concealment will prove to become stronger in the aftermath of *Being and Time* and hence, in my view, Heidegger has to give up on fundamental ontology.

2 Fundamental Ontology, Phenomenology and Dasein's Self-Investigation

However profound the focus on Dasein and its world use of tools and equipment seems to be, "[t]he real theme [of *Being and Time*] is being." (SZ: 67/67) At the end of *Being and Time* Heidegger thus points out that the thematic analytic of Dasein is one way to approach the question of being. "Our *goal* is to work out the question of being *überhaupt*." (SZ: 436/413 *ta*) This is crucial because it points to the question whether the fundamental-ontological investigation necessarily requires the ontic foundation, called Dasein, as Heidegger seems convinced it is at the beginning of

---

[10] Müller's *Existenzphilosophie* and von Herrmann's *Hermeneutische Philosophie des Daseins* deliver more in-depth accounts.

the book. At the end of *Being and Time* Heidegger however points out the crux of the argument: "Our *thematic* analytic of existence [of Dasein] needs in its turn the light from a previously clarified idea of being *überhaupt*." (ibid. *ta*) The idea of being in *Being and Time* is a regulative idea. On the one hand, the idea of being can only be clarified by explicating Dasein and its existentials. Thus, this is to say that Dasein as ontic foundation is necessary within the context of the approach of *Being and Time*. On the other hand, Dasein's analytic is only possible, if the idea of being has already been clarified. This is a prime example of the hermeneutic circle, of simultaneity and equiprimordiality, and points to the problem of beginning that philosophy struggles with since the days of German Idealism. The beginning of *Being and Time* is what is ready-to-hand, is the seemingly immediately given, where some vague understanding of being is already active. That which is immediately given must be investigated to show that which lets beings be present. Dasein's self-investigation begins with what is initially ready-to-hand, for example, the daily use of a hammer or driving a car. Even such ordinary everyday dealings imply a pre-ontological understanding of being in which Dasein always already is and thanks to which Dasein can have any access to the world. Thus, being *qua* regulative idea is presupposed in *Being and Time*. It is this presupposition of being which Heidegger will try to reel in in his later writings on *Ereignis* and this is one of the main reasons why Heidegger will give up on the analytic of Dasein.

On the face of it there is hence a certain givenness of the meaning of being. Dasein's immediate understanding of being is presupposed. Yet, the presupposition at work is not logical, but existential-ontological. For Heidegger to pre-suppose means to project a possibility of being and *let* the phenomenon show itself (cf. SZ: 314f/300f). Thus, the investigation cannot stop at what is seemingly "given" because the text looks for a proper, determinate understanding of the idea of being as that which regulates any and all presence. Dasein and the hermeneutics of Dasein, i.e., the way in which Dasein interprets itself and the world, is the path Heidegger chooses to clarify being because being is an issue for Dasein. Dasein is the being that asks questions. Heidegger also chooses Dasein as the ontic foundation in order to free the human being from the Cartesian paradigm and thereby clear the way to think being itself. Post Descartes, philosophy must first get beyond the subject-object-dichotomy, which reduces being to presence-at-hand, and places the human being in the world. As Heidegger points out on the last page of *Being and Time*, pre-echoing the thinking path: "We must look for a *way* to illuminate the fundamental ontological question and *follow* it." (SZ: 437/414) The reference to illumination is crucial. Being, here as the regulatory *idea of being*, provides light. Yet, there remains a significant tension at this early stage of the thinking path precisely because being and the understanding of being are quasi-identical. Heidegger will later attempt to solve this issue by speaking of *Lichtung*, the clearing of being thanks to which beings appear without Dasein's initial disclosure. Dasein's transcendental self-investigation, in turn, presupposes the light of being that its self-investigation at once brings to light. Put differently, *as* Dasein investigates itself, Dasein brings to light that there is a regulatory idea of being. Yet, the proper idea of being is not simply always already given beforehand, but rather results out of Dasein's fundamental self-investigation. In this sense Dasein as ontic foundation enables the ontological investigation. This also stresses that the ontological would be empty without the ontic. In *Being and Time*, "[b]eing is [therefore] always the being of a being." (SZ: 9/8) In *Being and Time* being is always the presence of some being (*Seiendes*). Being itself comes into focus only later. What is required in context of *Being and Time*, is *a* being, called Dasein, that can understand the being of beings insofar as Dasein investigates them and asks, *what are beings?, what is it to be?* Dasein can ask these questions precisely for its essential relation to being. From this presupposition called Dasein no one can escape, Heidegger thinks at the time of *Being and Time*. In fact, "the question of being is nothing else than the radicalization of an essential tendency of being that belongs to Dasein itself, namely, of the pre-ontological understanding of being." (SZ: 15/13) My claim is that Heidegger undertakes this radicalisation in the analysis of death. Yet the fact that Dasein is the necessary presupposition does not mean that Dasein posits itself or even being. It is a tendency of Dasein to understand being pre-ontologically. That tendency is a result of the interplay between Dasein and its understanding of being and the regulative idea of being.[11] But in *Being and Time* the onus is clearly on Dasein, whereas in later texts it is being that self-discloses, while the responses of the human being participate in and co-respond to the occurrence of clearing.

Heidegger argues that also in Aristotle we find something like Dasein's ontic-ontological primacy, insofar as "[t]he soul (of the human being) is in a certain way beings." (SZ: 14/12 *ta*) This does not mean that everything exists only because the human being exists as the subject (ground) of all beings. Instead, this says that the soul as the being of the human being is able to disclose beings *as* beings in a *hermeneutical* way, i.e., beings are meaningful phenomena belonging to a world only through that disclosure. The "as" here is not the "as" of judgment. That is to say, Dasein does not primarily encounter world by making value judgments about a given totality of objects. Nor is the world structured in a propositional way. The hermeneutical "as" is the performance of disclosing something as meaningful. Dasein is in the world insofar as Dasein continuously discloses and lays bare that which is—primarily in a non-propositional way. Furthermore, Aristotle understands the human being as the ζῷον λόγον ἔχον, the living being "whose being is essentially determined by its ability to speak." (SZ: 25/24) *Speaking* lets us encounter and disclose beings in their being. Through discourse Dasein discloses (ἀλήθευειν) and brings phenomena to light (λόγος). Following Aristotle, Heidegger calls Dasein "the being of the human being" (ibid.) The being of the human being is such that it discloses beings. The being of the human being and its relation to being as such is the explicit thematic focus of *Being and Time*.

Dasein is the *being*, *das Sein*, of the human being. This is a crucial claim because Dasein is not a present-at-hand entity like a hammer or a tree. Yet, at the same time Heidegger keeps referring to Dasein as *a being*, *ein Seiendes*. Unfortunately,

---

[11] Heidegger will later articulate this more clearly. In *Introduction to Metaphysics* Heidegger says: "Dasein is *itself* by virtue of its essential *relation to being* as such." (GA 40: 22/31 *ta*; translated by G. Fried and R. Polt).

Heidegger does not appear to be rigorous enough in his use of the term Dasein. Which one is it? Is Dasein the being [*Sein*] of the human being or is Dasein a being [*ein Seiendes*]? The answer is that Dasein is both, which is potentially dissatisfying on the face of it. Yet, there is a profound philosophical reason for this. *Qua* care Dasein is the "between" between being and beings. (SZ: 374/357) We can think of Dasein as the *place* of the ontic-ontological difference. As such Dasein is the place of mediation between being (presence) and beings (that which is present). On the one hand, Dasein is *a* being in the sense that Dasein extends historically and temporally and insofar as Dasein makes sense of itself and its world in those terms. On the other hand, Dasein is *the* being of the human being as Dasein denotes the way in which the human being exists. To a certain degree the German word "Dasein" expresses that. The word "Dasein" means both presence *and* existence. Presence pertains to being as disclosedness and existence pertains to all that is insofar *that* it is. Dasein continuously interprets itself and the world by projecting possibilities of existence against its horizons of understanding. In this way Dasein's self-relation simultaneously enables the disclosure of other beings *as* beings. Both Dasein's horizons and possibilities ultimately arise from Dasein's directedness towards its death.

There is a further reason for Heidegger to *posit* Dasein as the ontic foundation for the investigation. In the introduction to *Being and Time* Heidegger mentions the crisis of the sciences and that "tendencies to place research on new foundations have cropped up on all sides in the various disciplines." (SZ: 9/9) The forgetting of being has crept into the sciences. Heidegger thus wishes to provide a new foundation for the sciences. The crisis stems from the reductive ontology of Cartesianism. Post Descartes the sciences operate with an ontology grounded in the subject-object-dichotomy and the *cogito sum*. Hence, they operate with an ontology that, maintains Heidegger, has failed to ask for the meaning of being. The "new" foundation for all ontologies is what Heidegger calls Dasein. This being now wants to investigate itself and at the same time *found* itself so as to provide the foundation for all other ontologies of the beings this peculiar being called Dasein investigates. Dasein is the "there" of being and therefore Dasein can understand beings in their respective being. In *Being and Time* Heidegger further develops the claim from his *Prolegomena* that death is the source of meaning for the *sum*. In its self-investigation Dasein finds death to be what constitutes it as a whole and only as a whole can Dasein properly serve as the foundation for the ontologies of beings unlike Dasein (cf. Demske 1970: 23). Ontologies are founded on the ontic structure of Dasein insofar as Dasein dis-covers and so mediates between being and beings: "Thus *fundamental ontology*, from which alone all other ontologies can originate, must be sought in the *existential analytic of Dasein*." (SZ: 13/12 *ta*)

Dasein takes itself as its hypothesis. Dasein then interprets this hypothesis in *Being and Time* by means of a phenomenological hermeneutics that asks: *what is it to be*? This hermeneutical phenomenology is hence an ontological investigation. Heidegger's decisive claim regarding methodology is found in the decisive §7 of *Being and Time*:

> Philosophy is universal phenomenological ontology, taking its departure from the herme-
> neutic of Dasein, which, as an analysis of *existence [Existenz]*, has fastened the end of the
> guideline of all philosophical inquiry at the point from which it *arises* and to which it
> *returns [zurückschlägt]*. (SZ: 38/36)

Heidegger aims at a universal fundamental ontology. The existential analytic of
Dasein is neither an anthropology nor an exercise in social philosophy nor existential philosophy as already pointed out above. This is especially important to note
with regard to the analytic of death. Everything Heidegger says is meant as a gateway into being. The descriptions of, say, handling a hammer are directed toward the
disclosure of the phenomenon of world, i.e., of the rising of being as universally
constituting any and all horizons of meaning. In *Fundamental Concepts of
Metaphysics*, a lecture course given in 1929/1930 where he deepens his conception
of world, Heidegger explicitly denies anthropological readings of *Being and Time*:
"It never occurred to me, however, to try and claim or prove with this interpretation
[of world] that the essence of man consists in the fact that he knows how to handle
knives and forks or use the tram." (GA 29/30: 263/177)[12] Dasein is not "what"
human beings are. Nor is Dasein some reified homunculus. *Dasein*, rather, is the
ways in which we exist. Hence we understand why Heidegger in his Hegel lectures
points out that *Being and Time* is concerned with λόγος in its original content. In
§7B of *Being and Time* Heidegger explicates his understanding of λόγος that originally means "to make manifest [*offenbar*] "what is being talked about" in speech"
(SZ: 32/28) and to make manifest what is present. Thus the aim is an original let-
ting-see and making manifest of original phenomena that are universal, for they
arise out of existence itself and return to existence in a circular movement.

This circularity is indicated in the beginning of *Being and Time* which always
takes its lead with Dasein's immediate, indeterminate and fuzzy everyday modes of
being, i.e., the ontic, leading unto the ontological and back up to the ontic. Yet, these
are not observations from the outside objectifying Dasein and its world. Rather,
Dasein self-investigates from within its world performatively. This also means that
as readers of *Being and Time* we cannot take the text to contain propositions about
Dasein, but rather formal indications *of* Dasein. Still the text aims at universal statements. Yet, those are universal not in the sense as talking *about* "what it means to
be." Instead, they are universal as they begin from within the world and lead back to
the fundamental structures enabling "that which is" and always return to the ontic.
The ontic, the inauthentic and the everyday, even if not identical, are all on the same
level, as it were.[13] Yet, they are not lower kinds of phenomena or lower than the level
of being: "the inauthenticity of Dasein does not signify a "lesser" being or a "lower"
degree of being." (SZ: 43/40) The authentic cannot be without the inauthentic. The
ontological cannot be without the ontic. In fact, we can only arrive at the authentic
from the inauthentic and the attempt of the text is to show the ontological

---

[12] Translated by W. McNeill and N. Walker.

[13] Heidegger points out that Aristotle's *Rhetoric*, far from being a catalogue of methods for giving
speeches, is "the first systematic hermeneutic of the everydayness of being-with-one-another."
(SZ: 138/135).

significance of the ontic. Dasein in its inauthentic modes *formally indicates* deeper goings-on. Formally here means fuzzy and imprecise. This is especially the case in the analysis of death where Heidegger does not wish to provide us with a normative guideline on how to deal with, say, moral concerns regarding mortality. Instead, the analysis of death pushes the text to that which Dasein is always already furthest removed from, i.e., to being as such. Thus, the universal phenomenological ontology is not an objectification of Dasein's structures and its attunements. Rather, the disclosed structures are a continuous "structuring," more precisely an attuned structuring that is formally indicated in the ontic and the everyday. The ontological shines through the ontic and vice versa.

The phenomenology of *Being and Time* thus discloses being as Dasein's understanding of the being of beings. Note that this does not mean that this is the only dimension of the truth of being Heidegger would accept at the time of writing *Being and Time*. The truth of being Dasein discloses is what Heidegger calls "*veritas transcendentalis*"[14] precisely because Dasein can range above beings and thereby disclose them in their being and articulate what it is to be. In brackets Heidegger here adds "disclosedness [*Erschlossenheit*] of being" (SZ: 36/36 *me*) I understand the "*of*" here as a genitive subjective and not a genitive objective. That is to say, Dasein is open to being and this is why Dasein can at all begin to investigate the being of beings and its own being. Dasein is most radically pushed towards its own being, in a non-propositional and non-general way, but in a radically unique, *einmalig*, way when Dasein confronts its death: "*I have to die*" is the loneliest and most urgent insight into the uniqueness of *my* being. Rather than the propositional claim that "all men are mortal." Nevertheless, this uniqueness translates into a universal (but not generalised) ontology, for Dasein cannot be thought of without being-without-others and without being-in-the-world. As soon as *I* say Dasein those are always already indicated.

3 Being as *Transcendens Pure and Simple*

As we are in search for an answer to the question *of* being and since my claim is that a preliminary response can already be developed out of the analysis of death in *Being and Time* we must not ignore Heidegger's own assertions regarding being in the text. In a highly contested passage, which I quote here in full, Heidegger writes:

> As the fundamental theme of philosophy being is not a genus of beings; yet it pertains to every being. Its "universality" must be sought in a higher sphere. Being and its structure transcend every being and every possible existent determination of a being. *Being is the transcendens pure and simple* [*schlechthin*]. The transcendence of the being of Dasein is a

---

[14] Heidegger later abandons the notion of *veritas* when he radicalises his diagnosis of truth as ἀλήθεια. *Veritas* is too close to verification and correspondence truth and Heidegger begins to see *veritas* as a Roman distortion of the original Greek experience of truth as ἀλήθεια.

distinctive one since in it lies the possibility and necessity of the most radical *individuation*. Every disclosure of being as the *transcendens* is *transcendental* knowledge. (SZ: 38/35f)

What is at stake here? Is this a reification of being? Is this an attempt to speak of *pure* being as Stambaugh's translation suggests? Does being as *transcendens*[15] refer to a world "beyond"? In order to gain a clearer understanding, I first provide a summary of readings of this passage from different schools of thought. I then present a synthesis of these interpretations and add the aspect of the experience of finitude, which finds expression in Heidegger's notion of being as *transcendens*.

The first interpretation I turn to comes from the Dreyfus camp. For William Blattner being is "the "*transcendens* pure and simple" because everything that shows up in any way, the world, Dasein, the available, or the occurrent, all show up in terms of some ontological framework." (Blattner 1999: 23) The notion of an ontological framework together with Blattner's claim that *Being and Time* is a case of temporal idealism is highly problematic. "Some framework" suggests something stable surrounding beings, a prefixed givenness, which, for the supposed idealism at work, turns out to be of the mind! A temporal-mental framework, as it were, with which Dasein supposedly perceives beings. Note also Blattner's questionable and seemingly careless stringing together of Dasein and the available, as if Dasein were something available, i.e., something present-at-hand. When engaging with Heidegger's philosophy, one must attempt not to objectify his insights, which is however precisely what Blattner is doing here. In effect, Blattner calls being a framework and hence turns being into something present-at-hand, too! The very notion of framework also appears rather awkward when we think of Heidegger's later critique of technology as "*Gestell*," a literal frame. Thus, this is a reification of being. Blattner removes the performative character of being and of Dasein's understanding disclosure of being. I shall carve out the performativity of being in more detail in Sect. 1 of Chap. 3. Let me add, though, that yes there is a frame, always already a frame insofar as that thanks to which Dasein can disclose something is to a certain frame. However, assuming a fixed framework reifies being. This is to say there is not initially or originally a given or fixed framework, for being is only in disclosing itself and insofar as Dasein discloses. This double-movement brings about a certain frame and it is precisely the danger of technology that it presents everything in a frame that is not further questioned and not further disclosed.

In my interpretation I rather follow Otto Pöggeler (1983: 96) and Daniel O. Dahlstrom (2005: 34). Both argue that Heidegger in this passage marries Kant's notion of the transcendental with the scholastics' notion of *transcendens*. If Heidegger were here to speak of being as *transcendens* only in the scholastic sense, then he would be equating his notion of being with the beingness of beings. As Dahlstrom argues, Heidegger, therefore, "applies the notion [of scholastic transcendence] to a specific sort of being, [Dasein]" (ibid.). That is to say, to a being that *transcends* the world and categorises beings. Heidegger then combines this with the Kantian "transcendental" insofar as Heidegger looks for necessary conditions of

---

[15] In the *Letter on Humanism* Heidegger admits to a failure of language in *Being and Time*. The language was too metaphysically charged. This holds true for being as *transcendens*.

experience *a priori*. However, the purely Kantian "transcendental" is not quite what Heidegger has in mind either, as he does not look for *epistemic* conditions of knowledge, but rather for *existential* conditions of experience. This is where I disagree with Dahlstrom who takes the notion of transcendental in too much a Kantian sense, i.e., in an epistemological sense. Friedrich-Wilhelm von Herrmann disagrees with such readings and argues that transcendental cognition is to be taken purely in the sense of a transcending cognising and that it has nothing whatsoever to do with Kant's notion of the transcendental (von Herrmann 1987: 380). True, in 1926 Heidegger explicitly argues that *veritas transcendentalis* is not to be taken in the Kantian sense (GA 22: 10). Rather, being as *transcendens* is to indicate the ontological difference, that being is not at all a being. Nonetheless, I wish to stress that the "transcending" of Dasein is the necessary condition *a priori* for any world access and experience and it is in this sense I speak of Dasein's transcendental self-investigation of its being to which no category pertains. The transcendental then is not Kantian, if transcendental means conditions for the possibility of knowledge. But transcendental is broadly Kantian insofar as *Being and Time* does investigate conditions for the possibility of experience. It is primarily the *Über-steigen*, transcending, of Dasein that makes possible philosophical truth. Dasein can transcend and therefore approach being as such.

It is certainly true, as Dahlstrom maintains, that Heidegger singles out Dasein in its being. I would, however, challenge the notion that what is at stake in *Being and Time* is only and primarily the being of Dasein. In a similar fashion as Dahlstrom, Magnus points out that if we did not understand Heidegger to make a claim exclusively about the being of Dasein, which is performative, Heidegger would in fact reify being as definite beingness. Magnus thus concludes that being in *Being and Time* is "humanistic Being [sic.]" (Magnus 1970: 85f) since there is no being (disclosedness) without the human being. This is true to the degree that being is disclosed insofar as Dasein continues to disclose being. Yet, this is not a unilateral process. Human beings can disclose beings only insofar as also being as such moves by disclosing itself. The passage in question is the following: "However, only as long as Dasein *is*, that is, as long as there is the ontic possibility of an understanding of being, "is there" [*gibt es*] being [*Sein*]." (SZ: 212/203) I should point out—*contra* Magnus—that also in Heidegger's later philosophy the human being *qua* thinking being still participates in the *Entbergungsgeschehen*, the occurrence of disclosure. Still, there is something to Magnus' critique, which has also been made by others. Heidegger himself later claims for example in *Time and Being* and the *Letter on Humanism* that the language of *Being and Time* failed at saying what he tried to say. Magnus does not believe Heidegger's later claims that *Being and Time* already speaks of being's "it gives" in this passage. Here now again lies the crux of the matter of how to read Heidegger. If we follow the thinker Heidegger and his later claims, then we can interpret him as saying something like the following. In *Being and Time* Heidegger makes the *experience* in his thinking which lead him away from fundamental ontology. I am not trying to argue that everything of the later philosophy is contained in *Being and Time*. Quite the opposite. I argue that Heidegger here comes across the limitations of his first attempt and hence has to move on. Yet, if we take

Heidegger himself seriously, then I should also point out that he will begin to see something in his own text *Being and Time*, from his new perspective, that he did not see before and hence re-interpret the "es gibt" as the "Es gibt" of being's clearing. Of course, this is not yet present in *Being and Time*. Hence in my reading I am not following Heidegger and assume anachronistically that in *Being and Time* the later "Es gibt" is already contained. It is not contained and here I agree with Magnus and others. Nevertheless, we can still appreciate Heidegger's own hermeneutic re-reading of *Being and Time* and beginning to see something else in it.

However, I do not follow Magnus' claim that "being" in *Being and Time* is humanistic or mildly subjectivist. Heidegger here is in line with the ontological tradition of the occident and will remain so throughout his philosophical life. Being would be "humanistic", *if and only if* it is Dasein *who* is the mover of being and history. Dasein, however, is not some rational mind that moves all. Instead Dasein is the initial openness for being—the initial openness in which the human being participates. Heidegger speaks of being as *"transcendens"*. By this Heidegger does not mean the beingness of beings, which is for example categorised by the human being. Instead, *transcendens* indicates the "rising of being" *qua* world. *Being*-in-the-world, more precisely, *In-der-Welt-Sein* speaks of *Sein* first. Thanks to this initial openness beings can appear and Dasein can disclose beings *as* beings. Note that being is not earlier than Dasein, but always only accessible in a temporal disclosure and response. Being needs human beings and vice versa. For Magnus, the "es gibt" passage is clearly a humanistic claim. As outlined above I read this differently. Human beings are not at the centre of history, they are not the movers of history and being. Being and the being of the human being, i.e. Dasein, are necessarily related, in such a way, in fact, that Dasein *is* the place of the mediation between that which *allows* Dasein to disclose being and beings insofar as they can be disclosed. That is, the "*es gibt*" in *Being and Time* points to the possibility to disclose beings as meaningful in the world and as belonging to the world. As such being is the initial openness and Dasein is the necessary receiver or responder and carries out or performs that very disclosing. *Dasein ist der lebendige Vollzug des Erschliessens des Seins.* But being also needs Dasein and Dasein's disclosing, for being is not a self-sufficient substance. Hence, there is here no reification because "giving" and "disclosing" are events and being *is* as that very giving and disclosing. The "giving" of being to Dasein confers to Dasein the possibility of disclosing phenomena as meaningful. The "giving" itself is not given, but only in disclosing by Dasein *is there* disclosing. Thus, *Being and Time* already points to the openness *of* being thanks to which beings appear and this openness *transcends* beings, i.e., being is distinguished from beings and this distinction is what allows Dasein to bring beings into focus in the peculiar way that Dasein does this.[16] There is one being, called Dasein, the ecstatic-temporal existing presence of the *there*, in which this openness finds an anchor. Hence, as Dahlstrom puts it, what Dasein does is "to transcend (range over

---

[16] De Gennaro, therefore, suggests that the notion being as *transcendens*, which indicates the ontological difference, suggests being without beings. Thus, De Gennaro argues, this is an early "flashing" of being as *Ereignis* (cf. De Gennaro 2013: 14).

and characterise) itself and the world, others, and any other entities and modes of being that it encounters within the world." (Dahlstrom 2005: 35) Yet, this is not a humanist claim precisely because being as *transcendens*, in an interdependent manner, opens that possibility for Dasein and its ways of being. There is something more at stake though than Dahlstrom's reading permits: finitude. Let me point out what I mean by this.

The limitations of *Being and Time* and its language are further stressed by Heidegger himself shortly after the publication. In the seminal talk *What is Metaphysics?*, which Heidegger held in 1929, Heidegger is already beyond the language of *Being and Time*, already further removed from traditional language and restrictions. He writes: "If in the ground of its essence Dasein were not transcending, which now means, if it were not in advance holding itself out into the nothing, then it could never adopt a stance toward beings nor even toward itself." (GA 9: 115/91) Furthermore, he argues that being and nothing belong together not for their "indeterminateness and immediacy [*sic*. Hegel], but rather because being itself is essentially finite and manifests itself only in the transcendence of a Dasein that is held out into the nothing." (ibid.: 120/94f) Thus, Dasein's transcendental self-investigation, with *Being and Time* as its first culmination, is an articulation of Dasein's relation to being and nothing. This tension-filled relation, in turn, is the *a priori* condition for Dasein to enter into any encounter with beings. It is crucial to note that Heidegger here determines being itself to be finite. By way of Dasein—the being that transcends as it asks, the finite being, *Seiendes*, determined in its sense and direction by its ownmost possibility, i.e., death—the investigation is brought before being. And, as we shall see, Heidegger will later in his philosophy determine being as *possibility* precisely because this allows him to think being as that which continuously *gives*.

Thus, I disagree with Dahlstrom and Magnus that only the being of Dasein is at stake in this decisive passage and elsewhere in *Being and Time*. True, Heidegger there does refer to Dasein's being as distinctive. Yet, he does so as a specific proof of the transcendence of being as such, i.e., of its disclosure, because Dasein is the being that understands other beings in their being. That is, Dasein is the being that can follow, comprehend and perform (*nach-vollziehen*) that movement of being. Only as such, and this is crucial for our purposes here, is there in the transcendence of Dasein's being "the possibility and necessity of the most radical *individuation*." (SZ: 38f/35f) This means, first, that Heidegger aims at disclosing being *via* Dasein's being precisely because, second, Dasein's being is such that it can radically be singled out. Dasein *is* itself the possibility and the necessity for radical individuation, i.e., Dasein exists as the possibility and the necessity to ask the question of being. Descartes did precisely that, yet (to no fault of his own) his response to the question fell short of properly expounding the meaning of being. Dasein's possibility for radical individuation is then precisely not purely self-referential, but always already only possible in light of the world. As Dasein self-individuates, and Dasein does that in the text *Being and Time*, Dasein ranges over its being, i.e., over who it is, and thereby Dasein finds the conditions for the possibility of existence. This casts Dasein back into the world, out from the subject-object-dichotomy: "This individuation is a way in which the "there" is disclosed for existence." (SZ: 263/252 *ta*) Dasein's self-individuation takes place in running forth towards death. By this *Transzendenzbewegung*, transcending movement, Dasein becomes authentic: "The ownmost possibility is *nonrelational*. Running forth lets Dasein understand that it has to take over solely from itself the potentiality-of-being in which it is concerned absolutely about its ownmost being." (ibid.) Only when Dasein is properly concerned with its ownmost possibility to be, does Dasein open itself to the question of being in general and that means Dasein, as the questioning being, is authentically in the world only when it asks, *what does it mean to be?* But Dasein can properly ask that question only if Dasein radically singles itself out which happens most forcefully in the realisation that no one can die *my* death in *my* stead.

Not only death, but also angst (or anxiety, as it is often translated) plays a pivotal role here because "[a]ngst individuates Dasein". (SZ: 187/182 *ta*) Angst is neither a psychological state nor fear of, say, demise. Instead, angst as fundamental attunement is "a distinctive disclosedness of Dasein." (SZ: 184/178) Attunement is not a contingent mood for Heidegger, but is an existential one. Attunement determines Dasein in its being. Disclosedness is the decisive term here. Angst does not have an object but its "before-which," *Wovor*, is "*being-in-the-world as such*." (SZ: 186/180) Angst literally and strictly "comes over" Dasein only during its transcendental-hermeneutical self-interpretation. Consider the following claim by Heidegger: "The nothingness before which angst brings us reveals the nullity that determines Dasein in its *ground*, which itself is as thrownness into death." (SZ: 308/295 *ta*) Rather than describing the experience of someone in their lifeworld, from a transcendental perspective—i.e., from the perspective of the *That* of Dasein's existence[17]—this means that the fundamental-ontological conception of angst allows Heidegger to disclose Dasein in its nothingness. The fact that nothingness permeates the being of Dasein, however, does not mean that there is no self. This rather points to the essential tension between being and nothing which Dasein *holds itself out into* in advance and which is what enables any encounter of beings in the first place. This also points to the "not" of the "not-yet" of the ecstasy of the future that predominantly constitutes Dasein's horizon of understanding. That is, Dasein is ecstatically (out of itself) toward that which *is not yet* and this movement constitutes the present moment thanks to which Dasein understands itself and the world. The analytic of angst (and death) reveals Dasein's solipsism. This, however, does not mean that Dasein is "an isolated subject-thing [transposed] into the harmless vacuum of worldless occurrence". (SZ: 188/182) Quite to the opposite, singling out Dasein, i.e., separating Dasein from beings unlike Dasein, most radically discloses that Dasein is always already in the world and always already with others. That is because singling-out is an abstraction and is immediately pushed back to who Dasein is. Abstraction cannot remain where it is, for then the result of the analytic would be empty and formalistic. Put differently, the solipsism is not a static result of the investigation, but is a

---

[17] See also the following claim by Heidegger: "Angst is anxious about naked Dasein thrown into uncanniness. It brings one back to the sheer *That* of one's ownmost, individuated thrownness." (SZ: 343/328 *me*; *ta*).

momentary abstraction in the course of Dasein's self-investigation. Dasein's self-investigation, then, depicts an experience of transcendence in the sense of an experience of finitude. This experience at once brings Dasein before its own finitude and before being as such in its finitude. Here we see the striking difference between Epicurus and Heidegger. For Epicurus the analysis stops short of an ontic fear of demise and breaks off Dasein's self-investigation. For Heidegger proper angst is what fundamentally attunes Dasein to be authentically in the world and pushes Dasein to investigate further.

Chapter 3
Understanding Being and Dasein's Temporality

When I first introduced the *understanding* of being earlier in this part, I presupposed the specific meaning of "understanding." Yet, it is crucial to carve out what Heidegger means by "understanding" to grasp being to its full extend. I shall here now also carve out how the understanding of being relates to Dasein's temporality. I tie my findings to the role death plays in this regard. As we know from the *Davos Disputation*, *Being and Time* posits death as utmost limit in order to develop Dasein's radical and "primordial" futurity. I thus also address the question why Heidegger thinks it necessary to posit a radical futurity of Dasein's understanding of being and how death is at all supposed to enable Dasein's futurity. In order to do so I need to explicate Dasein's temporal *ecstasies*, a term Heidegger bases on the Ancient Greek word ἐκστατικόν. Heidegger understands ἐκστατικόν to indicate Dasein's *"primordial "outside of itself"."* (SZ: 329/302) The analysis of Dasein's ecstatic temporality serves to move the analytic beyond Dasein's pre-ontological and nonthematic understanding of being. My main argument in this chapter is that both Dasein's pre-ontological understanding and its thematic grasping of being are conditional on being-toward-death.

Before I begin with my interpretation of Dasein's temporal ecstasies, let me briefly point out that there are, of course, religious and today also psychological echoes in the word ecstasy. The former speaks to experiences of the divine that are out of ordinary. The latter speaks to a state that is extraordinary. For Heidegger, however, only the original Greek meaning of ἐκστατικόν as "outside of itself" is relevant and speaks to how Dasein's temporal ecstasies of that which has been, that which currently is, and that which is to come, so perfectly flow into one other that none of them is for itself, but each is outside itself and in the other. The ἐκστατικόν also refers to how Dasein is outside itself in this temporal manner already pushed into the world.

© Springer Nature Switzerland AG 2021
J. A. Niederhauser, *Heidegger on Death and Being*,
https://doi.org/10.1007/978-3-030-51375-7_3

1 From Understanding to Disclosedness and Resoluteness

The project of *Being and Time* is to move from Dasein's vague, pre-ontological understanding to a proper ontological *and* temporal understanding of being. By "understanding" Heidegger does not mean the cognitive capacity to perceive and recognise objects as objects. Heidegger neither defines "understanding" in epistemological nor in logical terms, but as a "fundamental existential … which constitutes the being of the there." (SZ: 143/138) Thus, the understanding co-constitutes the very openness of the there thanks to which anything—even in the pre-ontological manner—appears as meaningful. By determining "understanding" in this way Heidegger avoids an objectification of the world. Marinopoulou's recent claim that understanding means that Dasein attempts "to formulate true and valid judgments" (Marinopoulou 2017: 41) about the world could not be further from what Heidegger has in mind. Readings like Marinopoulou's objectify understanding and that which is understood. Furthermore, such readings are based on the prejudice that world is but the objectively given totality of beings. Dasein then supposedly makes value judgments about that available totality. But world means something else for Heidegger.

Dastur puts it as follows:

> For Heidegger the world is not the totality of beings, but the *horizon* in terms of which beings may be comprehended as what they are. It is therefore a constitutive moment of *Dasein* itself, not a receptacle into which the latter may be inserted. (Dastur 1996: 43)

The world is neither given, objectively present totality nor some state Dasein is in. World rather continues to arise as Dasein's horizon, as Dasein projects possibilities of being. But world also, on the reading of Dastur, constitutes Dasein. Again we see the interrelatedness Heidegger sets up that allows him to avoid objectification. World arises, for Dasein continuously projects possibilities into the future. But world *qua* horizon also constitutes Dasein, i.e., Dasein's very openness for the projection of such possibilities. The very direction towards the future is enabled by Dasein's fundamental structure being-towards-death. By presupposing Dasein's fundamental being-in-the-world, Heidegger effectively annuls the problem of knowledge of modern epistemology: how does the subject have access to the world? For Heidegger, the subject-object-relation and -dichotomy is only possible on the ground of Dasein's fundamental disclosure of world. The subject-object-dichotomy must presuppose world before abstracting from it. The subject-object-dichotomy is already an abstraction from being-in-the-world. This dichotomy only makes sense when implicitly presupposing Dasein's being-in-the-world. For Heidegger *understanding* then does not mean to cognise an object and verify that one's representations of the object correspond to it. Instead, understanding means that Dasein is always already dis-covering world, i.e., beings in their being (SZ: 220/211) Put differently, Dasein always already makes present. As a fundamental existential, understanding belongs to Dasein's structure. Understanding is primarily nonthematic and non-propositional since it does not specifically need to ask the question of being in order to disclose beings.

Insofar as Dasein *understands*, Dasein projects itself towards its possibilities-of-being. This projecting is not to be confused with planning. Planning requires actualisation and effectuation, but Heidegger wishes to retain a sense of pure possibility that, on the most fundamental level of sheer projecting, does not *per se* require actualisation. In the existential-ontological sense projection is "the existential constitution of being in the *realm* of factical potentiality of being." (SZ: 145/141) Projection hence spans open a realm of possibilities for Dasein's factical existence. For its projecting character, understanding is of a toward-structure. Dasein understands, insofar as it projects possibilities onto a primordial spatio-temporal openness called future. On the ontological level this projection is without content. The ontological level thus requires the ontic factical decisions of Dasein. The bare, ontological projecting is directed toward Dasein's ownmost possibility, death, as that which limits Dasein but which as that limit discloses to Dasein its possibilities-of-being. This is why Heidegger argues that "[a]s long as it is, Dasein has always understood itself and will understand itself in terms of possibilities." (ibid.) This is a crucial claim regarding Dasein's self-referentiality. Dasein relates to itself insofar as it understands itself, i.e. insofar as it projects itself toward the future as the horizon of its possibilities. Dasein understands itself most authentically, though, only when Dasein projects itself towards its utmost possibility death whence all other possibilities arise. These possibilities are, however, not to be actualised. They are to remain purely possible and thus abeyant. This is already an indication of the abyss that will be pivotal for the thinking of *Ereignis*. This abeyant, purely ontological projecting enables any ontic, factical projecting. Thus, the primordial understanding "does not thematically grasp that upon which it projects, the possibilities themselves." (ibid.)

Here Heidegger introduces the idea that being is possibility, insofar as Dasein's understanding (thematic grasping) of being is equivalent to being. But with the notion of possibility Heidegger also seems to introduce a certain contingency that is not helpful, if the goal is a thematic analysis of being. This leads to the question, how being as possibility can properly and thematically be grasped. The short and for now rather unclear answer: through the ecstasis of the future (cf. SZ: 327/312). Dasein understands its ability-to-be as it projects itself toward the open possibility-horizon of the future, which is ultimately constituted by Dasein's utmost limit: death. In order to arrive at a thematic grasping of being the text must hence bring Dasein's futural temporality into focus.

Dasein's ontological directedness towards its death means that Dasein is always already ahead of itself in its ways of being. Being-ahead-of-itself "concerns the whole of the constitution of Dasein." (SZ: 192/185) Dasein is ahead of itself also because of its care-structure which conditions Dasein always to be concerned with…, to be with beings innerworldly, care for others and itself. "Innerworldly" is an adverb. It articulates the way in which beings appear and how Dasein encounters them in the world. Care is the being of Dasein. This articulation of being shows the performative character of being. Being is or rather takes place as taking care of…, being concerned with …, etc. Thus, the understanding of being is not the understanding of some highest entity called Being. Rather being is only understood in the acts of Dasein understand*ing* its ordinary everyday dealings. Death plays a pivotal part here: "[c]are is being-toward-death." (SZ: 329/315) Dasein's directedness suggests, first, that Dasein is outside itself and, second, that *being* as Dasein's understanding of being is temporal. In order to make the pre-ontological understanding of being thematically explicit, that is, in order to grasp the meaning of being, the temporality at work must specifically be carved out. Ecstatic temporality is what enables Dasein's toward-directedness of disclosing (being) in the first place, since temporality generates the presence (being) at work in any disclos*ing*. This is why in the *Contributions* Heidegger says that in *Being and Time* ""time" is a directive toward, and a resonating with, that which takes place in the uniqueness of the ap-propriation [*Er-eignung*] as the truth of the essential occurrence of beyng." (GA 65: 74/59) Note, then, that in understanding and disclosing (of being) there is nothing given, for being is not something present-at-hand. Rather, only *in* the event of disclosing being is as self-disclosing.

Besides understanding, attunement and discourse co-constitute Dasein's openness to the world. "*Discourse is existentially equiprimordial with attunement and understanding.*" (SZ: 161/155) This, in turn, means that being as disclosedness is constituted by understanding, discourse and attunement. The claim to equiprimordiality means any understanding is always already attuned. Dasein is always already in a mood and that mood predisposes and co-determines understanding and hence world-disclosure in discourse.

If, for the sake of illustration, we put the movement of the disclosure of meaning in logical terms, then disclosing takes place *ex negativo*.[1] Dasein's fundamental attunement angst plays a pivotal role here. Expanding on what I argued above, angst is a prime disclosedness of being. Angst is the name Heidegger gives to the existential-ontological phenomenon of a *seeming* collapse of meaning. Angst is "utter insignificance" (SZ: 187/181) of anything ready-to-hand and present-at-hand. The before-which or the about-what, *Wovor*, of angst is being-in-the-world itself, is the very possibility of anything being present. The *Wovor* is not an object, but again a case of formal indication, an immanent occurrence. Angst is most intense before death as the possibility of not-being (cf. SZ: 254/244). Angst hence brings most radically before nothingness. *There is nothing* in angst, no object, no ground, nothing to hold on to. In the analysis of angst Heidegger, then, discloses a prime way of thinking outside the realm of beings! Angst introduces Dasein to the difference between being and beings. As I argued above, angst discloses that a "not" determines Dasein in its ground. Thus, any presence and disclosure, including the horizons in terms of which Dasein discloses, are conditional on a "not," a non-availability. Angst, then, does not simply refer to an ontic collapse of meaning. Rather, angst as fundamental attunement, as utter insignificance, together with the nihilation of the nothing, death, the not-yet, is co-constitutive of disclosedness, i.e., of a proper grasping of the *meaning* being that Dasein must disclose. In moments of

---

[1] See my paper on the possibility of establishing an existential logic by explicating death in *Being and Time* (cf. Niederhauser 2017b).

experiencing "angst" Dasein reaches down to that fundamental attunement angst that always already co-constitutes Dasein. Thus, meaning arises out of a non-availability. When Heidegger argues that angst "discloses, primarily and directly, the world as world" (SZ: 187/181), I understand him as saying that the meaning of the world arises out of the nullity of Dasein, and this nullity is ultimately conditional on death. Dasein can properly disclose the meaning of being only by accepting its thrownness. In sum, the fundamental attunement angst, which is intimately related to death, discloses the ontological difference, the "not" between being and beings. Moments of experiencing angst can then be moments of breaking free from the prevalence of beings, tools, equipment, and the modes of the everyday and in this way a radical openness of the horizon of the future unfolds out of Dasein's nullity. For the ontological difference, Dasein can tear open new temporal horizons, i.e., new modes of presence which grant a different meaning of beings, and this includes history. Dasein's nullity, then, is not an unsurpassable abyss, but the reference point between being and beings. Moreover, the "not" that is here involved prohibits an indeterminate and chaotic openness, for the "not" limits what can be.

This is crucial because it defies claims that the understanding of being amounts to a sheer positivity or a prefixed givenness of meaning waiting to be discovered. Such readings are common among Hegel scholars who stress the necessity of negativity for history and world-access. I will have more to say on Heidegger's critique of Hegel's negativity and Heidegger's attempt to think "the negative" more radically and originally than Hegel in Part II of this book. Note for now that Stephen Houlgate maintains that *Being and Time* establishes "a definitive horizon of understanding within which all thought of being … must occur." (Houlgate 2006: 106f) Houlgate maintains that Hegel's *Phenomenology of Spirit* breaks down the ordinary consciousness of the definitive horizon and shows that absolute knowledge is radically open. Heidegger's account, however, closes being off and hence is a case, claims Houlgate, of ordinary consciousness. In the language of *Being and Time* this would mean that *Being and Time* on the whole provides but an inauthentic understanding of being. This is not the case. True, there is a determinateness of the horizons of Dasein. The very term "horizon" indicates that. But the horizon is not definitive once and for all and but a sophisticated reformulation of ordinary consciousness. If the understanding of being were fixated, then Dasein would be "static" as well. Yet, to counter with Müller, Dasein is "as living understanding of being the site of being." (Müller 1964: 89) Houlgate's claim only holds true for the inauthentic mode of the they. The they is truly trapped in a fixed horizon of understanding, in a historically encrusted understanding of being. Heidegger himself explicitly says in *Being and Time* that we must question what is self-evident and given (cf. SZ: 49/48). Dasein must, however, wrench itself free from what the mode of the they takes for granted. The proper understanding of being is a horizon that self-constitutes out of the structural totality of Dasein's temporal ecstasies, and primarily out of the future, *as* Dasein projects possibilities of being. That is to say, a "not-yet" and a "not" constitute Dasein's horizon of understanding because the future is not yet. Thus, Dasein does not encounter a definitive prefixed horizon, but a truly radical openness of the future that is conditional on death. The negativity Hegelians look for is found in death and angst in *Being and Time*. Note, however, also that the radical openness of the future is not detached from Dasein's past. More on this below.

A central problem of *Being and Time* is rather how, or if at all, Dasein can access its fundamental structures and become authentic and whether *each* Dasein that we each are must and *can* do so. For Heidegger even calls carrying out being-toward-death "existentially a fantastical demand" and an "ideal of existence" (SZ: 266/255). If Dasein is in fact perfectly capable of making itself authentic, then Dasein would be precariously close to being capable of positing itself. Moreover, on the ontic level this would imply that Dasein is heroic and tragic. This cannot be the aim of a phenomenological project. This is why Demske argues that *Being and Time* itself is a text that has an authentic and an inauthentic side. Demske points out that *Being and Time* is inauthentic precisely when it comes to the question whether and how Dasein can achieve authenticity (Demske 1970: 113). This is most obvious, Demske maintains, in Heidegger's talk of the necessity for Dasein to choose its hero (cf. SZ: 385/367). Yet, if we consider *Being and Time* a transcendental self-investigation, then the transformation takes place in the text, insofar as the text uncovers Dasein's existential-ontological structures that enable Dasein's authenticity. The text then is a preparation for the transformation. Hence Heidegger's analytic of death is not a normative guideline for action. This, however, leads to the problem that we cannot seem to make any of the existential-ontological adjustments Heidegger at times seems to be demanding. Dasein simply does not posit itself in its being. Heidegger will consequently move away from the possibility that each Dasein can self-transform according to the ideal of existence when he begins to talk of "the few and rare" in the *Contributions* (cf. GA 65: 11/11). There, only a select few are required to carry out the transformative tasks and this means only a few are required to carry out being-toward-death. More on this in Part II.

In *Being and Time* Heidegger introduces the notion of *resoluteness*, *Entschlossenheit*, as Dasein's mode of authentic disclosedness. As "decisive" and "strong-willed" the English "resoluteness" and the German "*Entschlossenheit*" sound, in the existential-ontological sense Heidegger means something else than our ears would have us believe. Heidegger often uses ordinary words that carry certain, immediate connotations. He then reverses the meaning of these words. But this is not arbitrary. The reversal in meaning moves the ordinary word out of its ontic meaning toward something as yet unheard-of, something that is in that sense primordial and that has little to nothing to do with the word's ordinary connotations. Ignoring its ordinary meaning, we hear in *ent-schlossen* the root verb *schließen* which means "to lock." To be *ent-schlossen* then literally means to be *un-locked, dis-closed*. At the same time "resoluteness" does retain a sense of decisiveness for Heidegger. Dasein decides to be itself according to what it has learnt about itself during its self-investigation. That is, with resoluteness Heidegger assumes to have disclosed Dasein's ownmost ability to be. *Resoluteness* is thus the most primordial way of Dasein's authentic being-in-the-world. Heidegger writes: "Now, in resoluteness the most primordial truth of Dasein has been reached, because it is *authentic*." (SZ: 297/273).

This claim by Heidegger is crucial because it stresses the fact that he means by *Entschlossenheit* the full disclosedness of Dasein. Dasein's world, its "being-in" and Dasein's self are all at once disclosed here. Note that *entschlossen* always means both "opened up" and "resolute", where the former takes primacy. Being resolute opens Dasein to hear the call of conscience and to be with others and in the world now determined "in terms of [*Dasein's*] ownmost ability-to-be." (SZ: 298/274) Dasein's ownmost ability-to-be is directly related to Dasein's ownmost possibility, death. Only if Dasein runs forth towards its death as its ownmost possibility can Dasein be *resolute*. Yet, Heidegger reminds us that this full disclosure of Dasein's world, self, and being-with-others is still only possible thanks to Dasein's simultaneous "*Unentschlossenheit*", "irresoluteness" (cf. SZ: 299/275). As should have become obvious by now I do not hold to the view that Dasein is ever an individual. Dasein is the attuned openness of the human being to being. As such the diagnosis of *Entschlossenheit* does not treat of some "Dasein's" authenticity or one can reach the "state" of authenticity. Instead, Dasein *qua* this fundamental openness has here come into its own and stands revealed. This is what the German word "*eigentlich*" means.[2] Again, this "standing revealed" of Dasein does not mean pure authenticity but shows that Dasein is equiprimordially in truth and untruth, authenticity and inauthenticity. Resoluteness is then a first decisive step towards grasping being thematically. Still, Dasein is the focus here and hence also Dasein's understanding of being, not being itself.

The text arrives at resoluteness from the analysis of Dasein's conscience and the call of conscience. Dasein encounters conscience in a persistent call, which calls upon Dasein to enter into a relationship with its most authentic possibilities and its own self (cf. SZ: 273/252). But Dasein for the most part always already listens to the they-self, to its non-authentic possibilities.[3] It is in an interruption, a breach away from the they-self and calls Dasein towards its being-in-the-world. In my view this does not so much say that Dasein is supposed to become an authentic self-sufficient, self-certain individual through the call of conscience. On my reading this rather suggests that Dasein begins to leave behind the subject-object-dichotomy. That is to say, the *there* of being, i.e., the temporal openness for the question of being, the very openness in which humans *ecstatically* participate, is thrust open in the call of conscience and radically brings Dasein back into its world, more precisely into the uncaninness of being-in-the-world (cf. SZ: 277/255f). The uncanniness at the heart of being-in-the-world, which Heidegger sees—and which also tells us that he is far from idealising Dasein's authenticity—this fundamental uncanniness points to the *uncertainty* of existence contra the self-certainty of the enclosed Cartesian subject. The only certainty of Dasein is the uncertainty of the hour of its death.

---

[2] Obviously, a sense of *eigen* is also present in *Ereignis*.

[3] One could point out that Heidegger writes *Being and Time* in the 1920s. Perhaps then the public they-self of that decade is what Dasein is to break away from in order to achieve again a genuine stance in and relationship with its history.

The call of conscience introduces at least two significant trajectories for the later thinking path. First, Heidegger returns to the call of conscience in *Being and Time* as the most significant sense. The shift away from the *intuitus* is crucial for the rest of the thinking path. This is because, second, in the later philosophy it will be *being* which calls upon man and man will respond to the calls of being. While the call of being is not yet present in *Being and Time*, Heidegger stresses the significance of hearing: "Hearing even constitutes the primary and authentic openness of Dasein for its ownmost ability-to-be [*Seinkönnen*], as in hearing the voice of the friend whom every Dasein carries with it. Dasein hears because it understands." (SZ: 163/153 *ta*) Hearing in the ontological sense then is not some ontic capacity to receive soundwaves. Hearing opens Dasein to its most authentic possibilities to be itself. The ominous "friend" Heidegger here mentions is not further explicated and we find no clues for it elsewhere in the text. It remains speculation but it may well be that this "friend" is death and that Heidegger here takes inspiration from Rilke. After all Heidegger here also addresses Dasein's ownmost ability-to-be which Dasein presses into the most when it runs forth towards its ownmost possibility, death. On this reading, then, it is death calling on Dasein and Dasein's ontological hearing harkens to the voice of this most intimate "friend".

This would also explain that the content of the call is "nothing" (cf. SZ: 273/252) There is no propositional content of the call. Instead, there is an appeal [*Aufruf*] to Dasein to be itself. Note that Heidegger here talks of Dasein's *eigenstes Seinkönnen*, ownmost ability-to-be into which Dasein only presses forth when it is authentically towards its death. But this is not some heroic "state" one enters. Rather, as conscience speaks in the mode of silence, Dasein itself becomes silent. It is precisely this *stillness*, though, which is key to be awoken again to the significance of the question of being. A question which is itself open and remains a question. Most crucial for our endeavours here then is Heidegger's argument that it is care which calls upon Dasein in the call of conscience. Care *qua* the being of Dasein is the fundamental attuned structure thanks to which Dasein is always already ahead of itself, toward …, thrown into the world and always already in a certain web of meaning Dasein has to disentangle—and of course thanks to care Dasein is also always already prone to fall for its they-self. Not only is care the being of Dasein. As Heidegger explicitly argues, "[care] is being-towards-death." (SZ: 329/303) Heidegger says this in the pivotal §65 of *Being and Time* which brings together the entire analytic of Dasein under the header of *Temporality as the Ontological Meaning of Care*. Care *is* being-towards-death means that Dasein's *being*, that which Dasein is always already concerned with, *is* its being-towards-its-death as its ownmost possibility, as the possibility of its impossibility of existence. That is to say, as is the main argument of this part, Dasein can at all ask the question of being precisely because of its relationship with its death, because this is how Dasein exists—as finitely *towards* … The utter finitude of Dasein—and of being and time— is what Heidegger is after contra the metaphysical tradition. The authentic future of Dasein which is here *ent-schlossen, dis-closed*—translated as "resolute" in the official English versions of *Being and Time*—is finite.

Thus, resoluteness, or better resolute self-disclosedness, comes about when Dasein *understands* the call of conscience and recognises its lostness to the they-self. The they-self is however not some ominous Other. Instead, the they-self is an existential-ontological structure of Dasein. Hence when Dasein is resolutely self-disclosed the they-self does not disappear but is integrated in the full self-disclosure in which Dasein finds a hold for itself in the midst of beings. It is crucial to note that the call directly addresses Dasein and calls Dasein to decide for its ownmost ability-to-be by running forth (indicating the futurity of resoluteness) toward death (cf. SZ: 272 and 305ff/262 and 292ff). I shall return to the silent call of conscience in more detail in Part IV of the book. Note for now that literally "nothing" calls upon Dasein to be itself in the call of conscience. That is, the "not" that fundamentally constitutes Dasein and its future calls upon Dasein to become itself. Heidegger calls this accepting one's ontological guilt. To accept guilt is tantamount to found oneself on "a being [*Sein*] which is determined by a not" (SZ: 283/272). That is to say, Dasein does not choose itself out of thin air. Dasein rather recognises that its existence is fundamentally determined by what it is "not" and this "not" limits Dasein's possibilities. Moreover, ontological guilt also implies that Dasein is infinitely indebted to all others who have come before it and who will come after it. Far from being a moralistic claim, guilt is an articulation of love for one's ancestors and one's descendants. The "not" of ontological guilt is not privative or negative in a dialectical or logical sense (cf. SZ: 286/274). Nor is the "not" of ontological guilt a lack. For lack only applies to something present-at-hand. Instead, for the ontic-ontological difference Dasein can only experience lack in its ontic concerns and dealings with beings and others. Ontologically the "not" of guilt is entirely incorporated and does not speak to a lack or failure of Dasein at all, but rather to the true richness and fullness of Dasein. The "not" of ontological guilt is also related to thrownness. Dasein does *not* make or choose itself. Dasein is therefore forever indebted to others, who Dasein is not, for its own being. Ontological guilt ensures that Dasein is not closed off. The "not" of guilt in a very genuine sense connects Dasein with others. In resolute self-disclosure Dasein accepts this guilt as the ground of its own being. Dasein is only who it is for its thrown, lasting indebtedness to others. Thrown into its guilt Dasein, Dasein does not choose itself. But when Dasein discloses itself resolutely, the possibilities-of-being that Dasein finds, is what Dasein has to take over in order to exist truly and authentically. To exist truly and authentically and appreciating the indebtedness to those who came before us and those who will come after us indicates a temporality—but a non-linear temporality.

Bret W. Davis thus makes the crucial point that the "later Heidegger often hyphenates the word as *Ent-schlossenheit*, stressing this etymologically original ecstatic meaning." (Davis 2007: 41) Dasein's ecstatic temporal structure, to which I shall presently turn, means that Dasein comes towards itself in view of what it has been and if it does so properly, then Dasein is authentically in the world, with others and with itself:

> As *authentic being a self* [*Selbstsein*], resoluteness does not detach Dasein from its world, nor does it isolate it as free-floating ego. How could it, if resoluteness as authentic disclosedness is, after all, nothing other than *authentically being-in-the-world*? Resoluteness

brings the self right into its being concerned [*besorgende Sein*] with what is ready-to-hand, and pushes it toward concerned being-with with others. (SZ: 298/285 *ta*)

Resoluteness is thus an ecstatic-temporal process rather than a state Dasein can arbitrality and at will reach. Resoluteness is Dasein's authentic being-in-the-world because it unfolds from Dasein's ownmost possibility. Methodologically we require Dasein's authenticity, together with Dasein's inauthenticity, because only when Dasein is fully disclosed, is there a possibility to gain a full ontological grasping of what it means to be. Ecstatic resoluteness, then, is the first attempt to leave behind the forgetting of being.

2 Dasein's Ecstatic Temporality

Being and Time aims at an understanding of being that is temporal, for the early Greek insight into being as presence and even the Cartesian reduction of being to presence-at-hand point to time. More precisely, time seems to be structuring presence. What is present, is present temporally. However, the tradition failed to think time properly and in its own right and instead interpreted time as linear. The ecstatic temporality of Dasein in question is not time in the ordinary sense of fleeting or passing time. Instead, ecstatic time *arises*. How these ecstasies work and how they are united is the question of this chapter.

In order to understand Dasein's ecstatic temporality, and as a result of that in how far time *is* the horizon of the meaning of being, we must begin with what Heidegger calls the ordinary (or vulgar) understanding of time. The ordinary understanding of time is conditional on original, ecstatic temporality (cf. SZ: 425/404) In a nutshell, the ordinary understanding of time represents time as linear. Ordinary time is the time of passing homogenous now-states: t_1, t_2, … t_x. As such ordinary time is the time of the they-self and structures the everyday. The three modes of the inauthentic understanding of time are called past, *Vergangenheit*, presence, *Gegenwart*, and future, *Zukunft*. As Heidegger notes in the decisive §65 of *Being and Time*, these are represented as separate from one another. Nonetheless, Heidegger takes the ordinary modes to be indicative of the unity of Dasein's ecstatic temporality, for they are derivative of the primordial ecstatic unity of temporality. Dasein's three proper ecstasies, which the ordinary modes of time are conditional on, are *Gewesenheit* as having-been, *Gegenwart* as good presence, and *Zukunft* as that which is to come. Other than in the ordinary understanding of time, these ecstasies are separate from each other. Instead, they are equiprimordial and, what is even more difficult to comprehend, they are simultaneous. Strictly speaking these are not proper modes that somehow are interrelated. Instead, arising out of the future and returning into the past and thereby letting the presence unfold is how time temporalises itself.

Dasein's ecstasies are reflected in its relation-of-being (*Seinsverhältnis*) with itself insofar as Dasein always already relates to itself out of what it has been and what it projects itself to be. This is a finite process because Dasein is finite. In the prevalent mode of the they, as Dasein falls for the world, Dasein forgets its finite ecstasies and makes time a linear and end-less flow of arbitrarily available now-states. Hence the prevalent talk today of "saving time" and the need to be "time efficient," as if time were a present-at-hand resource we can at will operate with. The only thing these expressions reveal is that we are running out of time, that we have less and less time precisely because we think of time as a scarce resource that continuously passes us by. It is beyond the scope of this book, but I should note that we have not even begun to appreciate what Heidegger has seen in the workings of time in with his notion of the ecstasies of time. Ecstatic time cannot be measured. Ecstatic time does not pass. Ecstatic time *arises* and *gives*. There is a wellspring of abundant riches in ecstatic time, there is a possibility to exist in accordance with it precisely because ecstatic time structures any presence. Ecstatic time is time in excess of itself.

Beginning with §65 Heidegger aims to provide the final argument for why time is supposed to be the horizon of Dasein's proper thematic grasping of being. The analysis of understanding as co-constitutive of resoluteness has pointed to the toward-structure of Dasein in any primordial understanding of itself, others and world. Heidegger now has to lift the analysis of Dasein's "ahead-of-itself" and "out-of-itself" on ontologically sound grounds. That means that Heidegger must now be able to answer ontologically why it is that Dasein is of that toward-direction and what enables this directedness *towards…* As argued above, Heidegger posits death as the utmost limit and ownmost possibility in order to establish Dasein's toward-structure. Yet, this must now be shown to cohere with Dasein's temporal structure as well. Hence, I now address why the ecstasy of the future has priority, what unifies Dasein's ecstatic temporality and what role the phenomenon of death plays in this regard. Following Heidegger's remarks in Davos, I argue that death opens Dasein for its radical futurity and as such death in fact enables Dasein's disclosing of being.

The ordinary understanding of time, maintains Heidegger, is not just the time of the they, but also the way in which even philosophy, post Plato and especially post Aristotle, has often interpreted time.[4] Hegel's conception of time, Heidegger argues, is "the most radical way in which the vulgar understanding of time has been given form conceptually." (SZ: 428/407) This is because Hegel's account of time depicts the most sustained formalisation and philosophical justification of linear time. Hegel first equates time with space. This allows him to posit now-states as points in space. The point posits itself as the now and as the point posits itself it negates itself. For Hegel time is intuited becoming, the movement from being to non-being and vice versa, for every now is already no longer itself when it posits itself. Becoming is the interplay between *Entstehen und Vergehen*, generation and corruption. Hence for Hegel "[t]he being of time is the now." (SZ: 431/409) This is the crucial claim. With the being of time as the now and the being of the now as the point, the Hegelian conception of time formalises the vulgar understanding of time. Hegel formalises and philosophically justifies—in a most abstract and redundant way—what everybody always already knows, but never cares to question whence this assumption comes: that time passes and passes us by. The future passes into the present and the

---

[4] Heidegger mentions Augustine, Aristotle, and Hegel as examples of vulgar time. Heidegger takes from them the positive insight that the ecstatic temporality of Dasein can only be appreciated in relation to vulgar time (cf. SZ: 427/406).

present passes into the past, indifferently so and so on forever. Whatever is actual, will no longer be actual as soon as the next now comes around and what has passed disappears into the past never to return. Hence Hegel's *Logic,* to which I shall turn in Part II, is timeless precisely because Hegel's understanding of time is deeply metaphysical. For Heidegger this is the time of the they. To put it bluntly, Hegel simply formalised the they's understanding of time. The time of the they is only that which is currently present. Thus, the they forgets how that which has been and that which is to come are formative for that which is now. "The vulgar understanding of time sees the fundamental phenomenon of time in the *now,* and indeed in the sheer now, cut off in its complete structure, that is called the "present"." (SZ: 426f/205) In vulgar time there is a certain indifference at work because of the assumed homogeneity of "now-states." There is also a certain scatteredness about it since every "now-state" is cut off from all other "now-states." This finds expression in the idle talk about passing time that has even made it into Hegel's metaphysical system and logic of everything. Hence, as Heidegger says in his lecture course on Hegel's *Phenomenology* and as quoted above, the need to think *being and time* arises. Yet, Heidegger's revolutionary question is: "Why do we [at all] say that time *passes away* [*vergeht*] when we do not emphasize *just as much,* how it comes into being [*entsteht*]?" (SZ: 425/404) The reason for this, as Heidegger explicitly says, is death, more precisely the inauthentic being-towards-death:

> *Dasein knows fleeting time from its "fleeting" knowledge of its death.* In the kind of talk that emphasizes time's passing away, the *finite futurality* of the temporality of Dasein is publicly reflected. And since even in the talk about time's passing away death can remain covered over, time shows itself as passing away "in itself." (ibid.)

Thus, the they's idle talk helps the they to isolate itself from its finitude. The they's fleeing from death finds expression in common phrases like "time flies."

Piotr Hoffman reads the just quoted lengthy passage as saying that Dasein knows its time is passing by because it is mortally finite (cf. Hoffman 2005: 334). In my view this reading does not only fail to account for the depth of the claim in question, but also rather distorts Heidegger's project. Heidegger here provides the reason for how the ordinary understanding of time as *passing* has come about in the first place and he also suggests that authentically being-toward-death could bring about an access to ecstatic time! That is, authenticity comes about by running forth toward death. Hoffmann's reading, however, reinforces the vulgar understanding of time. The passage illustrates that Dasein always already knows of its death. This knowledge is "fleeting" as long as Dasein has not yet taken over its own death as its ownmost possibility. What is reflected in the idle talk about "fleeting time" is Dasein's inauthentic stance towards its mortality. Death is at once the hidden ground of the chatter about fleeting time, and death provides the way toward disclosing authentic primordial temporality. The vulgar understanding of time as fleeting then, which Heidegger also suspects to be dominant in most, if not all, of philosophy, is a direct result of not having faced up to human mortality as the ownmost possibility. This in turn means that philosophy is inauthentic when it does not properly consider human mortality, for example by taking death to be a passageway. We shall see in Parts III and IV that in his writings on the fourfold Heidegger begins to argue for the necessity of the human being to become the mortal being. The ontic talk of fleeting time, however, also positively indicates something—namely, that time cannot be reversed. This is the case precisely because of Dasein's ontological directedness toward the future.

The passage furthermore stresses that Dasein's existential finite futurity is conditional on death. This is why Dasein's fundamental toward-structure is most radically apparent in what Heidegger calls being-toward-death. Death is the limit toward which Dasein exists, but that limit always already determines Dasein in its being. As Daniela Vallega-Neu notes, Heidegger understands death as limit in the Greek sense of πέρας, which is "a limit that gives something free in its limiting. Death is a limit that frees Dasein's ownmost potentiality of being" (Vallega-Neu 2003: 13) That is to say, as πέρας death belongs to Dasein rather than being its other. If Dasein falls for the they, Dasein is precisely not free, because Dasein then isolates itself from its death. The future then has priority because it is *from* its finite futurity that Dasein derives its meaning.

What Heidegger means by future, however, is something else entirely than how we usually think of it. "Here "future" does not mean a now that has *not yet* become "actual" and that sometime *will be*." (SZ: 325/311) Authentic future hence is not a "now" that is not yet and that has to be actualised or will self-actualise. Instead, future is understood as "the coming [*Kunft*] in which Dasein comes toward itself in its ownmost potentiality-of-being." (ibid.) Heidegger here understands future very closely to the origin of the German word *Zukunft*. *Zu-kunft* literally means "that which comes toward," *das Zu-kommende*. When Dasein is authentically towards its finite futurity, Dasein comes toward itself as its ownmost *Seinkönnen*. That is to say, Dasein comes toward itself as authentic resolute disclosing of its understanding of being. In that sense the future constitutes the horizon against which the meaning of being is disclosed, for Dasein "is futural in its being in general." (ibid.) The future then is not a "not-yet" to be actualised. Instead, future means that Dasein is fundamentally directed and oriented toward its utmost limit in such a way that Dasein can authentically and meaningfully disclose world. This is also how Heidegger understands meaning: "Strictly speaking, meaning [*Sinn*] signifies the upon-which of the primary project of the understanding of being." (SZ: 324/310). This is to say that "[m]eaning is an existential of Dasein, not a property that is attached to beings" (SZ 151/147). The world is meaningful for Dasein because Dasein is ecstatically directed towards its ownmost possibility and thereby Dasein is able to disclose beings in their being.

On the face of it the talk of the priority of the future appears to be contradictory to Heidegger's claim that "an *a priori perfect* [characterises] the kind of being of Dasein itself." (SZ: 85/83) Let me briefly clarify Heidegger's peculiar use of the *a priori*, the "before-structure" (*Vor*), and the "always already". For Heidegger these are not timeless notions. Instead, they point to the methodological necessity of presupposing *a being*, Dasein, that understands being. The "before," the *a priori* perfect of Dasein, i.e., *that* Dasein has always already existed, is not a transtemporal claim, and especially not a claim made in terms of linear time. This is an ecstatic-temporal claim. As soon as Dasein is, it is already *in* the world, with others, fallen for the world and the world's factical possibilities. In this sense an *a priori* is what structures Dasein. This is Dasein's having-been and having-been-thrown (cf. SZ: 327/312). As long as Dasein is, it exists according to its having-been-thrown. Moreover, "[*b*]*eing*-thrown means existentially to find oneself in such and such a way." (SZ: 340/325) Thus, Dasein is attuned on the ground of its having-been, which is never of the past in the ordinary sense, but which continues to come towards Dasein, i.e., Dasein's having-been co-constitutes Dasein's future (cf. SZ: 326/311) The fact that Dasein is thrown means that there is a "not" in Dasein's being because Dasein is who it is, for it is *not* everything else that Dasein could have been, for Dasein is not all its other possibilities. This "not" frees Dasein to who Dasein is. There is hence an immeasurable abundance of possible horizons in excess of themselves, limited *and* enabled by Dasein's thrownness and Dasein's ownmost possibility, death, for Dasein "*is always already its not-yet* as long as it is." (SZ: 244/235) This "always already" is not outside of time but takes place *out of* time, out of the ἐξ of Dasein's unitary ecstasies that fundamentally structure Dasein and that let Dasein *transcend* and range over beings. Dasein's ecstasies push Dasein out of itself. Horizons of understanding thus are not given because Dasein is fundamentally determined by a "not:" "Care, the being of Dasein, thus means, as thrown projection: being the null ground of a nullity." (SZ: 285/273 *ta*) Hence, the "not" as having-been has two functions: first, it delimits the contingency of the radical openness of the future. Second, it indicates that meaning is not previously given, but must always be wrested from what is coming towards us. Dasein's coming toward itself in its ownmost ability-to-be means that Dasein comes toward itself as the possibility not to be and this im-possibility of existence is precisely what determines and mediates Dasein's horizons of understanding. When Heidegger thus determines the meaning of existentiality to be the "future" (cf. SZ: 327/312) he argues that existence is meaningful because abundant but finite horizons of possibilities coming to Dasein from that which has been constitute existence.

Unlike the ordinary understanding of the modes of past, present and future suggest, which takes them to be separate, Dasein's ecstasies are unified and the presence results from the interplay of that which has been and that which comes toward Dasein (cf. SZ: 326/311). Thus, Heidegger argues that "[t]emporalizing does not mean a "succession" of the ecstasies. The future is *not later* than the having-been, and the having-been is *not earlier* than the present. Temporality temporalizes itself as a future that makes present, in the process of having-been." (SZ: 350/321) The future and that which has been are simultaneous in authentic original temporality insofar as that which is present *now* is always present only against the horizon of the future, but in order for understanding to work the future must ground that which has been. The past is not only not cut off from the future, but the past is grounded in the future. This interplay of future and having-been structures the "good presence" of Dasein. The mode of ordinary presence is one of Dasein "being swept along, [a mode where Dasein] never acquires another ecstatic horizon of its own accord." (SZ: 348/320) Unless Dasein faces up to its death, to its boundary situation and is thereby "brought back from its lostness." (ibid.) Only by pushing itself into its ownmost possibility, does Dasein become aware of its lostness and hence Dasein can tear open authentic horizons again. This brings about a "good presence". This "good presence" is not the presence of a passing now-state that disappears into oblivion. Good presence rather *arises* and unfolds out of the tension between what is to come and what has been. Heidegger calls this ecstatic unity "temporality."

On the most fundamental level Dasein's ecstasies are not successive but simultaneous (cf. SZ: 350/334) Temporality as the unity of the ecstasies is the meaning of Dasein's being because temporality makes any disclosure of world and being possible. Original temporality is finite because it is bound up by Dasein's utmost futural limit, death, and therefore being, as it manifests phenomenologically, is "itself" finite (cf. 331/316). Dasein's understanding of being is not contingent because Dasein's understanding is conditional on throwness and therefore on tradition and origin. At the same time there is no prefixed set of horizons since new horizons can be torn open from within Dasein's ecstatic moments. This is possible precisely because of the workings of ecstatic temporality. With every new birth of Dasein new possibilities of interpreting tradition are born. This is how the future takes the lead and returns into the past. Moreover, Heidegger argues that as "[a]uthentically futural, Dasein is authentically *having-been*." (SZ: 326/311) Thus, only if Dasein is authentically open for its future, and that also means that Dasein is authentically towards its own death, can there be an authentic understanding of what has been, i.e., of *Geschichte*. What Heidegger calls *existence* in *Being and Time* is then not existence in the metaphysical sense but the ecstatic-temporal openness for the meaning of being, which the human being does not posit, but for whose advent the human being is the site. The care-structure of Dasein in turn is only possible for the finite temporalizing itself of primordial finite time (cf. SZ: 331/304). That is to say Dasein understands itself, the world and others as continuous and is concerned with these precisely because of how ecstatic temporality structures all that is present as belonging-together. That primordial time is finite always already pushes Dasein back into its abundant but finite possibilities and lets Dasein appreciate what is: the wonder of world. Now we can also appreciate more that world is a continuously arising horizon: "Temporalizing itself with regard to its being as temporality, Dasein *is* essentially "in a world" on the basis of the ecstatic and horizonal constitution of that temporality. The world is neither present-at-hand nor ready-to-hand, but temporalizes itself in temporality." (SZ: 365/334 *ta*)

By privileging the openness of the future Heidegger breaks with the prevalence of the actual and therefore with the metaphysics of presence. Pöggeler argues that "metaphysics is not guided by an openness of the future as an exciting and tense possibility that arises from an utmost impossibility. Instead, metaphysics is guided by "actuality"." (Pöggeler 1983: 105).[5] Pöggeler's remark points precisely to what I shall address next: death as Dasein's ownmost possibility which is at the same time the possibility of Dasein's impossibility. Death as that possibility tears open the horizons of Dasein's understanding of being, without giving Dasein anything to actualise.

---

[5] My translation.

Chapter 4
From Death as Possibility to Being as Possibility

Possibility, *Möglichkeit*, is a central but problematic notion in Heidegger's thinking. It is problematic not least because the German *Möglichkeit* is of an entirely different origin than its English translation *possibility*. The way we understand "*Möglichkeit*" impacts not only our interpretation of death and being in *Being and Time*, but also how we understand Heidegger's turn and the thinking *of* the event. It is pivotal to bear in mind the difference in the origin of the words "*Möglichkeit*" and "*possibility*." In what follows I shall explicate Heidegger's notion of *Möglichkeit* in light of the analytic of Dasein's death. The core argument of this chapter is that death as ownmost possibility brings Dasein before being. Moreover, I shall carve out how this early vicinity of possibility and being introduced in *Being and Time* later leads Heidegger to determine being *itself* as the possible. He does so most prominently in the *Letter on Humanism* and in the earlier lecture on *Plato's Doctrine of Truth*. I shall consider both texts here.

1 Death and Dasein's Being-Whole

Besides bringing out Dasein's futurity the analytic of death in *Being and Time* allows Heidegger to establish Dasein's "being-able-to-be-whole," *Ganzseinkönnen*. The hermeneutical situation after the first section of the text is such that Dasein has been revealed as always already "ahead of itself," which, as outlined above, turns out to mean that Dasein is fundamentally determined by a not-yet. In existentiell terms Dasein hence appears to be unwhole. There always seems to be something lacking, there is always something Dasein could still be doing. Apparently, Dasein is complete only when Dasein demises. The same can be said of something ready-to-hand like a ripening fruit (cf. SZ: 243f/234f). The ripening fruit is also determined by its not-yet being a ripe fruit. The fruit's becoming-ripe is conditional on this not-yet. On the face of it, the same seems to be valid for Dasein. Dasein appears to be complete only when it has demised because demise makes it impossible for

© Springer Nature Switzerland AG 2021
J. A. Niederhauser, *Heidegger on Death and Being*,
https://doi.org/10.1007/978-3-030-51375-7_4

Dasein to continue to project possibilities. Yet, Dasein is not something ready-to-hand: "In death, Dasein is neither fulfilled nor does it simply disappear; it has not become finished or completely available as something ready-to-hand." (SZ: 245/236 ta) We can die before our time, too young, with unfinished projects. Yet, even when Dasein dies old and fulfilled, there is still a sense of lack, even if only the lack felt by others. Dastur hence stresses that after someone has died they are more present than "he or she ever was in life." (Dastur 1996: 46) In Chap. 2 I pointed out the difference between ontological death and demise. The conception of death Heidegger is after is such that it allows for Dasein's toward-structure, its being-ahead- and out-of-itself, but also for Dasein's wholeness, as long as it is. Even though demise cannot account for Dasein's wholeness, this ontic phenomenon still formally indicates ontological death as Dasein's limit determining Dasein's wholeness.

Heidegger introduces the notions of *Ganzsein*, being-a-whole, and *Ganzseinkönnen*, being-able-to-be-whole as descriptions of Dasein's totality. He wishes to demonstrate the possibility of authentic being-able-to-be-whole precisely because that would provide Dasein's primordial being, which is unitary (cf. SZ: 234/224). There are certainly echoes of Husserl's practical *I can* in *Ganzseinkönnen*. The *I can* is Husserl's response to the Cartesian *ego cogito*. Husserl anchors the *I can* in the body. The *I can* introduces an element of potentiality that underlies all activity. As such the *I can* constitutes the ego's practical freedom (cf. Husserl 1989: 129) The ego never completely gives in to a mere course of action the ego is accustomed to. Instead, since the ego always retains the potentiality of the *I can*, there remains a certain freedom. The *I can* implies a positive freedom in face of any negative constraints that might arise with new affections. The "consciousness of the free "I can" and not the mere consciousness that "it will come," "it will happen" frees the subject's "immediate horizon"" (ibid.: 270) for any future action beyond the current most immediate horizon. In everyday dealings the subject is drawn into a mode of acting where the subject merely executes, but does not really choose what it does. The subject's most immediate horizon determines the subject's actions. However, thanks to its constitutive *I can* the subject can transcend beyond the most immediate horizon. Transcending discloses new possibilities for the subject. For Husserl this possibility is not "merely [a] *"logical"* possibility … [but a] *practical* possibility as the to-be-able-to [*Können*]." (ibid.: 273) This is similar for Heidegger's notion *Seinkönnen*, being-able-to-be, which is best thought of as transcendental ability that guarantees Dasein's positive freedom. While Husserl places weight on the influence of affects on the body and subsequently on the subject's choice-making, Heidegger investigates the anonymous they-self, which Dasein falls for in its most immediate horizon called everdayness. In everydayness Dasein does as *they* do, Dasein speaks as *they* speak. Dasein does so because the they is an existential of Dasein (cf. SZ: 130/122). In order to be free Dasein must wrench itself from the they-self and transcend towards new horizons. Dasein *can* do so because of its self-understanding as being-able-to-be. This is "the idea of existence" (SZ: 232/221) as regulating transcendental idea. The idea of existence as being-able-to-be means that this idea contains the possibility for Dasein to take on its own being as an issue for itself. The talks of the "idea of existence" also indicates that

Dasein is not its own principle, but that Dasein is about experience, thinking, and being-in-the-world. In forerunning, i.e., in projecting itself into the future and transcending itself, each Dasein "can wrench itself free" (SZ: 263/252) from the they. Dasein *is able to be whole* by wrench*ing* itself free. This, in turn, is possible if Dasein faces death. For the they never dies.

By "holding death for true" (SZ: 265/254) Dasein runs forth toward its ownmost possibility and only in this way can Dasein "first make certain of its ownmost being in its insuperable totality." (ibid.) This is how "[d]eath is a way to be that Dasein takes over as soon as it is." (SZ: 245/236) Running forth toward death enables "the possibility of existing as a *whole potentiality-of-being*." (SZ: 264/253) Thus, Dasein can be ontologically whole because of death. As Lehmann, I think, rightly puts it: "Death, as limit, determines Dasein as a whole. If this limit were the absolute other of Dasein, then it could not reach this limit as long as it is." (Lehmann 2003: 410) Moreover, Heidegger argues that "[t]he existential-ontological constitution of the totality of Dasein is grounded in temporality." (SZ: 437/414f *ta*) Dasein can be whole insofar as it runs forth to its utmost limit that determines it as soon as it is. This takes place on the ground of Dasein's toward structure, put differently, on the ground of Dasein's ecstatic futurity, which death enables, insofar as death is the ultimate "not" and "not-yet" of Dasein. Heidegger speaks of *Seinkönnen* and *Ganzseinkönnen* rather than merely of Dasein's totality, *Ganzheit*, in order to denote Dasein's immeasurable possibilities limited only by its ultimate possibility, death. There is infinity in finitude for Dasein. The convoluted claim that the future is "the arrival in which Dasein comes towards itself in its ownmost being-able-to-be" now reads: the future is a mode that lets Dasein authentically relate to itself and the world, if and only if Dasein recognises its ownmost possibility: death. I should mention here that Alejandro Vallega therefore, and in my view rightly so, identifies Dasein's futurity with being-toward-death (cf. Vallega 2003: 8). Thus, at the most fundamental level Dasein can at all relate to anything because Dasein is mortally finite and directed towards that finiteness: *sum moribundus*. The future gives meaning and weight to Dasein's ability-to-be, for the horizon of the future ultimately arises out of death. Dasein is always already constituted as a whole on the ground of being-toward-death, but Dasein must specifically hold that possibility for true in order to assume itself as whole. Realising its ownmost being-able-to-be-whole lets Dasein properly grasp *being as possibility*.

2   Dasein's Ownmost Possibility

It might be a rather strange claim that death supposedly is Dasein's ownmost possibility. Even though in the melange of the everyday death could not be further removed from Dasein. What should death have to do with possibility? Is death not the breakdown of any and all possibility? Is death not the most obvious *fact* of life? We all die sooner or later and until then we need to act on as many opportunities as possible, but death certainly is not one of them. In its everyday dealings Dasein falls for the world, for the next-best opportunity and possibility. But none of those are death. In the public space death has nearly no room. Death is at best an occurrence, at worst bad luck. Death is something that happens but something that does not concern *me* for now. Death is of an "inconspicuousness characteristic of everyday encounters." (SZ: 253/243) Dasein's everyday being-toward-death reveals that death is for the most part understood as something not yet present-at-hand. Even though only *I* can die *my* death and no one can die in *my* stead, the they dictates death to be something so ordinary and irrelevant that death entirely "veils its character of possibility" (ibid.) Nonetheless, the fact that only *I* can die *my* death, already formally indicates that death is *ownmost* to *me*, no matter how strongly the they wants to tranquillise its fear of its impending demise and fall back into blissful carelessness.

To speak of death as possibility must, of course, at first appear paradoxical. Heidegger, however, introduces death as possibility when he points out that the ordinary "possibility of representation" entirely fails, when it comes to death. "*No one can take the other's dying away from him.*" (SZ: 240/231) This indicates to Heidegger that death "signifies a peculiar [*eigentümliche*] possibility of being" (ibid.) precisely because death allows for a most radical individuation. Death cannot be taken away from Dasein. Moreover, Section 1 of *Being and Time* showed Dasein to be "*thrown possibility* throughout" (SZ: 144/139) Thus, as death is in fact a possibility of being that can impossibly be referred to someone else, death must be grounded more fundamentally in Dasein's existential-ontological structures. To refer to death as possibility is hence not as arbitrary as it may at first seem. The existential-ontological determination of death *as* possibility, in turn, allows Heidegger to disclose "the character of possibility of Dasein ... most clearly" (SZ: 248f/239) because "[d]eath is a possibility of being that Dasein always has to take upon itself." (SZ: 250/241) Yet, and this is crucial, "[a]s possibility, death gives Dasein nothing to "be actualized"." (SZ: 262/251) That is, in the analytic of death where death is determined as Dasein's ownmost possibility[1] (where Dasein comes toward itself *as* possibility), Heidegger can fully establish that Dasein is not something present-at-hand, but pure possibility.

Heidegger determines the full existential concept of death as follows: "*as the end of Dasein, death is the ownmost, nonrelational, certain, and, as such, indefinite and insuperable possibility of Dasein.*" (SZ: 259f/248) This conception of death anchors in care as Dasein's being, i.e., in the fundamental ecstatic structure that determines Dasein's ecstatic being-ahead-of-itself. Death is ownmost to Dasein because only *I* can die *my* death. Dasein's being is here most radically individuated. This also means that by running forth towards death Dasein can fully accept its ontological guilt. Accepting death is a nonrelational act just like listening to one's conscience and taking over one's ontological guilt is. No one can do so for *me*. *I* cannot do so for anyone else. Thus, the resoluteness (Dasein's authentic self) that is disclosed

---

[1] Even though death is Dasein's "ownmost possibility" in *Being and Time*, Heidegger does not reduce possibility to death. In a lecture course on the *1st Critique* in 1927 Heidegger calls "philosophy the freest possibility of human existence" because philosophy articulates life and existence (cf. GA 25: 39).

here means a breakdown of "all "worldly" status and abilities of Dasein" (SZ: 307/293). From renouncing beings and worldly status an authentic understanding of being arises. This renunciation is tantamount to running forth toward death as utmost possibility.

On the face of it, it is trivial to say that death is certain. We obviously all have to die. However, by the term *certain*[2] Heidegger means that only when Dasein self-investigates and self-founds its being-in-the-world and being-with-others, can Dasein reach proper certainty about itself. This certainty is precisely not purely self-referential because it arises from the care-structure. Thanks to this non-self-founded certainty Dasein becomes free for authentic factical possibilities of being. Factical possibilities are in fact to be actualised. Facticity[3] is Heidegger's term for *Wirklichkeit* in the existentiell sense. We do not set the conditions of facticity, but *qua* Dasein we are free to investigate those conditions. From the perspective of Dasein's transcendental self-investigation this means that in the analysis of death Dasein has been thematically disclosed in terms of the necessary conditions of Dasein's factical freedom. Thus Heidegger speaks of Dasein's "*passionate, anxious freedom toward death, which is free of the illusions of the they, factical, and certain to itself*" (SZ: 267/255) This freedom arises from resolute running forth. In resolute running-forth Dasein comes "*face to face with the possibility to be itself.*" (ibid.) With the analysis of death, the text reaches into Dasein's most fundamental structures and here Dasein is pure possibility. Through realising itself as pure possibility Dasein can assert itself as being fundamentally *open* for its authentic, factical possibilities of being. Once Dasein has disclosed for itself its potentiality-to-be in this way, Dasein cannot overturn or surpass this finding. As this is the full account of resoluteness, death shows itself to be Dasein's "*most original possibility*. Death determines Dasein in its ground," as Wolfgang Müller-Lauter puts it (Müller-Lauter 1960: 25)[4] Death does so, in fact, not despite but because "Dasein has … always already turned away from it." (ibid.) Death is thus, as Müller-Lauter calls it, Dasein's "*Ur-Möglichkeit*" (ibid.: 31), which I translate as "ur-possibility" Note that Wolfgang Müller-Lauter's book "*Möglichkeit und Wirklichkeit bei Martin Heidegger*" published in 1960 is so far one of the few studies entirely devoted to possibility and actuality in Heidegger's philosophy.

Yet, there is an important twist. Even though Dasein is now fully disclosed in its being, Heidegger reminds us that "Dasein is equiprimordially in untruth." (SZ: 308/295) That is to say, even though Dasein has found its authentic self, this does not eradicate inauthenticity. Dasein is still "open for its constant lostness … which is possible from the very ground of its own being." (ibid.) On Müller-Lauter's and my readings that ground is death. Thus, if death is that very ground and Dasein always remains open for lostness etc., then death here also shows itself to be utterly

---

[2] Note that the German *gewiß* is the root of *Gewissen*, conscience.

[3] Facticity is one of the places where Heidegger mentions the body. Facticity breaks up Dasein's neutrality into female and male (cf. GA 26: 173).

[4] My translation.

uncontrollable, inaccessible and unavailable. As such death can, however, fully disclose Dasein's being *and* retain Dasein's "untruth," i.e., concealedness, of which inauthenticity and fallenness are possibilities. Untruth also points to the simultaneous concealment in every disclosure. For that self-concealment, which is conditional on death as "ur-possibility," Dasein's being is never static and objectively available but retains its performativity.

Yet, Müller-Lauter argues that death loses its character of "ur-possibility" (cf. Müller-Lauter 1960: 42f) when Heidegger states that death "is constantly certain and yet remains indefinite at every moment as to when possibility *becomes* impossibility."(SZ: 308/295 *me*) The fact that death *becomes* impossibility, claims Müller-Lauter, refutes death's original character of possibility, for it temporalizes death and because death is now apparently actualised as impossibility. True, Heidegger is quite unclear here and by saying "becoming" one could infer that Heidegger seems to suggest that death as possibility is actualised as impossibility. The question hence is whether there is a sudden reversal in the character of Dasein's ur-possibility. If that were the case, then that would mean the breakdown of Dasein's existential self-investigation because as an existential possibility is not a modal category applicable to beings present-at-hand. The ur-possibility must retain its nonactuality and possibility-character. Furthermore, note also that possibility as existential is not contingent as modal possibility is. Rather, possibility as an existential "is the most primordial and the ultimate positive ontological determination of Dasein" (SZ: 143f/139) This, in turn, means that Dasein is not free floating and perfectly at liberty to self-actualise as it wishes (*libertas indifferentiae*). Even though Dasein is pure possibility, Dasein does not choose itself absolutely freely in its actuality (factical existence) at any given moment. This was Sartre's grand misunderstanding. Instead, "Dasein exists as thrown, brought into its there *not* of its own accord." (SZ: 284/272) Hence, as a *positive* ontological determination of Dasein possibility is what *posits* Dasein. Death is that possibility that posits[5] Dasein so that Dasein is always already determined by its "not." However, this positing does not take place from out of a timeless sphere, as Müller-Lauter suggests (cf. Müller-Lauter 1960: 51) *Qua* limit, he maintains, death is outside Dasein, and hence outside time. I have argued the exact opposite. Death *qua* limit is integral to Dasein and as possibility death immanently posits Dasein. Death is only as long as Dasein *is* (this is a complete reversal of Epicurus). Thus, when Heidegger says that death *becomes* impossibility, this does not mean that death loses its character of *existential* ur-possibility. Instead, "becoming impossibility" now says that death *qua* possibility is of an abeyance continuously oscillating between possibility and impossibility. This movement thus rather enforces the character of death as ur-possibility, precisely because as such death gives Dasein nothing to actualise. What always and essentially oscillates between two poles cannot be grasped and cannot be reduced to either side. To say that death *becomes* impossibility, that death is "the

---

[5] Heidegger later calls death the *Ge-setz*, the concentration of all positing, the Law. This will be discussed further in Parts III and IV.

possibility of the measureless impossibility of existence" (SZ: 262/251), emphasises that the being of Dasein is never something present-at-hand; that Dasein's
being *is* always purely *an event*. Precisely this *becoming im-possibility* thus guarantees Dasein's withdrawal from reification. This, in turn, guarantees Dasein's freedom. Death as *existential* possibility must, for the law of equiprimordiality and
simultaneity, contain its opposite within itself. By becoming impossibility death
shows itself as "ur-possibility" because the movement from possibility to impossibility and from impossibility to possibility is only possible insofar as the "ur-possibility" contains the impossible. Thus, I understand the notion that possibility
becomes impossibility as saying that this fundamental possibility always already
and at once self-differentiates (in the sense of *auf-* and *aus-differenzieren*) as possibility and impossibility.

Death as hovering possibility *and* impossibility conditions all of Dasein's factical possibilities: "*Even in average everydayness, Dasein is constantly concerned [es
geht um] with its ownmost, non-relational, and insuperable potentiality-of-being,
even if only in the mode of taking care of things in a mode of untroubled indifference ... that opposes the most extreme possibility of its existence.*" (SZ: 254f/244)
Death structures Dasein's average, everyday existence and thus permeates Dasein's
world. That is, death gives rise to world as the horizon against which beings appear
as beings. Bearing in mind Müller's claim that world is the rising of being, it is
death as ur-possibility that brings most radically *before* being as the non-available
presence in excess of itself thanks to which beings appear.

Seen from the perspective of the history of being the analysis of death and
ecstatic temporality together with Heidegger's interpretation of ἀλήθεια as unconcealment depict a milestone for the thinking path. They allow Heidegger to think
equiprimordially, simultaneously, and ecstatically rather than dialectically or linearly. This is the reason why death will retain its central place in the thinking of
Ereignis. In Part II we shall see that Heidegger transfers over his findings especially
of Dasein's being-toward-death to being itself.

3 From Death to Being

In this chapter I am tracing Heidegger's move from his early conception of possibility in terms of death to his later determination of being itself as the possible. There
is a significant trajectory, I argue, that begins precisely with the analysis of death as
ownmost possibility in *Being and Time* because death fundamentally enables Dasein
to properly disclose being. The analysis of death allows Heidegger to think being as
possibility, more precisely, as realm of the possible. I shall carve out in more detail
in Part II what I introduce here.

In *Being and Time* there is a crucial passage I already referred to above and that
I now quote in full because it epitomises Heidegger's conception of death as
"ur-possibility:"

> As possibility, death gives Dasein nothing to "be actualized" and nothing which it itself could *be* as something actual. It is the possibility of the impossibility of every mode of behaviour toward…, of every way of existing. In anticipating this possibility, it becomes "greater and greater." (SZ: 262/251 *ta*)

From what I argued above it is clear that death as "ur-possibility" is not to be actualised. John Sallis has interpreted just quoted passage as saying that "death is the possibility that suspends all others." (Sallis 1990: 129) This is true to a certain degree, but not entirely. On the one hand, yes, death is that utter abyss that suspends everything. On the other hand, on the most fundamental level of ur-possibility, exactly the opposite does take place. I here follow Demske who argues that death as ur-possibility "enfolds and engulfs all other possibilities, just as it enwraps Dasein's total being-in-the-world, wholly and entirely." (Demske 1970: 26) Thus, Dasein's ur-possibility death spans open a realm and enables all factical possibilities of Dasein. In the context of *Being and Time* it is death in the existential-ontological structure of Dasein that makes possible all of Dasein's possibilities precisely because of the abeyant oscillation between possibility and impossibility. This *turning* leaves Dasein open, directs Dasein toward the horizon of the future, and brings Dasein most radically before its being. What being itself does *after* the turn is similar to what death does in *Being and Time*. Reading this against Müller's notion referred to in Chap. 1 that being itself *is* after the turn the possibility that makes any possibility possible, we see how the conception of death as non-actualisable possibility guides Heidegger to think being itself as realm of the possible. This is one of the reasons why Heidegger in *Contributions* calls death "the highest testimony to beyng". (GA 65: 230/181) When Heidegger turns to his attempts to think *from* being what happens, in my view, is the following: Heidegger radicalises the insight that possibility stands higher than actuality and unites this with the insight into thinking death as "ur-possibility" that forbids any actualisation. The analytic of death in *Being and Time*, then is what opens for Heidegger the horizon to think being neither as presence-at-hand, actuality, nor as beingness but as sheer possibility. Thinking being as pure possibility allows Heidegger to think being no longer as the "constant presence-at-hand [*Vorhandenheit*]" (SZ: 98/96 *ta*) he sees prevalent in modern metaphysics.

The representation of being as constant presence-at-hand, argues Heidegger, diminishes Dasein's world access because world is here reduced to the objectified totality of beings. The world is turned into a present-at-hand object that the subject commands over at will. His early and profound worry about that particular trajectory of the interpretation of being as present availability comes into full force when Heidegger begins to think after the meaning of technology critically. Technology's inherent motivation is to turn everything into something readily available, into standing reserve waiting to be exploited. In Part III on the relation of death and technology I shall hence carve out that it is precisely death that withdraws from the demand of availability and presence-at-hand. This is why death continues to be significant for Heidegger's late philosophy of technology and of the fourfold.

In *Being and Time* Heidegger is, of course, aware that there have been other interpretations of being, which are less reifying than assuming being as sheer presence-at-hand. For example, the ontic "talk ... about the *lumen naturale* in human being" (SZ: 133/129) points to Dasein's ontological structural disposition to understand itself and other beings in their respective being. Heidegger in this passage also introduces the notion of *Lichtung*, clearing, which will be a thematic focus of his later philosophy. Clearing is not a function of human reason, as is the *lumen naturale*. Instead, clearing is the way in which being itself essentially provides a realm of appearance. Even though being clears itself, its self-concealment remains in place. The movement of clearing is the movement of ἀλήθεια. Despite the talk of *lumen naturale*, which indicates previous darkness, there is in metaphysics a tendency to reify being. Yet, considering being in terms of ἀλήθεια and possibility allows Heidegger to think being itself performatively.

His analysis of truth as ἀλήθεια in *Being and Time* is also what leads Heidegger to develop his interpretation of being with regards to Plato's Idea of the Good. Heidegger tries to bring to light the original experience the Greeks might have made when they coined the word ἀλήθεια. In *Plato's Doctrine of Truth*, which is pivotal on the way to the turn, Heidegger says: "The expression "idea of the good" ... is the name for that distinctive idea which ... enables everything else. The good may be called the "highest idea" in a double sense: It is the highest in the hierarchy of making possible; and seeing it is a very arduous task of looking straight upward." (GA 9: 228/175) Seeing the highest idea is a tedious task because making the Idea, or being, the thematic focus of investigation is difficult, if one wishes to avoid reification. Still, this is a metaphysical understanding of being and this is not how Heidegger understands being as the possible or what he means by being enabling something. The Idea of the Good actualises all that is. Being as the possible does not do that. Nevertheless, the thought that being itself as the possible could enable all that is, stays with Heidegger, but he re-interprets it in a non-metaphysical way. In the *Letter on Humanism* Heidegger presents this thought most clearly, when he says, in contrast to metaphysical being:

> Of course, our words *möglich* [possible] and *Möglichkeit* [possibility], under the dominance of "logic" and "metaphysics," are thought solely in contrast to "actuality"; that is, they are thought of the basis of a definite - the metaphysical - interpretation of being as *actus* and *potentia*, a distinction identified with that between *existentia* and *essentia*. When I speak of the "quiet power of the possible" I do not mean the possible of a merely represented *possibilitas*, nor *potentia* as the *essentia* of an *actus* of *existentia*; rather, I mean being itself, which in its favoring presides over thinking and hence over the essence of humanity, and that means over its relation to being. To enable something here means to preserve it in its essence, to maintain it in its element. (GA 9: 316f/242)

Being, he continues, is "*das Mög-liche*," the possible or the likely, as the "*Vermögend-Mögend*."[6] That is to say, being is that which at once is enabling and loving, but not actualising, and itself not available. In *Contributions* Heidegger in this regard speaks of the "*Erzitterung*" of beyng, its trembling or oscillating (GA 65: 262/206). Being

---

[6] De Gennaro therefore translates *Möglichkeit* as likelihood, as that which initially likes and pleases humans (2013: 26).

as possibility, or rather as enabling love, is not a possibility containing its actualisation. Nor is it in any sense proto-actual. Instead, being as possibility is in excess of itself. For its abundance being oscillates and opens the realm or dimensionality of all possibilities and thus also the realm of the actual. As Heidegger says in the *Letter on Humanism* this is a realm of thinking and, I may add, of echoes and that means that being needs the response of human beings.

Heidegger's early diagnosis of death as ur-possibility leads him to question the Aristotelian potentiality-actuality-schema that is prevalent in onto-theo-logy. Thus, the claim that possibility is higher than actuality truly becomes a ground-breaking notion for Heidegger that leads him to challenge not only the Aristotelian, but also the slightly different Hegelian schema. For Hegel what is possible is contained in and consumed by the actual: "What is actual [*wirklich*], is as such possible," Hegel states in the *Science of Logic* (Hegel 2010: 480). According to Dastur, Hegel articulates here what is true for all of modern philosophy where "the possible has always been defined as inferior to the real and the actual." (Dastur 1996: 54) The actual is how history unfolds, the actual is the place of rationality, only the actual is *real*. Max Planck carried this to its logical conclusion, when he said that only what is measurable, is real (cf. GA 7: 52). However, with Heidegger the story becomes: *What is possible pure and simple, is what enables and loves the essence of human beings.* Heidegger's critique of metaphysics then, as an ontology of presence that forgets latency and concealment, begins with his early analysis of death as oscillating, abeyant "ur-possibility." Like death latency and concealment are inaccessible and withdrawing, yet they make everything possible that is *actual*. It is crucial to note that Heidegger begins to call death the *Ge-Birg* of being in the late 1940s. That is to say, death comes to be understood as the concentration of all concealment.

Here we can also trace an important trajectory from Paul Natorp to Heidegger. In his *Philosophische Systematik* Natorp points out that *the* question of philosophy is the question for the unity and meaning of being (cf. Natorp 2004: 72). Although their approach is different—Heidegger does not logically deduce categories, as does Natorp—they both appear to make similar attempts at articulating the meaning of being. Take this claim by Natorp: "In possibility being already speaks, or at least it wants to speak." (Ibid.: 90)[7] Furthermore, Natorp defines possibility as "always simultaneously [!] the possibility of A and not-A." (ibid.: 94) "Therefore, possibility is the ur-ground." (ibid.: 90) In possibility being hence announces itself insofar as possibility is the abeyant simultaneity of A and not-A, or (with Heidegger) of the possible and the im-possible. I cannot here follow this trace any further, but both thinkers, each in their own way, seem to be responding to something similar.

In *Being and Time* there is even already an announcement of being itself as possibility, as that which grants and gives. This is most obvious in the diagnosis of being-toward-death as an existential possibility, a possibility that is to remain possibility:

---

[7] My translation.

[I]f being-toward-death has to disclose understandingly the possibility which we have characterized as *such*, then in such being-toward-death this possibility must not be weakened, it must be understood *as possibility*, cultivated *as possibility*, and *endured as possibility* in our relation to it. (SZ: 261/251f)

Dasein is stretched along that abeyance, and by facing this as true Dasein can bring its factical possibilities into view.

Chapter 5
Dasein's Historicity

Until now I have not mentioned a phenomenon which one might expect should play a pivotal role when dealing with the question of death. That is, of course, the phenomenon of birth. To a certain degree birth is enshrined in the notion of thrownness. Thrownness is, as it were, the existential-ontological notion of birth, for thrownness means that Dasein is and that Dasein is always already factically in the world, bound up in indebted relationships (cf. SZ: 135/127). But Heidegger does appreciate birth in its own right and he does so in the analytic of history in the fifth and last chapter of *Being and Time*. This last chapter is arguably the culmination of ecstatic temporality. In fact, Heidegger develops Dasein's historicity in light of his analysis of birth. I shall now reconstruct this final argument of *Being and Time* and bring to bear its importance for Heidegger's later idea of the history of being. Note that Heidegger later speaks of "another beginning" of the history of being and of thinking that human beings need to heed. In the context of the history of being I understand "another beginning" as a name for "birth." Heidegger's focus on Dasein's historicity plays a pivotal part for his later articulation of *Seinsgeschichte*. The history of being will be a central issue in Part II.

1 On Birth

Heidegger brings birth into play in §72 where he notes that in order to arrive at a proper thematic grasping of Dasein's understanding of being, which ultimately allows access to something like the meaning of being itself, a sufficient original interpretation of Dasein is necessary. Heidegger admits that many structures of Dasein are still obscure. A temporal being-whole, he writes, seems to require not just an "end" but also a "beginning." (cf. SZ: 372/341) Thus something like birth is still missing. But why does Heidegger bring birth into play only now and not only earlier in the analytic of temporality? Is this not a bit arbitrary? In the analytic of temporality only death seemed to play a role. Are critics of Heidegger right after all

© Springer Nature Switzerland AG 2021
J. A. Niederhauser, *Heidegger on Death and Being*,
https://doi.org/10.1007/978-3-030-51375-7_5

who say that Dasein is only born to die? Has Dasein really been established as a whole if birth as Dasein's beginning has been neglected?

Heidegger brings birth into play in the form of a critique of *Lebensphilosophie* which understands life, birth and death in a rather ordinary way. Life is the linear timespan between birth and death. The self is whole or fulfilled when it has died. A common trope at the time of Heidegger writing the book was the question for the "*Zusammenhang des Lebens*," the "connection of life." (cf. SZ: 373/343) Between the contingent events of birth and death the self accumulates a number of *lived experiences* and as long as the self represents itself along the linear stretch between its birth and death the self can establish its clear context and is a totality. In this view, "Dasein" is temporal because it lives from moment to moment but Dasein can always fall back on its pre-established totality between its "birth" and its "death." Yet, this is a representational account of Dasein and turns Dasein's being into something present-at-hand that can be reduced to the number of years Dasein lives and the experiences Dasein makes during that measured time. This does two things. First, it takes time as something that is, i.e., has being, and as something that is only insofar as it is measured. Second, as Dasein is turned into something present-at-hand, a proper conception of its understanding of being is impeded. This can only be found immanently, from within the structures and attunements of Dasein, but not by objectifying Dasein. An objectified Dasein means an objectified understanding of being and that impedes access to being as such. This is because of the difference between being and beings, i.e., because being is not an entity. Once Dasein is reified, for example, as a *res cogitans* somehow attached to a *res extensa*, its understanding of being—by way of Dasein's self-understanding—is also necessarily directed towards being as a "thing." As the human being becomes an object in his self-interpretation, so do world and being. Regardless of Heidegger's criticism here, the ordinary understanding of birth and death indicates to Heidegger that Dasein must be in some sense stretched out. What enables the ontic appearance of Dasein's "stretchedness"?

We usually think of birth as something that lies in the past, as some biological process that takes place at a perfectly measurable present at-hand date. Death, on the other hand, is ordinarily understood as the end of our biological existence, some present-at-hand event at some later point in life. As we have seen, death is not some event waiting to self-actualise, but the continuous oscillation between possibility and impossibility, the abysmal abeyance of the open future itself. The future is here the very source of temporality itself that returns into the past and thence structures the present moment. In order to understand Heidegger on birth *and* death fully, it is necessary to follow his own advice that *Being and Time* is neither an anthropology, social philosophy nor existential philosophy, if existential philosophy means that what is at stake in *Being and Time* is Dasein's lifeworld. We can only fully appreciate Heidegger's remarks on birth when we consider Dasein exclusively as the attuned structuring of the "there" of being—and the human being participates in this structuring. This also frees the way to appreciate that what is at stake in *Being and Time* is being as such, as its history and meaning. Thus, for Heidegger birth is not some event of the past: "Understood existentially, birth is never something past in the sense of what is no longer present-at-hand" (SZ: 374/246) Existential here means two things. First, it means that we are to understand birth in existential-ontological terms, i.e., as that which makes the ontic possible. Second, we also have to understand this in light of Dasein's ecstatic temporality. As ecstatic, birth is never of the past as something that lies behind Dasein, but rather birth continues to work through Dasein. Unlike death, birth is not the ur-possibility of Dasein. Instead, birth together with death is, existentially seen, co-constitutive of Dasein's factical possibilities. Heidegger writes: "Factical Dasein exists as being born [*existiert gebürtig*], and in being born it is also already dying ... in the sense of being-toward-death." (ibid.) This, again, seems to imply that Dasein exists from birth toward death. Yet, the ecstatic structure is different.

Dasein is at once toward death *and* toward birth. Dasein does not stretch out from its initiation point, birth, toward its end point, death, but it simultaneously stretches out toward birth *and* toward death. Heidegger speaks in this regard of Dasein's "*stretched stretching-itself.*" (SZ: 375/358) Dasein's birth is *now* just as its death is *now* and its birth is intimately related to its death and vice versa: "In the unity of thrownness and the fleeting, or else anticipatory, being-toward-death, birth and death "are connected"." (SZ: 374/357) Birth and death belong together, they are simultaneous in the existential-ontological sense and, thereby, they generate a field of tension within which Dasein stretches itself out. More precisely, Dasein itself is that attuned field stretching-itself, originally spun open by Dasein's birth and death. The ontic talk of life as that which is between birth and death reflects that to a certain degree, but at once also covers over that Dasein itself is immanently this stretched-stretching-itself. This stretched-stretching-itself from within Dasein is what enables the "movedness of existence [which] is not the movement of something present-at-hand." (SZ: 374f/358) This stresses the performative character of Dasein's being and hence of being itself. Based in his insight into Dasein's ecstatic stretching-itself-along Heidegger begins to develop Dasein's historicity.

I should note that besides these structural insights into Dasein there is something else to be learned from Heidegger's understanding of birth and from the claim that Dasein "exists *gebürtig*," i.e., as being born continuously. This means that birth is a gift and that Dasein in an ecstatic appreciation of its birth recognises its birth not as a simple *factum brutum* of its existence but as continuously enabling its existence. The gift of birth works through Dasein and it is only because of this gift that Dasein is set on course towards the future. Dasein is then not just born to die, but can only appreciate the gift of its birth by also appreciating the necessity of its ownmost possibility. Birth is a gift only when birth is unique and the uniqueness of birth is equiprimordial with the uniqueness of *my* death.

2 Dasein's Historicity

Heidegger calls the distinct temporal movedness and constancy of Dasein "*stretched out stretching itself along.*" (SZ: 375/358) More precisely, Heidegger calls this the "*occurrence [Geschehen] of Dasein*" (ibid.). To say that Dasein *is* temporally stretched out and stretching itself along, then, means to articulate the way in which Dasein fundamentally *takes place*. This fundamental *occurring*, *Geschehen*, is what allows for any ontic reflections we ordinarily consider "historical events." It is crucial to note that in the German Heidegger distinguishes between *Geschichte* and *Historie*. The latter is an object of research. It comes after the fact, as it were. The former is the way in which Dasein's being unfolds in an ecstatic-temporal way. Thus, *Geschichte* for Heidegger comes from the verb *geschehen*. The difference between *Geschichte* and *Historie*, which Heidegger develops in the German, does not translate well into English with any available standard dictionary translation. For the sake of understanding I shall follow Stambaugh and translate *Geschichte* as "history" and *Historie* as historiography. Note, however, that the crucial traits of *Geschehen* and its ramifications are entirely lost in the now standard translations of *Geschichte* as "history" and of *Geschichtlichkeit* as "historicity." On the other hand, the translation of *Historie* as historiography is quite helpful because it points to the scientific nature of *Historie* and to the general backward-looking attitude of the field. Historiography objectifies that which has occurred and never once seems to be wondering how its access to "history" is at all possible. Heidegger thus makes a distinction between existential-ontological *occurring* or *taking-place*, i.e., *Geschichte*, and ontic *Historie*. *Historie* is inauthentic historicity, *Geschichtlichkeit*, because it makes events and occurrences linear and takes history to be a receptacle Dasein is placed in. In view of Heidegger's later notion of *Seinsgeschichte*, of being itself as *essentially occurring as its history*, the term "history of being" must be seen in sharp distinction from historiography. *Seinsgeschichte* is to be understood close to *Geschehen*, taking place and occurring. It will become clearer in Part II that Heidegger develops his conception of the history of being out of his early insight into the difference between *Historie* and *Geschichte*.

Dasein, then, is not historical because it lives *in* the receptacle history understood as succession of historical events. Rather, Dasein is historical, *geschichtlich*, and Dasein can write history and historiography "*because it is temporal in the ground of its being.*" (SZ: 376/359) That is, Dasein is historical as stretched out toward birth *and* toward its death, toward that utmost possibility that holds nothing to be actualised, and which as such determines Dasein in its being. Thus, also in his analysis of Dasein's historicity the notion of a possibility that does not need to be actualised but that rather provides the ground for factical possibilities and hence the actual, plays a pivotal role. Death *and* birth push Dasein into history, as it were, for Dasein's stretched-stretching-itself spans open the horizon against which possibilities-to-be appear as historical and related.

As Dasein's historicity is conditional on Dasein's temporality, all three ecstasies are at stake here, too. In ordinary terms history is that which lies behind us. History is the past, *vergangen*, and as such it no longer has any real bearing on us. For Heidegger, however, history works through Dasein because Dasein *is* fundamentally historical. Heidegger thus argues that Dasein's original historicity does not primarily look back at the past as something that is inescapably lost. Rather Dasein is properly historical when it considers history as something worth repeating and as something that comes toward us. Nietzsche's distinction between the antiquarian, the critical, and the monumental understanding of history is in the background here (cf. SZ: 396/362). Dasein's authentic historicity is best thought of as an ontologisation of Nietzsche's monumentalism. Dasein authentically discloses history when Dasein regards history as a realm of possibilities worth repeating and to live by. Dasein can do so because it is mortally finite: "The finitude of existence thus seized upon tears one back out of endless multiplicity of closest possibilities offering themselves—those of comfort, shirking and taking things easy—and brings Dasein to the simplicity of its *fate [Schickals]*." (SZ: 384/365) Note that repetition in the ontological sense does not constitute a definitive horizon of the understanding of being, but a tearing open of horizons out of what has been precisely because the basic movement is *ecstatic* and not linear. Dasein is futural first and only from this futural directedness can Dasein make present what has been and relate to the gift of tradition:

> Only a being that is essentially futural in its being so that it can let itself be thrown back upon its factical there, free for its death and shattering itself on it, that is, only a being that, as futural, is equiprimordially having-been, can hand down to itself its inherited possibility, take over its own thrownness and be in the Moment for "its time." Only authentic temporality that is at the same time finite makes something like fate, that is, authentic historicity, possible. (SZ: 385/366)

The notion of shattering is crucial here. Dasein pushes itself against its utmost limit and ownmost possibility. This leads to Dasein shattering itself on that limit not only because death is Dasein's limit but also because there is nothing to actualise there. This shattering is not utter self-destruction of Dasein, is not suicide, or demise, but the destruction of inauthenticity. Facing the abeyant openness of the future at once opens up the authentic possibilities of that which has been and lets Dasein rid itself of inauthentic modes of being. This is not heroic but sobering. By appreciating the openness of the future authentic repetition becomes possible. It is important to note that this is not a guideline for any individual on how to live their lives. This is a philosophical claim first and foremost. Thus, when Heidegger says, "[r]etrieve [*Wiederholung*] is explicit handing down [*Überlieferung*]" (SZ: 385/352) we are reminded of §1 of *Being and Time*: "*The Necessity of an Explicit Retrieve of the Question of Being*." (SZ: 2/1) Authentic repetition or retrieve of earlier Dasein then means that *Being and Time* here at the end pushes into the necessity and possibility of asking the question of being and the text does so with the explicit reference to death! This is hence not some heroic call to action by Heidegger, but rather shows the profound relationship between being and death. Dasein can ask that question because it is mortally finite. On some level Heidegger here also already speaks of the history of being and the other beginning, without yet naming them so. The retrieving Dasein engages in is the continuous need to ask the infinite question of being again and again as a finite being. This could mean, thinks Heidegger, a way out of the nihilism, boredom and carelessness of our age:

> Only factically authentic historicity, as resolute fate, can disclose the history that has-been-there in such a way that in retrieve the "power" of the possible [!] breaks into factical existence, that is, comes toward it in its futurality. (SZ: 395/360)

Here being is the possible realm of that which has been and which as such is possible again. There is a need to retrieve the question of being and free being from the reification of (modern) metaphysics. By opening the future (as opposed to the closure of metaphysics) those other possibilities of that which-has-been light up and that, simply put, is the case because of the hermeneutic circle out of which Dasein interprets itself. That is to say Dasein projects its future from that which Dasein has been.

Dasein is thus a fundamentally *historical* being in the sense that Dasein first forms history and only secondarily writes historiographies. Everything Dasein does is historical. Dasein is historical in the sense that Dasein is ecstatically towards a finite future that spans open a horizon of possibilities which are equiprimordially informed by Dasein's having-been. The presence of Dasein is never a sheer available "now" but is always constituted (and fuzzily so) by that which has been and that which comes toward Dasein. After the turn Heidegger places even more weight on origin and that which has been. In *Being and Time* Dasein's ur-possibility death ultimately enables Dasein's historicity. This early insight will lead Heidegger to make a similar argument about the history of being, which, as we shall see, is the realm that, in excess of itself, grants the possibility for history to manifest itself in finite articulations of the history of being as, for example, rationality moving progressively toward freedom. In Part II, I shall argue that death is testimony to being's epochs. In context of *Being and Time* death is Dasein's ground of history: "*Authentic being-toward-death, that is, the finitude of temporality, is the concealed ground of the historicity of Dasein.*" (SZ: 386/367) It is on the ground of its historicity that Dasein can disclose itself historically and understand the being of beings in a historical way. For example, in form of "world history" or the "history of nature." After the turn, Heidegger will be able to bring the history of being into perspective precisely because of his early focus on death as possibility.

Chapter 6
Signs of the Turn

In hindsight we can already identify in *Being and Time* signs of the turn. Being *itself* is the aim of the investigation, and, as I noted above, toward the end of the book Heidegger himself wonders whether there needs to be an ontic foundation for an ontological investigation into being itself. The problem is, as Houlgate notes, that Heidegger presupposes that being always means "being of beings." Instead of trying to think being directly this unchecked presupposition leads Heidegger to posit *a* being called Dasein which can investigate the being of beings (cf. Houlgate 2006: 105f). It is true that Heidegger in *Being and Time* says that "being" is always the being of some being. Yet, I do not fully endorse this reading, as this makes Heidegger sound too subjectivistic. I do not argue that Heidegger knew where his initial project would take him. But I would still hold to the initial claim of this part that Heidegger first has to establish a way to get over the subject-object-dichotomy—and the Cartesian understanding of being as presence-at-hand—in order to arrive at being itself outside the Cartesian matrix, which according to Heidegger none of the thinkers before him have been able to achieve. There is also to some degree an emphasis on concealment in *Being and Time* which indicates that Dasein responds to certain possibilities of disclosure rather than being the centre and sole actor of disclosure. Take for example *Being and Time*'s interpretation of equipment. Heidegger does not approach equipment in an instrumental sense. Rather, the analysis of equipment looks at equipment in its own right and being. Equipment like a hammer withdraws into inconspicuousness after all. Thus, there is some degree of concealment and withdrawal at work here, too, and Dasein is not the sole actor of the occurrings of disclosure. If Dasein were the sole actor of disclosures, *Being and Time* would present a case of idealism. Nevertheless, Dasein's *understanding* appears to take primacy and to lead Heidegger astray from considering being directly. In the introduction to this part, I have argued that Heidegger first needed to free Dasein from the subject-object-dichotomy and this is why Heidegger focussed on Dasein in *Being and Time*. That is to say Heidegger in this text focuses on the peculiar being that he will come to call the "shepherd of being" rather than the "lord of beings". Of course, this is not to say that Heidegger knew where this path would lead him.

© Springer Nature Switzerland AG 2021
J. A. Niederhauser, *Heidegger on Death and Being*,
https://doi.org/10.1007/978-3-030-51375-7_6

The peculiar being, called human being, which at the dawn of modernity revolts against being must be put in its place again. Heidegger does so by showing that the existence of Dasein is radically predicated on its death, on its impossibility of being. Thus, to a certain degree Dasein is already in *Being and Time* dethroned and dethroned precisely by death. Hence readings, such as those of Houlgate and Magnus, which focus on Dasein as the primary source of disclosure fail to see what is already at stake in *Being and Time*: being itself.

Then again one could argue that positing world as a horizon constituted by Dasein's futural projection introduces a significant threat of subjectivism. Beings are *as* beings insofar as Dasein discloses them in their being, it seems. Hence, even if not being itself, so at least the *meaning* of being is dependent upon Dasein. But this is not how Heidegger puts it. The world as horizon is constituted by the interplay of the ecstasies of temporality and death. Still, is there a shadow of a subjectivism in *Being and Time* leaving something to be desired? Heidegger explicitly addresses this problem in §264 of *Contributions* where he speaks of the ambiguous meaning of the notion "understanding of being." On the one hand, the understanding of being is truly subjective stretching back to Plato's ἰδέα, Heidegger there points out. On the other hand, Heidegger claims in hindsight, understanding defined as *Ent-wurf*, as Dasein's thrownness and standing out into the world, already refers to Da-sein, i.e., to the realm of grounding of the truth of being, its concealing unconcealment. Seen from this angle, in *Being and Time* Dasein hence exists as living *Seinsverständnis* insofar as it is analogous to being. Still, being itself does not appear to be at work enough in *Being and Time*.

Lehmann, in turn, argues that there is precisely in the analysis of death in *Being and Time* the greatest danger for a reinforcement of the power of the subject. This is because, Lehmann argues, it appears to be entirely within Dasein's power to run forth towards death and make death *qua* possibility available to itself. Hence, Lehmann suspects, Dasein here makes itself absolute (cf. Lehmann 2003: 423f). One of the ambiguous aspects is precisely the question whether Dasein makes *itself* purely authentic by running forth towards death. After all the experience of the death of others is not helpful to get to the ownmost possibility. But does Dasein not need to be inauthentic as well? Does being not need to be concealed as well? Does Dasein make *itself* in running forth? How does Dasein know that it is authentic? If Dasein is to be transformed, does it transform itself, and would that not turn Dasein into the almighty subject Heidegger wishes to overcome? Heidegger even speaks of the power of death and the "superiority" Dasein gains by running forth toward death (cf. SZ: 384/366 *ta*). Superiority over being? Over the world? William Richardson, however, argues that in *Being and Time* "authenticity is achieved in re-solve by acquiescing in the finitude of one's transcendence in complete freedom unto death." (Richardson 1963: 512) This is the case precisely because realising one's finitude shows that death is more powerful than the subject. Nevertheless, in order to overcome subjectivism Heidegger will need to begin to think differently. It appears as though Heidegger was aware of the manifold tensions of his text, when he, toward the end of *Being and Time*, points out that Dasein is but one way to approach the question of being.

Similar as Lehmann Miguel de Beistegui argues that there remains "a kind of subjectivity [in place] as the "singular" "I", emerges from the individuating power of death." (de Beistegui 2003b: 29) Yet, we should also keep in mind that Heidegger later argues that the "metaphysical meaning of the concept of the subject has, in the first instance, no special relation to man and has none at all to the I." (GA 5: 88/66)[1] Dastur also stresses that "[s]ubjectivity must not be confused, as there is a natural tendency to do, with the ability to say "I"." (Dastur 1996: 43f) In fact, continues Dastur, "Dasein because it is not indifferent to its own being, is able to indicate itself by means of the personal pronoun "I"." (ibid.) For Heidegger it is not the enclosed subject that addresses itself as "I," but "[c]are expresses itself with the "I"." (SZ: 322/308) We must acknowledge that Dasein as care and *Seinkönnen* is already outside the enclosedness of the subject. As death is Dasein's ownmost but also utmost, *äußerste*, possibility, it is on the path toward death that we leave the enclosedness of subjectivism.

Hence there is in *Being and Time* at least a partial solution to the apparent problem or threat of subjectivism. This solution is found precisely in the analytic of death, for death disempowers the subject. This is why the formula *sum moribundus* is crucial, for this formula says that *I* am, that my existence can be and is only meaningful insofar as death always already holds power over *me*. Here the *ego* does not posit its being insofar as the *ego* thinks of itself. Instead, the formula *sum moribundus* already includes the negativity of being and it is this negativity that is the source of meaning. This is Heidegger's early revolution against modernity and its positivistic and positing tendencies.

There is yet another way in which already in *Being and Time* being is at work. In the discussion of the first prejudice Heidegger mentions Aristotle's unity of analogy. Dasein is in an understanding *of* being insofar as Dasein is analogous to being as such and corresponds to being. Yet, precisely this notion of a correspondence to the call of being is at best underdeveloped in *Being and Time* while Dasein's ambiguous *projection* is privileged. There is talk of the call of conscience, but not really of the call of being itself. With the thinking of *Ereignis* co-responding to being takes a primary role. There, analogy is understood not in terms of comparability of two different objects. Instead, being as the possible opens a historical play of time-space in which all beings, including the human being, correspond to and are analogous to the fate of being. We shall see that this is especially the case in *Ge-Stell* and *Geviert*. Yet, what will have to happen first is a further focus on that which remains concealed, and which has also remained concealed in *Being and Time*. This focussing is what takes place in what has come to be called the "turn" in Heidegger's thought. Let me stress again, however, that it is Heidegger's analytic of Dasein's death as the impending possibility of the impossibility of its existence that Heidegger's distinct thought is initiated. For Heidegger here in this moment of the analytic of Dasein makes the experience that being *essentially* withdraws, that being itself is withdrawal. This is what Heidegger will begin to think after during the so-called turn— and it will turn out that "turning" describes that movement of being well.

---

[1] Translated by J. Young and K. Haynes.

Part II
The Testimony of Being: Death in the Thinking of the Event

Lang ist Die Zeit, es ereignet sich aber Das Wahre
—Hölderlin

Abstract This part is the foundation for the rest of the book. Heidegger's thinking comes into its own with his thought of the history of being and the *Ereignis*. His later work on technology and language can only be fully appreciated, if one takes into consideration what Heidegger means by the history of being and how the *Ereignis* moves. The tension between concealment and unconcealment is well known as the driving factor of that history. However, and this is where this interpretation seems to be unique, death is at the core of the thought of concealment. In fact, Heidegger goes so far as saying that death is "the testimony of being" and that human thought can think concealment for they know of "being-away" from their relationship with death. One could go as far as saying that without considering death the talk of concealment and withdrawal lack justification and basis for thought. The history of being then as a history of withdrawing presence can be thought thanks to the relationship humans have with death. If we take into consideration the strong focus on death in texts like *Contributions to Philosophy* and *The Event*, but also of *Über den Anfang*, then we can see more easily why Heidegger will later say that mortals have to become mortals.

Keywords *Ereignis* · Event of appropriation · The Event · Event-thinking · History of being · *Seinsgeschichte* · The turning · Death · Withdrawal of being · Concealment · Clearing · *Lichtung* · Da-sein · Heidegger's *Contributions*

Introduction: Truth and The Turning

Im Wesen der Gefahr *verbirgt* sich darum die Möglichkeit einer Kehre, in der die Vergessenheit des Wesens des Seins sich so wendet, daß mit *dieser* Kehre die Wahrheit des Wesens des Seins in das Seiende eigens einkehrt. (GA 11: 118)

Before I can properly address death in the main body of Heidegger's texts on the *Ereignis*[1] it is necessary to reconstruct which direction Heidegger's thought takes after *Being and Time* and why. The talk of a "turn" in context of Heidegger's philosophy usually refers to what scholars have referred to as the shift from "Heidegger I" to "Heidegger II". (cf. GA 11: 152/304)[2] This clear-cut distinction is a representational account that stifles a genuine access to the thinking path precisely because this distinction suggests that the "turn" is an abrupt caesura in Heidegger's philosophy. As if Heidegger suddenly just shifted from one approach to the next and that both approaches can and must be clearly and neatly kept apart. The trouble is that Richardson's definition of the "turn" is prevalent up until this day. This commonplace perception of Heidegger would mean that *Being and Time* is divided from the rest of his philosophical body. Misunderstanding the turn can also show itself in a different way. This is when commentators remain stuck, as it were, on the level of the thought of *Being and Time* and hence on the level of Dasein's understanding of being. But in the "later" Heidegger being itself is at work and there are profound structural reasons for why his thought moves in that direction. The shift from "Heidegger I" to "Heidegger II" remains superficial if we do not trace the inherent turning of this thought itself that pushes itself further and further into the thought of being itself. What is it that Heidegger means by *die Kehre*?

Heidegger does not per se intent to move abruptly beyond his initial attempt at the question of being. Rather, his original experience with the thought of being pulls him further in a direction where the initial approach via the understanding of Dasein fails. With Dasein as the ontic, adverbial foundation *Being and Time* addresses the meaning of being predominantly in terms of the horizons of Dasein. Now, the declared project of the text is to awaken again an understanding for the necessity of the question of being. Yet, with Dasein as the primary focus there arguably is the threat of reducing being to the *Verstandeshorizont* of Dasein. If Dasein's *understanding* of being is the primary focus, then there is the risk of subjectivising being. Heidegger admits to that in *Contributions* (cf. GA 65: 295/233) Considering Dasein's understanding has advantages because this allows Heidegger, first, to think being without hypostatising it and, second, to lead Dasein back into its world. The latter is the case because anything the text reveals of Dasein only makes sense when considering Dasein in its world and from the standpoint of Dasein's understanding of world. The disadvantage is that being appears to be concealed behind Dasein's horizon. What pulls Heidegger towards the inherent turning of being and thus towards a thinking of being directly is ἀλήθεια. Yet, as I shall argue here, death is also pivotal in this move towards being itself. The turn or rather the inherent *turning* of being is already present in *Being and Time* and it is the way in which being itself moves. In the moment of the greatest intensity of being, of getting closer to being, which is when Dasein runs forth towards its death, being withdraws. This is why

---

[1] I hesitate to translate the word *Ereignis* just yet because I shall give Heidegger's justification of the term below and this only works in German.

[2] Translated by J. Veith.

Daniela Vallega-Neu argues that already in *Being and Time* "[b]eing is thought, thus, in terms of a presencing out of a withdrawal." (Vallega-Neu 2003: 30) Or as the later Heidegger says this is the way being occurs, *sich ereignet*. In the following I shall carve out why death and ἀλήθεια are pivotal for the thought of the turning and hence also for the direction the thinking path takes post *Being and Time*.[3]

In the *Letter on Humanism* Heidegger speaks of the failure of *Being and Time*'s metaphysical language to articulate the necessary belonging-together of being *and* time (GA 9: 328/250). A thinking in terms of horizons and necessary conditions for the possibility of experience fails to think being as such.[4] In the *Letter on Humanism* Heidegger also claims that the planned third section of *Being and Time* "Time and Being"—where "everything would be turned around [*Hier kehrt sich das Ganze um*]"—had to be withheld because "thinking failed in the adequate saying of this turning [*Kehre*]." (GA 9: 328/250) Note that Heidegger admits the impossibility to continue the project of *Being and Time* in the metaphysical language. Hence another language had to be found that could speak ecstatically of the simultaneity of presence and withdrawal. On the face of it this seems to imply that Richardson is right to claim the turn to be a radical caesura and that the "first" approach has little to do with the "second". Heidegger himself, however, in a letter to Father Richardson points out that what Richardson calls "Heidegger I" and "Heidegger II" are interdependent: "Only by way of what Heidegger I has thought, does one gain access to what is to be thought by Heidegger II. But Heidegger I only becomes possible if it is contained in Heidegger II." (GA 11: 152/304). The thinking *after* the turn then does not eliminate *Being and Time*, but serves to disclose the historical, "hitherto altogether concealed realm" (GA 65: 3/5) thanks to which Dasein can at all self-investigate and self-found as Dasein does in *Being and Time*. With the publication of texts such as *Contributions* and *The Event* we are now, of course, in a different position than Richardson was and it is easier to reconstruct the turn properly. I do not mean to say that Heidegger does not leave behind the fundamental ontology of Dasein and its transcendental investigation in order to think beyng itself as history. He certainly does and there is, in fact, no longer a (quasi-)transcendental approach in the thinking of the *Ereignis*. For the *Ereignis* self-ascertains, self-mediates, and occurs. More on this later. Nevertheless, it is crucial to see (and actually so obvious that it is almost trivial to mention) that the move toward the *Ereignis* takes place *out of* fundamental ontology. If we hence take into consideration ἀλήθεια and death as crucial moments, then we begin to see the continuity and unity of Heidegger's thought.[5]

---

[3] It is necessary to point out that there are several "turns" or "turnings" in Heidegger's thought and that this can only present one of the many ways Heidegger arrives at the thought of the *Ereignis*.

[4] Heidegger also admits to Richardson that in *Being and Time* his thought "inevitably remained captive to contemporary modes of presentation and language." (GA 11: 148/301)

[5] See, for example, the Zollikon Seminars delivered between 1959 and 1969. The seminars develop Daseinsanalysis from the perspective of the "*transcendence of Dasein* [which] remains determined from the transcendens *qua* being (*Unterschied*)" (GA 89: 240) That is, the seminars develop a

In *Being and Time* death is what gives meaning to Dasein. Death is *qua* Dasein's utmost limit the necessary condition for Dasein's world to arise as the meaningful disclosedness of beings. Yet, remember that death is simultaneously possibility *and* im-possibility of existence. Hence there is an oscillating abeyance about death and this, in turn, co-enables the rise and breakdown of world and meaning. Thus, on the ontic level this means that death not only enables Dasein's authentic being-in-the-world, but also Dasein's fallenness for the they and inauthentic world disclosure. In purely ontological terms what the phenomenon of death as possibility of impossibility reveals is precisely that double-movement of bursting out and folding back into-itself. This double-movement that unfolds from death is a reflection of Heidegger's retranslation of the Greek word for truth, ἀλήθεια, as *dis-covering* or *un-concealment*. The thought of a presencing out of a withdrawal is the thought of ἀλήθεια. More to the point: in *Being and Time* being as such stands revealed precisely in the analytic of Dasein's being-toward-death, where Dasein faces the possibility of not-being. Dasein is here most presently with itself, for it faces its ownmost possibility, but this presence at once withdraws. Thus, death to a certain degree already in *Being and Time* does what Frank Schalow sees death as doing in Heidegger's later philosophy: "Heidegger points to death as marking the tension between presence/absence whereby the *events* of world and truth come to pass." (Schalow 2001: 12) I should, however, point out that I disagree with this "schema" of presence/absence, which is exactly the schema of metaphysics. That is to say, metaphysics' forgetting of being's inherent withdrawal lets metaphysics think of that which withdraws in terms of an absence of some thing that should be there or was there. Death in *Being and Time* is therefore at the very limit of transcendental-horizontal thinking, as Eric Nelson notes (cf. Nelson 2011: 276). This very limit is the thought Heidegger further pursues after *Being and Time* and the name of that thought is *ἀ-λήθεια*. While *Being and Time* introduces ἀλήθεια as unconcealment, as revealedness, Heideggerd does not yet fully explore the thought of simultaneous concealment. Heidegger does this in a pivotal lecture course on Plato.

The structure of Part II is as follows: First, I shall focus on the "turn" in Heidegger's thought. Second, I shall address the unfolding of *Ereignis* in view of death. This serves as the foundation for the third chapter where I develop, in light of death, Heidegger's interpretation of being as essentially fissured. The fourth and final chapter explicates the relation between the history of being and death.

---

theory of Dasein's self-investigation out of being as difference and this is spoken from the perspective of the history of being.

Chapter 7
The Turn

1 The Turning and ἀλήθεια

Heidegger's first pursuit of the question of being took its direction from Plato's warning that we do not properly seem to grasp the meaning of being, even though we always already have an understanding of being. In 1931 Heidegger devotes a lecture course to Plato's Analogy of the Cave in order to initiate a thoughtful return to what he later calls the "first beginning."[1] In this lecture course and in a talk on the same matter from 1930 Heidegger radicalises his early interpretation of truth as ἀλήθεια. Plato's Analogy is an archetype of the revealing character of truth. However, Heidegger sees precisely in the Analogy also the epitome of the loss of the primary experience of truth as ἀλήθεια. He sees the Analogy as a loss of the simultaneity of unconcealment *and* concealment. The word ἀλήθεια, claims Heidegger (cf. GA 34: 120/87),[2] becomes "powerless" with Plato. This is of a profound impact for Occidental thought, argues Heidegger, because here a sheer presence gains the upper hand and the forgetting of concealment sets in. When Heidegger by way of destruction thinks through the history of metaphysics the experience he makes is that (self-)concealment has been forgotten.

In what follows I reconstruct how the radicalisation of ἀλήθεια with reference to Plato's Analogy of the Cave[3] leads Heidegger to think being as such—and that

---

[1] This takes place by way of destruction. Far from being "deconstruction" of imagined constructed ways of understanding of being, and far from being a literal destruction of history or the tradition, "destruction" in terms of fundamental ontology wishes to bring to light again the origins and sources of Dasein's ecstatic temporality. A proper destruction would have been the task of the 2nd volume of *Being and Time* that was never completed.

[2] Sadler translation.

[3] Bogdan Minca's work on Heidegger and Plato, and especially his careful translations, have been very helpful for my understanding of the philosophical issues at work here.

© Springer Nature Switzerland AG 2021
J. A. Niederhauser, *Heidegger on Death and Being*,
https://doi.org/10.1007/978-3-030-51375-7_7

means to think being's self-concealment. Bret Davis[4] argues that there is an "immanent overturning and radical twisting free [from metaphysics] ... at work in Heidegger's turn" (Davis 2007: 60). It is this line of thought that I follow here without claiming to reconstruct the turn in full.[5]

Heidegger's first approach to the question of being is by way of the phenomenology of Dasein's fundamental ontology that *discloses* being as the being of beings. The Greek word for truth, ἀλήθεια, encapsulates the process of disclosure. Here truth does not have the meaning of correctness and correspondence. Heidegger *destructs* the ordinary meaning of ἀλήθεια and translates ἀλήθεια literally as disclosure. While the thought of concealment is not fully developed in *Being and Time*, Heidegger does point to the necessity of concealment. Already in the decisive §7 of *Being and Time* Heidegger says: "The "being true" of λόγος as ἀληθεύειν means: to take beings that are being talked *about* in λέγειν as ἀποφαίνεσθαι out of their concealment; to let them be seen as something unconcealed (ἀληθές); to *discover* them." (SZ: 33/31) Note that Heidegger says that the ἀποφαίνεσθαι of speech takes place out of concealment. In ἀ-λήθεια we find several important connotations that let us understand Heidegger's translation better. The word ἀλήθεια is the negation of the verb λανθάνω, which means "I forget" or "I am concealed." In Hades *Lethe* is the river of forgetting. Thus, ἀλήθεια denotes moments of unconcealment, disclosure or unforgetting. Dasein's disclosing of the being of beings, which takes place in discourse, is, before any propositional claim is made, conditional on the movement from concealedness to unconcealedness. This is why Heidegger says that ἀποφαίνεσθαι takes place *out of concealment*. While this may indicate that concealment is not negated in moments of disclosure, there is still a clear tendency in *Being and Time* to understand disclosure as the abandonment of concealment. Nevertheless, there is still room to see even here the simultaneity of unconcealment and concealment in any temporal process of disclosing. That is also to say that already in *Being and Time* concealment is indicated as primordial and of a temporal dimension.

In *Being and Time* the simultaneity of unconcealment and concealment is reserved to Dasein's discovering and disclosing, for example, in scientific findings. Note that this does not limit the process of disclosure only to Dasein. Being as such must be structured in such a way that it makes possible an openness where

---

[4] Davis' extensive study on the will in Heidegger's thought is one of the most profound reconstructions of *The Turn* in recent years. In a nutshell, Davis argues that Heidegger by *gradually* giving up on a philosophy focused on the will (to power) he achieves to think the *turning* in the *Ereignis* itself. This is so because in giving up the will the human being is opened for the realm of the counter-resonance of *Ereignis* (cf. Davis 2007: 60ff).

Daniela Vallega-Neu points out that Heidegger's engagement with Hölderlin, especially with the question of the godly as a question to be posited out of beyng, also plays a pivotal role for the turn (cf. 2003: 8).

[5] I do not claim to provide here an exhaustive discussion of ἀλήθεια in Heidegger. I rather wish to carve out the direction Heidegger's thought takes thanks to ἀλήθεια and where it leads him: to the *Ereignis*. For more detailed account of Heidegger on truth see, for example, (Dahlstrom 2009).

disclosure takes place that Dasein enacts. The disclosure and simultaneous conceal-ment is reflected in Dasein in existential-ontological terms insofar as Dasein is simultaneously in truth and untruth. This paradoxical claim is not a claim about Dasein's epistemic capacities to recognise objects and make judgments about them. Heidegger writes: *"Because it essentially falls prey to the world, Dasein is in "untruth" in accordance with its constitution of being."* (SZ: 222/213) In existential-ontological terms Dasein is always already also in "untruth," i.e. concealment, and this is reflected on the ontic level when Dasein falls for the they and its opinions and—most significantly—when Dasein forgets the question of being.

In his diagnosis of truth in *Being and Time* Heidegger refers to Parmenides and the two paths the goddess offers him. The path of discovery, ἀλήθεια, or the path of "concealment," as Heidegger writes. The original Greek text speaks of δόξα. This clearly indicates that Heidegger here still thinks in terms of the meta-physical privileging of disclosure over concealment. The shift away from this traditional schema towards concealment itself is what ignites Heidegger's unique thought. Heidegger points out that Parmenides shows how Dasein has from early on been understood as being "always already in the truth and untruth." (SZ: 222/214) Therefore, Dasein must engage in κρίνειν λόγῳ, a differentiating understanding of *what is* and what it means *to be*. Dasein always responds to these two paths one way or another. To decide for truth means to be able to dis-tinguish between what is and what is not, what only seems (e.g., shadows) and what properly is. This also points to the difference between being and beings. To speak of the *way* of truth as the *way* of being indicates that being is not some-thing reified, is not something present-at-hand. The *way* of truth indicates the process of being's self-unconcealing thanks to Dasein's disclosure. Being is not previously given and then disclosed, rather being *is* in disclosing itself. Note also that the goddess in section 2 of Parmenides' poem says that he should con-sider the ἀπεόντα, the absent, as equally *present* as the present: Λεῦσσε δ᾽ ὅμως ἀπεόντα νόῳ παρεόντα βεβαίως (cf. Coxon 2009: 60f). One could understand this according to the standard reading of Parmenides as saying that the absent really *is* not. Contrary to what the standard reading suggests, Parmenides here, however, says that the present can only come into focus thanks to the non-present. In his later lecture course on *Parmenides* Heidegger thus explicitly stresses that the early thinkers remembered both unconcealment and conceal-ment when they tried to think being (cf. GA 54: 90f/61).[6] In *Being and Time* Heidegger, however, is not there yet. Only thanks to that which withdraws can the present be in focus. That is to say, with Parmenides being is articulated in terms of simultaneous concealment and unconcealment. Heidegger sees in Plato's Analogy of the Cave the most forceful canonisation of this early thought of Parmenides—a canonisation that, however, covers over concealment at work in disclosure. It is in the Cave Analogy that death explicitly comes into play with ἀλήθεια.

---

[6] Schuwer and Rojcewicz translation.

2 Death in the Cave

Heidegger's lecture course on the Analogy of the Cave depicts a deepening of his early encounter with "primordial" truth. Heidegger finds the Analogy to be decisive because it raises the fundamental question of the essence of truth. The *truth* that is at stake here comes before any propositional claim or judgement. This *truth* is what makes possible propositional and correspondence truth because before any correspondence or proposition about something are at all likely beings must disclose themselves in the whole. The occurrence of disclosure presupposes concealment and, as Heidegger argues, beings are primarily experienced as concealed because beings are not readily available as a whole (cf. GA 34: 13/9).[7] The unconcealment of beings, so that they fully make sense, is the exception. Hence the "Greek expression [of truth] is *privative*." (GA 34: 11/7) Note that beings are neither exclusively nor even primarily objects. Instead, beings are "human history, the processes of nature, divine happenings." (GA 34: 13f/9). Unconcealment must be wrested from beings.

The Analogy of the Cave articulates that unconcealment is not given. One person, more precisely the philosopher who has the urge to know beings, leaves the cave, i.e., leaves concealment, only to realise that he had not seen the light of truth before. Those down in the Cave only perceive shadows, which are but copies of imitations. This does not mean so much that they are not *real* or *actual*. The shadows are very much actual and it is crucial to understand that they do co-constitute the world of those imprisoned in the Cave. However, what is lacking is the insight into that which grants presence to them. As Plato describes the philosopher's way out of the cave he speaks of ἀλήθες, which Heidegger understands as moments of disclosure. The further the philosopher walks up, the more is disclosed to him. At first the torches and then those unnamed masters of shadows who carry the clay figures, which are the sources of the shadows on the wall. Once the philosopher—that is, the one who by definition diagnoses that which is—sees the Sun, the Idea of the Good discloses itself to him as the ultimate source of openness. Seeing the truth though is not a moment of inspiration or joy, but a moment of shock. Looking right at the light of the Sun is painful. Hence, Plato says that the philosopher first has to spend a night outside the cave in order to be properly able to see the light and what is outside. Plato, it seems, appreciates the necessity of the interplay of darkness and light. When the philosopher returns into the cave—which he does out of compassion for his fellows down in the cave—he takes the light of the Idea of the Good down with him into the cave. It is this light that for the first time allows him to see the shadows *as* shadows. The philosopher sees the shadows for what they truly are because only after having seen the truth, he sees the shadows as the mimetic seeming they are and no longer as proper things. There is, even though Heidegger does not yet explicitly speak of it, a call, *Zuruf*, at work in the Analogy. Something calls upon the philosopher to leave and to return and the philosopher responds to that call. Returning into the cave is not a pleasant experience either. Blinded by the light the philosopher stumbles and falls down in the dim light of the cave.

---

[7] Sadler translation.

Thus, the Analogy tells us of the movement of unconcealment and also of a necessary re-turn. That is to say, of a turning that has always already captured and that always already demands something of the human being. Heidegger points out that the Analogy "as a whole treats of an *occurrence* [*Geschehen*] and this occurrence involves a *return* [*Umkehr*]." (GA 34: 81/59 *ta*) Hence Plato describes truth as something that takes place and that turns within itself. Just as seeing the Idea all at once would not be enough, or more precisely, would not even be possible. Truth is that event of disclosure *and* withdrawal that the human being is always already witness to and to which we respond one way or another. Not responding is a response all the same. The hiddenness of the cave, its shadows, fuzzy boundaries, secluded and unknown tracks are necessary for one to arrive at truth. Once one has arrived at truth one does not leave the cave once and for all, but one must return into the cave, i.e., one has to move back into concealment.

The return into the cave not only forces the philosopher to face the shadows, but also something else: "How does this occurrence end? With the prospect of *death*!" (GA 34: 81/59) Why? Because seeing the shadows and the shackles and the torches for the first time fully for what they are is equivalent to death and because the fellow prisoners are disturbed by the thought that what they are looking at might not be what it seems. Yet, this *death* is the beginning of philosophy. Philosophy only begins when we face death and renounce what is immediately presented to us and begin to diagnose our time. This is why Schelling says that whoever wants to achieve "truly free philosophy" must leave everything behind. Schelling continues that this is "a great step that Plato likened with death." (Schelling 1979: 12)[8] As the freed person has seen the light, he will be blinded by the shadowy and gloomy cave and others will only see him stumble, seemingly incapable of seeing. The return into the cave demands the freed person to face "the actual (*actual* I say) constant having-before-oneself of death ... not just death in the physical sense of dying, but the forfeiture and rendering powerless of one's own essence." (GA 34: 84/61) Death here throws the human being into naked powerlessness because death is the most actual reality of human existence. But this very naked powerlessness, this shock, when it is seen for what it is, is at once what frees the human being into his most vivid possibilities. That the freed person ultimately faces death also indicates that truth is finite. Furthermore, the stages of the cave are not linear, but ecstatic. In the return, which has its beginning and its end in the tension of death as the human being's most fundamental reality, truth is at work as the simultaneity of unconcealment and concealment. There is no cave without the Sun and there is no shining of the Idea of the Good without the darkness of the cave: "Concealment belongs *essentially* to unconcealment, *like the valley belongs to the mountain*." (GA 34: 90/66 *ta*) The beginning of philosophy, following Plato, Schelling, Heidegger (and Hegel) is *death*. But it will be Heidegger who will bring death and concealment together and radicalise the necessity of the thought of concealment.

The necessity to radicalise concealment is the result of Plato's forgetting of something crucial in Analogy of the Cave. He does not forget that shadows appear

---

[8] My translation.

as shadows only in light of the Sun. Thus, he respects this moment of simultaneous unconcealment and concealment *and* return. To no fault of his own, since he only responds to what had disclosed itself to him, Plato, however, forgets the initial concealment of uttermost unconcealment. That is to say, he forgets the initial concealment of the Idea of the Good and posits the Sun as the ever-present and the *absolutely* unconcealed that (once found) requires no longer disclosure and knows no self-concealment. Plato forgets the moments that lead to the unconcealment of the Idea. The availability of the Open is so vast that it appears to eradicate concealment. The λανθάνω becomes insignificant (cf. GA 71: 15/9). Even though Plato initially describes ἀλήθεια as a *Geschehen*, occurrence, he begins to ignore that aspect precisely at the end of the Analogy. The Sun is posited as stable, fixed and given. Thereby ἀλήθεια, truth, is established as something fixed, ever-present and as absolute. According to Heidegger this forgetting has tremendous consequences, for this moment impedes the occidental human being from properly entering into *Geschichte* (cf. GA 34: 119f/87). This is the case because "[t]ruth is not static possession ... but unconcealment [truth] *occurs* [*geschieht*] in the *history* [*Geschichte*] of continuous freeing [from concealment]." (GA 34: 91/66*ta*) Note how early Heidegger makes use of this vocabulary. This is a first crucial hint at *Seinsgeschichte*. By the early 1930s Heidegger hence thinks of history in terms of ἀλήθεια, i.e., as a continuous strife between unconcealment and concealment and an inherent turning. This early insight is decisive for the realisation of the history of being. There cannot be, for Heidegger, the eternal light of the Idea of the Good as something ever available since this would preclude human being from what his tasks are: creating and preserving. There can only be, if a true understanding of *history* is looked for, the unitary, but ecstatic movement of ascent and return; an erring and finding that always also face death. The searching person cannot stay outside the cave staring at the Sun precisely because every true seeing requires shadows and darkness and the Sun must be found *again and again*. There must *again and again* be searching, erring, finding, creating and preserving. For there is no ultimate saving grace that will absolutely and once and for all free us. With Plato the Parmenidean and Heraclitean insight into the necessity of the "ἀπεόντα" for all that which is present and that which abides is covered over in favour of an a-historical absolute. Plato's forgetting of concealment indicates that the "first beginning" is a history of loss. The "other beginning," which Heidegger sees, would be one not of loss, but one in tune with being and its withdrawal and therefore in tune also with death. In the way that Heidegger reads it, the Cave then speaks of an ecstatic re-turn, a movement of unconcealment that only occurs when there is self-concealment. Here in this lecture course Heidegger has already gone beyond metaphysics, for he sees and tries to articulate that "something else" or "something more" that has been at work, but that has been forgotten.

Heidegger's quest for primordiality leads him into the Cave where searching, finding a path, and dis-closing truth are most formidably gathered and articulated; but simultaneously the event of truth is covered over. His reading of the Analogy is a crucial moment for Heidegger's thinking because his intensified engagement with the origin of Occidental thinking leads Heidegger to develop his *aletheiological* thinking. This is where Heidegger's unique thinking truly begins and it must be stated again that death here comes to bear.

Heidegger's reading of the Analogy of the Cave is decisive for the thinking path also because Heidegger here begins to understand the implications of mimesis and its effectuation in modernity. In a text entitled *Das Ereignis* published as volume 71 of the *Gesamtausgabe* Heidegger sees a clear continuation from Plato's Cave to the age of the world picture, i.e., the reduction of world and earth to a representation as an organisable and manageable resource (cf. GA 71: 107f/90f). Our epoch, which is the epoch of the finalisation of metaphysics, is also a manifestation of the Cave. Heidegger comes to see the prevalence of the image, or the mimetic shadow, in photography, in film, and also in scientific models as the fulfilment of the Cave. In our age that which is pictured, *is* considered real for the seeming perfect presence of the picture. He goes so far as to say in our epoch "[t]he "cave" is the genuine world, the one and only world, but is now illuminated by the light of planning." (GA 71: 107/91) The absoluteness of the posited positivity of the Idea is now found in the claim to absolute planning power of the human subject. In being-historical terms the Cave works and acts through the history of being and through us. The Cave Analogy is not a metaphor by which we understand our epoch, but the Cave Analogy *is* our epoch. Note in this regard that the shadows in the cave are *not* not real. They are real, they are actual, and they co-constitute the world of the prisoners. Similar to how mimetic representations like scientific models do not simply re-present but also interfere with the world. But Heidegger wishes to show that there is in any representation always something that withdraws and refuses itself. In *Contributions* Heidegger hence begins to try to think in an imageless fashion. In *Das Ereignis* he writes: "Thinking—through the imageless saying of the beginning." (GA 71: 283/246) The attempt to think being in an imageless fashion, put differently, in a non-propositional way, means to think being without beings and thus without giving us anything to represent. As we shall see, the language of *Contributions* and *The Event* attempts to speak out of the unfolding of *Ereignis* in a non-propositional way.

It is important to note that none of this is meant as a "critique" of Plato. Plato does not intentionally ignore concealment and thereby sets us on the wrong track, as if there was some causation or some inevitable teleology at work in metaphysics. Instead, after the conscious completion of metaphysics by Hegel Heidegger begins to see even in Plato what Heidegger comes to call Ereignis, i.e., what turns within itself. Nevertheless, the word ἀλήθεια and the experience it transports begins to wane, says Heidegger. The openness of being, i.e., of the Idea of the Good, begins to be a sheer openness and lets beings appear as available. For Heidegger this means that the human being becomes the being that determines what is true and what is not (cf. GA 34: 120/87). Understanding ἀλήθεια again in its original purport for humans would mean to appreciate that humans are not in charge of determining truth, but are always already thrown and have to respond to the current epoch over which they have no power. Put differently, we are thrown into an opening whose origin and ramifications are concealed to us. This thought is decisive to understand the workings of the *Ereignis*.

In the lecture course on the Cave Heidegger also refers again to Plato's dialogue *Sophists*. Heidegger points out that Plato here understands being, or the Idea of the Good, as δύναμις. This is not the place to trace this further in great depth, but it is important to note that Heidegger translates δύναμις as *Ermächtigung*, enabling power rather than possibility, as δύναμις is usually translated (cf. GA 34: 110f/80). In the German word *Ermächtigung* we can hear what Heidegger sees at work in all of metaphysics—from Plato to Nietzsche's Will to Power—the continuous increase in power and availability paired with the simultaneous forgetting of concealment. Thus, when Heidegger speaks of being as *das Mögliche* then he does not have δύναμις in mind. Instead, Heidegger attempts to be mindful of what Plato forgot: being's aletheiatic withdrawal.

In sum, there is really a turn in Heidegger's thinking that takes place as soon as his thinking is properly ignited. This happens when Heidegger begins to see what metaphysics forgets. But this turn by Heidegger—which on the one hand is a turn away from the previous language of *Being and Time*, and on the other hand is a turn toward the thought of ἀλήθεια—is not just the turn of someone looking for a language better suited to express something. Instead, the turn or better turning on a more fundamental level is the turning of the *Ereignis* itself. Thus, Heidegger's turn is ignited by the turning of *Ereignis* itself. This will become clearer when I explicate the meaning of the word *Er-eignis* and its ramifications. In his letter to Richardson Heidegger writes: "If instead of "Time" [in *Time and Being*] we substitute the clearing of the self-concealing of presence, then being is determined by the scope of time. Yet, this only results insofar as the clearing of self-concealment makes use of a thinking that corresponds to it." (GA 11: 151/303 *ta*)[9] Heidegger here himself clearly states that by "turn" he rather means a *turning* and he brings this turning into relation with the turning of ἀλήθεια and time in touch with clearing and concealment. The turn properly understood then is not Heidegger moving away from something but a structural necessity of thinking being as it presented itself to Heidegger: "The *turning* itself is the essence of "*beyng*"." (GA 71: 180/153) I argue that human beings can think the turning of ἀλήθεια because they are mortal beings. For death is, on the one hand, closest to us while, on the other hand, always withdrawing from human control. As such death as the always utterly non-present, unavailable and concealed comes into focus, for death is the other side turning away.

3   Death in the Turn

In order to understand better what happens in the turn the lecture course *Introduction to Metaphysics* is another seminal text to consider. This is because this lecture course further takes away powers and capacities from the human

---

[9] In *Time and Being* Heidegger calls the *Ereignis* the word which says being *and* time: "Was beide, Zeit und Sein, in ihr Eigenes, d. h. in ihr Zusammengehören, bestimmt, nennen wir: *das Ereignis*." (GA14: 24).

being. Here I have to leap ahead a bit and will already speak of the *Ereignis*. It will become clearer further below what I now address. In Heidegger's discussion of Plato's Analogy the event of truth is still conditional on human discovery. With the turn this is reversed and this is the turning of the *Ereignis*. Now the *Ereignis* appropriates human beings and human beings are involved in disclosure and must own up to it. Put differently, being lets human beings participate in its ways of occurring. The way human beings participate in being is by corresponding to its occurrences. Language and death, for example, are of being first but they touch human beings. Heidegger calls this surrender and renunciation of human subjectivity *übereignen*, transferring over. If we follow Heidegger, then this is how being itself works. Transferring over is then not Heidegger's arbitrary doing so. What was supposed to be a distinct human feature is transferred over, or surrendered to beyng. The chapters on the grammar of being in this lecture course are pivotal for the development of the thought of this process of transferring over. Take Heidegger's example in the German of "*Er ist des Todes.*" (GA 40: 95) This literally means, *he is of death*, which the English vernacular translates as "he is doomed to die." *Des Todes sein* literally means to belong to death, to be dedicated to death, and also to be taken by death. Just as death takes the human being, so does being.

This example is not an invention of Heidegger. It is how the German vernacular speaks. In this way of speaking Heidegger hears that death is more powerful than man. More powerful not only when man dies, but as soon as man is. Reading Sophocles Heidegger points out that in all human activity, in all human world-building and dwelling, there is also violence at work. This, he says, is the shocking insight into the tragedy of what it means to be human. In *Being and Time* Heidegger already mentions the "unhomeliness," the eeriness that can befall Dasein even in its most familiar surroundings. That eeriness is "the *flight* from [Dasein's] ownmost being-toward-death." (SZ: 252/233) While Heidegger sees an existential-ontological structure in *Being and Time* his later thought is radically different. It is a tragic insight into what it means to be human. But it is not simply tragic in a traditional sense of the hopelessness of abandoning oneself to mortality and finitude. Rather, tragic human being is now tied up with being and its inherent turning. Most radically though Heidegger's insight into human tragedy is not that everywhere human being roams and builds and dwells violence not only ensues but violence is a necessary precondition. Only death limits that violence. For death "over-limits [*über-grenzt*] all limits." (GA 40: 167/168) The tragedy of what it means to be human is the violence in all human activity and that that fundamental violence can only end with death. However, now death is no longer Dasein's ownmost possibility enabling and at once limiting all of Dasein's other possibilities. Instead, death is now *of* being and as such not only entirely out of the hands of man, but the very reason for the un-homeliness of Da-sein that man has to carry out (ibid.). This is why Heidegger calls death the testimony of being in *Contributions*. Death is testimony to being's self-concealment and turning.

4   The Decentring of Dasein

After *Being and Time* Heidegger begins to reformulate the question of being so that the question asks after being directly and no longer for Dasein's understanding of being. The decentring of Dasein finds expression in the shift from Dasein to Da-sein. Now the task of the human being is to respond and correspond to the call of being, to its turning and epochs. Man's response *grounds* the "there" as the site where being reveals itself historically. Da-sein is not a being and cannot be. It will prove to be the grounding of a way of mortal thinking necessary for both the arrival of being and the essential transformation of the human being. Thus, Da-sein is not a noun, but an adverb. Da-sein points to how grounding essentially occurs.

The decentring of Dasein might lead one to think that death is no longer an issue. This is true to the degree that death is no longer an existential-ontological phenomenon belonging to the structure of Dasein. Nevertheless, death remains central. I shall hence carve out how death itself changes, what new roles it takes on in the thinking of *Ereignis* and why. As argued above death is now an interest of being itself.[10] Heidegger's attempt is to think *out of* being itself (cf. GA 65: 3/5). Heidegger argues in *The Event*, and this claim must for now seem rather extraordinary, that "[f]or the first and only time in the history of beyng, the essence of death must now be experienced and interrogated out of beyng itself, i.e. in terms of Dasein." (GA 71: 190/162) In this part I shall investigate this extraordinary claim by Heidegger and show why death is significant for the history of being. I shall argue that death provides an entry point to think being and its history directly. That is to say death lets us think the concealment of being and thus death is related to ἀλήθεια. Death does so precisely because death as the utterly inaccessible and uncontrollable is the source of concealment for the human being. Death also grants to human beings the possibility to renounce beings. Heidegger's experience with being is that being refuses itself and death is what first leads Heidegger to make that experience.

To think being's concealment specifically is necessary in order to achieve a "pre-metaphysical" thinking. That is to say, a thinking outside the claim of a metaphysics that, as Beistegui puts it, "wants presence, full presence, absolute consumption, unlimited, unrestricted access to the world and things within it"[11] (the world, in its view, is nothing more than the sum of things to be found within it)." (2004: 165) With the possibility to think pre-metaphysically Heidegger does not make a linear temporal claim. Rather, by thinking being's self-concealing he can take the history

---

[10] Michel Haar (1993) argues that Heidegger took it too far when he attributed a variety of core human qualities to being itself. There is in fact something uncanny about that. Heidegger even speaks of *Entmenschung*, dehumanising, in *Contributions* (cf. GA 65: 510/401). I shall return to this troublesome notion in Part IV. Note, however, that the thinking of being and *Ereignis* is only possible in view of the human being. It is not the case that death becomes an attribute of the object "being" and is taken away as a property from the subject "man." But human beings can only be because they are touched by being and death alike.

[11] Metaphysics can achieve this, for example, by determining all life as self-willing will to power (Nietzsche), or all life as life and life only where death is entirely impossible (Fichte).

of metaphysical epochs into perspective. Heidegger understands metaphysics as that which "grounds an age," (GA 5: 75/57)[12] insofar as metaphysics gives a foundation to beings as such. Yet this can only be brought into view from the perspective of the history of being. No longer is Dasein's historicity the ground of history. Rather, being itself is now inherently historical (*geschichtlich*) and metaphysics responds to the epochs of being.

In *Contributions* and surrounding texts on *Ereignis* Heidegger writes *Seyn* with a "*y*" to differentiate it from metaphysical beingness and sheer presence (cf. GA 65: 436/344). I shall follow Heidegger's spelling and write "beyng." Beyng indicates the simultaneous concealment and withholding in all presencing. Hence the question of being is no longer how Dasein, insofar as its being is an issue for it, temporally discloses the being (presence) of beings. Now the question of beyng is how beyng self-discloses and self-conceals, in one word how beyng *turns*, and how the human being responds to that turning. In the language of *Contributions to Philosophy*, the question of being now reads: *How does beyng essentially occur historically? Wie west das Seyn, wie ereignet sich Seyn geschichtlich?* Perhaps one could add to this: *How does the human being respond to this occurring?*

Far from historicising beyng, Heidegger wishes to provide an opening to reconnect with the fundamental question of being without aiming to establish an ultimate ground and without falling for a metaphysical humanism where the human being is at the centre. Rather, Heidegger sees the possibility or even necessity of another beginning. The other beginning is necessary, says Heidegger, because of the profound nihilism and aimlessness that befalls all beings and man. In *Contributions* Heidegger hence mentions that "[t]he hidden goal ... [of modernity and technology] is the state of complete boredom." (GA 65: 157/123) I shall argue that death plays a pivotal role in Heidegger's attempt to ignite another beginning, to ignite again a love for thinking because it is precisely by way of death that the human being can enter into a thinking of beyng itself as withdrawing presence, as that which gives as it refuses. Heidegger, therefore, calls "death the highest testimony to beyng." (GA 65: 230/181).

The thinking of *Ereignis*, Heidegger writes on the first page of *Contributions*, "is no longer to be "about" something [i.e., Dasein's understanding of being] ..., but to be appropriated over to the appropriating event. That is equivalent to an essential transformation of the human being: from "rational animal" (*animal rationale*) to Da-sein."[13] (GA 65: 3/5) Heidegger gives a clear indication who the human being will be after the transformation: "The grounding of Da-sein transforms the *human being* (seeker, preserver, steward)." (GA 65: 230/181) Somewhere else in the book he writes: "the human being steadfastly becomes [Da-sein] through an essential transformation in the transition." (GA 65: 489/385) This takes place, as will become clearer as Part II progresses, in that concealment is specifically thought, for this is

---

[12] Young and Haynes translation.

[13] Heidegger argues that the animal rationale is the differentiation of the human subject into animalistic "substance" or foundation (think genetics) and "culture" (the rational part) (cf. GA 65: 90).

what *preserves* beyng's truth, i.e., concealment and withdrawal. This is open to human thinking for their relationship with death. As "shepherds of being" humans are also stewards of concealment.

It is helpful to note what motivates the thinking of *Ereignis* and of the history of being. Again, his letter to Richardson points to something crucial in Heidegger's thinking. In the letter Heidegger, viz., writes that the question, "[w]hat is the simple, unified determination of being that pervades all of the various meanings?" (GA 11: 146/299 *ta*) has moved his thinking from the beginning. Far from trying to abandon metaphysics Heidegger wishes to bring into harmony the various metaphysical determinations of being. Those include being as possibility and actuality, as order, as will etc. There must be a realm whence the determinations of being have come. This realm itself is "pre-metaphysical," i.e., metaphysics for its reliance on presence cannot think that realm. The realm will prove to be captured in the word *Ereignis* for reasons that will become clearer in Chaps. 8 and 9 of this part, and it is *Seynsgeschichte* that at once unifies and lets us see all determinations of being.

Chapter 8
The Unfolding of *Ereignis* in Light of Death

Heidegger interprets the Cave Analogy as an occurrence of the self-differentiation of unconcealment and concealment, which in one word is captured in ἀλήθεια. This reading is decisive for his path toward thinking being as such. The forgetting of concealment is the history of the first beginning, which is, therefore, a history of the loss of concealment. This loss ultimately reduces being to something present-at-hand. The other beginning, which Heidegger sees as necessary, considers and safeguards concealment. But how can one meaningfully think being in harmony with concealment?

This is where difference and *Ereignis* come into play. As we shall see, the choice of the word *Ereignis* is not arbitrary. The thinking of *Ereignis* opens the realm where beyng and human beings encounter each other. In that realm human beings correspond, *entsprechen*, in a thinking manner to beyng's claim, *Zuspruch*, and showing, *Zeige*. This chapter is foundational for the rest of this part. We can gain a clear understanding of the history of being, of death as beyng's testimony, and of Da-sein, only if we take the unfolding of the *Ereignis* into consideration. By unfolding I mean that I shall try to think through the *Ereignis* in its turning: "the truth of [beyng] is thought as [*Ereignis*] because this is the way being occurs and is experienced *in* thinking if this thinking abides in the truth of [beyng]." (Vallega-Neu 2003: 33)

What follows is by no means a complete account of the *Ereignis* and the variations it undergoes in Heidegger's thinking. I wish to provide a reconstruction of the *Ereignis* in view of the history of being, i.e., a reconstruction of *Ereignis* as opening a realm where beyng in its current fate and epoch and human beings encounter each other. Most crucially, this requires us to think withdrawal and this, in turn, is open to human thinking because of death. I take lead for the importance of death for the thinking of *Ereignis* from a note found in GA 97. This is one of the few places

© Springer Nature Switzerland AG 2021
J. A. Niederhauser, *Heidegger on Death and Being*,
https://doi.org/10.1007/978-3-030-51375-7_8

where Heidegger explicitly engages with the question of death in the *Black Notebooks*. The note reads: "In death the essence [*Wesen*[1]] of *Ereignis* conceals itself." (GA 97: 289).[2]

When assessing the *Ereignis* one fundamental question is whether *Ereignis* is a singular event that happens once and which thereby induces another beginning; or whether the *Ereignis* is a "realm" that is as long as human beings are, but which human beings have to consider and enter anew with every epoch. I shall follow the latter understanding of *Ereignis*.

1   The Word *Ereignis*

The commonplace translation of the German word "Ereignis" is "event." Events are sometimes more, sometimes less contingent. Some events are public, some are private. If announced in advance, one can plan to attend an event at a definite point in time. Events take place on a linear timeline and they demand full presence. Heidegger's *Ereignis* is not in any way an occurrence or event in the ordinary sense. He explicitly says: "By no means, however, may *Ereignis* be *re*-presented as an "incident" or a "novelty" [*Begebenheit*]" (GA 65: 256/201 *ta*). Why would Heidegger make such an arbitrary choice for a fundamental word of his thinking? What does *Ereignis* mean? Let me point out straight away that the essential *Ereignis* retains a sense of occurring. Yet, Heidegger wishes to differentiate ontic events from the proper, essential event because the *Ereignis* does not occur on a linear timeline.

For Heidegger the choice of the word *Ereignis* is not at all arbitrary. He notes that *Ereignis* is properly "thought of … as a key term [*Leitwort*] in the service of thinking." (GA 11: 45/36)[3] Heidegger's experience with the word *Ereignis* is such that *Ereignis* is a guiding word, untranslatable "like the Greek key word λόγος and the Chinese *Tao*." (ibid.) What are we to make of such grand claims? In how far, if at all, is the *Ereignis* as pivotal as the Tao or the λόγος? The Tao has arguably sustained and inspired various Chinese schools of thought. The λόγος ignites the entire history of occidental thought including Christianity. Can that really be said of *Ereignis*? If there is anything to that claim, if we want to be sympathetic to it, then we must consider how Heidegger explicates the *Ereignis* and how his thinking arrives at it.

---

[1] I translate *Wesen* as "essence" only for convenience, but "essence" could not be further from what Heidegger has in mind. The German word *Wesen* is by no means only of metaphysical import. Heidegger rather follows the vernacular and what *Wesen* means in the German vernacular. I will address this further in Part III, but for now note that *Wesen* in the relevant sense means something the staying time of a space. There is nothing metaphysical whatsoever about the word *Wesen* neither in German vernacular nor in Heidegger's use of the word.

[2] My translation. "Im Tod verhüllt sich das Wesen des Ereignisses."

[3] Stambaugh translation.

In his lectures on the Cave Analogy Heidegger points out that anyone who leaves the cave must return into the cave because one would lose a true understanding of the Idea if one only ever saw its light. We could say that one would be exposed to a sheer positivity, a givenness, which would turn even the Idea itself into something trivial and thus into something negative in its own right. Light needs darkness, as darkness needs light. Note that the difference between the two comes "first." The art is to "behold," "catch sight," *er-blicken*, of the Idea in such a way that concealment is overcome yet without forgetting concealment: "That which is the highest to be beheld [*Er-blickende*] requires the deepest beholding." (GA 34: 111/80 *ta*) Heidegger here stresses the prefix "*er-*" of *er-blicken* by hyphenating the word. In general, the prefix *er-* indicates that something is being achieved or reached. In this case something is being reached by looking at it. But *er-blicken* also points to an aletheiatic turning, since *er-blicken*[4] is ever only possible out of the simultaneous differentiation of concealment and unconcealment. *I* can catch sight only of what has previously been obscure, concealed, or rather what had been at a distance to me. The "*er-*" thus here rather speaks of a letting or enabling. The prefix "*er-*" is also contained in the *Er-eignis*. What does Heidegger hear in the word *Ereignis*?

For Heidegger hearing is the most important sense, rather than the *intuitus*, which is the most important sense for metaphysics. The importance of seeing is obvious in the Cave. Note that Heraclitus (cf. Hahn 1987: 28) in his first fragment says that all people are in a *hearing* relationship with the λόγος, but that they that do not *listen* to the λόγος. With Plato not only concealment is concealed, but also the importance of hearing. Of course, philosophy after Plato knows of hearing. Just think of Augustine or Kant's inner voice. But with Heidegger hearing becomes relevant in a different sense since he *listens to* words and what they tell us. Haar, therefore, rightly stresses that we should not judge Heidegger's engagement with language and with the meaning of words by the standards of etymology or philology. Instead, "[w]hat is at stake is to rediscover hidden possibilities in language" (Haar 1993: 103). Thus Heidegger is not a nominalist either. He does not look up the earlier nominal meanings of words. Nor does he merely posit concepts out of thin air only to subsequently become a conceptual realist who believes his own positing. *Ereignis* is neither a new word nor does Heidegger merely posit it. Instead, Heidegger invites us to make an experience with language, which is totally out of the ordinary. Thereby we escape the automatism of everyday communication and begin again to hear the exuberant abundance of simple words like *Ereignis* and *Wesen*. In that sense the thinking of *Ereignis* is an original thinking.

The word *Ereignis*, as Heidegger points out in the *Identity* essay, is taken from grown language, from spoken vernacular (cf. GA 11: 45). There will be more to say

---

[4] The "*er-denken des Seyns*, inventive thinking of beyng" works in a similar fashion. This does not mean to invent beyng out of thin air, but for Heidegger this rather means to *let* beyng in its original turning take over.

on Heidegger and language in Part IV. For now, it may suffice to point out the following in order to understand more clearly how Heidegger encounters language.
Heidegger tries to show with his "etymology" that the genesis of language and of
words literally moves history. For Heidegger words unfold and human beings correspond to that unfolding. That is why Heidegger speaks of *Leitworte*, of words that
guide thinking. It is along these words and their unfolding that thinking takes place.
It is the task of human beings to respond and correspond to key terms. *Ereignis* is a
Leitwort, a "guiding word," insofar as *Ereignis* speaks of the historical relationship
between humans and being. This claim will make more sense when we look at the
meaning of *Ereignis* in Heidegger's philosophy. Note for now also that the encounter with a word such as *Ereignis* is an act of *Ent-sprechen*, ergo a corresponding and
a speaking out of... Acts of *ent-sprechen* are not passive repetitions of something,
but there is room for dialogue in corresponding, even objection. I shall return to this
in more detail in Part IV.

By hyphenating the word *Er-eignis* Heidegger points to a meaning beyond the
ordinary one. Now the prefix "*er-*" is as emphasised as the stem of the word. The
hyphenation also brings to the fore that the stem of *Ereignis* is apparently the
adjective "*eigen*," which means own. Yet, *ereignen*, the verbal root of *Ereignis*,
does not come from *eigen*. Instead, Heidegger notes in *The Sentence of Identity*
that *ereignen* "originally means: *er-äugen*, peering *toward*, looking at, i.e.,
erblicken [!], calling toward oneself while looking at something, *aneignen*, appropriating." (GA 11: 45)[5] This is a crucial passage that makes public what Heidegger
had noted down earlier in the only recently published book *The Event*. In this text
written in the 1940s Heidegger says: (1) *Er-eigen* comes from *ereugen* or *eräugen*
which in English means "to catch sight of ... to catch the eye." (GA 71: 184/156)
Heidegger mentions further crucial meanings of *er-eugen*: "to manifest itself, to
take place, to give forth, ..., *to clear or to disclose* [*lichten*]." (ibid. *ta*) (2)
Heidegger then considers what appears to be a confusion regarding the meaning
of the word that occurred at some point. The syllable "*eu*" of *eugen* was softened
to the syllable "*ei*" of *eigen*, which was subsequently confused "with the unrelated
"own" [*eigen*], "*proprium*"" (ibid.). Thus, the verb *eignen*, which means "to
appertain to," is now found in *ereignen*. All of this could simply be regarded a
mistake that distorted the nominal, original meaning of the word. Yet, Heidegger
sees something else at work here, and in language more generally, which he tries
to uncover. Heidegger does not arbitrarily combine the two elements of the verb
ereignen. Instead, by granting equiprimordiality to the two elements Heidegger
lets the inherent errancy of this word unfold. Hence the verbal root of *Ereignis*,
ereignen, turns out to mean: "*To eventuate* [*Er-eignen*] = to come into its own of
the appearing and at the same time self-concealing." (GA 71: 185/157)[6] A

---

[5] My translation, as this crucial sentence is not included in Stambaugh's translation. "Er-eignen
heißt urprünglich: er-äugen, d.h. erblicken, im Blicken zu sich rufen, an-eignen."
[6] The German original is helpful here. Too much is lost in the official translation. The original
reads: "*Das Er-eignen* — das in die Erscheinung kommende und so zugleich sich verbergende
Sich zu eigen werden."

different way of saying this is *turning*. I shall refer to this passage as the "unfolding passage" in this part. The *Ereignis* then is that which turns within itself by coming into its own as it at once withdraws and refuses itself. This sounds less arbitrary and abstractly poetic, if we consider this in terms of history. The epoch we exist in is never fully disclosed to us, even though we are always already thrown into an epoch (and multiple layers of "interwoven" epochs at the same time) that is our own and that we have to make our own and live up to.

The verb "*er-eignen*," to eventuate, also refers to how Heidegger begins to understand "difference" after *Being and Time*. Heidegger no longer assumes the rather representational "ontic-ontological difference" between two different "levels" of phenomena. This "difference" is representational, for it is assumed beforehand and distinguishes clearly between two kinds of phenomena. This is the approach of fundamental-existential ontology of Dasein. Instead, Heidegger now understands difference as the self-differentiation of *Bezug* and *Entzug*, as the simultaneous coming into one's own *and* withdrawing. Note that this is not a dialectical movement of one against the other ultimately leading to sublation. The figure of thought of *Bezug* and *Entzug* as well as the *Ereignis* are best thought of as turning and counterswinging, as *tiding* in a heterological way. Instead of considering Dasein's fundamental ontology Heidegger now thinks after the *aletheiological* turning of being as such. As we shall see in the last chapter of this part, this is also the basic movement of the history of being.

Another crucial, simultaneously occurring moment speaking to the turning captured in the word *Er-eignis*, is *Irre*, errancy. Rather than understanding history as a teleological process that proves to be inherently rational leading us to greater freedom, errancy is, even if not on its own, co-constitutive of the history of being.[7] Heidegger fully incorporates errancy into that history insofar as human beings respond to it. As he writes in *On the Essence of Truth*: "The errancy through which human beings stray is not something that, as it were, extends alongside them like a ditch into which they occasionally stumble; rather, errancy belongs to the inner constitution of the Da-sein into which historical human beings are admitted." (GA 9: 196/150) Errancy is not another name for untruth, hence for concealment. Rather errancy is a mode of concealment that comes about by the responses of finite human beings to the staying question of being. The errancy of the "conflated" meaning of *Ereignis*, as Heidegger refers to in GA 71, is reflected in the errancy of the history of being.

Heidegger here provides quite a thorough, even if idiosyncratic, λόγον διδόναι for the *Ereignis* as a key term of his thinking. In what follows I shall explicate the important moments captured in *Ereignis*. I refer to the way in which the *Ereignis* turns as "*aletheiatic*." Since I have now clarified the German origins of *Ereignis* I shall from here on refer to it as essential event.

---

[7] Heidegger sometimes writes *Seinsgeschichte* and sometimes *Seynsgeschichte*. It will become clearer in the last chapter of this part why there is a history of *beyng* and a history of *being*.

2   The Oscillating of *Ereignis* and Human Correspondence in "Da-sein"

Eventuating can always only be thought *in actu*. This does not mean the event unfolds successively, as if clearing lead to withdrawing, which then leads to clearing and so on. Rather, eventuating is simultaneous. Heidegger calls the inherent turning of the essential event "*Gegenschwung*," counter-resonance, or that which "oscillates in itself." (GA 65: 261f/206). Here one oscillation does not linearly follow the other. Rather any oscillation is always only possible insofar as the sway in one direction *at once* means a sway in another direction. Counter-resonance is another name for turning. This is the most fundamental movement of the essential event. Heidegger calls the essential event the *Wesen* of beyng (cf. GA 65: 32/27f). It may be helpful here to point out that *Wesen* cannot be easily translated into English. The standard translation "essence" could not be further from what the German vernacular means by *Wesen*. *Wesen* is best thought of as biding dimensionality, as something that opens up a realm, wherein which possibilities abide for human beings—the few and rare at least—to respond to. Thus "*Wesen des Seyns*" does not ask for the *essentia*, the *quiddity* of *Seyn*, but for *how* beyng by its counter-resonance spans open a realm of possibilities. As we know from Heidegger's artwork essay, this is reflected in the genuine artwork that carries out the strife of world (clearing) and earth (concealment) and thereby spans open a world for a historical people.

The notion of *counter-resonance* implies, first, that this is the inherent motion of beyng. Second, this implies that beyng can also occur as its *un-essence, Un-Wesen*, i.e., that beyng can withdraw, can even act against itself. To speak with the later Heidegger: the fourfold is the essence of beyng, while the *Ge-Stell* is rather the unessence of beyng. Nevertheless, both are simultaneously possible occurrences or dimensions of beyng. The fourfold, as I shall argue in Parts III and IV, is only possible together with *Ge-Stell*. The essential event is opening up—as a letting into free play—the realm of appearance thanks to which beings appear in a certain way while the event simultaneously self-conceals. Only in this turning can the event come into its own. This thinking does not absolutise the clearing of disclosure but regards the truth of beyng as self-refusal *in* clearing. Thus, Heidegger here tries to think inventively[8] what began to be covered over with Plato. This thinking is "the inception of history as owning and estrangement," as Richard Polt (Polt 2006: 84) puts it. To this I just want to add that "owning" and "estrangement" are simultaneous and interwoven, not running parallel or occurring one after the other.

Furthermore, the essential event is not the ground of everything that is. The essential event does not underlie beings. The expression *coming-into-appearance* and *simultaneous withdrawal* defies representation and speaks of a motion of differentiation taking place *out of itself*. They also emphasise the non-foundationalism of Heidegger's thought. That which "*lets*" something occur does not *ground*

---

[8] "To invent" comes from Latin *invenire* which means to enter into, to discover, rather than to construct out of thin air.

something. Rather, *letting* indicates the space of a time in which something is allowed to *be* in its own right of its *own* accord. The essential event *lets something happen* and the essential event *is* only insofar as it occurs and unfolds. In this sense the event is *abgründig*, abyssal in the sense of the ground withdrawing and as such the event is oscillating. As we shall see below, this is why the event needs the grounding of Da-sein. Beyng thus needs the human being, for beyng is not a self-sufficient substance.

In *Being and Time* the call of conscience is a first pre-echo of abysmal beyng insofar as "nothing" calls Dasein, and if Dasein accepts that call, Dasein is on the way to authenticity. Yet, Heidegger does not further develop that call there. His later talk of appropriation suggests that the event calls on the human being. Thus, the *er-äugen* or *er-blicken*, a leitmotif of the Cave, is reversed in the thinking of the event. Now, it is no longer the human being who looks at the Sun and who makes his way to see more. Instead, it is now the event that looks at the essence of human beings, calls upon and appropriates human beings but this appropriation "swings back" and "resonates" according to the way in which human beings respond. As a realm that resonates and vibrates within itself, the essential event is that "through which man and being reach each other in their respective dimensionality." (GA 11: 46/37 *ta*) This does not mean that the essential event is a receptacle into which being and human beings are placed. Instead, the oscillating indicates the historicity of human responses to the disclosures of being. The realm Heidegger speaks of is the realm of the possible as self-concealing realm of possibilities. Heidegger thus also speaks of the *Eigentum* of the event which we are to understand as we understand *Fürstentum*, i.e., "realm" or "principality" (GA 65: 311/247). Human beings are addressed and to this claim (*Anspruch*)—as something that concerns human beings—there is a response that comes back to the initial claim. Yet, in the moment that there is a response—and human beings always respond even if with indifference—a counter-swing and -resonance has already set in and is already coming towards humans. This is why humans are the site of history. It is, therefore, upon human beings to "ground" the truth of being *again and again*. These *groundings* can fail as much as they can succeed, but the first opening for their possibility is not upon humans but upon beyng. *Da-sein*, now with a hyphen, is the name Heidegger gives to the site of those groundings. Da-sein is not the human being, but Da-sein is itself a moment of the essential event and as such Da-sein is the way in which a grounding for the history of being takes place. Da-sein, then, is a "time-space" in the sense of *Augenblickstätte*, the place of the proper moment of "the grounding of the truth of beyng," as Heidegger puts it in *Contributions* (GA 65: 323/255). I thus understand Da-sein as a way of thinking and therefore of grounding. As such Da-sein is the site where the possible takes its course: "the inventive thinking of beyng, as soon as and insofar as it will have been successful [*geglückt*] in its leap, determines its own essence, as "thinking," on the basis of that which being as appropriating event appropriates [*er-eignet*], [*aus dem*] Da-*sein*." (GA 65: 452/356 *ta*) With this reformulation of *Da-sein* the talk of Dasein's understanding of being is obsolete because Da-sein is the adverbial site of the grounding of the truth of beyng and human beings enter that site as seekers, preservers, stewards.

Hence, the task of human beings is now to safeguard the counter-resonance of the essential event. That means to enter "into this oscillation" (GA 65: 239/188) in a thinking manner. Thereby Da-sein becomes *the grounded one that grounds the ground*." (GA 65: 239/189) That is to say that Da-sein is the temporal occurrence which beyng needs in order to find an anchor, for beyng is "unsupported and unsecured." (GA 65: 482/379) But Da-sein is not a static ground (noun) for an abysmal event (noun). Rather Da-sein is an adverb and thus addresses the way in which beyng (verb) unfolds. This unfolding is an oscillation between appearance and withdrawal and it creates a realm where every response triggers a resonance and counter-resonance, even if silently. Human beings are thus not passive in the grounding and the subsequent transformation. On the contrary, every response matters. The response is first of all one of thinking.

However, Heidegger does reserve the task of profoundly corresponding with beyng to the so-called "few and rare" (cf. GA 65: 11/12). In the Cave corresponding is exclusively reserved for the philosopher. Heidegger does not restrict the "few" to the philosopher but has also the artist and the artisan in mind, and, as of the mid-1930s, especially the poet. Polt maintains that the talk of the few and rare boils down to esoteric elitism (cf. Polt 2006: 16). Polt argues that the "few" supposedly span open and sustain a realm of possibilities where the many can merely reproduce the possibilities granted by the few and rare. In my view, this is rather a misleading illustration. The few do not on their own span open a realm of possibilities. The event itself is what spans open such realms (through the strife or earth and world). True, for the course of the history of beyng the way in which the few respond, and whether their attempts at grounding succeed or not, is pivotal. Yet, Polt's claim seems to suggest that there are some selected human beings who are nearly trans-historical, outside of human history, beyng's chosen ones who can conspire and steer the course of history. My worry is that Polt's claim implies control of a few over the many. This would be a humanist account of history which is not Heidegger's understanding of history. I think Heidegger means something else with his talk of the few. The few are those who are more open to the call of beyng and respond to it sooner than others. Their response, say, in a work of art, is not the act of a rare genius expressing their subjectivity. Instead, the response of the few, of a poet or a philosopher, brings forth what has been shown to them in a sign, *Wink*, of beyng. The work of art generates a space for others to dwell in. The few are beyng's medium. As they bring forth an artwork, they wish the artwork farewell, they let the artwork depart, they let the artwork be on its own. They *let* go of the artwork and do not claim it as their own or try to possess it. *Letting* as *Gewähren-lassen* is crucial. This "letting" appreciates that thinking and its occurrences in art and poetry cannot be controlled. It appreciates that thinking must take its course, and that we as mortal beings can only follow it. In that sense human beings become seekers, preservers, stewards, and this is potentially open to anyone, not just to "elitist" professions such as artists and poets. The figure of the few also indicates that the few are not participants of the public realm. For Heidegger truth happens very much on the sidelines, concealed and hidden away. The few seek for beyng, they try to preserve and steward its truth (clearing concealment), mindful that they cannot possess and control beyng. As preservers human beings act at the behest of beyng but they hold no power over beyng. Groundings then are historical tasks and the term grounding echoes the notion of throwness in *Being and Time*. In *Being and Time* each Dasein has to accept its inevitable throwness. Now a few have to take over the grounding of the truth of beyng in Da-sein is and this is where death comes in, for death allows humans to let go of beings.

Note that the stance of creative letting-go is not quietism, as, for example, Allan Megill has argued (cf. Megill 1985: 185). This is because there is always something that addresses us and hence something we respond to. In my view, Megill's claim that Heidegger ends up in a position of passive quietism is not helpful. For Megill Heidegger provides a modern form of quietism, i.e., the position that beyng will do as it wills and that humans have to succumb their will to beyng. True, there is a gradual surrender of the will in Heidegger. Bret Davis' study of the will in Heidegger shows this vividly and conclusively (cf. Davis 2007). Letting go means to disempower the will. Yet, there is no surrender of human activity or responsibility. Take the example of the German idiom, "*das geht mich nichts an*" in order to understand what Heidegger means when he speaks of humans as addressed by beyng. The English translation of this idiom reads: *this does not concern me*. Taken literally in both languages, these expressions indicate that there is something that addresses and moves us, even if we react with indifference (cf. GA 79: 24/23f). Beyng always addresses human beings and it is always only a few that can respond and correspond to that call in any given epoch. It is easier to understand why there can be only a few in every given epoch, when we take into account how beyng itself "turns". If there is continuously refusal and presence, then it is always only a few who can appreciate the refusal in every presence. This is because of how beyng as such vibes. The mood, however, of an age overcomes all. But how one responds to the general attunement of an age is up to everyone themselves. The response of the few is such that it allows for an opening to see and understand something about our epoch that had remained concealed before. As will become clearer in what follows this can only properly happen to those human beings who take a mortal stance. In other words, human beings must renounce beings in order to be open for beyng and its abyss. Taking a mortal stance means just that: renouncing the prevalence of beings and letting-go of them. But this is what in the first place allows one to appreciate the true abundance of beings in their own accord—without trying to possess or perfectly control beings by establishing their common ground (beingness; i.e., ground as noun).

Regardless then of allegations of passivity, quietism and elitism, there is room for humans to respond to being and that means to act. We cannot steer the course of the history of being, but since this history is neither a linear nor a cyclical process, there is always room for alternative ways of existence in any given epoch. How such openings or "exits" occur has to do with concealment and death is crucial when it comes to considering concealment and refusal.

3   The Self-Mediation of the Event

In *Contributions* Heidegger writes that "for us today, it remains difficult in every respect to experience the projection as event out of the essence of ap-propriation [*Er-eignung*] as refusal." (GA 65: 448/353). Moreover, Heidegger says that we are inventively to think forth beyng out of the essential event and this thinking is supposed to induce the transition from metaphysics to the history of being (cf. GA 65: 456/359). What does it mean to think inventively out of the essential event, i.e., to think self-concealment and self-refusal? Is that at all possible, not least because we are used to a metaphysics of presence? In my view, we find in §34 of *Contributions* the decisive hint for thinking the essential event. It reads:

> The event is the self-eliciting [*ermittelnd*] and self-mediating center in which all essential occurrence [*Wesung*] of the truth of beyng must be thought back in advance. This thinking back in advance to that center is the inventive thinking of beyng. And all concepts of beyng must be uttered from there. (GA 65: 73/58f)

How is this thinking back in advance[9] supposed to be possible? How can we know that the essential event moves as such if we do not yet have any notion of it? In order to address these questions, it is necessary to go beyond the *Contributions*. It is also necessary to understand that Heidegger is here in dialogue with German Idealism.

In a note or rather a poem entitled *Das Unvordenkliche* Heidegger says that *das Unvordenkliche*, the immemorial, "is not a byname of beyng—but is the "former [*einstig*] name" of beyng" (GA 81: 200). This is a highly important remark by Heidegger and how we understand his remarks on the immemorial, or the un-pre-thinkable, is pivotal for the history of being and for the thinking of *Ereignis*. At least since Gadamer's identification of Dasein's facticity with Schelling's notion of the immemorial, scholars have assumed that Heidegger's history of being is a systematic succession of that which Schelling calls *unvordenklich* (cf. Gadamer 1986: 103). Moreover, this assumption allows one to identify Schelling's *Ages of the World* with the history of being, insofar as both supposedly originate out of an abyss prior and inaccessible to human thought. In recent years Gadamer's reading of Heidegger as a direct heir of Schelling has resurfaced again. Konstanze Sommer's (cf. Sommer 2015: 419f) and Sylvaine Gourdain's (cf. Gourdain 2017) comparative studies of Heidegger and Schelling are just two recent examples for the identification of Heidegger with Schelling. Sommer argues that what Heidegger means by beyng or *Ereignis* is what Schelling means by immemorial, insofar as there is a non-availability about beyng and beyng withdraws. Gourdain argues that Heidegger's notion of *Lichtung* is equivalent with the immemorial. True, on the face of it, this is exactly what Heidegger appears to be saying. Both philosophers speak of the abyss, of contingency, of non-availability and of excess. Both even speak of some sort of dark or hidden history. In terms of Heidegger it seems to be clear that we do not have access to beyng in its entirety, and that we do not have full knowledge of the

---

[9] Remember that in *What is Metaphysics?* Heidegger already speaks of being and nothing into which Dasein stands out *in advance*.

history of being as a consequence, i.e., that there is always something hidden for finite beings such as ourselves. But, is not Heidegger the thinker who brings concealment into focus? In fact, Heidegger in a late seminar says the following: "[t]he forgetting of being [could] "sublate" itself with the awakening to the essential event. Yet, concealment, which belongs to metaphysics as its limit, must be of the event." (GA 14: 50) That is to say that with the thinking of the event concealment comes into focus, i.e., precisely that which a metaphysician such as Schelling must call the "immemorial"! To metaphysics there is an echo of beyng itself here, but as metaphysics remains directed at beings, metaphysics does not have access to beyng and the event as that which self-elicits and self-mediates. Note especially that Heidegger says here that one must think back *in advance* into that centre. The immemorial of Schelling says exactly the opposite. In fact, for Schelling thinking always comes too late. In my view, what Heidegger's note quoted above on the immemorial says is the following: (1) beyng is, like Schelling's notion of the immemorial, without presupposition; however, (2), beyng is only that which *once* could not be thought when metaphysics was prevalent, which is directed at beings. Note in this regard that Sommer explicitly claims that Heidegger's *Seyn* is Schelling's "*unvordenkliches Seiendes*", "immemorial beings" (cf. Sommer 2015: 419). This makes perfect sense from a metaphysical perspective that tries to level the thought of Heidegger into something already known and therefore something that can be just as easily historicised. For the metaphysical eye what Heidegger talks about must be something inaccessible in the sense of something *Seiendes*, something present-at-hand that is not present, absent. But Heidegger does not at all quest after that. Concealment is not absence. That is how metaphysics understood the matter. What Heidegger attempts in his response to German Idealism—and that also means to the logic of positing prevalent with these thinkers—is to think through how their responses factor into the event.

See the following crucial passage from the *Contributions* where Heidegger mentions the immemorial:

> Thoughtful meditation on this that is unique (namely, the truth of beyng) can only be a path on which what is unable to be thought in advance [*immemorial*] is nevertheless thought, i.e., a path on which there begins the transformation of the relation of the human being to the truth of beyng. (GA 65: 415/329)[10]

---

[10] See also this note from Heidegger in GA 81: 297
Gegnet noch Gegend
rufend den Aufenthalt?
Läuten noch Stimmen der Stille
Ruhe spendend, Erfüllung verschwendend?
Wartet noch ein Gefüge
ferner Bestimmung
bindenden Brauchs?
Kommt noch ein Welt-würdig Geschlecht
gründend den Gang
unter die Weisung
abschiedlichen Wanderns

Thus, with the event there is an entrance to think the nearly unthinkable "that" of beyng, which literally means to enter into the truth of beyng. That is to say into the simultaneous movement and unfolding of concealment and unconcealment. It is only with this thought that the history of being comes into focus. No one saw this particular "history" before Heidegger. I shall explicate this further below, but note for now that the history of being can *only* be thought because of the thought of the event! As Heidegger says, beyng's *former* name was the immemorial precisely because metaphysics could not think *beyng*. Beyng, however, can now be approached by thinking out of the figure of the event, i.e., out of the turning that comes into its own as it self-conceals. The human being can think that movement because of death. As Heidegger writes: "Only the human being "has" the distinction of standing in front of death, because the human being is steadfastly in [*inständig in*] beyng: death the highest testimony to beyng." (GA 65: 230/181). Death testifies the traceless draft of beyng and as human beings are towards their death, they are steadfastly in beyng. To a metaphysical thinker such as Schelling this occurs as something unthinkable, something that thought cannot get behind. For Heidegger thinking is always already *there* in this draft insofar as it is mortal thinking. Thus "being-towards-death" now means that human beings can enter into that realm of thinking the groundless, the ground withdrawing.

Beyng is now to be thought and understood by thinking back into the original realm of the essential event.[11] For Schelling the incomprehensible, called immemorial, can only be made comprehensible *a posteriori*. As Axel Hutter (cf. 2003: 118f) points out, Schelling's positive philosophy can thereby avoid facing the abyss of the unconditional (that which is unsupported). Yet, for Heidegger thinking the immemorial is supposed to be possible *in advance*. On the face of it, this means that Heidegger's thinking here looks for the presuppositions of beyng and that beyng can be understood *a priori* as conditioned. But, contrary to Schelling's *a posteriori* fixation of the immemorial, beyng is to remain without presupposition and unconditioned. Moreover, Heidegger does not think in terms of the metaphysical schema of *a priori* and *a posteriori*, since this schema is directed at beings in their beingness. Instead, Heidegger thinks the *Ab-grund*, the withdrawing ground, and thinks without beings. Hutter (ibid.), moreover, notes that Schelling's notion of the immemorial wants to avoid Kant's warning from the *First Critique* that "[u]nconditioned necessity, which we so indispensably require as *the last bearer of all things*, is for human reason the veritable abyss." (A613/B641 *me*) Heidegger, on the other hand, argues that we "must take seriously [Kant's] reference to the abyssal." (GA 65:

---

durch die Wende
des Seins
in unvordenkliches Gelände,
wo Dasein im Tode sich fände?

I understand this as Heidegger's call for a few and rare who are able to move into "immemorial territory" where death is pulled and welcomed into existence, which means to say that death allows mortals to think concealment. Hence, the "unthinkable" becomes thinkable.

[11] There are echoes of χώρα in the talk of the essential event as realm.

448/353) Hence we are specifically invited to think the abyssal dimension of beyng in terms of the *self*-eliciting and *self*-mediating centre that is totally unsupported and that grants no support in any metaphysical sense. To accept this simple thought that the event is nothing that provides a ground for beings, but that the event is simply that which *lets* beings occur in a certain way in a certain epoch, is ultimately that which allows us to think beyng without presupposition. Metaphysics sees this "abyss" as an abyss because metaphysics looks for the ultimate principle or ground. Kant obviously sees this "abyss," and so do Schelling, Plato, and certainly Hegel. But metaphysics shies away from thinking the abyss. Heidegger thinks the abyss as the withdrawing ground and as beyng as that which withdraws. For its withdrawal however beyng is that which allows for any occurrence of a dimensionality thanks to which beings appear as meaningful in the first place. Heidegger thus speaks of a foreboding that opens a glimpse at concealment already at work in metaphysics (cf. GA 65: 14/13). Withdrawal, self-concealment and self-refusal point to beyng's abyss. Thus, with the essential event as self-eliciting centre beyng in its self-clearing and self-concealment, i.e., in its truth, can specifically be brought into thematic focus—and death will prove to be the locus of all concealment and the gateway into that which appears to be an abyss for metaphysics.

The nuanced reading of the vicinity of Heidegger's and Schelling's thought I would thus like to present is the following. Heidegger clearly speaks of the immemorial and that it is of systematic importance to his thought. This is the case because the immemorial is the way in which metaphysics would respond to the echoes of beyng as the beings-less, as that which withdraws. Heidegger responds to the immemorial, but already from the perspective of the thinking of the event and the history of being. Hence to identify Heidegger with Schelling is neither of historical nor systematic significance. It rather distorts both their respective places in the history of Occidental thought. To a certain degree human beings, finite and mortal as they are, are always already also captured by something immemorial, something that has come before them, something that is covered over. But with Heidegger's thought, and especially with taking death into account in the way in which Heidegger does, there is, he thinks, the historical opportunity to enter into another beginning, another history, where the tempest and self-withdrawal of beyng becomes transparent to the human being. That is to say the play in which humans inevitably take part, and of which they are victims, too, is now transparent and this openness and clarity—a clarity that takes concealment into view—tears open the possibility for the other beginning. The other beginning, however, is nourished from the first beginning and only possible in dialogue with the first beginning. Schelling, then, does respond to the event when he speaks of the un-pre-thinkable, the immemorial, but Schelling does not know what he is responding to, which is why "the ages of the world" remain in the dark and humans are merely at the mercy of the irrational forces that rule from within darkness. With Heidegger it is all about how the human being responds to the event and not leaving concealment in the dark. True, there will remain something unfathomable and especially something uncontrollable, and there is no access to absolute knowledge with Heidegger. Nevertheless, that which metaphysics calls "un-thinkable" or that which metaphysics tries to steer away from by calling it "un-pre-thinkable" is precisely that which Heidegger calls event and which Heidegger begins to think. The thinking of concealment and withdrawal then is tantamount to striding through the immemorial, to which humans inevitably also always belong. In sum, yes, there is mystery in Heidegger's question of being. The question of being is that mystery itself. Yet, Heidegger does not stop there. That would be the end of thinking. Heidegger, instead, aims to think precisely that which must appear as abyssal or "un-pre-thinkable" to metaphysics, even though those two notions are, of course, not identical. The word *Ereignis* allows him to think what metaphysics has responded to—and what human beings still respond to. The question of being, however, remains mysterious and the question remains a question to which humans have to respond again and again, for humans are finite. But this does not mean that Heidegger pushes beyng into the realm of the "un-pre-think-able". Quite the opposite! Beyng itself only now comes into focus and can be named for this other thinking can think concealment and withdrawal, which to metaphysics must appear as though it cannot be thought.

What must appear as a "leap" for metaphysics is a letting-go of the beingness of beings, i.e., of ground. This "leap," which is the thematic focus of the third "fugue" of the *Contributions*, is not Jacobi's *salto mortale* and hence not the demise of thinking. In the fugue "Leap" we also find the most sustained treatment of death in *Contributions*. This leap is coined by the attunement of "shyness" or "awe" (cf. GA 65: 227/179). Thus, it is not a triumphant abandonment of metaphysics, but a reverent letting-go of the ordinary, i.e., the supposed ground metaphysics can provide, but that Kant rightly refers to as "abyss"!

In §34 Heidegger therefore speaks of the event as *selbst-ermittelnd*, i.e., as that which finds its own centre or middle. "Self-eliciting" speaks solely to the abyss of beyng, where there is nothing to hold on to. Furthermore, *ermitteln* does not mean the same as *ver-mitteln*, to mediate, which means to generate a synthesis between two opposed poles. *Ermitteln* rather means to find and own oneself and one's centre. A Hegelian critique of that would be to point to the apparent pure and therefore empty and abstract self-referentiality of the event. Hegel's response to the self-referentiality of immediate being that is just itself is negative dialectics. Being must negate itself and hence be mediated. This is similar in the life-death-dialectic. Heidegger's thought, however, should not be flatly compared with the language and the thought of German Idealism. There is something else at stake for Heidegger. When Heidegger speaks of the event as self-eliciting, then Heidegger speaks of the way in which the event occurs, or eventuates. This eventuating of the event is such that the event always already unfolds as concealment and unconcealment and this unfolding spans open the realm of the event, a realm that is historical. Note also that Heidegger does not advocate for a sheer givenness with the history of being precisely because the ways in which humans respond facture into that history.

For Heidegger the thinking of the event is initiated when we "leap" into that middle or centre, which is tantamount to letting-go of beings, *to be without beings*, but needed by beyng. For the human being this means to take a mortal stance, i.e., to learn how to die. Before anything thinking means and requires humans to accept the abyss and humans do so as they learn how to die. Thinking is creative when it lets the event's self-eliciting and self-mediation take their course in its responses to those. Hence "to think back in advance" is the leap into the centre and being-historical thinking takes its direction from and is enriched by, *schöpft sich aus*, this very centre. The "un-pre-thinkable" becomes thinkable *in advance*. This is why, and I shall explicate this further below, the *Ereignis* itself is not "historical", is itself without "fate". This is the experience Heidegger made in his thinking. Mortal thinking can enter that centre where concealment and unconcealment are equiprimordial and simultaneous precisely for its vicinity with death. From the poverty of abyssal beyng, the perspective for the abundant wealth and riches of beings in their *own* right emerges; proper beings arising out of themselves as they each and uniquely are—not shadows, representations, instantiations, not appearances of noumenal things in themselves. Thinking is therefore ignited by "the abyssal ground of the unsupported and unsecured" (GA 65: 482/379). Beyng is entirely unsupported and unsecured. The essential event is unsupported, withdrawing centre. Thus beyng "needs those who go down" (GA 65: 7/8) into the abyss and those who are prepared to serve as the "there" of beyng, as an anchor for it, i.e., to serve *qua* care as a momentary grounding of beyng's truth (cf. GA 65: 16/15) These groundings are not metaphysical principles that give a ground to beings. These groundings are rather historical occurrences of a certain time-space that lets beings appear in a certain way and with a certain sense and meaning. These groundings are fundamentally dependent upon the ways in which humans respond to the "vibrations" of beyng that require humans to act. That is to say that the essential event is precisely not absolute Idea, nor Spinozist substance, nor *causa sui*, all of which are perfectly self-sufficient and independent. Taking a mortal stance is what lets human beings enter into the middle that not only self-mediates but also self-conceals. In order to gain a better understanding of §34 and the thinking of the event in general, it is necessary to clarify what Heidegger means by concealment. This is also where death comes into play.

4 Concealment and Death

In my interpretation of the thinking of the event I have so far assumed the specific meaning of *concealment*. Yet, what precisely does Heidegger mean by concealment? How, if at all, can we think concealment? This question needs to be answered, because if thinking concealment is not possible, then we cannot at all think the essential event. These questions are crucial also because they address how meaning constitutes according the thinking of the essential event. As I will show, death is crucial for a proper understanding of the motion called "un-concealment" and thus for the essential event. I should point out straight away that instead of asking *what* concealment is, we should rather ask *how* concealment essentially occurs.

Heidegger sees three modes of *veiling* (*Verhüllung*) in which concealment is at work in the current epoch of the abandonment of beyng. These modes of veiling, which hinder a genuine access to being, are "calculation," "acceleration," and "the outbreak of massiveness." (GA 65: 120f/95f) These are the ways in which beyng conceals itself in the current epoch. It is fair to speak here of a "double-concealment", as it were: beyng self-conceals in that it abandons itself in these modes of veiling. But at once also beyng's abandonment is concealed. This happens because beyng's inherent self-withdrawal has not yet been properly thought and hence metaphysics has vehemently pushed beings in their beingness to the fore. This is reinforced by human self-aggrandisement and the assumption that technology can at will manipulate and control beings. There is, Heidegger says in *Contributions*, something that concerns us and that indicates to us beyng's self-concealing abandonment. He sees this manifest in the fact that we do not know our historical goal, that we lack a greater purpose, put simply, nihilism rules (cf. GA 65: 11/12). Heidegger thus sees it as our task today to think that utmost concealment of meaning, i.e., to think beyng's abandonment. The latter has come about precisely because metaphysics has forgotten to think *self-concealment* in its own right. Thus, the self-eliciting, self-mediating centre has to be thought back in advance, we have to think self-concealment and abyss. Human beings can do so, argues Heidegger. by thinking the "away," *das Weg,* which human beings know from death (cf. GA 65: 324/257). This is precisely what the *grounding* of Da-sein is to achieve, which is to provide again a meaning of history, which finds its ultimate meaning in the history of beyng. This would include overcoming those three "veilings" Heidegger here speaks of. The three *Verhüllungen* of beyng can be understood as *dissimulations, Verstellungen,* of beyng. Beyng self-conceals by dissimulating. But is that the original sense of concealment, *Verbergung*?

In traditional terms one could understand the concealment (*Verbergung*) of beyng, as *occultatio* and *dissimulatio. Dissimulatio* is sinister, since what dissimulates pretends to be something that it is not and thus conceals what it is, but that which dissimulates also of course conceals that concealment. *Occultatio*, on the other hand, suggests that there is something there that is hidden or hiding itself. To a certain degree some sense of *occultatio* is active in what Heidegger means by concealment, but I think *occultatio* is only secondary with *dissimulatio* being tertiary to the most fundamental sense of concealment.[12] Heidegger also explicitly says that "deception and dissimulation … are not the only opposite to truth [unconcealment] at all." (GA 54: 88/59 *ta*) Thus there must be a more fundamental sense. For Mark Wrathall concealment simply means that the world *qua* object of enquiry momentarily eludes the possibility to make propositional claims about it (cf. Wrathall 2010: 19). Once the world is again determinable we can again make truthful propositional judgements about it and this eliminates concealment. The talk of propositionality and judgement in context of concealment and ἀλήθεια distorts the entire Heideggerian project. Ἀλήθεια has got nothing to do with propositional truth.

---

[12] In a recent paper Ionel (2017) argues that as of the mid-30s Heidegger primarily understands concealment as *dissimulatio* because withdrawal supposedly cannot be thought. I would argue just the opposite because, as Ionel himself points out, earth is that which conceals. Hence if concealment is exclusively *dissimulatio,* then there would be something sinister about earth; but there is nothing that suggests that.

Even in *Being and Time* propositional truth is derivative to interpreting the world (cf. SZ: §33) There is something different at stake. The unfolding passage is specifically non-propositional, but rather *poietic*.[13] The language intends to bring forth the truth of beyng as the strife between concealment and unconcealment.[14] The language of *Contributions* and surrounding texts is poetic and non-propositional also in the sense that it withdraws from representation. The language attempts to ground Da-sein. As quoted above, the inventive thinking of beyng begins with that grounding. If in this grounding, which has to take place *again and again* (cf. GA 65: 415/328), the truth of beyng is to be brought forth, then *concealment* is at its heart. Put differently, there is no clearing and no openness without concealing at its heart precisely because the opening is not something present-at-hand (cf. GA 65: 304/240f). With the thought of radicalised "self-concealment" Heidegger attempts to twist being free from *Vorhandenheit*, from the reification of metaphysics and technology.

In my view, Heidegger proposes a most primordial sense of self-concealment which is neither *occultatio* nor *dissimulatio*. Both of them suggest something given that is covered over or distorted. Both of them are also directed at beings. Moreover, concealment is neither negativity nor negation of presence, for this, too, would suggest that concealment is directed toward beings. Primordial concealment is precisely not concerned with beings, with something that is hidden or absent or something that dissimulates either itself or something else. Even though it is often argued that concealment is absence, Heidegger in *Contributions* makes clear that concealment is not absence (cf. GA 65: 340/269). This is the case also because absence is still concerned with beings. As argued above, absence is the way in which metaphysics understands withdrawal. Yet, Heidegger is after the "beings-less", beyng as such. Heidegger also makes a distinction between *Verborgenheit*, concealment, and *Verbergung*, concealing. The former is more directed towards beings than the latter. The latter is an event. *Verbergung*, concealing, is an event, is something that primordially occurs and that can only occur together with openness. Heidegger thus speaks of the clearing for self-concealing, *Lichtung für das Sich-Verbergen*. This is to indicate not something that is pre-given, but this clearing is that which grants the non-available space-time of occurring, i.e., the free letting-be of beings without an absolute ground which metaphysics wants to provide. The "clearing for self-concealing" is the turning of the event, its simultaneous counterresonance. Yet, there is also now after metaphysics, Heidegger thinks, the need to think concealing as such. Thus, the "clearing" of concealing also indicates that concealing as such begins to show itself as that which has remained in the dark in metaphysics, as that

---

[13] Sacha Golob hence rightly argues that already in *Being and Time* Dasein experiences the world in a non-propositional way (cf. Golob 2014: 2f)

[14] Vallega-Neu hence argues: "The language of *Contributions* is poietic in a twofold sense: it enables the event of being to appear as it appears in thinking and—in turn—it enables language and thinking to appear as events of being. What the language of *Contributions* says is found in the performative motion, that is, in the occurrence of thinking and language, and not in something that this occurrence would present objectively." (2003: 3)

which is at the limit of metaphysics. Concealing has shown itself, *hat sich gelichtet*, to Heidegger's thinking as that which is now necessary to be thought specifically. This is because in metaphysics, in Plato's response to the demands of ἀλήθεια, the privative –ἁ takes the upper hand while λήθε is forgotten. Heidegger focuses in on concealing as such. At once the clearing for self-concealing is thus also the articulation of how the event turns and *grants* a space of a time thanks to which phenomena of an epoch are possible.

It is crucial to understand that concealment, refusal, withdrawal *and* the "possible" all are related. Something can only come into its own through refusal. In order to become ripe so that something can gift itself to the world at some undetermined moment it needs to refuse itself and withdraw itself. As argued in Part I, Heidegger thinks *Möglichkeit* not in terms of *potentia* or *posse* but in terms of *mögen*. The German *mögen* is related to being and to gifting. Something can only gift itself in the right moment, the proper kairos, when it has properly refused and kept itself before. This speaks to the rarity of proper moments and proper clearings. To let something *be* so that in a rare moment true clearing can occur. From the very beginning of the thinking path death determines *das Mögliche*, for death is that which utterly defies actualisation. The later thought then exemplified in the notion of the "clearing *for* self-concealing" requires the thinker to partake in the clearing by letting something be. When I speak of "mortal thinking" this is exactly what I mean: the capacity to let something be, also to let oneself ripen so that one can gift oneself in an unexpected unique moment. Mortal thinking is the capacity to let something be of its own accord and to let something come into its own, for death is that which is profoundly related with "possibility", with nothingness, and *das Unverfügbare* (the non-available). Mortal thinking is that thinking which appreciates inherent withdrawal, for it stands closest to death, concealment, and the possible in which nothingness sways.

We are faced here, of course, with the problem of translation. For Heidegger the German verb *ver-bergen* is related to the verb *bergen*, which is difficult to translate. *Bergen* can mean "to shelter," "to recover," "to rescue," "to retrieve." Thus, in my view, when we wish to arrive at an understanding of *Verbergung* we need to heed that Heidegger has something like sheltering and recovering in mind as well. In context of the argument of this book, this is especially important because after the war Heidegger begins to refer to death as the *Ge-Birg* of being, i.e., as the concentration or gathering of all modes of *bergen*. There will be more to say on this in Part III. For now it may suffice to point out that death and truth are therefore related for Heidegger, and that means, as just outlined, that death and thinking are related. However, if we wish to understand how Heidegger arrives at this strange formulation of death, then we must understand his struggle with *Verbergung* in the late 1930s. Besides the problem of translation, there is a certain intensification at work when one tries to think after concealing. This intensification indicates the possibility of what Heidegger means by an original beginning, which is never historiographical, but an initiation of something else, of that which has been forgotten and is now being salvaged.

Primordial *bergen*, sheltering-recovering, which is human activity, then reaches into the utterly *beings*-less and non-available: into that which is abyssal. Heidegger calls this abyssal *Leere* (emptiness): "a temporal-spatial emptiness, an originary yawning open in hesitant self-withholding." (GA 65: 381/301) The yawning open is the source of beyng's abundance, precisely because of primordial concealing. Hence Vallega-Neu points out that in the late 1930s and early 1940s "Heidegger's thinking *goes down* (*geht unter*) into concealment." (Vallega-Neu 2015: 3 *me*) That is tantamount to saying, she continues, that Heidegger's thinking "lets go of something; something that we may preliminarily think of as a tension that held his thinking back in *Contributions*." (Vallega-Neu 2015: 15 *me*) It is true that Heidegger in *Contributions* is not quite there yet, but his talk there of the "unsupported and unprotected," to my mind, suggests that Heidegger already tries to think that which is utterly abyssal, i.e., beyng without beings. Thus, on my reading, on the most fundamental level *ver-bergen* is utter withholding, refusal and withdrawal. A different way of saying this is Heidegger's notion of "*nichten*", in English "nihilating". As he writes in *Über den Anfang*: "Being itself nihilates in that it shelters [*wahrt*] and protects [*verwahren*] and conceals." (GA 70: 49)[15] This nihilating, *Nichtung*, which Heidegger is at pains to point out that it is not negativity, as negativity grounds in subjectivity, this nihilating *is* concealing [*Verbergung*]. As such nihilating and concealing are the "intimacy of the be-ginning of the beginning." (GA 70: 49)[16] Note that Heidegger here stresses the German verb *fangen* in *An-fang*. That is to say that the original beginning throws itself open and catches itself. The task of the thinker is to shelter this truth of beyng in the midst of beings as they tower up around the thinker. That is to say, the thinker is to heed the self-concealing withdrawal in all presence. Even or perhaps especially in the most objectified reality of real things there is something that refuses itself. The name of this withdrawal is beyng. For beyng *is* the utterly non-available. This most primordial sense of *nihilating-concealing-sheltering* occurs on the level of beyng, more precisely, this is *how* beyng essentially occurs and therefore beyng *needs* to be sheltered and preserved (*geborgen*) itself and this is the task of thinkers (cf. GA 65: 19/17). Note also that this *bergen* always already self-differentiates as *entbergen* and *verbergen*, in English unconcealing *and* concealing; or perhaps it is better to say "disabsconding" and "absconding," for beyng is essentially elusive. This is also why Heidegger says that beyng is lonely. Beyng "casts round about itself only the nought, whose neighbourhood remains the most genuine one and the most faithful guardian of the solitude." (GA 65: 471/371 *ta*) Hence Heidegger here also points out that "beyng essentially occurs in relation to "beings" always only mediately, through the strife of world and earth." (ibid.) The fact that beyng is unsupported makes beyng hold on to Da-sein as a site where beyng can find a grounding. This grounding has to be performed by the few and rare. In terms of "beings", *Seiendes*, concealing however does take on another meaning. In terms of "beings" concealing can mean *occultatio* and

---

[15] My translation. "Das Sein selbst nichtet, indem es wahrt und verwahrt und verbirgt."

[16] "Die Nichtung als Verbergung ist die Innigkeit des An-fangens des Anfangs."

dissimulatio (cf. GA 65: 354/279). Yet, this is only possible through primordial concealing and nihilating and beyng's loneliness. Thus, *Bergung* always already also returns to beings and lets them become beings: "How, in sheltering [*Bergung*], beings first become *beings*." (GA 65: 354/279). That is to say by heeding the self-concealing of beyng beings are allowed into their free play and thereby they are sheltered. The human response is thus fundamental to how beings occur. If the response is such that the human response tries to establish an absolute ground, the beingness of beings, then beings in this age become artefacts producible at will according to parameters that the will sets. If the response is a mortal response mindful of the nihilating in every occurrence and presence, then beings are let to roam freely and according to their unique way of being.

The thought of concealment (and the history of being) is Heidegger's attempt to think history and "negativity" more radically than Hegel. Heidegger tries to show that the completion of metaphysics that sets in with Hegel is to some degree an extinguishing of the great fire of thought. Yet, this situation also provides the unique chance to consider what lies in darkness for metaphysics: beyng. That is to say, Heidegger tries to think entirely without beings, he tries to think the withdrawing ground. But this is what opens the possibility to gain a perspective for the simple wealth of beings again without the urge to manipulate and optimise them. In his notes on Hegel's negativity from 1938/1939 and 1941 Heidegger argues that *absolute* philosophy "must *enclose* negativity ... and that basically means *not* to take it seriously*." (GA 68: 24/19) On death in Hegel Heidegger thus says that death "can never become a serious threat; no καταστοφή is possible, nor is any downfall and subversion ... Everything is *already unconditionally* secured and accommodated." (ibid.) The supposedly unconditional and independent, the self-sufficient absolute shows itself to be always already *secured*. But what secures and supports the absolute? The absolute is always already secured by its total consumption of death and negativity. The absolute needs them in order to become absolutely unified. The absolute must consume all opposites and contradictions. This thinking cannot, rather, does not want to enter the abyss. Note what Hegel says about death in the preface to his *Phenomenology*: "Death, if that is what we want to call this *non-actuality* ..." (Hegel 2018: 16 *me*) Death is non-actuality. Thus, Hegel appreciates that death is the utterly unavailable and that which defies actualisation, i.e., death is close to possibility and the "not" here, too. Still, absolute thinking immediately consumes this non-actuality, and does not let this non-actuality take its course. Even though death is the "most dreadful thing" (ibid.) for Hegel, on Heidegger's reading of this passage it is always already clear that death is what allows Spirit to secure and complete itself. Death is here not an irreducible non-availability. Instead, death is integrated in the total consumption of Spirit. Heidegger does not buy the presuppositionless nature of Hegel's thought. The negativity of death as absolute master serves to mediate the immediacy of positivity. Spirit fully attains itself when it strides through death and thereby makes this non-actuality less or not at all dreadful. Thus, Spirit domesticates death. As such death cannot be *the* transformational moment (in the sense of *Seinsgeschichte*) that Heidegger sees in death. Hegel rather uses death to secure against the abyss because by withstanding this "*Unwirklichkeit*"

Spirit finds itself and thus provides a ground to beings. Heidegger attempts exactly the opposite. His thinking remains in the abyss, in the "unsupported and unprotected." Death is the window toward that thought of beyng, for death is the non-resolvable, non-sublateable tragedy at the heart of existence. By withstanding that tragedy and accepting that ultimate frailty and weakness mortal thinking enters into the thought of the unsupported and unprotected that always already needs human responses. Let me quote again what Heidegger says in *The Event*: "[w]e devastate the abyssal ... event-related essence of death if we seek to calculate what might be "after" it. Thereby we degrade death to a null passageway." (GA 71: 194/165) This, then, means that death must remain that unresolvable tension at the heart of who we are, for this allows us to think the draft of beyng. Death is what lets mortal thinking experience the possibility not to give a foundation, as metaphysics *qua* onto-theology has always tried to do, and therefore death in that being-historical sense is what lets thinking leave behind metaphysics.

Hegel's negativity even as absolute disunity, already secures the mediation of the immediacy of life, of positivity. Heidegger in this regard thus speaks of "the complete conciliation in everything." (GA 68: 19/19) The negativity that is death as absolute master serves to repress the immediacy of positivity. As such death cannot be that transformational moment that Heidegger sees in it. Death for Heidegger hence is *cata-strophic* in the Greek sense of the word where κατά means "down" and "under" and στρέφειν means "to turn". Death as catastrophe is the καιρός of the down-turn or subversion of metaphysics and therefore of the transformation of human being. Death so vehemently brings before the intensity of beyng as the "not" that the outcome is precisely not yet certain as it is in Hegel's ultimate articulation of the truth of metaphysics. This un-certainty is what must take place to transform modernity fundamentally. Heidegger thus often speaks of *vor-denken*, of thinking ahead toward the other beginning, toward that which has remained in the dark in metaphysics. This, as Heidegger writes in the first volume on Nietzsche, allows us also to see what has been (cf. GA 6.1: 356). What has remained dark is not anything mystical or fancy. It is the *"qua"*, the "as" in the formula of the *ens qua ens*. Metaphysics has never specifically thought the unconcealedness of the *qua*. This unconcealedness has remained concealed because metaphysics has not thought the "as such". In plain sight something rather simple withdrew for millennia. The unconcealed remained concealed and hence the task is now to think this simple thought.

In his notes on *Overcoming Metaphysics* Heidegger also remarks that the other beginning is not a simple return to the so-called history of philosophy. Instead, the attempt here is to think ahead, to think possible futures out of that and in relation to that which has been (cf. GA 67: 39). Futures that are, I may add, coined by limitations and finitude and not fantasies of an endless-and-so-on progression towards ever greater superlatives. The negativity of the absolute master then cannot be in the least similar to the "not" that death indicates according to Heidegger. Nonetheless, death, rather being-toward-death which points to the utmost, shall serve "not to negate "beyng," but rather to endow [*stiften*] the ground of its complete and essential affirmability." (GA 65: 284/223 *ta*) What must occur, however, is that death is not consumed, but brings before beyng in its unwontedness. This cata-strophe, this turn of events, shows the difference between beyng and beings, and only this difference allows for the affirmation of beyng, for out of difference is how beyng comes into view.

What metaphysics in the articulation of Hegel sees is that there is a "not" at work in death. But metaphysics does not see the activity of the "not" and therefore that of differencing and unfolding. The "not," which death indicates and which Heidegger has in mind, is therefore more primordial than Hegel's negativity. As mentioned before Heidegger refers to the "not" in a crucial addendum to *On the Essence of Ground*. I quote Heidegger again: "The nothing is the "not" of beings and is thus being, experienced from the perspective of beings. The ontological difference is the "not" between beings and being." (GA 9: 123/97) On the reading I have provided so far, there is strong reason to suggest that it is for their being-toward-death that beings appear as beings, i.e., as meaningful phenomena for humans. As Heidegger writes in *What is Metaphysics?*: "For human Dasein, the nothing makes possible the clearing of beings as such … [thus the nothing] originally belongs to their essential unfolding as such." (GA 9: 115/91 *ta*). This is not to say that there is literally nothing in front of *me*, but that the difference between being (withdrawing abyssal ground, temporally occurring) and beings (present but ephemeral), i.e., that the very "not" itself, lets us encounter beings. This is to say that the world occurs as meaningful to humans when they are properly mortal. An example to illustrate what Heidegger means is the artist who is able to see on the empty canvas what is already there, but yet hidden, e.g., the calmness of a natural scene. As Michelangelo said, "I saw the Angel in the marble and carved until I set him free." In his book on Heidegger and art Thomson puts the nihilating of the nothing as follows: "experiencing this "noth-ing" is to become attuned to something that is not a thing … but which conditions all our experiences of things" (Thomson 2011: 85). This statement betrays a misreading of what is at stake in Heidegger's later thinking. To speak here of "conditioning" fails to appreciate that the thinking of the event is not transcendental at all. The nothing nihilates and this nihilating is enough for itself. This nihilating does not condition or enable. This kind of thinking remains stuck on the level of beings. Instead, the thought of nihilating is concerned only with beyng and nothing, not directed at beings. The true power of genuine artworks is therefore that they are the mediators of the nihilating of beyng and nothingness—and death. Hence in a world deprived of death, of an authentic being-toward-death, there can be no wholesome world for humans who are essentially world-builders. That is to say that death is not the void of nihilistic nothingness, not merely a sign of the "absurdity" of "life". Death rather is such a nothing that allows for any beings to arise as meaningful to human existence. Death is then not sheer negativity opposed to positivity, a negativity which Spirit consumes in order to evade the immediacy of life. Rather the "not," which death indicates, belongs to being itself. In this sense Heidegger thinks the relation of being and nothing more fundamentally than metaphysics, for he considers this relation without beings.

My claim that Heidegger tries to think negativity more radically than Hegel and non-dialectically is also supported by a note from 1946/1947. There Heidegger says "negativity" is not to be thought dialectically as the opponent of positivity. Instead, the "negative" is to be thought out of beyng as its refusal, withdrawal and concealing. Heidegger's "negative" cannot be sublated, nor does it negate itself. Its proper name is thus "δεινόν," the unsupported uncanny (cf. GA 97: 261). The abyss remains abyssal and death indicates that most fundamental being-away. This is where Hegel and Heidegger part ways, as Schmidt notes, or rather where Heidegger parts with the entirety of Occidental thinking since Plato: "Heidegger's challenge to thought is to release thought from its ancient relation to the will to an unconditioned ground." (Schmidt 1988: 149)[17] There is a sense of an "away," "*das Weg*," at work here that is beyond the schema of presence/absence, something present-at-hand lacking or being absent. What is this fundamental sense of "away"?

In *Contributions* Heidegger deliberately writes on being-away without using the verb "is" the following sentence that is worth quoting in German: "*Vor* dieser [die Offenheit] das Weg-sein und dieses sogar ständig." The translation reads: "*Prior* to this dislodgment, being-away occurs and indeed even occurs constantly." (GA 65: 304/241) The "prior" is not temporal in a linear sense, but it indicates the primordial primacy of being-away in any appearance. "Away" then, Heidegger says, does not mean "mere absence [!] of something hitherto present-at-hand" (GA 65: 324/257 ta). Instead, the "away" fundamentally belongs to the "there." The away "is the completely other of the "there," entirely concealed to us." (ibid.) This tension between the "away" and the "there," where the "away" has primacy, is what opens the *possibility* for any act of grounding in the first place. Heidegger continues by saying that we know the "away" and thus concealing from "the various forms [*Gestalten*] of death." (GA 65: 324/256) Put differently, in the occurrence of Da-sein as the adverbial site of the grounding of beyng's truth the name of concealing is "being-away." As humans know this from death, humans can enter the thought of beyng as the unsupported and unprotected because of their vicinity to their death. Humans—or rather again, the few and rare—can reach into the self-withholding and yawning emptiness because of their relationship with death. To be sure, humans have a relationship with death. But death is *of* beyng first and as such death touches humans, insofar as they belong to the "there" of *Da-sein* as the site where the history of being articulates itself. Mortal thinking is that abyssal thinking, that thinking of a simple but exuberant wealth. What Heidegger tries to think is the "other" of metaphysics. Plato does think openness and even concealing, as we saw in the Analogy of the Cave. Yet, Plato thinks this counter-resonance with regard to beings. Heidegger's insight is that there is a pure *bergen* and a pure *verbergen* on the level of beyng and this must be thought first in order to ignite another beginning.

Thus, at the very heart of Heidegger's thinking, where we find the focus on concealing and the clearing of concealing in the afore-mentioned double-meaning, we find death and its various gestalts. Death is the window unto thinking the event of

---

[17] Schmidt concludes that it would be short-sighted to look for a victor between the two. Instead, both Hegel and Heidegger struggle with finitude and negativity, albeit from different angles. I do not wish to portray Heidegger as superior either. But by illuminating their differences here, the difference between metaphysics and being-historical thinking become apparent.

beyng as withdrawing presence. As Heidegger says in *Über den Anfang*: "Death *is* going-down [*Untergang*] and that *is* utmost beginning, *is* utmost concealing, *is* being." (GA 70: 139)[18] It cannot be overstated, what Heidegger says here: Death *is* beyng. That is to say that death as such is now an interest of beyng, death is of beyng, rather than human. Remember that beyng is a traceless draft for Heidegger. Hence, Heidegger continues to point out here, any anthropology or theology cannot properly grasp death. Death itself is of beyng-historical essence (cf. GA 70: 138). It is only by considering death that the history of beyng begins to light up. Yet, just how are we to understand death here? It will be helpful to consider Heidegger's lecture course on *Parmenides* for a sounder understanding of concealment and its relationship with death.

In *Parmenides* Heidegger argues that "death is not a "biological" process [for the Greeks], any more than birth is." (GA 54: 88/60) For Greek thinking "[b]irth and death take their essence from the realm of disclosiveness and concealment." (ibid.) There is a "pre-eminent level of the essence of concealment" where "the essential connection between death and concealment is starting to appear." (ibid.) This concealment is more fundamental than that of the earth because the earth is the "in-between ... between the concealment of the subterranean and the luminosity, the disclosiveness, of the supraterranean." (ibid.) The concealment of death is also more fundamental than the concealments of the everyday where, for example, a ship harbours goods which we do not see when we look at the ship from outside. The most fundamental concealing is open to human thinking because the human being is the mortal being and stands in a special relationship with death. This is the case precisely because, as outlined above, humans partake in Da-sein as the site of the history of being. Death touches only the human being. Hence Heidegger says in *Being and Time* and in later writings on the fourfold that the animal perishes but the human being *dies*. The understanding of death Heidegger argues for is not the measurable end of biological life. Nor is death here still Dasein's ownmost possibility. Birth is now the name of clearing or disclosing and death for concealing and absconding. Both birth and death touch the human being and grant and withdraw. There is an essential relation between death and concealing, i.e., between death and beyng, and this is why mortals experience loss when someone dies. Because then abruptly the inherent withdrawal of beyng shows itself, i.e., the fact that there is no substance, no ultimate ground that holds beings. "Mortals", of which Heidegger speaks here as does Parmenides in his poem, can appreciate that when they go "through the mortal journey on earth." (GA 54: 178/120) In my view, Heidegger here does not depart from his original position in *Being and Time* where he argues that the dying of others does not provide an insight into the ontological death of Dasein. Note that Heidegger does this precisely because this would reduce death again just to the biologically measurable end of someone's life. In fact, to refer to Dastur again, Dasein must always already be in touch with its own ontological death *qua* way of being so that the death of others at all touches Dasein. This is what Heidegger

[18] "Der Tod *ist* Untergang und das *ist* höchster Anfang, *ist* äußerste Verbergung, *ist* Sein."

argues for in *Being and Time*. What I argue here then is not to say that it is because of someone else dying that humans appreciate withdrawing. Rather, it is because humans are touched by death *qua* concealment that they, first, can at all experience loss when someone dies. Second, this fundamental withdrawal shows itself, or flashes, when someone dies, i.e., when someone is taken by and is then *of* death. In *Being and Time* Dasein can only relate to the dying of others because of Dasein's original relationship with its ontological death. In the thinking of the event there is a similarity insofar as mortals relate to the death of others only insofar as they are always already touched by death. The belonging of the human being to *Ereignis*, or the way in which humans can bind themselves to *Ereignis*, is thanks to their relationship with death. Heidegger thus writes in *Contributions*: "Only the human being "has" the distinction of standing in front of death, because the human being is steadfastly in [*inständig in*] beyng: death the highest testimony to beyng. (GA 65: 230/181)" I will return to this claim below because Heidegger here also ties death to the history of being. Death as the highest testimony to beyng means that death testifies that beyng is inherently withdrawal. In this sense death is the window unto thinking beyng. To be "standing in" beyng then means to stand in this inherent *withdrawal* which has the name "*Seyn*". What Heidegger attempts to show in the above quoted part of his Parmenides lectures, but also in *Introduction to Metaphysics* for example, is not that human beings die at the end of their lives and that the death of others reveals something about being. That would be rather a banal point. Instead, Heidegger here reminds his students and readers how the Greeks thought of birth, life, and death. "Life" as the mortal journey already points at death where this journey is a gift of birth. The mortal journey also points at that which Heidegger calls "the unsupported unsafeguarded", i.e., *Ereignis*, to which human beings always already respond.

However, there is not just a sense of loss. Withstanding this groundlessness by becoming mortal lets beings appear in their richness and in their own right. The towering up of the wealth of beings, in the midst of which the human being is, takes place out of itself. Schmidt hence argues that "[t]his connection between death and concealment defines the original form of forgetfulness upon which all other forms rest." (Schmidt 2013: 169) That means that death—and birth—structures any space of a time thanks to which phenomena occur in certain ways insofar as there is always also forgetting at work. Thus, only when human beings appreciate "a concealment and a withdrawal of beings [then beings properly appear in their wealth because] at the same time and in opposition to this concealment and this withdrawal there also prevails an unconcealedness in which the unconcealed is conserved." (GA 54: 178/120) This is also important to understand why Heidegger in the writings on the fourfold will call on human beings to become mortals. I will return to the fourfold in Parts III and IV. Death and concealment give rise to all forms and it is the task of the mortal being to be mindful of the withdrawal in all presence, a withdrawal that technological production and replication works against.

As I have already indicated above, there is in *Contributions* an even more fundamental relation than that between concealment and death: the relation between beyng and the nought as its neighbour. I write "nought" to indicate that this nothing is precisely not directed at no-thing or no being, but is utter *nothing*, or as Heidegger experimentally says in *Über den Anfang*, it is the *nothingless, das Nichtslose* (cf. GA 70: 9). The tension between beyng and the nought is reflected in the tension between being-there and being-away and the strife between world and earth. The latter tension, in turn, impacts the essential transformation, i.e., the grounding of Da-sein in order for the human being to become the seeker and preserver of beyng's refusal and withdrawal. The essential transformation comes about when being-away is specifically thought. In the thinking of being-away, which is open to human thought because of its acquaintance with death, "the deepest essence of nothingness" (GA 65: 325/257) shows itself. In contemplating death human thought reaches into the utter abyss. The nought, however, "nihilates" which is to say that the nought sways and thereby structures the "there". Death discloses the "not" to the human being, the "not" that belongs to beyng. Beyng's non-availability finds in human existence its only equivalent in the non-availability of death. The simplicity of beyng also finds its equivalent only in the singularity of death. To put this in the language of *Being and Time*: every Dasein has to die its own death. The threat of death, the most radical possibility of impossibility, shows us that "[b]eing *is not* [but that] nevertheless, we cannot equate it with nothingness." (GA 65: 286/225) Thus the sense of abeyance that death introduces in *Being and Time* is transferred over to beyng as such and the history of beyng. The fact that beyng as essential event inherently oscillates, i.e., is that which withdraws and so releases into appearance, was first indicated in the figure of being-toward-death. Death, then, introduces mortals to the thinking of the abyss and this thought opens the path towards the self-mediating centre called *Ereignis*.

Much of this might remind some readers of Hegel. Hence Hegel was brought up before to show how the metaphysician Hegel differs from the being-historical thinker Heidegger. Nevertheless, such misunderstandings persist and it might therefore be useful to point out in more detail the sharp distinction. Francisco Gonzalez has argued that Heidegger in *Contributions* silently slips back into a negative dialectic (cf. Gonzalez 2008). In a nutshell, Gonzalez maintains that Heidegger must recur to a negative dialectic precisely because Heidegger's attempt to speak of beyng directly and not in a mediated way fails. Heidegger's talk of primordiality, however, suggests that he assumes that beyng can be immediately and directly said. Thus, Gonzalez does not buy that Heidegger here in the "other beginning" attempts to speak from beyng. To Gonzalez this indicates a negative stance, as it denies the familiarity of beings and attempts to leap into beyng itself. Gonzalez' criticism points to something else that is crucial when he argues that one of the fundamental tensions of *Contributions* is their apparent oscillation "between a characterization of thinking as always transitional and a characterization of it as transitional only now" (Gonzalez 2008: 376).

Gonzalez' criticism of *Contributions* as a negative dialectics raises two important issues. The first relates to the question how we understand *Contributions* in the body of Heidegger's work. In my view, *Contributions* is a declared first attempt at the thinking *out of* the essential event. We find in *Contributions* crucial insights for reconstructing the thinking path, but the text is necessarily experimental. This explains the oscillation of the text, but the inherent turning of the event itself also explains the oscillation of the text. Second, Heidegger does not wish to speak only of beyng. His thought is always and simultaneously directed toward both beyng *and* beings.[19] Heidegger even denies that beyng can be "said directly at all if all language is language of beings." (GA 65: 78; as quoted in Gonzalez 2008: 358) Gonzalez understands this as Heidegger's implicit admission of defeat of speaking of beyng directly. I read this differently. Gonzalez omits that Heidegger here stresses the need to return to simple, ordinary words and cherish them, as he does with *Ereignis*. Note that words are not beings or entities as a naïve realism might claim. To cherish simple words, is, thinks Heidegger, tantamount to a transformation of language and grants the possibility to speak out of beyng, rather than saying anything *about* beyng. Hence the non-propositional and non-representational character of the language of *Contributions* and surrounding texts. For Heidegger this non-propositional, poietic language, for example of the unfolding passage, *is* the language of beyng. The language is of a withdrawing character as that language gives us nothing to represent. The language *of* beyng ("genitive subjective") is also inherently historical insofar as the multi-layered, interwoven and interspersed concealed ramifications of words are specifically appreciated. Heidegger's focus on the leap is, of course, also important. The leap lets go of everything familiar, e.g., of the representation of the human being as rational animal and of the modern definition of being as the ground of beings (cf. GA 11: 41/33). Therefore, the leap is liberating. But it is not a sudden abrupt reversal. The non-propositional language of passages like the unfolding passage emphasises the leap-character of the thought.

In *Identity and Difference* Heidegger makes the leap explicit when he interprets the German word *Satz* (sentence) as *Satz* in the sense of *Sprung*, leap. This leap leaps away from being as ground and leaps into the abyss. The leap occurs, Heidegger points out, precisely by a *Sichabsetzen*, a distancing-oneself, a leaping away from ordinary representations regarding the necessity of a mediation between subject and object. This is a distancing-oneself from metaphysics and another example of a language that is freed from informational values and ordinary connotations. By pointing out that *Satz* has a different meaning in ordinary German vernacular, Heidegger attempts to liberate the philosophical "concept" "*Satz*" from its philosophical connotations and return to an original meaning this word has in the vernacular. The abyss, Heidegger continues, is then an abyss only for metaphysical thinking, for metaphysics always requires a stable ground. But this "abyss" is at once the realm where human beings and being encounter each other. Heidegger here in *Der Satz der Identität* also speaks of the *brückenlos*, bridge-less or un-bridged, encounter between being and human beings. That is to say, the encounter is not one of mediation between subject (human beings) and object (being), for human beings are for their very mortality always already in this withdrawing ground, but forgetful of it. Appreciating that human beings and beyng belong together initiates appropriation and that mean humans are "transported [*entrückt*] into beyng." (GA 65: 489/384) But Heidegger

---

[19] See also Vallega-Neu (2015: 4f).

here in *Contributions* also notes that appropriation goes together with "loss," i.e., no appropriation lasts for good and there is always the possibility of forgetting.

Hegel's *Logic* begins with an immediate statement *about* pure being (cf. Hegel 2010: 59f). Being is, says Hegel, indeterminate and immediate, and "nothing" to the intuition. Hence the "nothing" already comes in as soon as one says being. Thinking cannot remain with being. If it did, then there would be no thinking. Being itself is initially the immediate and indeterminate, which is why being shows itself to be identical with "nothing" and this is how dialectics necessarily begins for Hegel without any presuppositions. But Heidegger thinks "beginning" differently. For Heidegger thinking "from within" beyng as beyng, i.e., as it is on its own, *Er-eignis*, means that beyng is that which actively withdraws and conceals. Note that also Hegel says that being "vanishes" into nothing and nothing "vanishes" into being and hence becoming comes about. Heidegger radicalises this thought of vanishing, *verschwinden*, with the thought of beyng itself, with that which he names *Seyn* but that which in fact is just that *vanishing*, that utter withdrawal. Hegel appears to see this as well, but from the perspective of metaphysics (in its highest form no less) this vanishing must be between two poles, being (permanent, stable) and nothing (not-being, not-active), which sets forth becoming. But Heidegger stays with *beyng* which is "pre-metaphysical", i.e., that which metaphysics does not see. The inherent self-concealment of beyng is that which is also the "presupposition" of the presuppositionless thought of Hegel's dialectic. Beyng for Heidegger withdraws and conceals *of its own accord*. The negativity, which Gonzalez seems to suspect, simply is not at work in Heidegger, since concealment and withdrawal are nothing negative. Beyng is not something positive waiting to be negated. *Beyng itself occurs insofar as it withdraws.* The nothing that beyng is surrounded with, is not ever identical with beyng. There is not identity of non-identity for Heidegger, but only a sheer schism. For Heidegger, therefore, finite mortal beings cannot immediately and properly say anything *about* beyng. The only claim mortals can make about beyng, with caution, is that "beyng is finite" (GA 65: 269/211). What remains is the leap into the essential event as the place of thinking. The essential event is precisely not immediate but it is always already mediated in and by itself and in that sense the essential event is the "self-mediating centre" out of which everything unfolds and into which everything folds back and which Da-sein "in-abides in" (*inständig*). The *inventive thinking* of beyng is a mortal, finite thinking that does not pretend to achieve absolute knowledge. Beyng withdraws from such attempts as it self-conceals. Precisely with this thought Heidegger does not only push the boundaries of metaphysics, but his thinking is already outside of it. If we take this seriously, then notions such as immanence and transcendence as well as logic and (negative) dialectic no longer apply. This is because now concealment is specifically thought. This centre called essential event self-elicits out of the possibilities of its historical occurrences and it does so finitely, for this centre withdraws, self-refuses and self-conceals. The responses of human beings are nevertheless crucial to this self-eliciting centre. The task is to appreciate in all thought and deed the sheer withdrawal at the heart of beyng itself.

In the current being-historical epoch, to which Heidegger responds, the arrival of a last god announces itself, while machination—i.e., the total organisation and mobilisation of the world in terms of scientific control, a manipulation that deprives beings of their unique being, insofar as everything is reduced to a measurable aggregate—appears to dominate. Hence, there is possibility of "being rescued", but also of abandonment. But both of them are only possible out of the very turning of the event.

The turning of the event is open to mortal thinking because of its vicinity to death. There is a certain pull from death that draws human thinking into this realm insofar as death opens the possibility to begin to grasp concealment. It is death that lets mortal thinking do this and grasping concealment means to see "a reflection of the turning in the essence of being itself." (GA 65: 325/257) Mortal thinking experiences death and so experiences beyng, for, remember, death *is* beyng. Death is not absence of something previously present-at-hand. Nor is death a zero-point. Instead, death itself is active, insofar as concealment is active in any appearance. Death is at once also that which explains mortal forgetting and confusion and therefore the simple fact that groundings need to take place *again and again*. The vicinity of human beings with death also opens to them the intensity of beyng. Death brings humans closer to the withdrawal of beyng. Heidegger does not describe this as a wholesome experience. The encounter with concealing and withdrawal leads to confusion even anger: "The intimacy of being has wrath as its essence, and the strife is always at the same time confusion." (GA 65: 325/257) Yet, by withstanding precisely this confusion that sets in when we are confronted with concealment and a concealment that does not disappear, the other beginning can set in. Death is pulled into the "there" and, as Heidegger writes, this invites us to understand "the end" no longer as the end of something present-at-hand, but as that where something begins and where something returns to. This is why I think that Heidegger argues in here quoted passage §202 of *Contributions* that another world is possible. A world in which beings are not reduced to resources standing ready to be exploited. Death invites us to appreciate finitude and limitation which we need to be reminded of first, when the destruction of the earth is to be stopped. As Heidegger puts it, the human being is the "there", insofar as the human being participates in grounding the history of being. Put differently, in every epoch a world needs to be built that can be inhabited by human beings so that the earth is not destroyed. As Heidegger writes: "Only as historical is the human being the "there," i.e., only as grounding of history and steadfast in the "there" by way of sheltering [*Bergung*] the truth in beings." (GA 65: 324/256) The sheltering of truth in beings then genuinely means to shelter beings and not exploit them and Heidegger for this is possible if we are mindful of our mortality and if we appreciate beyng's self-concealing, i.e., that in any clearing, in any act of disclosure concealing is and remains active. Beings can truly be appreciated if we begin from a realm of non-availability. This reveals the true wealth of beings and their temporal uniqueness.

There is "mediation" at work but not in a dialectical sense. Mediation takes place in the essential event as the unsupported that *self-elicits*, i.e., that finds itself, and that as such is the realm out of where being-historical sendings take their course. But the event self-elicits insofar as it is counter-turning and it can only counter-turn, or counter-swing, for the event is distinct from beings, i.e., distinct from that which "is grounded [*das Grundhafte*]" (GA 71: 148/128). Heidegger's thinking is not a thinking in terms of opposites and their sublation, a teleology striving towards, say, freedom as in Hegelian dialectics. Withdrawal is not the opposite of appearance. Nor are those two different aspects of the same. Instead, they *occur* simultaneously. Heidegger's is rather, as Dietmar Koch suggests, an account of finite teleologies, momentary equilibria reflecting successful groundings (cf. Koch 2012: 202). Their finitude suggests that death structures these teleologies. The "mediation" of the essential event is heterological, diverging and converging in immeasurable ways out of its ownmost unity and in this way the essential event is self-eliciting. In that sense "abysmal" means unfathomable, but only to metaphysical representation. The essential event is the centre, the yawning realm where that history takes its course, where its ramifications and possibilities merge, flow into each other and burst apart, and whence human beings receive *possibilities* they are called upon to respond to. The "other beginning" is hence neither the opposite of the first beginning nor does it sublate the first beginning. Nor is the other beginning a caesura-like new beginning out of thin air that begins at a measurable point in time. Instead, the history of beyng unfolds as continuous withdrawal and simultaneous re-turning. Beyng gapes open and thus provides the possibility for other beginnings. As Heidegger writes in *The Event*: "The first and the other beginning are not two distinct beginnings. They are the *same*." (GA 71: 28/21) For they are sendings of the same abysmal realm. This defies representational as well as dialectical accounts of the history of being.

Rather than empty nothingness, as it might appear to representationalism, Heidegger sees in beyng's self-concealment its "highest gift" (GA 65: 246/194). This is because the refusal, the inherent "not" in beyng, its concealment are what let beyng *be* in excess of itself and guarantee the continuous possibility of other inceptions. Thus at the heart of the movement of the history of being is a refusal of sheer availability (cf. GA 65: 268/210).

The realm called *Ereignis* is not a realm of perfection. Pain, suffering, failure, decay, erring, decline, and death all have and find their place in it. Death takes primacy because death is "departure-like [*abschiedlich*] the a-byss with respect to the beginning." (GA 71:193/165 *ta*) This is to say that in every beginning, for example, in the first beginning and the other beginning; that in any grounding that turns out well; that in any work (for example, a work of art) that succeeds to bring forth the truth of beyng, death already has a say. The *a-byss* is the "concealment of being," is its "nihilating, *Nichtung*." The abyss allows for the way in which beyng withdraws from objectification and ultimate metaphysical reification, e.g., as *summum ens*, as will, as will to power, etc. That is to say that historical metaphysical determinations of being are only possible because beyng withdraws. Those determinations are exemplifications of the attempt of metaphysics to hold on to beyng by determining beingness. This impedes access to the history of beyng (and being). But with Heidegger we can think the nihilating and concealment that give into the clearing, and therefore it is via death that human thinking can inventively think beyng and enter its history. A successful thinking of beyng is then a mortal thinking mindful of its finitude and fragility, its limitedness and openness to erring. This thinking begins with a released withdrawal from the prevalence of beings. This thinking thus begins with a mortal stance of receivership. That death is present in all beginnings, present in such a way that it withdraws, also means that breakdowns of meaning are inscribed in every beginning. Death in this fundamental role also plays into the danger that beyng can become to itself. Beyng is at once occurring in its essence and its unessence. The way in which mortals respond to its occurrences co-decides the fate of beyng.

In the remaining two chapters I shall explicate Heidegger's claim quoted above that death is now to be thought out of beyng itself (cf. GA 71:190/162). We can now more easily see, why the movement of the thought is not dialectical, purely twofold, but always moving between, unfolding out of and folding back into several dimensions *at once*, i.e. turning in a heterological way, held together by the self-differentiating fissure: beyng. Death is at once what leads into the thinking of beyng, but death also needs to be thought from the perspective of the history of being.

Chapter 9
Death and the Fissuring of Beyng

Heidegger suspects all of metaphysics to favour the sheer presence of the beingness of beings. The thinking of concealment is a gradual renunciation of the primacy of beings. Heidegger begins to see in *possibility* a distinct way to think outside the scope of a metaphysics of presence. Part I showed how the initial analysis of death leads Heidegger to think being as possibility. This chapter traces how Heidegger continues this thought in *Contributions* in light of the heterological movement of the history of being. In accordance with this history Heidegger in *Contributions* refers to the "structures" of beyng that allow for the revelations and concealments of beyng as *Zerklüftungen*, fissures (cf. GA 65: 244/192). Beyng *is*, or rather occurs, as fissured. Heidegger says that mortal thinking "can prepare the ... time-space (site of the moment) ... in Da-sein" (GA 65: 235/186) in order to make the figure of beyng's fissure graspable. In *Contributions* Heidegger refers to Dasein's structure of being-towards-death diagnosed in *Being and Time* in order to prepare for that time-space. That is, Heidegger returns to the analysis of death as possibility *and* impossibility, for here being briefly shows itself as split up. Heidegger further radicalises this thought and begins to think this inherent splitting of *beyng* in terms of fissures. Thus, the thinking that *Contributions* wishes to prepare is a thinking that carries out *beyng*-toward-death. This at once reflects back into beyng because death is *of* beyng. The discussion of the fissure of beyng will also allow me to touch on Heidegger's reformulation of the ontological difference. Note that the talk of the fissures of beyng indicates that there always are several dimensions at stake *in* beyng.

1 Beyng-Toward-Death and the Modalities

The sections on the fissure of beyng and beyng-toward-death are found in the joining "Leap" of *Contributions*. This joining prepares the timid leap into thinking the abyss of beyng (cf. GA 65: 278/218). Thus, Heidegger's experimental thoughts regarding the fissures are cautious attempts at leaping into the abyss. In *Über den*

© Springer Nature Switzerland AG 2021
J. A. Niederhauser, *Heidegger on Death and Being*,
https://doi.org/10.1007/978-3-030-51375-7_9

Anfang he continues what he begins in *Contributions*, when he tries to think the event as that which catches itself—"das Sichfangen und Sichauf-fangen im Ereignis selbst" (GA 70: 10)—as the inception, *der An-fang*, of the event. The event throws itself up and down its own withdrawing ground but it also catches itself again and again and this is how the event turns within itself. But it is in *Contributions* where we find the first significant attempts to think the abyssal fissure of beyng, approached in light of being-toward-death. Heidegger, however, also admits he is not the right thinker to perform the leap properly. It is, of course, philosophically dissatisfying to say that there might be some future thinker able to perform the leap and appropriately think the fissure. Nevertheless, I believe there is also in *Contributions* an attempt to think the fissure of beyng and this is precisely where death comes into play. In what follows I provide a reconstruction of beyng's fissures. This allows me to show how Heidegger arrives at his determination of beyng as possibility from his earlier determination of death as Dasein's ownmost possibility.

Heidegger notes that by means of the modalities metaphysics has to a certain degree pursued the fissures of beyng. Yet, the modalities have covered over the original fissures, since the modalities consider beings in their actuality. For Heidegger the modalities are a symptom of the encrustation of metaphysics. The modalities privilege actuality as that which properly is and thereby forget concealment. Possibility and necessity matter only insofar as they guarantee and secure the prevalence of actuality: "possibility and necessity [are]—so to speak—its [actuality's] horns" (GA 65: 281/221). They are what guarantee actuality's force and reinforce the actual over the potential. Still, the modalities indicate to Heidegger that beyng is inherently fissured.

The talk of beyng's fissures indicates that beyng unfolds in that it gapes open and yawns, withdraws, pushes, brings forth, holds back, collides—slowly but *at once* and always out of a onefold. To Heidegger these tidings of beyng are similar to fissures of a mountain range.

In order to think the fissure of beyng Heidegger returns to being-toward-death, i.e., to the figure of thought that revealed both the abeyance of Dasein's ur-possibility and that possibility stands higher than actuality. Being-toward-death is now seen from the perspective of beyng and Da-sein as the historical site of the grounding of the truth of beyng. Heidegger says that beyng-toward-death "harbors two basic determinations of the fissure and is its mostly unrecognized mirror image in the "there"" (GA 65: 282/222). It is worth quoting Heidegger here in full:

> In the first place, being-toward-death harbours the essential belonging of the "not" to being as such, *which here*, in the Da-sein that is distinctive as grounding the truth of being, shows itself only in unique sharpness.
> Secondly, it harbours the unfathomable fullness of the essence of *"necessity,"* which in turn is one of the fissures of being itself; being-toward-death again taken in terms of Dasein.
> The collision of necessity and possibility. Only in such spheres can it be surmised what truly belongs to that which "ontology" treats as the pale and vacuous *jumble* of "modalities." (GA 65: 282f/222 *ta*)

Does Heidegger here merely belittle traditional ontology? Or does he further develop the collision of necessity and possibility? Regardless of the choice of words, this is one of the most decisive passages of the *Contributions* and if we want to be sympathetic to Heidegger then we can understand his comments about "ontology" as saying that ontology calms itself about the fundamental collision of necessity and possibility by keeping them apart. The notion of collision is crucial because it provides a further hint at the motion of the history of being and consequently hints at the role of death in that history. Especially because death is now the ownmost possibility of beyng's rather than of Dasein.

In *Being and Time* being-toward-death shows that the ownmost possibility of Dasein is, in fact, at once Dasein's possibility of *im*possibility of existence. Being-toward-death brings Dasein most radically before its own being and before its understanding of being. As the understanding of being must of necessity indicate "something like being", as Heidegger says in *Being and Time*, Heidegger begins to "transfer" these insights over to beyng as such. *Beyng*-toward-death now reads literally that beyng as such is toward death and thus beyng is in the possibility of its impossibility. Remember that Heidegger in *Über den Anfang* says that beyng *is* death. Beyng itself occurs as finite and beyng occurs in its essence and unessence— always simultaneously. The "not" that belongs to beyng is the "not" of the possible, not so much of that which is not yet actual, but more fundamentally of that which is not at all to be actualised; of that which always remains an abyss for thinking, where thinking has nothing to hold on to. Heidegger says that the "not" becomes apparent precisely in the grounding of Da-sein as the site of the truth of beyng. This is why the grounding of Da-sein is only fully attainable if death is pulled into it. Da-sein, then, is "a-byssal Da-*sein*" (GA 65: 285/224). That is to say that Da-sein is not a static ahistorical foundation but is in the motion of grounding and withdrawing and as such opening itself up to the history of being. The reformulated beyng-toward-death need not be performed by each Dasein. Instead, "[t]he carrying out of being-toward-death is a duty incumbent only on thinkers of the other beginning." (GA 65: 285/224) That is, this running forth is the act of grounding the "there" which is initiated by a thinking that can think beyng's withdrawal and poverty—and therefore also beyng's excess. It is no coincidence that the notion of pain becomes quite crucial in *The Event* where Heidegger further develops the saying of the essential event and the history of being. Standing-in or inabiding in the history of being is a painful experience because standing-in brings most radically before inherent withholding and collision (cf. GA 71: 144/123). Standing-in *in* the history of beyng also brings before the intensity of beyng, its threat of abandonment. The pain in death, Heidegger writes, lets us experience the abyss of beyng: "Death is the purest nearness of the human being to being." (GA 71: 194/165) This is because death brings before beyng as pure possibility and hence abeyance. At the same time death reveals that the nought structures any opening, any unconcealment, beginning, and grounding, which therefore are all finite and fragile. That beyng is pure possibility introduces a tension-filled abeyance. It is now beyng that is toward death and in this way beyng self-appropriates (*sich zu eigen sein*). Beyng is thus toward its possibility and impossibility and this is why beyng can also lose itself. That is to say, beyng itself needs to come in touch with death in order to properly be itself. *Beyng essentially occurs as it is toward death: das Seyn selbst zum Tode.* In the thinking of the other beginning only the few will have to perform running forth. Their running forth, in turn, is possible because beyng itself runs forth toward death. Theirs is a reflection. Thus, the thinkers of the other beginning reflect how beyng itself runs forth towards death when they carry out being-toward-death.

Being-toward-death in *Being and Time* proves to be a necessary structure of Dasein because death is the necessary condition for world to arise. From this early analysis Heidegger sees a sense of necessity also at work in beyng, yet without the original transcendental import. The *Contributions* predominantly use the term "*Notwendigkeit*" in relation to "*Not*" which means emergency or distress: "All necessity is rooted in emergency." (GA 65: 45/37) In necessity there is then also a sense of pain. Heidegger understands "necessity" not in terms of a modality but in the way in which the vernacular understands the word. Here again we see the return to ordinary words. In *Contributions* we find a decisive section on "*The necessity of philosophy*" (GA 65: 45/37). Philosophy, Heidegger writes, begins only in utmost emergency, *Not*. Philosophy is, however, not to eradicate that emergency. Philosophy is rather to bear, withstand and even justify that emergency. Taken literally, as Heidegger appears to be doing, the German word *Not-wendigkeit* says "emergency that turns." Heidegger speaks of necessity as that which *umtreibt*, as that which bothers and animates. Thus Heidegger does not understand necessity in a modal sense but assumes that modal-logical "necessity" retains some sense of a more primordial necessity anchored in beyng's turning; a necessity that induces emergencies, for beyng occurs as danger. Emergency points to the philosophical need of the human being to know and understand. This is present in the first beginning in the θαυμάζειν as the fundamental mood of that beginning. The original question was, how does everything correlate, what are *beings in the whole*? As Hermann Cohen writes in the *Logic of Pure Cognition*, the question for the origin is what first places the human being in a meaningful web of beings: "Only then do beings *as* beings become a problem." (Cohen 1922: 79)[1] We can here clearly see how Heidegger's time in Marburg influenced his later thinking. A sense of wonder that something is at all initiates the original quest. But today we are faced with something different, something that makes the other beginning necessary. Heidegger argues: "This plight is what propels humans around among beings and brings them before beings in the whole … and to themselves and thereby lets history begin or perish." (GA 65: 45/37 *ta*) Those in the Cave are trapped in a state where all they know are singular shadows, apparently unrelated, because they have not seen the Idea, they have not asked for origin, they felt no distress, no need to leave the Cave. With Plato the Idea is established as the ground of beings in the whole. But seeing the Idea and truth is painful, is utter distress. It even entails having to leave one's home for an unknown place only to return and face death. Hence even in the first beginning, there is an emergency, a distress at work. With Heidegger a shift occurs. No longer are beings the beginning of the enquiry as are the shadows in the Cave. Now the leap into beyng is necessary in order to think difference specifically. Hence *Not* has nothing

---

[1] My translation.

to do with hardship, *Elend*, or lack, *Mangel*, in the ordinary sense, which would mean that something present-at-hand is currently missing. What Heidegger calls *Not der Notlosigkeit*, lack of distress, is the forgetting of being. In such an epoch we are numbed by lived experiences and the wonders of machination—there is too much of everything, so much in fact that we are blind to the sense of wonder that something is, that we *are*. But we are equally deaf to the call of origin, to that which at all brings into relation anything and all that is. For Heidegger death is the utmost emergency human beings always already know. As such death could reawaken the human beings' questioning stance and show them the lack of distress. Hence shock and terror are necessary.

Death at once terrifies and restrains, but also asks us to be attentive. Death is the last refuge where the reductive logic of machination does not yet—at least for now—rule, even though transhumanism and its ideologues already proclaim that death is just another technical problem the engineered solution for which will soon be available equally to everyone. Death shocks us back into what is. Shock, *Erschrecken*, is "[t]he basic disposition of the other beginning." (GA 65: 46/38) This shock suddenly makes us aware of the abandonment of beyng, of the emptiness of beings and the lack of world. But the shock is also a creative experience pushing us back into fundamental questions like, "what is truth?", "what is meaning?", i.e., questions that have to be asked again and again. In terms of the history of being, for Heidegger the current epoch is the epoch of the completion and self-fulfilment, ergo encrustation, of metaphysics. In this situation, in purely philosophical terms, a shock is necessary that lets us ask again the question for origin. Hence Heidegger reformulates running forth toward death as disclosing "the openness of beyng ... fully and out of what is most extreme." (GA 65: 283/223) Only through that openness of beyng, that concealing clearing, beings properly appear of their own accord, and not, say, as resources or units of energy. This is also a reformulation of how world arises again out of death now as the uttermost extreme. Yet, world now is the "self-opening openness" (GA 5: 35/26) which discloses paths and routes, where a people can err and find itself, rather than the horizon against which a singular Dasein projects its factical possibilities. World is in strife with earth, that which provides shelter, for earth it withdraws. There will be more to say on earth and world in Parts III and IV when I turn to the fourfold. Through bearing the utmost extreme, i.e., death, there is an opening of "the necessity of the highest possibilities, on whose paths human beings, in a creative and grounding way, go beyond themselves and back into the ground of beings." (GA 65: 46/38) This, the necessity of the highest possibilities, is the collision of possibility and necessity. The few, e.g., poets, carry out the collision in beyng-toward-death, thus they think beyng's abysmal fissures.

Possibility and necessity, then, are fissures of beyng as beyng unfolds and occurs *as* history. They occur and collide *before* there is any actuality. Possibility takes the upper hand in the fissures of beyng and I shall presently turn to Heidegger's notion of possibility in *Contributions* in order to make this clearer. The motion of the history of being is one of fissuring. Once one path bursts open, a multiplicity of paths are opened as well and a multiplicity of other parts are covered over. The history of being is literally, and not metaphorically, a never fully disclosed, ever uncharted mountain range in which human beings roam, hike, get lost, find themselves, ground and build worlds, go astray, fall, hurt, gain, reach peaks only to hike down again, learn—and die.

As I have already mentioned, Heidegger in the late 1940s begins to call death the *Ge-Birg*, literally the mountain range, of beyng (cf. GA 9: 374 *na*). This will be crucial for Parts III and IV. *Ge-Birg* is less estranging and arbitrary a term when we take into consideration the notion of the fissures of beyng and the role death plays there. Death is *Ge-Birg* in a twofold sense. First, beyng is fissured, unfolds and occurs as fissured because death as mountain range is fundamental even to beyng. Put differently, death is what lets beyng unfold historically and therefore death is in turn for mortals the window into the truth of beyng. This also explains why and how the history of being is finite. Second, as *Ge-Birg* death is the gathering or concentration of sheltering-harbouring, of *bergen*, i.e. of the way in which beyng fundamentally occurs as it conceals, refuses and shelters itself. *Ge-Birg* is also the gathering of *Bergung*, which human beings engage in, for example, through art and poetry. In so doing humans are preservers of the truth of beyng and therefore of beings in their respective exuberant simplicity and wealth. Beyng's self-concealment goads on acts of *Bergung* (cf. GA 65: 56/45); what is not available and withdraws spurs on creative acts that build a world for humans, rather than the sheer availability of what is presence-at-hand that lets us only drown in a growing multitude of indifferent things. To say this more drastically: we are drowning in garbage. For Heidegger the nihilism of our age means precisely that everything is available with seemingly little left to discover. This is what pushes us into circular optimisation and enhancement of beings in their beingness—including the human being—for nothing but optimisation's sake. When we take into consideration death as *Ge-Birg* and its role in the thinking of the event more broadly, we see that the notion that "[s]heltering [*Bergung*] belongs to the essential occurrence of truth" (GA 65: 389/307)[2] speaks out of death. That is, *bergen*, that most fundamental moment of ἀλήθεια, which always already unfolds as *Entbergung* and *Verbergung*, is itself an interest of death and concentrated in death. Death as *Ge-Birg* is then also related to time as "clearing of the self-concealment of beyng," as Heidegger calls "time" in his letter to Father Richardson. In *Contributions* death is the utmost extreme of the "there" of Da-sein, i.e., of historical man who takes on the task to carry out and bear the truth of an epoch. Death as such gives rise to the time-space that grants the *kairos* of responding to the sendings of beyng (cf. GA 65: 323/255). By facing death then the few enter into the ecstatic temporality of beyng itself and see what is possible beyond the currently prevalent occurrence of beyng. This is especially relevant to understand how Heidegger thinks of *Ge-Stell* and *Ge-Viert* as two possible modes of beyng occurring in the same epoch.

---

[2] See also: "Die *Bergung* selbst vollzieht sich im und als *Da-sein*." (GA 65: 71).

2   The Fissure of the Possible

Based on what I have argued so far, I can now reconstruct in more detail, how Heidegger arrives at beyng as the possible and what role death plays in this regard. As argued in Part I, death as the possibility that gives Dasein nothing to actualise leads Heidegger to privilege possibility in a distinct non-metaphysical sense. Thus, Heidegger's thought is not simply an inversion of the Aristotelian-Scholastic schema of potentiality-actuality. The German word *Möglichkeit* takes on another meaning, removed from connotations of power and potency. Heidegger's *Möglichkeit* speaks out of the verbs *mögen* and *vermögen*. Heidegger properly develops possibility, *Möglichkeit* in relation to those verbs in the lecture course *What calls for Thinking?* (cf. GA 8: 5). Yet, that sense of *Möglichkeit* is already active in *Contributions*.

It is important to point out here that *Möglichkeit* or *das Mögliche* is precisely neither infinite, eternal, nor limitless. There is a "not", which sways in the possible and this "not" Heidegger wishes to bring to the fore. For Heidegger the "possible" is limited, precisely because it is not some indefinite power that only waits to be actualised. The "possible" is to remain unhurt and mortals accomplish this by cherishing the earth rather than by exploiting it, as Heidegger says in *Overcoming Metaphysics* (cf. GA 7: 97). The Will to Will wants the opposite. The Will to Will wants the "possible" to be the impossible, i.e., to be limitless and infinite, Heidegger here continues. Thus, we could say that Deleuze with his notion of the "virtual" formulates the technical-instrumental rationality of the current age. Heidegger's "possible" is something else entirely. Thus, we have to be careful what Heidegger really means by *Möglichkeit*.

For Heidegger *Möglichkeit* has to do with the verb *mögen* first and foremost. That is to say, *Möglichkeit* does not have to do with power as do potentiality and possibility. These two have their etymological origin in the vulgar Latin verb *potere* which means to be capable of, to be powerful. Yet, Heidegger wishes to understand *Möglichkeit* in a similar way as he understands the German word *Wesen*. I will say more on *Wesen* in Part III when I address the *Wesen der Technik*. That is to say, he understands these words in a non-metaphysically charged way, but rather in the way the vernacular would understand them. He may not be entirely etymologically accurate since the German word *mögen*, in fact, does have to do with power and force. Nevertheless, Heidegger wishes to stress the meaning of "liking" and "loving" as prevalent in *mögen* and hence also in *Möglichkeit* and the pivotal verb *vermögen*. It is thus highly crucial to appreciate that Heidegger wishes to wrest *Möglichkeit* entirely free from any metaphysical connotations and hence also from prevalent connotations of power and *potential*. *Möglichkeit* is about love for Heidegger, but also about force (*Kraft*) in a non-metaphysical sense. Hence when Heidegger writes in *Why Poets?* that we have not yet learnt how to love (cf. GA 5: 274/204), in my view, what he is trying to say, is that we have forgotten being. Note that Heidegger continues here by saying: "But mortals are. They are so long as there is language." (GA 5: 274/204) This is an indication of the relationship between language and death and the possibility to return to being through the medium of mortals: language. I will return to this issue in Part IV.

In the context of Heidegger the verb *vermögen* is hence difficult to translate. In talks on the fourfold Heidegger begins to name mortals those who *den Tod als Tod vermögen* (cf. GA 7: 180/148).[3] The standard translation of *vermögen* here would be "to be capable of". Yet, I argue that *vermögen* here does not mean what the dictionary suggests. "To be capable of" is a misleading translation of *vermögen* because it suggests the capacity to actualise. In my view, Pattison makes the two following mistakes in his study on death that impede a proper understanding of what Heidegger is after (cf. Pattison 2016: 128). First, Pattison equates Heidegger's later notion of "mortals" with Dasein and Dasein's "capacity" to run forth toward death. That Dasein is capable of running forth toward its death is a controversial and problematic claim in its own right, but equating running forth with mortals learning to die and becoming mortals, is not accurate for reasons that will become more obvious in Parts III and IV. Second, and more important for the question after the meaning of *Möglichkeit* in Heidegger, Pattison relies on the standard English translation of *vermögen* as "to be capable of".[4] Thus, Heidegger's claim, which is admittedly strange, that mortals are those who *den Tod als Tod vermögen* becomes even stranger when we understand simply as saying that mortals are those who are capable of death. What does that mean? That mortals command over death? How do they do that? Where or what is death such that mortals could be capable of commanding it? True, even to a German ear or someone who is familiar with the German language Heidegger's claim at first seems to say just this, that mortals are capable of death as death. But *vermögen* means something else.

In fact, *vermögen* articulates an experience in which *I* have been addressed by something or someone and where *I* have dared to respond to that person or that thing in a certain way. There is *vermögen* only where there is something or someone involved who loves *me* and who or what *I* love in return. The odd claim about mortals and their death then tells us that death touches mortals and that they dare to respond to death—in a restrained, but also in a loving and caring way. That is to say, mortals are to begin to love their death and in this way *become mortal*.

When Heidegger calls being itself das *Mög-liche*, as he does in the *Letter on Humanism*, this indicates that beyng is *the* realm of realms, *the* historical dimensionality of dimensionalities, that always already addresses (*Zuspruch*) the human being and which the human being always already analogously responds to (*Entspruch*). There is then also a sense of love in beyng as *Möglichkeit*. In the self-differentiation of *Zuspruch* and *Entspruch*, address or claim and correspondence, the withdrawal of beyng is inherent. Beyng addresses through withdrawing. The proper human response is timid, mindful that mortal thinking can never have full manipulative control over all that is. This is also how I understand the following claims on "possibility" in *Contributions* in accordance with Heidegger's later remarks on *das Mög-liche*. Heidegger writes: "beyng is possibility, that which is

---

[3] Hofstadter translation.
[4] Nevertheless, Pattison acknowledges that there is a distinct poetic aspect to "mortals" and their community in Heidegger's later writings, which is lacking in *Being and Time* (cf. Pattison 2016: 151).

never present-at-hand and yet is always bestowing and denying itself [*Gewährend und Versagend*] refusal through ap-propriation [*Er-eignung*]." (GA 65: 475/374 *ta*) And: "in the other beginning beyng must first be thought in the form of the possible [*das Mögliche*]." (GA 65: 475/374) One of Heidegger's earliest motivations is to think being and the ontological *in actu, im Vollzug*, without reifying it. Beyng as the possible allows Heidegger to think beyng without reification: "Being is, and therefore it does not become a being—this can be expressed most pointedly by saying that beyng is possibility." (GA 65: 475/374) There is also a sense of subversion of metaphysics and its privileging of the actual at work here. Heidegger subverts the dominance of the actual and turns the focus toward the possible. In so doing we are immediately on a different level, one of experimenting, as Heidegger says here. But we are also on a level of thought that now only works by trying to articulate the activity of beyng and ultimately that of any occurrence such as world and thing. Hence Heidegger's later strange formulations of "the world worlds" and "the thing things." Beyng as the possible, not as actuality or reality, limited within and by itself, denies reifications such as *summum ens* or *genus* because now thinking begins not with beings, but with beyng as a realm of the possible. Metaphysics "makes the "actual," i.e. beings the point of departure and the goal of the determination of being." (GA 65: 475/374) In *Being and Time* Dasein is initially pushed toward the thought of being as possibility in being-toward-death. In the thinking of the other beginning a thinking *out of* beyng as the possible shows itself to be necessary in order to overcome the metaphysics of availability and actuality that objectifies the world and reduces all beings to contribute to the functioning of a continuous but aimless increase in power. Working toward overcoming metaphysics is necessary, thinks Heidegger, since metaphysics is what fuels the all-encompassing technological manipulation of all that is. The possible is, therefore, to be thought of as the "deepest fissure" (GA 65: 475/374) of beyng and death as utmost possibility of the human being is testimony to that. The possible then also refers to the abyss of beyng, to the non-presence of beings in the mortal thinking of beyng. There is, in fact as already in *Being and Time*, a profound connection between the possible and the nought. Thus, there is, as always with Heidegger, at once a great chance in thinking the possible for another beginning, but also the chance to get lost in it.

Thanks to the determination of beyng as possibility in a non-metaphysical sense, presupposing the representational schema of the ontic-ontological difference is no longer necessary (cf. GA 65: 250/197). Now beyng itself has been found in the way in which it unfolds. Yet, the talk of fissure still suggests something like difference, *Unterschied*. Moreover, beyng and beings are still not identical after the turn simply because beyng is not a being. There is a difference between the truth of beyng, i.e., the clearing self-concealing dimension of presence, and beings, i.e., what is present. With beyng as realm of the possible we can think of beyng as self-differentiating in such a way that there is *being* (*Anwesen*, presence, *Sein*) and beings. This presence, *Sein* with "i", indicates that beings *are* in their own right. In the *Onto-theo-logy* essay Heidegger says: ""being" itself says: being which is *beings*." (GA 11: 69/62) The "is" is intransitive, i.e., *beings* here is not the accusative object, but nominative subject. The "is" is similar to the German *blühen*, the Italian *piove*, or the Greek χρή: "In each case, the verb is pointing purely to that which is taking place or rather to the taking place or the happening itself, which is entirely indissociable from that which is actually taking place." (de Beistegui 2003a: 223) Beyng self-differentiates in such a way that there can be presence and something that is present. This is not to say that beyng is the ultimate ground. Instead, this says that beings are but spatio-temporal occurrences entirely without ground. "Presence" is the way in which beings are present and this presence is a projection of time itself. Thus, difference is now differentiation, or *differencing*, and this works precisely through beyng's self-concealing. Beyng as *Ereignis* is in one word "being and time." This is similar to how Heidegger understands the *Es gibt*, *it gives* or *there is*, in the talk *Time and Being* (cf. GA 14: 9ff). Whenever *I* say, "*I am here*," *I* already speak out of that *differencing* (cf. GA 11: 69). That is, differencing takes place in this saying and that differencing is being unfolding as self-differentiation. In *Contributions* Heidegger thus says, "beyng is not something "earlier"—existing in itself, for itself. Instead, the event is the temporal-spatial simultaneity for beyng and beings." (GA 65: 13/13) Koch in this respect notes that this suggests a unity in difference and that difference unfolds out of the simultaneity that is at work in the event (cf. Koch 2007: 97). Thus, the heterology emerges out of a homology but that homology is always already fissured and therefore fans out (*auffächern*). We can better understand this unfolding as self-differentiation when we take into account beyng as fissured and with the possible as its main fissure. Beyng unfolds as self-differentiating because it is temporally fissured. In truth, then, what speaks when we say *I am here*, *I am a thinking being*, or *Why is there something?* is death as the mountain range of beyng, as that which lets beyng self-differentiate: *sum moribundus*. Thus, when Heidegger says that the tiny word "is" moves the history of being (cf. GA 11: 79), what really moves that history is death as the mountain range of being where all its fissures are gathered. For death *is* beyng.

Chapter 10
Seinsgeschichte and Death

Throughout this part, I have several times indicated the important role death plays in the history of being. I shall now further explicate what I take Heidegger to mean when he says that "[f]or the first and only time in the history of beyng, the essence of death must now be experienced and interrogated out of beyng itself." (GA 71: 190/162) I do so by way of a discussion of my understanding of the history of being. One should not underestimate the scope of this claim by Heidegger. He very clearly here says that the *essence* of death, i.e., its historically unfolding dimensionality, has not yet been brought into focus in the history of thought. Moreover, death now is clearly an interest of beyng itself and even though human beings have been mortal beings since their very origins, they have not yet become proper mortals. By explicating this remark by Heidegger it will be easier to understand his later call for mortals to become mortals.

1   The Meaning of *Seinsgeschichte*

One of the major shifts after *Being and Time* is that history is now primarily the history of beyng itself, rather than of Dasein. The English translation of *Seinsgeschichte* as *history of being* could lead one to assume that Heidegger writes a history[1] of some meta-subject of general history called "Being" or that "being" is the stable, unmoving ground of that history. Demske, for example, in his book on death in Heidegger argues just that when he says that "being is the ground of all history." (Demske 1970: 127) To my mind, this is a direct result of failing to understand the "turning" of the event and depicts a regress into foundationalism and thus ultimately a metaphysical understanding of being. Moreover, the notion of the history of being

---

[1] Perhaps a more appropriate translation for *Geschichte* is "tidings" rather than "history". This would seem to come closer to what is meant by *Geschichte*.

© Springer Nature Switzerland AG 2021
J. A. Niederhauser, *Heidegger on Death and Being*,
https://doi.org/10.1007/978-3-030-51375-7_10

could suggest that Heidegger writes a historiography of the various "definitions" or ways of understanding being. It is helpful to clarify what *Seinsgeschichte* grammatically indicates. The history *of* being is not an objective genitive, but rather a subjective genitive. Hence, the history *of* being does not tell the story of how people in some epoch or other understood being so that we can neatly pigeonhole and investigate this history. There is an important hint at what Heidegger means by *Seinsgeschichte* in the *Onto-theo-logy* essay. Heidegger there says that the history of being is not on display "like apples, pears, peaches ... on the counter of historical representational thinking." (GA 11: 73/66) This would turn "being" into an object of historiographical investigation and on top of that make the history of being linear. This is why I disagree with interpretations of *Seinsgeschichte* such as that of Thomson who argues that *Seinsgeschichte* is nothing but a "historical series of ... epoch-grounding understandings of Being." (Thomson 2000: 298) True, they are epoch-grounding, yet whence do they come? The history of being is precisely not a linear and clear-cut "series" of various human understandings of being. Heidegger himself says in *Moira*, an essay on Parmenides, that the "history of being is never a sequence of events [*Geschehnisse*] which being traverses for itself." (GA 7: 257/98)[2] In the *Onto-theo-logy* Heidegger also clearly says that we can never reduce the history of being to just "*one* epoch of the history of the clearing of being [*Lichtungsgeschichte*]." (GA 11: 60/51) Readings like Thomson's suggests that there are clear-cut epochs and that those are for the most part just how humans have understood being. Notice Heidegger does not speak of *Sein und Geschichte* oder *Sein in der Geschichte*. Being, or rather beyng itself, is at work *as* its history, put differently, beyng with all its fissures *is* the history of histories, beyng occurs historically, *geschichtlich*, or *geschicklich*, as Heidegger sometimes says. That means that beyng sends possibilities which humans respond to and these responses push back into beyng.

Heidegger does say that there are various understandings of being. He mentions being as "Φύσις, Λόγος, Ἕν, Ἰδέα, Ἐνέργεια, Substantiality, Objectivity, Subjectivity, Will, the Will to Power, [and] the Will to Will." (GA 11: 73/66) Now, one could argue that these are simply ways of understanding being and that those occur as a succession in history. But this would defy claims of simultaneity and of the fissuring of beyng. Rather, as already argued above, these clearings of beyng, for lack of a better expression, flow into each other, they mingle and merge. Therefore, they are not reducible to just one at a time and they are not *of the past* in any ordinary sense. The history of being is not backward-looking, as Heidegger often says. Note also that only when the event has come into focus, can the history of *being* as its metaphysical determinations come into focus *at all*. No one saw this before Heidegger. Thus, I distinguish between the "history of being" and the "history of beyng". The former is in fact the epochal self-differentiation of being *as* Φύσις, Λόγος, Ἕν, etc. These indicate different ways of *responding* to beyng and subsequent different *understandings* of being. The latter are directed at beings. Yet, these are neither linear nor ever entirely lost, but continue to work through history and

---

[2] Translated by Krell and Capuzzi.

they are interwoven. The latter, in turn, is the realm thanks to which the former is possible. The history of beyng is not directed at beings. The history of beyng works by radical incisions, which in that history of histories are possible due to the workings of abyssal beyng as the possible. These incisions result in beyng's sendings and those, in turn, bring fates upon the human being, fates the human being must respond to.

Much of the confusion readings like Gonzalez' display, which I referred to above, is caused by the assumption that the "saying" of beyng is supposedly an immediate and perfectly direct access to some object "Being" about which we are to formulate truthful propositions. An access so immediate that it would require no history. In order to understand this saying *of* beyng as the event we must understand the history of beyng. Heidegger writes: "saying does not express *about* beyng something that supervenes to it in general ... on the contrary it says beyng out of itself." (GA 65: 473/372) This is possible only thanks to an access to beyng as its history. The fact that Heidegger can see *Seinsgeschichte* is the clearest indication that his is a saying *out of* beyng. *Seinsgeschichte* was not possible before Heidegger. Only through the thought of beyng as event can the history of being come into view. The saying out of beyng is then not an access to some object, but the insight into the *tidings*, the "turnings" of the event. The attempts of Heidegger to say these "turnings" are necessarily non-propositional and try to capture the simultaneity at work in the turnings. Yet, this does not mean that beyng is the meta-subject of history. Beyng is not something acting somewhere beyond or behind us and the world. To speak of a meta-subject would be a reification of beyng. Instead, beyng self-differentiates according to its fissures and these "sendings" give rise to the way in which beings occur (are present) in any epoch, and the way beings occur also always has to do with the way in which human beings respond to their thrownness. This finds articulation in metaphysical determinations of being as substance, will to power, etc., which all look for an ultimate ground of beings.

In a conversation with a Japanese scholar Heidegger says: "Origin always means future, *Herkunft aber bleibt stets Zukunft.*" (GA 12: 91) Yet, this does not mean that Heidegger's perspective or the perspective of the history of beyng becomes antiquarian and backward-looking. Quite the opposite. The ways in which beyng has disclosed itself still work and will continue to work themselves "through" history. "Origin" begins to take primacy insofar as that which has been presses back into that which will have been as that which is coming toward us. Any saying of beyng is a saying of the essential event as precisely that realm in which the manifestations of "being as..." are at war over prevalence. Heraclitus' notion that war is the father of all things is in the background here. Mortal saying out of beyng takes place in the tiny word "is," as Heidegger says at several places (cf. GA 65: 473/372 and GA 11: 79/66). The "is" determines the way in which beings *are* in these constellations. For example, in being as *Ge-Stell*, beings *are as* standing reserve, readily available for manipulation. Being sways in the "as". As such beings are analogous to being as the concentration of all challenging and positioning. In how far metaphysics is at work in *Ge-Stell* is the topic of the next part. For Heidegger it is, however, clear that the "end" of metaphysics does not mean that metaphysics is a thing of the past. Quite the opposite and in line with how he understands history metaphysics for him only just now begins. As he writes in *Overcoming Metaphysics*: "metaphysics only now accedes its unconditional domination over beings." (GA 7: 69) That is to say that the forgetting of the withdrawal now assumes absolute power over beings. The task that Heidegger hence sees for mortals is to respond to this problem and its destructive forces in such a way that metaphysics can be overcome and another beginning becomes possible.

In order for this to happen, concealing and withdrawal must be thought. The history of the first beginning is a history of withdrawal, but, as I noted above, Heidegger does not want to deny the importance of the first beginning. Instead, he attempts a *grounding* so as to be able to re-construct and comprehend the original experiences of thinking. That origin remains future means precisely that everything is meaningful. The gift that comes to thinking is, in fact, the tradition, is the first beginning. This gift and giving are not readily available, they deny us easy and immediate access.

In a recent extensive study of *Seinsgeschichte* Keiling argues, like Thomson, that the history of being is a series of *past* ways of how metaphysics understood and coined understandings of being (cf. Keiling 2015: 16ff). Keiling points out that in a seminar on *Time and Being* Heidegger declares the end of the history of being (cf. GA 14: 50). Keiling also claims that any meaningful interpretation of the history of being must read anything Heidegger had previously said on *Seinsgeschichte* against the background of this later essay. It is true that Heidegger in this seminar on *Time and Being* says that the "forgetfulness of being is "sublated" [*hebt sich auf*] by an awakening [*Erwachen*] to the essential event." (GA 14: 50) Heidegger here even explicitly says that there is the possibility for the end of the history of being for a thinking that is possibly entirely of the event, for the event is what had been concealed to metaphysics. The thinking of the event then is not just the end of the forgetfulness of beyng, i.e., of concealment, but also the end of the withdrawal. But I understand Heidegger as trying to say something different here. Namely that with the awakening, which is the equivalent of thinking the withdrawal in the word *Ereignis*, the *history of beyng* properly begins. The history of being, i.e., of the various ways metaphysics has coined, *ends* with the thinking of the *Ereignis* that is itself without fate and therefore that which sends and that which metaphysics has responded to. But this should not prompt us to historicise the history of being and the history of *beyng* as something of the past. Now is the time to think the dimension of concealment specifically and this can only be done in light of what has remained in the dark in metaphysics. This is to say that the human being enters into that history in a thinking manner. Hence Heidegger writes in a short note on the *Holzwege* anthology that the "future human being has to face up to dealing with the essence and the history of occidental metaphysics." (GA 13: 91)[3] The forgetfulness of being is sublated, i.e., harboured and transformed by the thinking of the *Ereignis* and hence a proper examination of the history of the first beginning can only now set in.

---

[3] My translation. "Dem zukünftigen Menschen steht die Auseinandersetzung mit dem Wesen und der Geschichte der abendländischen Metaphysik bevor."

Thinking is only just beginning. This is why Heidegger writes in *Contributions*: "Only now begin the history of being and the history of the human being." (GA 65: 454/358) The other beginning has the exuberant wealth of the first as its wellspring. Yet, this opening, which Heidegger sees, is neither guarantee for some promised utopia nor is this opening in any way at the mercy of human power. The history of being is not teleological. Instead, one could say that it is infinitely demanding of humans to respond to the claims of beyng. Most importantly though, as beyng moves by self-withdrawing, the oblivion, even abandonment of beyng are not ever fully sublated and cancelled out.

Guignon thus rightly argues that the history of being (and beyng) is precisely not "a series of past events or epochs leading up to today." (Guignon 2005: 391) If it were, then it would end as soon as it has been recognised. Heidegger, however, does not prophesy the end of history. Instead, Heidegger sees a window for the grounding of the history of beyng so that human beings become aware of this history, of which they are suffering participants, but not prime agents. The history of withdrawal is, then, not meant as something negative in the ordinary sense. As Heidegger says in *What is called Thinking?*: "*Entzug ist Ereignis.* Withdrawal is essential event." (GA 8: 10) If the first beginning is a history of withdrawal, then it is a history *of* the essential event. "[W]hat withdraws," Heidegger continues, "may even concern and claim man more essentially than anything present" (GA 8: 10/9).[4] However, there is something that was missed in the first beginning and that is precisely to specifically allow for and think withdrawal and concealment. As I have argued death is what lets mortals think "being-away." Thinking "being-away" lets mortals reach down into the abyss of beyng and its essential withdrawal. In this sense, as I have addressed above, death is the highest testimony to beyng.

2 Death as Testimony to Beyng's Epochs

The strange claim that death is testimony to beyng begins to make sense if we understand death as the concentration of concealment, or as Heidegger puts it in the *Contributions* as "being-away". As argued above, death as testimony to beyng leads into the thought of concealment which is at the heart of the thinking of the event. This also means that death is testimony to the history and the epochs of beyng. One should only carefully speak of the epochs of beyng because the notion of "epoch" invites the imagination to categorise various understandings of being neatly as historiographical epochs. Yet, when one understands "epoch" closer to Husserl's *epoché*, it is easier to see that the epochs of beyng are rather radical incisions bursting in and sending their silent and subtle shockwaves through the fates of human beings. Beyng's "epochs" then are self-reductions *of* beyng to which the human being responds and which are only subsequently historicised as *historiographical epochs*: "epochs of being are fundamental ways in which being occurs and humans

---

[4] Trans. by Wieck and Gray.

relate to this occurrence." (Vallega-Neu 2010: 151) There is a necessity to the epochs of beyng rather than contingency, as those self-reductions take place on the level of beyng itself as the utterly possible in excess of itself into which everything pushes back in tides, and beyng is in excess of itself for the collision of its fissures, possibility and necessity. The history of beyng and its epochs are, however, not self-actualisations of beyng. Here the notion of sending is crucial because it refers to beyng as pure possibility. Sendings are not actualisations. When Heidegger speaks of sendings, he appreciates that beyng remains the *possible* but sends human beings factical possibilities humans relate to. The plural here is crucial. There are always multiple and multidimensional sendings at play and the *question* is which one(s) do human beings respond to.

My claim now is that death plays a crucial role with regard to beyng's sendings. In fact, *Contributions* explicitly mentions death the first time when Heidegger speaks of the dying of a god:

> The most frightful jubilation must be the dying of a god. Only the human being "has" the distinction of standing in front of death, because the human being is steadfastly in [*inständig in*] beyng: death the highest testimony to beyng. (GA 65: 230/181)

Before I address how this is supposed to speak to death as highest testimony for beyng's sendings, I would like carve out what Heidegger means by the death of God. Even though Heidegger is at the time of writing this already deeply concerned with Nietzsche's thought, Hölderlin's notion of the departure of gods seems to be the focus here. Nietzsche's dictum *God is dead* is an abrupt caesura. It is an act, more importantly, of a subject that kills god, a subject that deludes itself into believing it is almighty and ready to become god. Hölderlin's stance is different. Hölderlin rather speaks of a disappearance of the divine in modernity and Heidegger calls this disappearance "dying." In the second composition of *Empedocles*, Hölderlin writes: "To be alone, And without gods, is death." (Hölderlin 2008: 548) What announces itself to Hölderlin is a desolate age, an epoch of transition. Heidegger notes in §105 *Contributions* entitled *Hölderlin—Kierkegaard—Nietzsche* that something uncanny addressed these thinkers in various ways. For Hölderlin it is an experience of a silent departure of gods, and as a consequence an emptiness, a period devoid of meaning is setting in. A profound worry about the prevalence of nihilism in modernity is what all three have in common. Heidegger also appreciates the fundamental nihilism of the Occident. Yet, in the *dying* of a god, also something else is announced: god's departure depicts the possibility of a return of the divine.

When Heidegger now says that death is the "highest testimony of beyng" and that the human being is steadfast in beyng because of his relationship with death, then Heidegger says that death is the window that bridges human being and beyng. Yet, as Heidegger makes this claim in context of the dying of god and the lack of the divine in our epoch, death also seems to be testimony to something else and that is to the sendings of beyng. Humans suffer those sendings because they are steadfast in beyng. Thus, in my view, death is testimony to the history of beyng, to the rising and collapsing of its sendings that form the fates of mortals. Again, it seems better to translate "*Geschichte*" as "tidings" rather than history. The notion of death as testimony to beyng shows more of its meaning when we consider Heidegger's later notion of death as the *Ge-birg* of being, i.e., as the gathering or concentration of concealing. Death as the concentration of concealment and harbouring is then the place into which beyng withdraws and thanks to these withdrawals into its "refuge" the sendings of beyng occur. For beyng works always by self-withdrawing and self-concealing. Thus, it is for beyng's relationship with death that the "turnings" of beyng occur. This is why Heidegger says that beyng-toward-death and the inherent collision of necessity and possibility, which it gives expression to, is "the goad of the highest historicality [*Geschichtlichkeit*] and is the secret ground of the decided-ness toward the shortest path." (GA 65: 282/222) Thus, what Heidegger is saying here is that mortals have access to the history of histories for their intimate relation-ship with death. Mortals can begin to think concealment and being-away because of death and this thinking is precisely what is necessary to begin to see what metaphys-ics has left in the dark: the clearing of concealing. Put differently, mortals need to think the unsupported and they do so by releasing themselves of beings. Again, death is not an anthropological phenomenon but occurs *within* and *of* beyng and mortals participate in that occurrence, for their essence belongs to beyng. For Heidegger death is thus the sting that ignites history. From the perspective of the thinking path this means that Heidegger realised the very possibility of the history of beyng because of what being-toward-death in *Being and Time* disclosed to him. For, remember, in being-towards-death, as also Vallega-Neu argues, being discloses itself as essentially withdrawing. There would hence be no history of beyng without death as *Ge-birg* and there would be no way of entering that history without death. Heidegger arrives at thinking the "essence of death" interrogated out of beyng itself when he thinks death as *Ge-birg*.

Nevertheless, beyng's sendings are always at first concealed to mortal thinking. That which has been sent is slowly, subtly, silently creeping into that which is to come. This is the slow and silent, *schweigend*, workings of the tidings of beyng. "The intrusion of beyng which is granted to historical human beings does not ever manifest itself to them immediately but only in a hidden way, in the modes of shel-tering [*Bergung*] of truth." (GA 65: 236/186) For mortals it is all about *Bergung*, *Bergung* is the way in which humans respond to those sayings. As Heidegger says, humans carry *sheltering* out "in art, thinking, poetizing, deed" (GA 65: 256/201).

3 Sheltering and Grounding

Bergung, harbouring-sheltering, is related to *Verbergung* and *Entbergung*,[5] i.e., to the self-differentiation of ἀλήθεια. The grounding of Da-sein as the site of beyng is in tune with harbouring-sheltering (cf. GA 65: 386/304). Running forth toward death, now performed by the few and rare, enables the grounding of Da-sein.

---

[5] Heidegger also interprets the λόγος as differentiation of unconcealing and concealing: "Der Logos ist *in sich zumal* ein Entbergen und Verbergen." (GA 7: 225)

Harbouring-sheltering is concentrated in death as *Ge-birg*. Running forth toward death is now performed in poetry, deed, thinking, and art; especially in those works of art that bring to the fore the nihilating of the nothing and of beyng. This also means that the groundings, which are of a sheltering mode, are performed *again and again*, for mortals are who perform those groundings. Hence those groundings are fragile and finite for their very vicinity to death. But before mortals can properly perform any grounding, they must let themselves in for mortal thinking and renounce beings only to come back to the wealth of beings in their respective simplicity. The thinking of the history of being, even though Heidegger sees a window opening up for mortals to enter into it, is not some magical tool by which the problems of modernity can be wiped away. Rather, for its vicinity with death the history of being reminds mortals of the errancy in which they also roam. The fact that death is so central also articulates the danger inherent in history, i.e., that collapse of meaning and world is possible at all times.

On my reading beyng's running forth toward death is therefore that which allows the original un-concealing, *entbergende Verbergung*, of beyng. This is why Heidegger says in *Moira* on Parmenides:

> Whoever expects of thinking some kind of a reassurance and therefore calculates the day when thinking can be ignored as it is no longer needed, demands of thinking to self-destruct. That demand appears to be strange, if we remember that the essence of the mortals is called to be aware and mindful of that behest that calls them to death. Death is as the utmost possibility of mortal *Dasein* not the end of what is possible, but highest *Ge-Birg* (the gathering *bergen*) of the secret of unconcealment calling on human beings. (GA 7: 261)

In order to learn how to think mortals need to become mortals, i.e., mortals have to learn how to die. This is what Heidegger also argues in his talks and essays on technology and the possibility of the fourfold. Note also that for Heidegger Socrates is the purest thinker because he learnt how to "place himself into this draft" (GA 8: 20/17), i.e., the withdrawal of beyng. Socrates was able to do so precisely because he learnt how to die. It is then, when concealment is appreciated, that all of a sudden there is a clearing of that concealment, put differently, all of a sudden something shows up that had been but that had been covered over before.

If death is that which opens the window for *Seinsgeschichte* in the first place, then death as *Ge-birg* could also grant a situation where mortals respond in ways that get us out of the current prevalent sending of beyng: being as *Ge-Stell*. In *Ge-Stell* everything can be manipulated and posited at will. In *Contributions* and the surrounding texts Heidegger does not yet speak of *Ge-Stell*, but rather of machination. While these are not identical, they have still important aspects in common. Like machination, *Ge-Stell* is an essential occurrence of beyng, but it is beyng's unessence, beyng's turning agaisnst itself and beings: "Machination is, in terms of the history of beyng, the abandonment of beings by beyng." (GA 71: 108/91) This holds true for *Ge-Stell* as well. For Heidegger the *stellen* of *Ge-Stell* is related to *bergen*. *Stellen* is a derivative mode of *bergen*, derivative in the sense that it forgets concealment. I will say more on their relation in Part III. Note for now that Heidegger added a footnote to *What is Metaphysics?* in 1949. There he writes: "Letting death come to oneself, holding oneself in the arrival of death as *Ge-Birg* of being." (GA 9:

374 *na*)[6] "Being" is here crossed out. It is for human mortality that the human being can engage in disclosing the sense of beyng. The footnote speaks of a stance of restrained releasedness human beings are to take. Heidegger sees the world at a crossroads. Either the human being remains stuck in encrusted metaphysics and becomes the "*technicized animal*" (GA 65: 275/216). Or human beings become *mortals* and so encounter the world as fourfold as another possibility of being. Death will prove to be central for a successful grounding of the fourfold and an exit from *Ge-Stell*.

In conclusion let me point out that Heidegger's focus on the abyss and on the unsupported is not the completion of his thought, but necessary for the further development of the thought of *Er-eignis* as the realm where being and human being meet. Heidegger has to stride through the sheer withdrawing ground, as it were, in order to carve out his non-metaphysical understanding of being and its history. When he begins to focus more on technology, the history of being does not take a backseat. Quite to the contrary, the history of being is what allows Heidegger to name the essence of technology in the first place and see something no one else saw.

---

[6] "Auf sich zu-kommen lassen den Tod, sich halten in der Ankunft des Todes als des Ge-Birgs des Seins." ("Sein" crossed out). This book is the result of wishing to understand this ominous quote which I read in the summer 2013 at the *Staatsbibliothek* whilst visiting my sister in Munich.

Part III
Gestell and *Gebirg*: The Relationship of Technology and Death

φύσις κρύπτεσθαι φιλεῖ
—*Heraclitus*

Sterbliches Denken muß
in das Dunkel der Brunnentiefe sich hinablassen, um bei Tag
den Stern zu sehen.
(GA 79: 93)

Abstract This part explores the relationship between modern technology and death. After introducing Heidegger's diagnosis of technology as the currently prevalent mode of being (and the history of being) I develop a response to the challenges of technology from Heidegger's notes on death from around the same time. Heidegger calls the essence of technology "*Gestell*", i.e., the concentration of positioning and placing. Death, on the other hand, he calls "*Gebirg des Seins*", which literally translates to "mountain range of being", but which I understand as the concentration of sheltering and concealing. Thus, I develop from notes Heidegger leaves along the thinking a response to the challenges of technology that Heidegger seems to see in death. In fact, his rather peculiar claim that mortals must become mortals, then means that mortals must think again the possibility of sheltering rather than trying to exploit. The limit that is death reminds mortals of their own limitations and hence of their impossible quest to dominate the earth. By "becoming mortal" humans are asked and reminded to shelter the earth rather than exploit it. *Gestell* demands the opposite of the human being: the total domination of nature which is reduced to a source of energy—precisely because *Gestell* knows no boundary.

Keywords Heidegger technology · Critique of technology · Gestell · Geviert · History of being · Mortal thinking · Thinking path · Heidegger Gelassenheit · Fourfold · Later Heidegger · Limitation · Positionality · Enframing · Heidegger environmentalism

Introduction

It is no coincidence that Heidegger begins to be concerned with technology when he begins to think in being-historical terms. In *Being and Time* and surrounding texts what is usually considered technological tools, e.g., cars, trams, and modern mass media, are mentioned, but do not play a significant role. They do not point to anything beyond Dasein's world. Heidegger does not problematise technology as an essential question for our age and what role technology might play for the forgetfulness of being. This changes fundamentally in *Contributions to Philosophy*, which is his first attempt to explicate what being-historical thinking might mean and moreover in which being-historical situation we are.[1] Thus, here the question becomes, how the situation of late modernity has come about and how the responses of metaphysics to the question of being[2] have opened the possibility for technology. This shift also means a shift away from "technology" in terms of tools or instruments towards the "essence" of technology. The strangeness of this thought is then that for Heidegger technology in the essential sense is neither primarily instrumental nor anthropological. Rather, technology comes toward humans today from millennia of interpretations of τέχνη and is hence a sending of beyng itself. Heidegger understands technology first and foremost as an essential occurrence and realm *of* beyng. That is to say technology in its essence is a dimension of beyng thanks to which beings occur in such a manner that they become a mere resource. Heidegger argues that in the currently prevalent, but not exclusive, disclosure of being the human being is challenged to *position, stellen*, all beings, including the human being, in such a way that they become resources readily available at all times and any place in a homogeneous, i.e., controllable fashion. Human beings act analogously to being as the *Ge-Stell*. As the *Ge-Stell* being occurs *un-essentially* in the current age. In other words, beings become artificial. Their unique unfolding must now follow

---

[1] The lecture course on *Fundamental Concepts of Metaphysics* is perhaps pivotal in this regard. It is here that Heidegger begins to diagnose boredom and how we experience boredom in the everyday and what this experience tells us about ecstatic temporality. However, Heidegger here also leads this discussion further and diagnoses our epoch as in the grips of a deep boredom that is the fundamental mood of our age. Thus, it seems to be here that Heidegger begins to think in terms of epochs, how epochs come about and how we can understand our epoch. The insight that there is a deep boredom about our age opens for the Heidegger the possibility to think in terms of epochs and hence in terms of the question whence our epoch comes and what fundamentally structures and attunes our epoch. In the lecture course Heidegger hence writes: "The *decisive question* now is: [...] Why do we find no meaning for ourselves any more, i.e., no essential possibility of being? Is it because an *indifference* yawns at us out of all things, an indifference whose grounds we do not know?" (GA 29/30: 115/77). Heidegger here begins to search not for that which has caused this situation, but for that which is hidden in our history such that one of the fates of that history is the nihilism of modernity.

[2] As Heidegger in most of the public talks and essays on technology spells *Sein* with "i," I shall follow his spelling. This means that technology is a metaphysical determination of being *as Ge-Stell*, just like being *as* actuality etc. Also, "being" denotes "presence" or the way in which beings are present. "Beyng" speaks of abysmal and self-concealing withdrawing beyng. Still, I shall write "beyng" where I think this is more appropriate.

the general demands of technology that disrespects the uniqueness of beings. As such technology is the current fate of being and a fate of metaphysics. When we approach the question of technology in Heidegger's thought, then we must approach this problem from within the history of being.

Despite technology's promises of human empowerment and liberation Heidegger argues that technology subtly subjugates human beings. The uncanny situation we face is that technology appears to give us powers previously reserved to gods. But those powers are for Heidegger an illusion. Technology does not empower human beings but replaces the human dimension with the epistemic-logical dimension. As such technology is an uprooting force. As Davis argues, there is a threat of the displacement of "the various peoples of the earth from their traditional contexts of dwelling and replacing them in a Euro-Americanocentric system of economic and technological manipulation." (Davis 2007: xxiv) Human beings are numbed by their seeming power and the control they can now exercise over the world. The human being, argues Heidegger, might even lose his self in technology: "*precisely nowhere does man any no longer encounter himself, i.e., his essence.*" (GA 7: 28/27)[3] Far from being at the centre of technological control, in this epoch the human being is challenged "to order the self-revealing as standing-reserve." (GA 7: 20/19) Luddism, however, is not the aim of Heidegger's diagnosis of the technological age. He rather wishes to provide a basis for a mindful relationship with technology in which the human being is not a slave to technology, but where technology serves the human being, as Heidegger points out in his essay on identity (cf. GA 11: 46).

Even though Heidegger's critique of technology and the history of being more broadly are not humanist accounts of history, the way in which humans relate, respond, and correspond to beyng's occurrences presses back into the histories and occurrences of beyng and human *being*. That is to say that the human being is never the acting agent of history, but always already the victim of history and if the human being is not mindful of that which is and that which constitutes the current epoch, then the human being is forced to enact what he is challenged to do. That is not to say, the human being is not free. Adding to what I have argued in Part II, the movement of this history is such that beyng sends and gives and the way humans respond creates waves and tidings within beyng that sways back and forth as its history— only to come toward us again. If there is no proper, mindful response to technology and its origins, then the human being is numb to that which is and that is tantamount to saying the human being is unfree. This is why Heidegger takes instrumental and anthropological explanations of technology to be limited in their scope. They can well explain how we interact with technology and how technological tools have evolved. These accounts take technology as something human and as a means by which humans achieve certain goals like securing food production. Heidegger does not deny that there is some truth to that explanation. Yet, they cannot tell us much about the origins of our epoch and what is at work in technology. How can Heidegger say that there is something at work in technology, something that is not human? In

---

[3] Lovitt translation.

the essay on *The Question Concerning Technology* and others Heidegger points out
that prevalent figures of speech that state the necessity "to master technology" tell
us something different (cf. GA 7: 8f). They tell us, viz., that technology currently
masters us and that we need to understand its origins in order to enter a free relationship with technology. But how to reach such a free relationship with technology?

Around the time of his most intense public engagement with technology
Heidegger determines the human being as "the one who waits" (GA 11: 118/42).
That is, the human being cannot forcefully or even by means of technology will a
change of being's epoch. We need to wait technology out. But that does not mean
that we are to remain passive. Waiting is related to *Gelassenheit*, releasement, and
to "letting-be" rather than willing and positing. Releasement and letting-be are, I
shall argue, anchored in human mortality and finitude. For human beings to lose
their essence, as Heidegger warns is possible, is tantamount to negating our fundamental possibility and limitation: death. The current being-historical situation and
our self-understanding sees the human being as the willing and commanding subject. The human subject positions itself as the master over the totality of objects. In
so doing the subject denies its mortality. Thus, Heidegger writes in *What are Poets
for?*: "The self-assertion of technological objectification is the constant negation of
death." (GA 5: 303/122) Yet, it is precisely death that comes to rescue, insofar as
death withdraws from the prevalence of *stellen*, positioning and positing. Hence the
craze to eradicate death in transhumanism. That and how death comes to rescue is
the main question of this Part.

In modern technology positioning (in the sense of imposing) takes over *bergen*,
harbouring-sheltering, for the age of technology assumes that anything can be positioned as readily available at any place at any time. Harbouring-sheltering in turn is
the way of disclosing and bringing forth in tune with the self-disclosure of some
phenomenon. Positioning, in turn, is the process of a challenging and demanding
bringing forth, more specifically of extracting energy for the production of a predetermined end. A production that no longer needs to respect the tides and the seasons. Its fundamental assumption, i.e., that everything can be posited and positioned
as standing ready for use anytime and anywhere, is a constant denial of finitude and
limitations. Heidegger calls the essence of technology the gathering and concentration of positioning *Ge-Stell*. *Ge-Stell* is the forceful concentration of all modes of
positioning. I will explicate this in further detail below. In *The Question Concerning
Technology* (hereafter: technology essay) Heidegger presents *Gebirg*, mountain
range, as an example of a natural occurrence of gathering (cf. GA 7: 20/19). As
mentioned in Part II Heidegger around the time of his intense preoccupation with
technology also notably begins to call death the *Ge-Birg* of being (cf. GA 7:
180/148).[4] Heidegger understands *Ge-Birg* as the gathering of all modes of *bergen*.
For Heidegger the verb *bergen* is the root for *Bergung*, and the verbs *ent-bergen* and
ver-bergen. Death as *Ge-Birg* is therefore intimately related to ἀ-λήθεια as unconcealing concealment, *ent-bergende Ver-bergung*. As *Ge-Birg* death is the hiding

---

[4] See also (GA 9: 374 *na*; and Arendt and Heidegger 1994: 80).

place of beyng. Beyng withdraws into death, death is the place where beyng self-conceals. Put differently, the self-concealment of beyng is possible because of beyng's relationship with death. The central argument of this part is hence that Heidegger sees in death a window out of the domination of technology, for it is by beyng's self-concealment and self-withdrawal that beyng's history opens new horizons and realms. Hence Heidegger begins to argue that humans need to become mortals in his writings on the *Geviert*, the fourfold. These texts on the fourfold are crucial to grasp the full scope of Heidegger's understanding of technology as the prevalent fate of this epoch. The fourfold is possible only during the age of the *Ge-stell* and humans need to become mortals in order to bring forth the fourfold.

In his recent, extensive study on the fourfold Andrew Mitchell translates *Ge-Birg* as refuge of being (cf. Mitchell 2015: 235ff). Perhaps in some contexts, certainly not in all though, "sanctuary" could be a possible translation as well. This emphasises the sacredness and wealth, which Heidegger increasingly speaks of in later writings, to be granted again to beings. As "sanctuary" *Ge-Birg* means a holy place of gathering and rest. Death as sanctuary is beyng's retreat from itself as *Ge-Stell*: "Death is the highest refuge and refuge of the truth of beyng itself." (GA 79: 56/53)[5] As *Ge-birg* death would then also be the place out of which *Bergung* is performed, e.g., in the act of poetising and in the act of doing artistic work. Here death as *Ge-birg* serves as a fountain of exuberant wealth precisely because it is always concealed and not-available. *Bergung* translates into human disclosing and bringing-forth in accordance with one (or possibly several) of the current fates of beyng. For its origin in ποίησις, i.e., in a sheltering bringing-forth, poetry can articulate in a sheltering way the truth of beyng *in* beings (cf. Vallega-Neu 2010: 147). Beings appear differently in a poem than they do in a production plan, for poetry cherishes something radically different about them, namely their uniqueness. Human articulations of *Bergung* try to discover meaning and mindfully respond to the current age, rather than merely enforce technology's demands like a functionary. Heidegger thus sees human beings in the distinct responsibility to initiate a free relationship with technology and this can come about by becoming mortal.

In terms of Heidegger's understanding of the history of being, the reason why Heidegger can name the essence of technology as the *Ge-Stell* is because a shift in the current epoch has already set in. Only when such shifts in the fissuring of beyng occur can mortal thinking respond and give a name to that which is. This is in tune with Heidegger's non-humanist understanding of history. Human intentions, consciousness, deeds are not the prime agents of history. Beyng comes *first*. Humans are thrown into its history and have to take over its sendings. Of course, this also says that human beings can fail. Think of Descartes' *ego cogito* as an example to illustrate the history of being further. Modernity does not begin because of that dictum. Instead, Descartes articulates what already announces itself, that which already is at stake: the inflation of the ego. Heidegger's understanding of the history of being, then, does not mean he makes himself a prophet of that history. He does not

---

[5] Mitchell translation.

pretend to know for certain what will happen. Nor does he believe that the future is whatever we want it to be. Nonetheless, the ways in which humans respond to technology creates waves flowing back into the tidings of beyng. Heidegger's response to the challenge of technology is what he calls *fourfold*.

Mitchell's study of the fourfold hence rightly begins with an analysis of technology and attempts to show how technology can be integrated into the fourfold and, more broadly, how the fourfold comes about. Mitchell appreciates the importance death plays in this regard. I wish to stress death's crucial role as refuge even more, for I shall bring to the fore the relationship between being as *Ge-Stell* and death as the *Ge-Birg* of beyng. I do so because Heidegger sees the possibility of the fourfold coming about if and only if humans become mortals, as Heidegger indicates in the essay *The Thing* (cf. GA 7: 180/148).[6] This paradoxical claim begins to make sense when we explicate the claim that death is the gathering of concealment. As argued in Part II, this means to appreciate the abyss of beyng. Once more the question of being, which is now the question concerning beyng's current fate, is intimately related to death. Becoming mortal means that humans respond to their mortality in such a way that beyng discloses a different realm of possibilities, called the fourfold. There is a need for a response of the few, who are for the most part poets, and who can help being to release itself, as it were, from its self-obstruction. But there also is a genuine call for forming communities of mortals in Heidegger's essays on the fourfold and those are open to everyone. Thus, the fourfold is of a distinct ethos. This does not mean that the human commands over being, but that that the human being is the "shepherd of being" (GA 9: 342/252), as Heidegger puts it in the *Letter on Humanism*. As such humans guide being. More precisely, they guide being to its refuge: death.

The structure of Part III is as follows: First, I shall address common misconceptions regarding Heidegger's critique of technology. The second chapter traces Heidegger's path to technology as a fate of metaphysics. The third chapter presents the full essence of technology as *Ge-Stell*. The last chapter introduces the fourfold and the role death plays in bringing about the fourfold. I argue that a proper encounter with the fourfold is only possible when we take the role of language into consideration. Language will be the topic of the fourth and last part.

---

[6] Hofstadter translation.

Chapter 11
Heidegger: The Luddite?

Contrary to a common misconception Heidegger's critique of technology is not an exercise in cultural pessimism. Nor is he a banal technophobe as some have argued.[1] Amongst others Mitchell, Dreyfus (2009) and Davis (2007) have recently argued against the standard reading of Heidegger as a luddite. Heidegger himself was well aware that his concerns with technology caused distress.

In a documentary film from 1970 the documentary filmmaker Richard Wisser asks Heidegger how he would respond to those who find his criticism of technology to cause severe headaches, *Kopfzerbrechen*. The German idiom "*jemandem Kopfzerbrechen bereiten* (to give someone a headache)" means to make someone think profoundly after some issue. This can cause a healthy worry with the inquirer. Heidegger responds: "I find *Kopfzerbrechen* very healthy! People do not at all worry enough. There is today even a great thoughtlessness that goes together with the forgetfulness of being." (Wisser 1970: 71)[2] For Heidegger today's thoughtlessness is tantamount to an ingratitude for the gift of thinking. This ingratitude is a most pressing danger, which is to say that we interact with technology without asking properly where it comes from. Heidegger then adds something crucial:

> I am *not against* technology. I have never spoken *against* technology nor against the so-called demonic nature of technology. I rather try to understand the essence of technology … I see in technology, in its essence, that human beings stand under a power that challenges them and in which human beings are no longer free—that something announces itself here, namely a relation [*Bezug*] between being and human being—and that this relation, which hides itself in technology, one day comes to light … Thus, I see in the essence of technology the first appearance of a much deeper occurrence (*Geschehen*) that I call *Ereignis*. (Wisser 1970: 73)

---

[1] See, for example, Gumbrecht (2003) and Buhr and Steigerwald (1981). Criticism of calling Heidegger a "technophobe" interestingly often are from Anglo-American Heidegger commentators.

[2] My translation.

© Springer Nature Switzerland AG 2021
J. A. Niederhauser, *Heidegger on Death and Being*,
https://doi.org/10.1007/978-3-030-51375-7_11

This is a dense summary of Heidegger's thought on technology and the history of being. The first thing to notice is that he refers to the *event* because in technology we can see beyng's self-reduction, a simultaneous withdrawal of a world that once has been and a world that is to come. We can see in the diagnosis of technology an epochal shift and transition that affects all beings. In the *Identity* essay we find a crucial statement by Heidegger in this regard. He writes: "the modern world of technology is a *prelude* of what is called *Er-eignis.*" (GA 11: 46/36 *ta*) The *Er-eignis* is the realm where being and humans can encounter each other such that the currently unchecked prevalence of technology is gotten over and transformed into a healthier relationship of human being and technology. This happens through the thinking of the *Ereignis*. Where the first beginning is a history of involuntary withdrawal, the other beginning takes concealment into consideration, properly focuses on the dimension of withdrawal, and thereby initiates another history. Technology is the fate of metaphysics insofar as metaphysics wants to keep beings in sheer presence and availability and forgets non-availability. With the thinking of the event another dimension is all of a sudden at stake and from that dimension another relationship with technology is possible.

Secondly, Heidegger is not *against* technology. Heidegger understands that an antithetical stance requires one to embrace what one is against. At worst this leads one to be consumed by what one despises most. A proper response to technology, Heidegger says in *Country Path Conversations* and *Gelassenheit*, is a simultaneous yes and no to technology. We can allow technological tools in our houses, but we ought not to let them take over our homes (cf. Davis 2007: xxiv). Thirdly, for Heidegger technology cannot be demonic in neither a Christian nor a Greek sense since technology is an essential occurrence of beyng, and beyng is not some demonic force that possesses us. Fourthly, technology overpowers the human being in such a way that the human being is no longer free. This overpowering goes together with the simultaneous seeming that technology gives the greatest powers *to* the human being.

Fifthly, Heidegger here says that technology goes together with the forgetting of beyng. The abandoning, however, also indicates a possible re-turn *of* beyng, i.e., a turning of beyng's prevalent way of occurring. Put differently, being as *Ge-Stell* already indicates other possibilities of how beings can occur. The withdrawal of beyng is greatest in technology but this intensification of withdrawal is precisely what primes the return of beyng—if mortals properly respond. The Open of beyng, into which human beings are thrown in each epoch, is not one-dimensional. Beyng moves historically insofar as both withdrawal and relation take place at once. Beyng's dimensions and tidings occur as *sfumato*, blending into one other. Thus, in the moment of beyng's greatest abandoning its re-turn is already enshrined, but not guaranteed, for it requires the help of its shepherd.

This is precisely not to say that we should abandon technology because, as Davis puts it, "the will to overcome technology by throwing away its devices would repeat the very problem it attempts to address: the will to mastery that characterizes human being in the epoch of technology." (Davis 2007: 184)[3] Condemning technology as

---

[3] See also Dreyfus (2009: 54f).

demonic and wilfully attempting to overcome it would mean to misunderstand what Heidegger is trying to tell us about the essence of technology. Heidegger (cf. GA 11: 118/39),[4] therefore, speaks of a *Verwindung des Gestells* rather than of overcoming technology. *Verwinden*, to get over, means to *let* arise out of positionality another possibility of world-encounter. This encounter he calls fourfold. But this does not do away with positionality. The fourfold is only possible as long as positionality is. Getting-over is then an internal rather than an external approach. Getting-over refers to another beginning possible out of that which is. Getting-over is not purely human and not initiated by the human being, but is still co-constituted by human responses and only possible thanks to them. The most important aspect of Heidegger's remark to Wisser, then, is that in technology as *Ge-Stell* another relation between being and human being, i.e., another beginning, is already showing itself as possible.

Nevertheless, technology, especially in its current and apparently unquestioned occurring, is a threat to human beings and their world. Technology challenges humans and could enslave us: "Human beings do not control technology. They are at its mercy [*ist ihr Spielwerk*] … In that respect modern human beings are a slave to their forgetfulnnes of being." (GA 15: 370) This is the crossroads Heidegger sees us at: either we move further into the sphere of machines, or we move towards the fourfold. Technology itself is not to be stopped. Once unleashed, once the ἄτομος has become divisible there is nothing to stop technology because now a sheer endless amount of energy stands ready for a continuous increase of energy that only serves to exploit nature further. This trajectory set in when the human being begins to revolt against being at the dawn of modernity. In the history of metaphysics this is most notably visible when Descartes posits being as the object posited by the subject, as Heidegger points out in a seminar held in 1951 in Zürich (cf. GA 15: 433). As argued in Part I this critique of Descartes is already present in the early Heidegger. The positing of nature as *res extensa* and the unquestioned *sum* of the *cogito sum* are articulations of this revolution of the human against being. This revolution even allows to posit the human being purely according to the genome. Once the genome has been decoded there is nothing to stop the artificial production, i.e., positing human beings for a specific technicist goal. Heidegger is fully aware of that. Hence, he tells Wisser: "In the foreseeable future we will be capable of *producing* human beings in any way—that is to say we will be capable of producing humans purely according to their organic nature just as we require them: skilled and unskilled, intelligent and stupid. It will come that far!" (Wisser 1970: 73) It is no coincidence that human beings must also make themselves a resource. Human beings are even the most important resource because they belong to the dimension of beyng and as such human beings carry out beyng's sendings. That is to say that *Ge-Stell* needs humans to enforce its will. It is for the essential relation between beyng and human that human essence is most open to the attacks of *Ge-Stell*. Hence, if we follow Heidegger here closely, then any wilful act over or against being leads to unintended consequences, to being itself subjecting the human, i.e., to consequences mortals cannot possibly hope to be able to see in full and with all their ramifications.

---

[4] Hertz translation.

In a paper defending Heidegger's stance on technology Dreyfus hence points out that Heidegger's concern with technology is ontological, but not a humanist critique of technology or a pessimistic view of the world: "The danger, then, is not the destruction of nature or culture but a restriction in our way of thinking—a levelling of our understanding of being." (Dreyfus 2009: 55) Heidegger himself writes: "The human being today is *on the run from thinking*." (GA 16: 519) I agree with Dreyfus that Heidegger is neither a humanist nor a pessimist. As Demske puts it in reference to Heidegger's diagnosis of the age of technology, for Heidegger "[h]umanistic subjectivism is the greater threat to mankind" (Demske 1970: 136) than technology. This is precisely because "humanistic subjectivism" is the hubris of the human being to assume absolute power over history and the world. I also agree with Dreyfus that Heidegger aims to provide an opening for a free relationship with technology. Heidegger explicitly does not want to purport that "fate means the inevitableness of an unalterable course." (GA 7: 26/25) There is at least one way out and Heidegger, in his response, calls this possibility the fourfold. However, I disagree with Dreyfus that Heidegger only worries about our understanding of being, as if Dasein were still at the centre. Dreyfus, I think, neglects the ramifications of the turning. There is something much more profound at stake. For Heidegger beyng itself is at work and thus the way we respond to this challenge must be more profound than Dreyfus' pragmatic example of drinking tea like the Japanese do. There is a practical side to the fourfold, but the response to *Ge-Stell* begins elsewhere.

The proper response to the challenge of technology is found first not in acting or, as Dreyfus suggests, mimicking another culture without being grounded in it. Instead, the proper response is mortal thinking, i.e., a thinking of the unsupported, of the abyss. For Heidegger, "[h]*ow must we think?*" (GA 11: 117/40),[5] is the essential question, rather than "how should we act?" In the same essay, entitled *The Turn*, Heidegger also writes: "So long as we do not, through thinking, experience what is, we can never belong to what will be." (GA 11: 123/49) Human beings first and foremost have the duty to think, and in this epoch this translates into asking what the essence of technology is and where technology comes from. Human beings have the duty to think after these fundamental shifts upon them, but we seem to be numb and unable to listen. The γιγαντομαχία περὶ τῆς οὐσίας Heidegger speaks of in the first paragraph of *Being and Time* now takes place in front of our eyes in technology. What it means to be, is currently decided. Thus, the crucial question is, how human beings can release themselves from the power of *Ge-Stell* and find a more thoughtful and mindful relationship with technology, one that is aware of the powers of technology as specifically non-human powers. For in technology the gigantic battle that determines the fate of the world takes place. Even though the encounter with the fourfold is at stake in Heidegger's writings on technology, this is still not an eschatological process since neither the rule of technology as *Ge-Stell* nor the fourfold will be the end state of history.

---

[5] Lovitt translation.

The thinking response begins with being *gelassen*, letting-go of beings (and of will) and leaping into the unsupported. Being *gelassen* is to be understood as a medial grammatical form. Being released is therefore beyond the active-passive distinction, it is rather between them. Medial verbs express that one's actions directly impact one's continued acting and that one's action has an immediate effect on the agent herself. In terms of *Heidegger*, being-released creates waves in the history of beyng. Far from condemning human beings to passivity, thinking for Heidegger means "genuine taking a hand, if to take a hand means to lend a hand to the essence, the coming to presence, of being. This means: to prepare (build) for the coming to presence of being that abode [*Stätte*] into which being brings itself and its essence to utterance in language." (GA 11: 117/40 *ta*) In Part IV I shall develop this claim further in light of Heidegger's assertion that there is an essential relation between death and language. In practical terms releasement means to let things be and this letting-be is the initiation of a free relationship with technology, one in which we can at any time let go of our technological tools. In theoretical terms freedom is achievable, if and only if the human being responds to the current fate of being by thinking the abyss. Merely using technological tools means that we "remain unfree and chained to technology, whether we passionately affirm or deny it." (GA 7: 7/4) I argue that the thinking that initiates releasement means to bethink one's death and one's mortal finitude. By letting-go of the grasp of beings, by renouncing them and leaping into the abyss, the true wealth of beings begins to appear. Thus, releasement lets human beings enter the world. *Gelassenheit* becomes *Eingelassenheit*, embeddedness in the world. The guiding thought for getting over positionality and encountering the fourfold is for Heidegger following Hölderlin: "[m]ortals die their death in life." (GA 4: 165/190) By this "dying" a certain releasement sets in and another possibility of world begins to occur.

True, Heidegger warns of technology and speaks of the "danger" of technology (GA 7: 27/26). In the essay *Überwindung der Metaphysik* Heidegger even calls our epoch the age of the "anarchy of catastrophes" (GA 7: 88). Yet, "danger" is primarily a philosophical term of art for Heidegger and must be addressed as such. If there is danger in the *essence* of technology, then there is danger primarily in beyng itself. Since beyng occurs as turning Heidegger in many of his writings on technology says, with reference to Hölderlin: "where the danger lies, there also grows that which saves" (GA 5: 296/222). Even in one of his seemingly most pessimistic texts, *What are Poets for?*, Heidegger says "[t]his epoch is neither decay nor decline." (GA 5: 320/240 *ta*) In this essay, where he reads Rilke and where Heidegger certainly also appreciates the metaphysical limitations of Rilke, Heidegger sees the distinct possibility in view of Rilke's thought in the *Elegies* to become true adults by appreciating death as the other side of being. What is required is another perspective directed toward the wholesome totality of all that is, i.e., of that which is turned towards us and that which is turned away from us. Presence and its echo: withdrawal. And only then does world light up in full and in its true wealth. A sheer availability deprives us of that wealth of world. For human thinking this is open thanks to its relationship with death. That which saves, then, can grow out of death as refuge and sanctuary. But death can also be, for the law of simultaneity, *qua*

Ge-birg utter loss of being and a moment of destruction. It all depends on how mortals respond to their death, for there to be a good death. Without becoming properly mortal, there is now the greatest threat of total destruction.

As Heidegger's question concerning technology is whence technology comes his is a perspective that looks for the origin of the technology that apparently only now emerges. This other perspective can provide possibilities to get over technology (cf. GA 5: 290/217). As already quoted in Part II, only if beyng's inherent self-concealment and abandonment is appreciated, then "[t]he forgetting of being [could] "shelter" [*aufheben*] itself with the awakening to the essential event. Yet, concealment, which belongs to metaphysics as its limit, must be of the essential event." (GA 14: 50) The "*aufheben*" as noted in Part II, is to be understood as sheltering-harbouring rather than "sublating". What I wish to stress now, is that concealment is the limit of metaphysics. Metaphysics cannot think concealment because metaphysics needs sheer presence. This is precisely where death as the utterly concealed and unavailable comes in. Technology is how a metaphysics of sheer presence occurs in this epoch, a metaphysics that is oblivious to the truth of beyng, to its withdrawing refusal. This is why carrying out being-toward-death as the gathering of sheltering is at the heart of getting-over of technology. Thus, getting over technology does not mean to overcome and do away with technology but to appreciate the dimension of concealment and the echo of withdrawal. This might well lead to a radically different, more wholesome technological world access that, for its very respect of concealment, appreciates finitude, tragedy, the impossibility of perfection, and that there cannot be a final answer to that which is. The threat and the danger of technology, then, are the abandonment of beyng prevalent in technological world access. There is, in fact, no proper world if all there is, is a sheer presence and availability, where everything is positioned in a fixed frame for the most useful and immediate consumption, where time and space are also resources for the control of beings, where beings appear to be empty and world itself, i.e., the deeply meaningful historical web, is diminished and makes way for the sphere of machines.

Chapter 12
Heidegger's Path to the Essence of Technology

1 Technology as a Fate of Metaphysics

Heidegger's path to naming the essence of technology as *Ge-stell* begins with his critique of subjectivism and metaphysics more broadly. According to Heidegger, metaphysics focuses on beings and then hypostatises the unique *being* of beings as definable beingness. By *being* I here mean to denote the way in which beings uniquely occur and *are present*. Take Heidegger's example of positivism as the "crudest of all "metaphysical" modes of thought" (GA 65: 172/136). Despite its declared aim to leave metaphysics behind positivism in fact is highly metaphysical, for it determines the beingness of beings as sense data. Hence all beings *are* data perceived by the senses. Positivism does not ask what constitutes the thing in front of *me* as a meaningful phenomenon, but rather *posits* the beingness of beings as simply given. Moreover, positivism "*surpasses* ... beings through the fundamental application of a homogenous "causality."" (GA 65: 172/136) Take genetics as another example of a crude metaphysics. All organic lifeforms are assumed to have a genetic code as their more or less static beingness. According to this assumption all organic beings can be reduced to their genome. But the process does not stop here. By virtue of the power of positing the genetic information of organic beings is assumed to be manipulable at will. This hypothesis comes before mashing up and arbitrarily re-combining genes in order to produce a desired organism. In a note entitled *Téχνη und Technik* from around 1940 Heidegger writes that technology is the "manipulation of "beings."" (GA 76: 288) Technology's "manipulation" is not accidental, "but is an assault on beings in the whole for the sake of preparing the self-assertion of the human being [*qua* rational and willing subject]." (GA 76: 288)[1] This does not mean that Heidegger blames metaphysics for anything. Nor does he

---

[1] My translation: "…Veränderung des Seienden und nicht nur "Veränderung" ganz unbestimmt undziellos, sondern Angriff auf das Seiende im Ganzen zur Eroberung der Selbstbehauptung des Menschen;"

© Springer Nature Switzerland AG 2021
J. A. Niederhauser, *Heidegger on Death and Being*,
https://doi.org/10.1007/978-3-030-51375-7_12

argue that metaphysics has caused technology necessarily. Rather, he sees the history of metaphysics as the failed responses to the dimension of concealment and withdrawal, i.e., to the full scope of *Ereignis*. Hence the first beginning is a history of withdrawal, more precisely, a withdrawal of concealment. As I have pointed out before, this withdrawal of the first beginning is, nevertheless, the fountain of the other beginning because once concealment comes into focus, once the other side becomes part of the play, paths open up towards different ways of being, i.e., ways of responding to being. While metaphysics is not to blame, there is still a certain encrustation that sets in as soon as Hegel finalises the dialectics of metaphysics. This encrustation is, however, what Heidegger sees as a possibility to think through the history of metaphysics again by focussing on what is at its limit: concealment, i.e., that which cannot be posited and positioned. That other side is known to mortals from their death.

The metaphysics that grounds the age of technology, then, operates by means of hypostatised representation, *Vorgestelltheit*, of being. In this regard, it is the same as metaphysics in its entirety, if metaphysics wants to provide a stable foundation for all beings. That foundation in modernity is the positing subject! Modern technology then is the rule of subjectivity in the peculiar sense Heidegger understands it. As Vallega-Neu puts it, for Heidegger subjectivity is the dominance of "representation (*Vorgestelltheit*) over the being of beings." (Vallega-Neu 2003: 60) Once the beingness of organisms is represented, literally placed before the subject, as, say, genetic code (which can be de-coded), organic beings can be positioned and repositioned, represented and produced (*vor-gestellt* and *her-gestellt*) as to the demands of the representing subject. "*Thus, technology is the genuine completion of "metaphysics"*" (GA 76: 294).[2] This is so because technology is the occurrence of the hypostasis of being as beingness under the hermeneutics of making, producing, and manipulating—a hermeneutics entirely forgetful of the dimension of concealment. Technology as the completion of metaphysics is the encrustation *of the history of loss of the first beginning*. The loss *of* being, initiated by beyng itself, but also influenced by human forgetting of being, manifests itself in the sheer presence of the technological world.

The world-enclosed, purely self-referential subject, estranged from its world, never quite certain whether God is not an evil deceiver, as Descartes suspects in his *Meditations*, the scepticism inherent in empiricism lurking in the background—that very subject now finds a possibility to satisfy its desire for absolute certainty and absolute knowledge in the means of total technological control. Technology is the subject's absolute positioning. Subjectivity, as Heidegger puts it in his notes on *Jünger*, is the "self-aggrandisement of humankind" (GA 90: 114).[3] Heidegger begins to dismantle the enclosed worldless subject in *Being and Time*. He extends his initial critique in a crucial way when he begins to devote more time to the problem of translation. In *Origin of the Artwork* Heidegger argues that the problem of

---

[2] "*Technik ist so die eigentliche Vollendung der "Metaphysik";*"

[3] My translation. "Selbst-herrlichkeit des Menschentums in der *Subjektivität*."

the subject begins with the Roman translation of the Greek ὑποκείμενον as *subiectum* (cf. GA 5: 8/6). This is a thoughtless translation since it does not respect that the Greeks made a specific experience of thinking which coined the word ὑποκείμενον. The original word ὑποκείμενον encapsulates the original experience of thinking. The Roman *subiectum* is however an imitation that lacks the authentic experience. The Romans only copied the word into their vernacular and they did so according to their understanding of truth as *veritas*, i.e., as correspondence truth.[4] The word *subiectum* is not just a sloppy translation, but a simulacrum. This mindless translation is a problem in its own right but the decisive and rather uncanny moment, as Heidegger points out in *The Age of the World Picture*, is when "the essence of humanity altogether transforms itself in that man becomes the subject." (GA 5: 88/66) *Qua* subject the human being is posited as the foundation of all beings in modernity. The subject, however, is a simulacrum. The subject *qua* foundation furthermore does not have an explicit relation to the human being or to the "*I*". Still, the human being *qua* subject becomes the simulacrum-ground of the objectivity of the world. Any theory of the human or of the "*I*" as subject remains stuck in this simulacrum. Heidegger wishes to show that the human being *qua* subject must necessarily transform all beings in their beingness so as to suit the subject's urge for certainty through control. It is the Cartesian *certitudo* of the *ego cogito* extending out into the world securing and certifying its existence by securing the beingness of beings whose very existence that *ego* first had to doubt in order to assert itself. The subject secures and controls beings in that it makes beings comply to its representations. This is the fate of modern metaphysics, the epoch that it grounds, insofar as metaphysics responds to that which is groundless and abysmal: beyng as *Ereignis*.

In the introduction to the B edition of the *1st Critique* Kant articulates the modern subject's quest for certainty when he calls for a "Copernican turn" in metaphysics: "the object (as object of the senses) must conform to the constitution of our faculty of intuition." (B xvii) In order to establish his Copernican turn Kant has to set up a noumenal realm of things in themselves which are not accessible in their being. Kant here answers to what shows itself to him. Kant does not cause the course of history to take a certain direction, he rather articulates the truth of Newtonian physics. That is to say, Kant articulates that which Newtonian physics has revealed to be possible, insofar as Newton does not cause anything either, but also articulates a response to beyng—and this response generates a subtle shift and crack in the fissures of beyng and brings about a new age. Metaphysics establishes the frame thanks to which beings occur in a certain manner, e.g., as resource to be exploited, and what always withdraws is concealment itself. What the Kantian subject has access to, is appearances of things in themselves and the subject's representations of those appearances. On some level, then, Kant even acknowledges the withdrawal. Things in themselves withdraw. But Kant articulates this in a way such that concealment itself does not become a problem. Instead, concealment is

---

[4] See Schmidt (2013) on the difference between Greek and Roman thought.

outsourced and controlled. This is the necessary step to ensure that appearances and the subject's representations conform to the subject's categories. If the subject had access to things as they *are* in themselves, then the subject would be capable of altering the very fabric of the universe. Kant did not promise too much. Technology functions by a transcendental logic that allows us to set the conditions and parameters we use to exert control over beings. As early as 1935 in the lecture course *Introduction to Metaphysics* Heidegger thus points out that modern technology is "*essentially* something different from every previously known use of tools." (GA 40: 202/207) This is the case because modern technology is not mere tool use at the hands of human beings but a system of parameters and thus itself nothing "technological", if by technological we have in mind the ordinary meaning of the word. I shall further expound the relation between technology and transcendental logic below.

This makes it seem as if the human being as subject were in total control, where control means certainty over beings in their beingness. However, Heidegger realises that this is an illusion. The self-aggrandisement of the human subject is a fantasy. Thus, Heidegger points out in *What are Poets for?* that "self-asserting man is a functionary" "[w]hether he as an individual knows it or not, wills it or not." (GA 5: 293f/220) Even though the illusion of being the foundation seems to grant uncanny powers to human beings, there is, for Heidegger, a fundamental shift taking place that threatens "man with death, and indeed with the death of his essence." (GA 5: 294/221) More precisely, "the absoluteness of his sheer willing in the sense of his deliberate self-assertion in everything" (GA 5: 294/221) threatens the human essence. As Demske notes, the human being "stands under an unprecedented threat of death" (Demske 1970: 135) in the present age. Not because of the nuclear bomb but because human essence is under threat. Human beings forget themselves as much as they forget beyng. Technology, therefore, means that what is dominant today is that beyng has left beings (cf. GA 76: 290) i.e., without rest and self-concealment. The human dimension is replaced by the epistemic-technical-rational dimension. I shall address below how time factors into that.

2 Φύσις, Τέχνη and Death

Heidegger's other access to the essence of modern technology is by way of the origin and meaning of the word τέχνη in Greek thought. Simply put, τέχνη is practical knowledge and world access. Τέχνη is a knowledge of production rather than theoretical knowledge. In the technology essay Heidegger reminds us that "[o]nce there was a time when the bringing-forth of the true into the beautiful was called τέχνη. And the ποίησις of the fine arts also was called τέχνη." (GA 7: 35/34) Heidegger here reminds his readers that a return to this understanding is necessary. In the note from 1940 I quoted above Heidegger determines τέχνη as "the knowing-one's-way-around in making." (GA 76: 290) As such τέχνη is first and foremost "a hermeneutics [*Auslegung*] of the beingness of beings" (GA 76: 290) in terms of practicability, operability, and manipulability. Machines and the mathematisation of the world are, for Heidegger, consequences of that interpretation of the world. There is nothing wrong with this way of world-access. There is, however, something that sets in, increasingly so in modernity, that privileges a purely technical and mathematical access to world. Technical here means that what we experience and encounter everything as according to a pre-established and posited end. There is a sheer positivity at work in that frame, a presence deaf to the echoes of concealment. Yet, τέχνη itself is not to blame. What is necessary instead, is to gain an understanding again for this initial response to how we can access the world.

Heidegger interprets Greek world access through τέχνη as follows. Τέχνη as making is of the human dimension, but as such it is also related to nature as φύσις. By means of τέχνη the human being can support the bringing-forth of φύσις, i.e., that which "naturally" occurs. Think of building a set of stone stairs by giving form to the natural occurring of the stone. Τέχνη here helps and supports φύσις. The stone mason uses a hammer to form the stone. In this example φύσις comes first and τέχνη comes to help and bring forth a useful form according to the four causes, material, formal, efficient, and final. The stairs are not an occurrence of φύσις at all, and yet τέχνη here only brings about what is there in the stone. The stone itself does not change. The stone does not become source of something else. The stone remains stone, resting in itself. With the beginning of modernity, τέχνη, however, seems to begin to take over under the rule of the representing subject. The relationship between τέχνη and φύσις is of a less and less supportive but of an increasingly demanding and forcefully challenging kind. Challenging in the sense that τέχνη now no longer seems to be in a free relationship with φύσις, but increasingly in a relationship where τέχνη tries to overpower φύσις. This is not to idealise premodern times. There may well be a plethora of historiographical examples, of how humans have interfered with "nature," e.g., by rearranging the course of a river. There is another significant and fundamental shift that fully sets itself forth with modern technology. That is, viz., the extraction of energy, the capacity to store that energy and to transform all that is into something to be consumed. This is also to indicate that this shift begins earlier than modernity, is already a possibility or fate of metaphysics, but that it only now comes into full force because of the specific constellation of modernity, where the human being begins to revolt against being. That is, where the human being assumes that he can at will posit being, as happens, for example, in genetic modification. For Heidegger, the origin of the threat to the human essence, mentioned above, lies in the relationship between τέχνη and φύσις.

In a particularly illuminating passage in *On the Essence and Concept of Φύσις* Heidegger demonstrates the interplay of τέχνη and φύσις and carves out in how far τέχνη can become dangerous for φύσις. He points out that a modern doctor certainly has better technological means at hand than any premodern doctor. But Heidegger also notes that in and of itself this says nothing about the quality of the doctor's understanding of health. To be sure, humans now live longer thanks to modern medicine. But an increase in the amount of years humans live reveals little about how humans live their lives. One could ask, for example, whether there are more wholesome communities today. To add numbers in years is no guarantee for a more fulfilled or meaningful life. Moreover, to the modern mind it might seem as though the αρχή, the origin, of the healing process were, in fact, *technological*, but not of φύσις. Thus, here a shift in perspective sets in, as Heidegger notes. Τέχνη is not in tune with φύσις, i.e., with that which brings forth on its own terms, but φύσις is now at the mercy of τέχνη. Yet, Heidegger also argues that "[τ]έχνη can merely *cooperate* with φύσις, can more or less expedite the cure; but as τέχνη, it can never replace φύσις; and in its stead become the αρχή of *health* as such." (GA 9: 257/197 *me*) The notion of cooperation is crucial here because it points to human correspondence with being (in this case as φύσις). Heidegger, however, here also warns that τέχνη might well be on the way to replace φύσις.

It is worth quoting Heidegger here at length also because the following passage epitomises what has been argued so far on the relation between technology and subjectivism:

> This [replacement] could happen only if life as such were to become a "technically" producible artefact [*Gemächte*]. However, at that very moment there would also no longer be such a thing as health, any more than there would be birth and death. Sometimes it seems as if modern humanity is rushing headlong toward this goal of *producing itself technologically*. If humanity achieves this, it will have exploded itself, i.e., *its essence* qua *subjectivity*, into thin air, into a region where the absolutely meaningless is valued as the one and only "meaning" and where preserving this value appears as the human "domination" of the globe. "Subjectivity" is not overcome in this way but merely "tranquilized" in the "eternal progress" of a Chinese-like "*constancy*." This is the most extreme unessence [*Unwesen*] in relation to φύσις—ουσία. (GA 9: 257/197 *ta*)

Heidegger says that the necessary consequence of human self-interpretation as subject will lead to artificial production of human organisms. But this production would mean that the explosion of modernity now also explodes the subject to a level of utter nihilism, where the only "meaning" is the continued securing of all resources for the sake of prolonging survival. This is the "endless-and-so-on" Heidegger already fears in *Contributions* will set itself into force. The subject's desire for absolute control would still not be overcome. On this reading, it can be seen why transhumanism must work towards digital immortality and the annihilation of death. One of the implicit goals, then, of the subject's will to power is to transcend the body, to become immortal by leaving behind the mortal prison of the flesh. Only if death is eradicated, and that implies, only if the human being becomes an artificial product, can the subject tranquilise its desire for total control. Why? Because death is the area technology cannot control and have any command over. In his interview with Wisser, given 30 years after he wrote the *Φύσις* essay, Heidegger seems convinced that the technological production of humanoid organisms is inevitably in store for us. If the replacement of φύσις with τέχνη were to happen, then this would mean an utter uprooting of human *being*. Human beings would become an artefact of the epistemic-logical dimension. Heidegger's term here is *Gemächte*. As something produced human beings would be at the mercy of machination, *Machenschaft*. This process, Heidegger points out, would make birth, death, life, and health meaningless concepts because this process would mean a radically new "ontology"—if such terms would still make sense at all. An "ontology"—rather a "logistics"—of sheer making and producing, circling around itself. A "logistics" in which the reification of being as the beingness of beings (e.g., as genetic code) would finally have taken the upper hand. The technological production of humans would be the victory of utter nihilism precisely because the human being would make himself an idol only to turn around himself aimlessly.

The logic of such endeavours is a logic of prolonging life for the sake of prolonging. This is a necessary consequence of what Heidegger calls the "will to will" that is operative in modernity. For Heidegger the technological production of organic life would mean the subject's victory. The purely self-referential subject must necessarily prolong itself, for all it knows with absolute certainty is itself.[5] However, as the human subject assumes itself to be the foundation of all beings, it is, according to Heidegger, in reality only an enforcer of a constellation of metaphysics that Heidegger calls *Ge-stell*.

3 Machination and the Will to Will

In *Contributions to Philosophy* Heidegger understands wilful making and producing to be technology's dominant trait and calls this process *Machenschaft*, machination. The German *Machenschaft* means manipulation and intrigue, yet Heidegger focuses on the verbal root *machen*, to make. *Machenschaft* is then the process of making (or producing) simply for the sake of producing more. At the time of writing the *Contributions* Heidegger understands machination as the dominant way in which beyng occurs in the present age. It is only secondarily something human beings engage in. In my view, *Machenschaft* as an essential occurrence of beyng retains a rather sinister connotation since machination is beyng turning against itself (cf. GA 65: 84/42). *Machenschaft* is beyng's "unessence" insofar as here beyng neglects its self-concealment. Heidegger first introduces machination in *Introduction to Metaphysics* (cf. GA 40: 168/169). But it is in *Contributions* that we find a more sustained explication of the term. Thus, it is with the proper beginning of being-historical thinking, which coincides with the claim of the abandonment of beyng, that machination becomes a central focus. Machination is crucial for a sound understanding of Heidegger's later notion of *Ge-Stell*.

Machination is a consequence of the first beginning and the forgetfulness of beyng's self-concealment. For that very forgetting there is "within machination …

---

[5] Fichte with his self-positing ego and its will that wills itself as its ground, therefore, ultimately and necessarily so ends up in a position where there can be no death, no mortality, and no immortality; but only all-consuming life (cf. Scherer 1979: 134). This is similar to Leibniz claim in §69 of the *Monadology*: "Ainsi il n'y a rien … de mort dans l'univers." (Leibniz 1991: 231) With Heidegger this is completely reversed: There would be nothing without death.

nothing question-worthy, nothing that could be deemed worthy through questioning as such." (GA 65: 109/87) Everything seems to stand ready as perfectly disclosed and given. In machination there is no need to ask what it means to be. We rather give in to the spectacle of lived experiences and amusement and numb our deep boredom with enchantment about the "wonders" of technology. As shepherd of being the human being's forgetting of concealment is not the primary reason for the beyng turning against itself as machination. Still, the human being *qua* shepherd has led beyng astray, as it were. If the essence of beyng as event is to let beings be and to let them come into their own in a free play respecting concealment, then beyng's un-essence, i.e., machination, is precisely the opposite. Machination is the forceful challenging of all beings to conform to organisation, to be homogenisable objects deprived of ownness, for everything to become an artefact. The imminent danger of machination is, as Vallega-Neu puts it, its potential for "closing down of the other possibilities of being and thus of essential history." (Vallega-Neu 2015: 12) The threat is that beyng becomes increasingly one-dimensional, that there is only the frame of technology, where no sense of wonder or awe seems possible, no dwelling, lingering and gaze, but only end-driven production.

Heidegger sees the will to power at work in machination: "[Machination] is the unconditional completion of being as the will to power." (GA 67: 150) By 1941/1942 Heidegger critically extends Nietzsche's notion of the will to power, when he, in *The Event*, begins to speak of the "will to will." Like the will to power this will is a will to domination, to ever more power over the earth, its resources and inhabitants. Yet, as Heidegger writes in his response to Ernst Jünger and with reference to Nietzsche, the will to will is the ""most uncanny" [guest] … because, as the unconditional will to will, it wills homelessness [*Heimatlosigkeit*] as such." (GA 9: 387/292) For Heidegger the will to will is a direct consequence of the closure of metaphysics that occurs with Hegel and Nietzsche. Hegel establishes absolute certainty and knowledge about the beingness of beings. Nietzsche determines being as will to power. Thus, beings in their being are absolutely secured as will to power and are accessible as such. Schmidt points out that Heidegger sees in Nietzsche, a great "attachment to this willing ground [which] led to the nihilism of the pure will to power willing itself uninhibitedly and unconditionally." (Schmidt 1988: 149) Heidegger thus sees yet another shift: the will to power actually wills itself—and necessarily so. Nietzsche is not the first and only to speak of the will. The will is an essential occurrence steering the course of modernity. The will to will is insatiable like Spinoza's *conatus* and Schopenhauer's *Will*. Schelling notoriously determines "Urseyn" as will (cf. GA 8: 95/90). Fichte rationalises the "acts of the will … in terms of the will itself, of which we can only say, "It is as it is, because it is so.""[6] (Beiser 2008: 275)[7] Of course, one has to make important distinctions between all these thinkers and their respective notions of the will. Still, they seem to be responding to the same phenomenon. But what does such a will want? This will wants itself, as Fichte seems to imply. This will

---

[6] As Shakespeare's *Caesar* says: "The cause is in my will."

[7] Quoting Fichte's *System der Sittenlehre, Werke* IV.

is its self-sufficient foundation. Hence, as De Gennaro argues, "the will in fact wills itself, so that … the ultimate sense of the will to power is the will to will." (De Gennaro 2012: 204) Heidegger brings the will that presents itself in modern metaphysics to its logical conclusion. The will wills itself, and it wills itself because it wills itself—because "it is so!" This circularity finds expression in the notion "will to will." In this epoch metaphysics responds to the abysmal occurring of beyng with the will as the foundation of all beings: a self-rotating will willing itself that wills itself simply because it wills itself and as such it sets itself into effect in technology. This will is not distinct from the subject, but rather *is* the subject's will. Pöggeler thus points out that "metaphysics as the science of grounds fulfils and completes itself in the technology of an absolute knowledge, which makes available an ultimate foundation." (Pöggeler 1983: 126)

Like machination the will to will means the rule of being's reification as beingness of beings, as the representation, *Vorgestelltheit*, of the subject (cf. GA 71: 79f/66f). In the essay *The Thing* Heidegger illustrates this process by the example of a now prevalent way of understanding beings as "states of aggregation of matter." (GA 7: 173/169) Wine is, according to the scientific worldview, not a wine with a unique being that cannot be perfectly reproduced. Wine is not a gift from the gods, something that mortals cherish by sacrificing the wine to the gods and by honouring the earth which gave the wine—the earth that also is the realm where a community's ancestors are buried. Instead, wine is a "liquid" (first level of abstraction) and "liquid" is a state of aggregation (second level of abstraction). The wine entirely disappears behind those abstractions. But those abstractions are precisely what allows industrial agriculture to produce the seemingly ever-same wine. This, in turn, means that the rotation of the will is effectively the neutralisation of time and history insofar as technology strives to make beings available by setting into actuality their ever-same beingness. The will to will is then also tantamount to the forgetting of being, as this defies the truth of beyng, viz., that withdrawal and denial are inherent to all appearance, that any access to beings takes place according to ecstatic time. This is why in his letter to Father Richardson, Heidegger says that time is to be understood as the "clearing of self-concealment." (GA 11: 151/303) Thus, in this uncanny historical constellation, there seems to be an eradication of time at work, if time is that which allows for beyng's self-concealment. The denial of concealment prevalent in the will to will is manifest in technology: "The universally unmistakeable consistency of the progression testifies that *the will to will* has become the actuality of the actual." (GA 71: 91/77 *ta*)

Hence Heidegger sees somethings at work in technology that, with reference to Nietzsche, he understands as a "steadily rotating recurrence of the same" (GA 8: 112/109). Their essence (metaphysical), their whatness, is the will to will. That is to say, *what* beings are (in their beingness) is owed to the representation of the willing subject. Their existence (metaphysical), their thatness, is the eternal repetition. That is to say, *that* beings are, means that they can be perfectly replaced. This shows how beings can be made available at will at all times. By means of a represented beingness technology makes *becoming* operational in the sense that technology forces all beings to recur ("become") as the ever-same ("beingness") in a controlled fashion. Rotation is also precisely what drives the *Ge-Stell* and, to quote Mitchell, "[t]o say that positionality [*Ge-Stell*] circulates is to say that it is without purpose." (Mitchell 2015: 52) *Ge-Stell*, then, is as an end-less will to will the realm of insatiable nihilism.

In *What is Called Thinking?*, Heidegger's last lecture course given around the same time as Heidegger's engagement with technology intensifies, Heidegger reads Nietzsche's *Zarathustra* as epitomising the problem of the hermeneutics of vulgar, linear time. Heidegger understands Nietzsche's eternal recurrence of the same as a means of the will to power to remain in power. According to the vulgar understanding of time, time is made up of homogeneous now-states that linearly flow from the future to the present and into the past. This continuous flow means that the current now-state is always already under threat of becoming obsolete. The will wants to hold tight to the current "now" but fails. Therefore, the will develops a resentment against time and its "it was" (GA 8: 97/93). The "it was" offends both representation and the will. Re-presentation needs presence. Only what is present can be represented and only what can be represented is real. What ceases to be present *is* not because only that which is re-presented *is*. This explains the prevalence and might of the picture in modernity. The will turns against the ephemeral nature of linear time because what the will needs is presence.

Heidegger quotes from *Zarathustra*: "This, yes, this alone is *revenge* itself: the will's revulsion against time and its "It was"." (GA 8: 97/93) As beings cease to be, the will seeks revenge and its revenge drives the will to want the ever-same and controllable outcome at all times, which the will needs for total control over beings. As we shall see, this is what *Bestand*, standing reserve, delivers. The German word Heidegger uses for "seeking revenge" is *nach-stellen*. *Nachstellen* can mean to position oneself behind someone else with the intent to chase after or even harm them. In *Ge-Stell* beings are without guard precisely since they are not allowed their own time and place but must stand ready at any time and anywhere. But *nach-stellen* also means to imitate. That is to say, the will to will operates by chasing after and imitating beings. Thus, the will produces the ever-same outcome it desires by producing imitations.

In *What is Called Thinking?* there is another crucial passage where Heidegger concisely presents his critique of representationalism and its connection to vulgar time. I quote Heidegger here at length because it shows how Heidegger's critique of representationalism leads him to determine the essence of technology as *Ge-Stell*:

> Since long ago, that which is present has been regarded as what is. But what representational ideas can we form of what in a way is no longer, and yet still is? What ideas can we form of that which was? At this "it was," idea and its willing take offense. Faced with what "was," willing no longer has anything to say. Faced with every "it was," willing no longer has anything to propose. This "it was" resists the willing of that will. The "it was" becomes a stumbling block for all willing. It is the block which the will can no longer budge. Then the "it was" becomes the sorrow and despair of all willing which, being what it is, always wills forward, and is always foiled by the bygones that lie fixed firmly in the past. (GA 8: 96/92)[8]

---

[8] Note in this regard also that Heidegger likens the developments of modern technology and society to Plato's cave (cf. GA 71: 107/90). In the cave all beings *qua* shadows are secured in their presence and they recur eternally in the same order.

4   From Vor-Stellung to Ge-Stell

In *Being and Time* Heidegger already criticises representationalism as an insufficient way of describing Dasein's being-in-the-world. Even just using a tool is too complex for representation to be able to do it justice. When a tool like a hammer breaks, Heidegger argues, perception and representation fail Dasein: "Even the most sharp and most persistent "perception" and "representation" of things could never discover something like damage to the tool. The using [*Handhaben*] must be able to be hampered so that something unhandy can be encountered." (SZ: 354f/325) Heidegger here understands representation as the linear succession of mental images of an object. The current representation is constituted by the present now-state. Hence, from an onto-logical perspective, representation cannot account for the inter-ruption, the hamper-ing, of the tool, because all representation ever perceives is the object in its present now-state. Representation does not disclose the being concerned in its being. Representation cannot account for what is between t1 and t2 and cannot synthesise the different time states on its own. What really takes place in moments of breakdown, according to Heidegger, is what he calls "making present," *Gegenwärtigen*. Making present on its own is not inauthentic. Rather, the problem is when making present takes prevalence, then the horizons of futurity and having-been begin to disappear. Dasein deals only with the immediately present rather than with that which self-con-ceals and self-withdraws. Representation on its own only provides a successive stream of what is "out there," but it cannot provide coherence. Representation (and con-sciousness) knows no unity of temporal ecstasies. But making present is of an "ecstatic unity … that awaits and retains." (SZ: 355/325) In order to repair a damaged tool, Dasein needs to make present what it has been and what it will be—and Dasein needs to do so simultaneously—for the tool to be made functional again. Ontologically, this is only possible out of the unity of the ecstasies of temporality. Dasein has to be out there in the world, deeply interwoven with the horizon of meaning against which the tool lights up in its being, and in this sense used to *handling* the tool with its hands. Representation by contrast is a purely internal mental process of representing pictures. Representation is a distanced observational stance operating on the level of correspon-dence truth.

Dasein's primary experience of being-in-the-world is practical rather than theo-retical in the modern scientific sense. Dasein uses tools with its hands, not with its mind. Tools are ready-to-*hand* and Dasein does not need to represent them mentally in order to use them. In moments of breakdown Dasein makes present a tool that is usually ready-to-hand. Thus, when in need of repair something ready-to-hand becomes something present-at-hand. Only then does Dasein have to ask itself, what the hammer is made of and how Dasein could repair the hammer. With the scientific revolution of modernity tools have become more complex and so they are prone to break down more often than tools like a hammer. The more complex machines are, the more often they have to be repaired and that means the more often they have to be made present. This shift in the tools available to human beings is not coinciden-tal, but necessary as a consequence of the response modern metaphysics gives to the event. The abstract, not that which is ready-at-hand, becomes the new regulative. At the same time, the "increased" presence of modernity, most visible with the Internet where everything that has ever been recorded can be stored and be made available at any place and time, bears another problem. As Heidegger writes in *Being and Time*: "When we just stare at something, our just-having-it-before-us lies before us *as a failure to understand* it any more." (SZ: 149/140) This has to do with the movement of ἀλήθεια. If something is right in front of oneself and perfectly available at any time, then understanding as dis-closing is—ironically so—impeded. Human beings must no longer engage in ἀλήθειν, when everything appear to be perfectly present and presented. In German "presented" would mean *vor einen gestellt*, i.e., placed before someone.

In *The Event* Heidegger interprets *vor-stellen* as follows: "To re-present: making present of something *as* something." (GA 71: 20/13 *ta*) For example, making present the world as an image, as a model. As Heidegger argues in *The Age of the World Picture*, the prevalent talk of worldviews, of the world *as* picture, indicates that the world *is* only "insofar as it is positioned by the representing-producing [*vorstellend-herstellend*] humanity." (GA 5: 89/67 *ta*) In the same essay Heidegger fully explores the manifoldness of the German verb *stellen*. The subject chases after and imitates, *nach-stellen*, what it wants to represent, *vor-stellen*, i.e., position before itself, in order to produce, *her-stellen*, which literally means to position something at the place where it is needed. "To represent means here: of oneself to set something before one and to make what has been set in place secure [*sicher-stellen*] as thus set in place." (GA 5: 108/82) Different than his account in *Being and Time*, Heidegger here appreciates that representation is not a simple picturing of what is out there, but rather an interference with the world. An interference operating with calculation in order to secure the predetermined desired outcome. Beings are now only insofar as they correspond to the represented *idea* (say, a production plan) according to which they are produced. This is the impoverished perspective of correspondence truth set to work (cf. GA 71: 20/13).

World access in modernity primarily takes place by way of representation, which is predicated on the subject-object-dichotomy. As representation means both picturing what is out there (resemblance) and *vor-stellen*, i.e., positioning before oneself, world-access now first and foremost takes place by preconceived representations. In one word: models. Thus, nature is now first represented "as an object of research," (GA 7: 19/19), and subsequently approached as such. Nature must obey the subject's models. Yet, as Mitchell argues: "The "picture" of the world is not really a picture at all, more a schematized and formal outline of it, a construction. The Cartesian mathematicization of nature would be the prime example." (Mitchell 2015: 30) The process can be formalised as follows: $A = B = A$, where A is the representation *qua* model by which nature is accessed and is posited in such a way that B—nature—must conform to A. Models by which human beings interact with the world, are precisely not mere representations *qua* resemblance of nature as it is itself or as it appears. They are rather directly transforming the very being in question, i.e., nature as something present-at-hand. Heidegger's insight into the manifoldness of *stellen* together with his interpretation of vulgar time inform his determination of the essence of technology as *Ge-Stell*, the concentrating of all modes of positioning.

Chapter 13
Ge-Stell: The Essence of Technology

1 The Word *Ge-Stell*

A first step toward a clearer understanding of why Heidegger chooses the word *Ge-Stell* to describe the essence of technology is via the word itself. The German word *Gestell* used to be a common word. A *Gestell* is a stand or supporting framework used, for example, in workshops or on farms. Until the second half of the twentieth century "*Gstell*" in Southern German dialects was also used to refer to machines like a circular saw. Yet, this is not what Heidegger means by *Ge-Stell*. By hyphenating the word Heidegger in a sense frees the word from its immediate everyday meanings. The interruption of the hyphen lets us rest on the prefix and simultaneously brings to the fore the weight and meaning of the root verb *stellen*: *Ge-Stell* is then the gathering of all modes of *stellen*, of placing, putting, positioning, setting (up), producing, chasing, imitating. Note also that the perfect tense of *stellen* is *gestellt*. As an adjective *gestellt* can also mean affected and artificial. The notion of *Ge-Stell* is inspired by Eckhart's *Gestellnis*, a translation of the Roman *forma* and the Greek μορφή. We always produce things according to preconceived forms, as Sheehan notes (cf. Sheehan 2010: 95). But *Ge-Stell* operates by homogenising and making uniform and in this way *Ge-Stell* eradicates ownness.

Ge-Stell is not to be understood as a general concept, genus or class under which all technological beings are subsumed. A radio or a smartphone, a plane or a computer are not *gestells* like cows and birds are animals or like telephones and letters are means of communication. In that sense the common English translation of *Ge-Stell* as *enframing* could be misleading since it implies that what technology essentially does is to *enframe* all beings, as though technology surrounded beings in such a way that all beings are in general enframed, as if coming to beings from outside. Mitchell, therefore, proposes to translate *Ge-Stell* as positionality precisely because *Ge-Stell* is not external to beings but rather an essential and currently prevalent essential occurrence of being, i.e., the way in which beings appear: "Positionality

© Springer Nature Switzerland AG 2021
J. A. Niederhauser, *Heidegger on Death and Being*,
https://doi.org/10.1007/978-3-030-51375-7_13

is not something distinct from the presencing of beings, but rather is their way of presencing in a post-modern era of circulative replacement." (Mitchell 2015: 51) It is also important to note that Mitchell identifies what Heidegger calls "machination" with post-modernity. Beings are analogous to being as positionality. In this sense *positionality* is the *essence* of technology. Note that this underlines the differentiation of beyng rather than denying it insofar as beyng self-differentiates as being (presencing) and beings (what is present). But what does Heidegger really mean by essence?

When Heidegger speaks of the "*Wesen*" of technology, he does not use the word in the metaphysical sense. In the technology essay Heidegger gives the examples of *Staatswesen* (state affairs) and *Hauswesen* (household matters) to illustrate what he means. In these cases, the German *Wesen* does not at all mean genus or *essentia*, but instead indicates, says Heidegger, "the ways in which house and state hold sway, administer themselves, develop and decay." (GA 7: 31/30) There is an old German saying that could be found in castles and farmhouses from Pommern to South Tyrol which reads: "*Mag draußen die Welt ihr Wesen treiben, Mein Heim soll meine Ruhstatt bleiben*." Now, if we translate *Wesen* here with essence, then this saying loses its meaning. *Wesen* here rather means something like *weben und streben*, weaving and striving. But *Wesen* can also have connotations of "to dwell" and "to linger on", of remaining, but *in time* and not in a transtemporal sense. Hence, the German saying could be translated as follows: "May world weave and strive in its ways, My home shall be my resting place." If we translated, "May the world drive its essence" we would have completely lost the meaning of what is at stake here. There is in *Wesen* in the relevant sense then a weaving a striving, and not "static" *essentia*.

Hence *Wesen* here indicates a realm, a dimensionality, and also refers to *how* a realm emerges, sustains and governs itself; *how* it organises, administers and rules over beings; and *how* it eventually declines. Thus, "essence" is finite. Positionality as the essence of technology is hence not a general whatness pertaining to all beings. Instead, positionality opens up a realm of possibilities such that things become circularly replaceable. To say that positionality is an essential "destining of the coming to presence of being itself" (GA 11: 115/37) hence does not mean that all beings are of the same metaphysical *essentia*. Instead, the way they are present is such that beings increasingly occur *as* positioned—as immediately ready for use and instantly replaceable. This is thus a being-historical conception of *Wesen* for which the English vernacular knows no word. If anything, then we should probably say the "dimensionality" of technology, rather than the "essence" of technology.

In the essay *The Turning* Heidegger articulates in full what he means by the word *Ge-Stell*. It is worth quoting the original German because it shows the manifoldness of the verb *stellen*:

Das Wesen des Gestells ist das in sich gesammelte Stellen, das seiner eigenen Wesenswahrheit mit der Vergessenheit nachstellt, welches Nachstellen sich dadurch verstellt, daß es sich in das Bestellen alles Anwesenden als den Bestand entfaltet, sich in diesem einrichtet und als dieser herrscht.

> The dimensionality of positionality is that setting-upon gathered into itself which entraps the truth of its own coming to presence with oblivion. This entrapping disguises itself, in that it develops into the setting in order of everything that presences as standing reserve, establishes itself in the standing-reserve, and rules as the standing-reserve. (GA 11: 115/36f *ta*)

2   Standing Reserve

Heidegger calls the peculiar way beings are present in positionality *Bestand*, standing reserve. Standing reserve is not a metaphysical claim about the beingness or quiddity of beings. Heidegger asks for the *how* instead of the *what*: "The name "standing reserve" ... designates nothing less than the way in which everything presences that is wrought upon by the challenging revealing." (GA 7: 17/17) Positionality places beings in a presence in such a way that that which appears finds no rest and is disclosed only if it can serve for the extraction of some use: "Air is now positioned [*gestellt*] to yield nitrogen, the earth to yield ore, ore to yield uranium." (GA 7: 16/15 *ta*) That is, beings *are* insofar as they can be ordered and calculated as to their projected effect. The standing reserve always stands ready. The uniqueness of beings is of no import in positionality. What matters is their readiness for use and manipulation. In the technology essay Heidegger points out the following: "Through this the other possibility is blocked, that man might be admitted more and sooner and ever more primally to the essence of that which is unconcealed and to its unconcealment, in order that he might experience as his essence his needed belonging to revealing." (GA 7: 27/26) The possibility that is blocked here, is the possibility to think concealment. Trapped in the sheer availability of the standing reserve, concealment cannot become the focus of the human being.

In positionality a more original relationship with being and consequently beings that are not positioned is covered over. In that sense Dreyfus has a point when he argues that the understanding of being is diminished. Yet, this is a consequence of beyng's *Selbst-verstellung*, its self-*dissimulation* and self-disguise. Thus, there is still concealment in positionality, but now concealment is truly a case of *dissimulatio*, a derivative mode of concealment. That dissimulation is the result of metaphysics' failure to think beyng's self-concealment. Beyng covers over itself and its "essential history" because "technology (metaphysical) and historiography forge ahead and fixate Everything [sic.] into an unknowable *delusion*." (GA 67: 56 *me*) Considering the movement of the event as that which withdraws as it arrives Heidegger can provide a being-historical explanation for the prevalence of what Baudrillard calls simulacra, a copy or imitation, the virtualisation of all that is. As beyng self-dissimulates, it essentially occurs as positionality. As beings are analogous to that occurrence they become simulacra. And positionality needs beings as simulacra so that it can operate nature "itself as a calculable complex of the effects of forces." (GA 7: 27/26) What we are dealing with in terms of the standing reserve is never a proper thing, a thing as it is in itself. Rather, "things" as standing reserve are every only mere semblances that can be positioned against each other in order to guarantee a continuous increase in energy-extraction and functionality. Thus, as Heidegger writes in *The Thing*, it is a mistake to assume that the natural sciences deal with reality (cf. GA 7: 172/168). What they really deal with are simulacra. The genuine, the proper thing remains concealed to them.

The role of human beings in positionality is twofold. On the one hand, as mentioned, human beings are the functionaries of technology, executing its demands. On the other hand, human beings as human material are standing reserve just like oil and timber are (cf. GA 7: 18/18). Human beings are challenged to make themselves standing reserve, for example, by growing human organs in half-animal, half-human chimeras.[1] Note that for this very participation in the ordering and organising of beings according to the demands of positionality human beings are closer to beyng than is obvious at first. But human beings, and this is the danger, are closer to beyng's self-dissimulation at work in these orderings.

In positionality our relationship with beings, or things, as Heidegger begins to say in his essays on the fourfold, is diminished. Things are predominantly accessible as standing reserve, but this means that their ownness is concealed, i.e., dissimulated: "The ordering belonging to positionality sets itself above the thing, leaves it, as thing, unsafeguarded [*wahrlos*]." (GA 11: 122/46 *ta*) The adjective "*wahrlos*" is crucial here. On the one hand, one can hear connotations of the interesting German adjective "*verwahrlost*" here. "*Verwahrlost*" means "depraved", "neglected", "desolate". Hence it indicates a certain vulnerability. But Heidegger writes "wahrlos". Thus, he seems to indicate that in positionality the thing is not *in truth* because the thing is supposed to be standing there fully disclosed and available and in that sense truly unsafeguarded. But even a simple thing like a jug or a stone bridge self-conceals. They are never fully accessible. Heidegger himself struggles to determine what makes the thing a thing in essays like the *Origin of the Artwork* or *The Thing*. That things self-withdraw is, however, what structures their uniqueness and is what defies attempts at perfectly controlling them. That which self-refuses, cannot be controlled. This is why the transcendental logic by which the technological sphere operates has to push the self-concealment of things into the noumenal realm of things in themselves. This very move of exiling concealment into the noumenal is the reason why Heidegger with the fourfold begins to return to *the thing* as it is in itself, to a simple thing like a jug. In *The Thing* Heidegger thus explicitly asks at the beginning of the essay: "What is the thing *in itself?*" (GA 7: 169/165 *me*). Heidegger there also points out that we can think the thing as it is in itself, if only we *let* the thing be and that also means to let its self-concealment *be*; for considering concealment implies sheltering and harbouring rather than challenging and forcing. Then the thing in itself as it stands before us can light up. The problem of our epoch is that the abstractions of the sciences interfere with the simple thing so that what we deal with are semblances, representations of appearances, which we confuse with the

---

[1] See, for example, an article by David Robson's on the *BBC* website from January 2017, where he describes the "The Birth of Half-human, Half-animal Chimeras."

actuality of the thing, with what the thing "really" is. Instead of seeing a stone bridge that bridges and hence unites places and brings forth a space; instead of appreciating a clay jug from which we drink wine to honour the earth and gods; instead of savouring the wine; we see the material "stone" or atoms; we see the material "clay", atoms, particles, electrons etc.; we see an aggregate fluid that happens to be wine. Heidegger asks us to return to the thing itself as it stands before us, but that thing, for example, the wine is never something on its own. Wine is only properly wine when in a proper world, a deeply interwoven web of meaning as is the fourfold. There the wine is a gift to mortals and at once gifted by mortals to the earth and the gods. This mirror-play is precisely what allows for the equilibrium and the measure of the fourfold. At the heart of this play is still the interplay of concealment-sheltering and unconcealment-disclosure. In this way the things of the fourfold and the fourfold itself are protected. This also means that death as *Ge-Birg* (together with ecstatic time) is that which structures the tempo-spatial occurrences called things. This is why positionality (and its ideology transhumanism) must work to annihilate death. This is why positionality must eradicate concealment so that everything can be made to stand ready and available for consumption.

3 Positing, Positioning and Sheltering-Harbouring

Heidegger draws inspiration for the word *Ge-Stell* from Eckhart and the manifoldness of the verb *stellen*. But he also provides a being-historical genealogy of the word *Ge-Stell* and a justification why positing and positioning take over in modernity. This takeover is the constant denial of death as the concentration of concealment and sheltering-harbouring. Death is what comes to rescue because death withdraws from the logic of positing. In what follows I shall demonstrate the relation between positioning and sheltering-harbouring. This will allow me to bring positionality into play with death as *Ge-Birg*. Note that Heidegger himself does not explicitly do so in his texts, but as *stellen* is a derivative mode of *bergen*, the mode that forgets concealment, there is here a trace of the thinking path to follow; a trace that Heidegger himself may not have been able to follow any further.

Heidegger provides, as he calls it in the essay *The Danger*, an "essential genealogy [*Wesensgenealogie*]" (GA 79: 65/62) of *stellen*. Contrary to an ordinary genealogy, an essential genealogy does not trace the historiographical development of a concept. A *Wesens-genealogie*, as Heidegger calls it, means to look for the being-historical *dimensionality* of the phenomenon in question. That is to say, Heidegger investigates the realms of possibility of beyng, its sendings and the responses metaphysics has given, and he tries to encapsulate his experience in thought in words that are specifically non-metaphysical. A different way of articulating this would be to say that Heidegger responds to a certain *claim*, *Anruf*. The presupposition of this specific essential genealogy is that modern technology is the completion and a fate of metaphysics.

Positioning itself is not something purely modern. Positioning has its origins in the first beginning. To Greek thinking being essentially occurred as φύσις, which Heidegger understands as follows: "to bring here from concealment forth into unconcealment. This bringing means letting something arrive and presence of its own accord." (GA 79: 64/60) Thus φύσις is that which allows (*lassen*) something to have free play or range, something comes into good presence from concealment by itself. To *let* something arrive in unconcealment of its own accord, to grant free-play is the act of being as φύσις. As argued above, τέχνη can contribute to and collaborate with this bringing-forth. This contribution is wholesome, when τέχνη supports the letting-into-free-play of φύσις. It is not wholesome when τέχνη forces φύσις. Dahlstrom describes φύσις as the "the constantly emerging presence of things, and their absences" (Dahlstrom 2011: 144). Dahlstrom also makes the critical point that absence and presence are not dialectical opposites, and that "talk of them as two sides or two aspects is fatally misleading" (Dahlstrom 2011: 144). This is the case precisely because absence and presence are not apart from each other, they are "at once." Note, however, as stated before that Dahlstrom appropriately speaks of "absences" of things, rather than of being itself. To speak of absence in terms of being would mean to still speak out of a metaphysical interpretation of the inherent withdrawal of being. In terms of being we need to speak of withdrawal, which is simply a different name of being. The "at once" is never simply given. It is, instead, the responsibility of mortal thinking, to appreciate and perform or carry out (*gedanklich vollziehen*) the simultaneity and equiprimordiality of presence and withdrawal. Heidegger says that "darkness is perhaps in play for all thinking at all times." (GA 79: 93/88) More precisely, what lies in darkness is "the origin of the principles of thinking" and this darkness guides thinking. That which is dark, however, is *not* a "mere and total absence of light." Instead, "[t]he dark keeps light to itself." (GA 79: 93/88) As the darkness at play in thinking, the very limit of metaphysics, is concealment, open to mortals from death as the refuge of being, i.e., as the utterly inaccessible. As death is forgotten, so are concealment and withdrawal which were then considered as mere absence by the tradition. But to this understanding of beyng Heidegger wishes to return. It is about the simultaneity and about the realisation that there is in any presence something not hidden, but rather a withholding-itself.

Heidegger's understanding of φύσις draws inspiration from Heraclitus' fragment B 10: "φύσις κρύπτεσθαι φιλεῖ". A possible translation reads: "φύσις likes to hide herself". But as κρύπτεσθαι is a medial grammatical form, not a purely self-reflective verb, this actually reads: "φύσις conceals herself in something else in a sheltering way." (*my translation*; original Greek text taken from (Hahn 1987: 32)) Through its medial self-concealing φύσις gives into the Open but is itself never available. Note, therefore, also the connotation of the German *geborgen sein*, which Heidegger often seems to have in mind when he speaks of *Ver-bergung*, and which does not mean "to be absent", but rather "to be home", "to be safe". At the heart of the Open there is concealment. Hence Heidegger speaks of clearing *for* self-concealment. Things are *sheltered* only if they also always retain a certain hiddenness. Things are then left at peace and are released into their free play. Hence Heidegger interprets the medial κρύπτεσθαι as a self-concealing that is "not a mere a self-closing but a sheltering [*Bergen*] in which the essential possibility of rising [*Aufgehen*] is preserved." (GA 7: 278/114) Heidegger writes this in a later essay on ἀλήθεια in Heraclitus' thought. With the course of the first beginning, this possibility of rising out of concealment began to be forgotten—as the search for the ultimate foundation of beings took its course. This forgetting is the forgetting of being (beyng), is *Seinsvergessenheit*, and this is why technology as a metaphysics of sheer presence is the manifestation and encrustation of the forgetting of being, which now means forgetting of concealment and sheltering.

According to Heidegger there is not only a "letting" at work in φύσις, but also a *stellen*. The positioning of φύσις is a "bringing-here-forth from itself of a letting persevere and a sheltering." (GA 79: 65/61) Φύσις "positions" in that it lets happen. Thus, its positioning does not show any of the forceful traits of the positioning of positionality. Heidegger argues that the original and, as it were, good positioning of being as φύσις makes possible θέσις which is human positioning and positing. Human positioning first of all means to produce something by the use of one's hands. Heidegger's example is a set of stone stairs as mentioned above. The stone itself is of φύσις, not in the sense that φύσις is the substance of the stone, but in the sense that the stone appears according to, or thanks to, a withdrawing *presencing*. There is an open presence, which itself withdraws, i.e., is not available, but which for that reason allows things like a bridge made of stone to appear *as a proper bridge that allows us to bridge the valley*. In positionality the bridge disappears and simply shows up as a means to the end of "I" getting across the valley. Human positioning, θέσις and τέχνη, is capable of forming the stone, of bringing something out, so that the stone changes its shape as well as the way it is present. The stairs made of stone present themselves differently than a block of rock. Heidegger argues that what human positioning does is that it can bring something to a stand and make it proper for use. Human θέσις forms a material not only according to human needs, but also in accordance with the material. Heidegger calls the positioning of φύσις "*zustellen*", which in English means "to deliver". What is of φύσις, is *zugestellt*, brought forth in the sense of "being delivered", or even in the sense of "being dedicated". What is of θέσις, is produced. That is to say that φύσις delivers and also lets beings persevere in such a way that their presencing is one of uniqueness. Beings appear of their own accord and are at the place where they can come into their own. In an epoch where θέσις and τέχνη collaborate with φύσις, things are of their own accord, truly unique, and precisely not of a circular replaceability.

The delivering of φύσις and subsequent human θέσις are for Heidegger also at the heart of the modern sciences. In *The Age of the World Picture* Heidegger quotes Newton's dictum "*hypotheses non fingo.*" (GA 5: 81/61) This means "I do not invent my hypotheses out of thin air." Scientific hypotheses are not ungrounded. Newton knew that his hypotheses stem from nature. Nevertheless, one of the fundamental shifts that occurs in modernity is the experiment. The experiment, Heidegger argues, does not wait for nature to show herself. Instead, the experiment functions by "anticipatory representation of the condition." (GA 5: 81/61). The experiment is the positing of anticipatory conditions *and* results. On Heidegger's understanding of history, the experiment becomes possible because being as positionality now spans open a realm where an anticipatory representation of conditions *and* results is possible. More precisely, the way in which modern man begins to respond to, or revolt against, being by beginning to posit the beingness of beings, is such that the experiment is necessitated in order to produce desired, i.e., posited, outcomes. The hypotheses for that certainly still come from nature herself, but the way in which the human being now sees nature is precisely as a resource positioned to deliver energy. We anticipate this because we posit being and because we take for granted that being is simply given and there; that there is nothing concealed about being.

Thus, technology is not the result of the experiment, but the experiment is the result of the shift in beyng. Operating with anticipatory representations is necessary in order to extract a desired result from nature. Hence nature has been turned into a "ground-plan" (GA 5: 81/61), as Heidegger says in *The Age of the World Picture*. In the technology essay Heidegger adds that "nature reports itself in some way or other that is identifiable through calculation and … it remains orderable as a system of information." (GA 7: 24/23) Nature can be turned into a ground-plan by reducing its beingness to information, i.e., collectable, quantifiable and qualifiable, in one word measurable, sense data. Science makes basic assumptions about a given phenomenon. Those basic assumptions science then proves by means of setting up an experiment and its parameters. The most important parameters are space and time. Every experiment has a certain, pre-determined and measured length of time and takes place within certain spatial conditions that are also carefully predetermined. Those wilfully set parameters serve to prove the very hypo-thesis that underlies the process of setting parameters. The revolution is, as Kant says, that the object must comply to the subject.[2] But this revolution does not happen out of thin air either.

In *The Danger* Heidegger writes that the positioning of positionality "is being itself" (GA 79: 65/62). Thus, positioning is always already a possibility of being. This finds expression in being as φύσις and its interplay with θέσις. But positioning as one of *beyng's* inherent sendings only comes into full force in the epoch of positionality. There are two main reasons for that: first, the forgetting of being, which means that beyng's self-concealing has been forgotten. Second, the way in which human beings begin to respond to positioning in modernity trigger positionality. This is why Heidegger says that Kant, the Newtonian, *echoes* the claim of being as φύσις, when he "pronounced the essence of being as "absolute position," as the positedness and positionhood of the object, i.e., of what presences." (GA 79: 66/63) Kant shows that there is always already mediation between subject and object. But he also determines that the transcendental ego, in order to get out into the world, must make the world follow its categories. Transcendental logic, and the positing of parameters for the sake of control this positing enables, is an echo of the

---

[2] Thus, as Houlgate notes, the Kantian position on nature is not too far away from Nietzsche who argues "that the world which we experience is made up of layer upon layer of human interpretation or fiction." (Houlgate 2009: 5)

relationship between being as φύσις and human θέσις. But this logic also depicts a response that reduces φύσις to human projection.

The positing that is at work in positionality discloses beings in such a way that access to simultaneous concealment is closed off. Hence, there is a double-concealment which plays out as dissimulation. Yet, this also indicates that even in positionality beyng's basic event, *Grundvorgang*, of *bergen* still takes place. *Bergen* always takes place in the simultaneity of its self-differentiation as *entbergen* and *verbergen*, the movement of ἀλήθεια. Positionality is then not a perversion of un-concealing and disclosing. Rather, positioning takes over unconcealing and assumes that beings can be positioned as utterly disclosed for an increase in efficiency at any time and anywhere. In so doing positionality disregards the simultaneous harbouring-sheltering, the concealing in every disclosure. Nevertheless, Heidegger also sees in our epoch the possibility for another mode of bringing-forth, for ποίησις, which is a bringing-forth in tune with ἀλήθεια (cf. GA 7: 21/20). Ποίησις would not have to work against the positing and setting of technology. For its very simultaneous origin in beyng together with the unconcealing of positionality, ποίησις is able to *turn* the current sendings of beyng around, i.e., ποίησις is able to respond to beyng differently. This other bringing-forth, which is not a forceful challenging takes place first and foremost in language and poetry. This is the case, as I shall argue in Part IV, because of the essential relation between death and language. We can already now see that ποίησις, for it respects harbouring as it brings forth, is near to death, has death as refuge as its source.

4 Danger and Salvation

In *The Danger* Heidegger writes that positionality is the completion of the forget-ting of being (GA 79: 51/49) Yet, there is no forgetting of being without forgetting ecstatic time, which is outside the time of technology that operates with time as a parameter. What I have referred to as the oblivion of time in Part I must hence also be at the heart of the danger of technology. In *The Turn* Heidegger writes: "But the danger is the *Nachstellen*, seeking revenge and imitating, that is the way in which being itself, in the mode of positionality, pursues with forgetting the safekeeping belonging to being." (GA 11: 119/43 *ta*) Thus, the danger is the forgetting of time, where time means clearing-concealing. The resentful imitation of beings, which forgets to shelter them, hence works by trying to eradicate time, and thereby also place and distance. Seasons no longer matter for growing vegetables. There are ski areas in the desert of Dubai and scientists at Harvard have plans to geo-engineer the global climate. The human subject assumes to be at the centre of everything and tries to imitate weather gods—entirely forgetful of the finite powers of humans. Resentful chasing imitation is *the* danger of positionality because it forgets conceal-ment (i.e., death). Therefore, imitation cannot interact with the world in a sheltering-harbouring manner, but must turn all things into a standing reserve, which is to stand ready for any subjectivistic fantasies.

Despite the seeming apocalyptic tone of many of his writings on technology Heidegger often quotes Hölderlin's *Patmos* on the possibility of salvation in danger. The possibility of salvation is even supposed to be equiprimordial with positionality: "The selfsame danger is, when it is as the danger, the saving power." (GA 11: 119/42) "Thus the coming to presence of technology harbors in itself what we least suspect, the possible arising of the saving power." (GA 7: 33/32) How could being itself come to its own rescue and what, if any, is the human being's role in this? The crucial term is *harbouring*. *Bergen* still takes place in positionality, but mortals must specifically think concealment in order to bring about again the wholesome poetic bringing forth. In my view, Heidegger's remarks on the possibility of a saving power from within positionality seem less arbitrary when we consider death as *Ge-Birg*. This is because the refuge of beyng is the place where that turning, that twisting free of beyng from its current prevalent dimension of occurring, takes place.

If the essence of technology is positionality and if positionality is a fate of being, then positionality holds its own saving grace because positionality is still *Entbergung*, unconcealment, and hence a response by mortals is still possible. In the ways of unconcealment of technology being even intensifies (cf. GA 7: 33/32) because its self-concealment takes over. In technology a disclosure is prevalent that covers over concealment. Ergo, concealment as dissimulation intensifies and this intensification of concealment—as paradoxical as it sounds—is the inherent saving grace. This is where death as refuge comes in. Beyng can *turn* at all because beyng itself can run forth toward death as its refuge. Human beings, in turn, can think beyng's movement because they are *mortal*, i.e., touched by death. Beyng has in death a place where it can rest and hide. But it is upon humans to help bring this about by becoming mortals. With reference to Lessing Heidegger understands salvation to mean: "to release [*lassen*] something into its own presencing." (GA 7: 152/148 *ta*) Hence the task of mortals is to release beyng itself into its essence and that means to think concealment. This releasing or letting-be *of* beyng is what grants free play to beings. This takes place precisely by thinking the withdrawing ground of beyng, by thinking the event as the unsupported and unsecured, as the self-eliciting centre, which frees beings, or things, into their richness and lets them arise and stand on their own accord. This thought at once also releases beyng from its self-dissimulation, which is its prevalent mode of concealing in technology.

Hence the human being is not passive for Heidegger, despite the talk of releasement and despite the claim that a supposed advent of beyng is abrupt.[3] The advent of beyng is abrupt insofar as we cannot decide for it. But the advent of beyng is not the arrival of some mystical entity that saves us at some measurable point in time. The arrival is a thinking stance that can come over us and it can come over us precisely through releasement, through renouncing beings and through waiting rather than willing. Thus, there are distinct stances human beings can take toward the sendings of beyng. These sendings neither call for hasty plans nor are humans condemned to stand. By lethargically and idly waiting for beyng to provide another

---

[3] See Marx (1983: 148) on this point.

realm. Releasement is a preparing comportment, responsible, humble, and aware of the limited powers of mortal existence. A sound mortal stance means to wait for the ripeness of the fruit instead of forcing the fruit to be ripe when it is not its season; to be mortal means to wait for rain instead of pumping gas into the atmosphere to generate rain; to be mortal means to wait for the immeasurable movements of the tides; to wait for the birth of the daughter, the coming-of-age of the son, the death of the parents. This does not mean to be passive. This rather means to let time *be*. But to become mortal, which is Heidegger's paradoxical task for humans, is not easily achieved. It is necessary to think death as refuge as the locus where being can twist free of its current prevalent occurring as positionality.

Chapter 14
Death as Shrine, Sanctuary and Law

Already in the early lecture course on *Fundamental Concepts of Metaphysics* Heidegger says that a proper "*mystery* [*Geheimnis*] is lacking in our Dasein." (GA 29/30: 244/163) What that mystery is, is perhaps not the right question. Instead, what Heidegger seems to have in mind with his continued reference to the *Geheimnis*, is a certain unavailability. In my view, death as refuge hence is, if not itself the secret of which Heidegger often speaks in later texts. Still, death is that which makes an openness for mystery possible, for death directly concerns us but is a source of uncertainty. The only realm that technology cannot control is death. This is why technology must work against death. In this chapter I shall first illuminate what Heidegger means when he says that we are to become mortals. Secondly, I shall explicate some of Heidegger's public remarks on the Holocaust he makes in the context of becoming mortals. In my view, his public remarks on the matter are more important and more accessible, as they are presented in a clearly argued series of talks that systematically engage with the question *what is today?*[1]

1 Becoming Mortals

The Thing contains a crucial passage regarding death as sanctuary. The passage also illustrates why I argue that that the sanctuary is crucial for establishing the fourfold:

> The mortals are human beings. They are called mortals because they can die. To die means to be capable of [*vermögen*] death as death. Only man dies. The animal perishes. It has death neither ahead of itself nor behind it. Death is the shrine of the nought, that is, of that which in every respect is never something that merely exists, but which nevertheless presences, even as the mystery of Being itself. As the shrine of the nought, death harbours within itself the sanctuary of being [*der Tod ist das Gebirg des Seins*]. As the shrine of

---

[1] Regarding Heidegger's notes on the Holocaust in the *Black Notebooks* see, for example, Trawny's (2016) recent paper.

© Springer Nature Switzerland AG 2021
J. A. Niederhauser, *Heidegger on Death and Being*,
https://doi.org/10.1007/978-3-030-51375-7_14

Nothing, death is the shelter of Being. We now call mortals "mortals"—not because their earthly life comes to an end, but because they are capable of death as death. Mortals are who they are, as mortals, present in the refuge of being. They are the presencing [*wesend*] relation to being as being. (GA 7: 180/176 *ta*)

That mortals are called mortals because they can die is, on the face of it, at best an existential truism. In the essay *The Danger* Heidegger makes the paradoxical assertion that we can only properly die, "when our essence is endeared [*mag* from *mögen*] to the essence of death." (GA 79: 56/53) Thus human beings apparently first need to become mortals. Yet, what Heidegger means by becoming mortal has nothing to do with a capacity for demising biologically. Hofstadter chose a poor and confusing translation of *vermögen*, when he translated it as "to be capable of." As argued in Parts I and II, *den Tod als Tod vermögen* means "to be open to death". Thus, what Heidegger aims for is a radically different hermeneutics of death. In what follows, I shall clarify what the expression "death *as* death" means as this allows me to provide a clearer understanding of the peculiar claim that we are not yet properly *dying*. Dying is a term of art for Heidegger. Dying does not mean to demise or deteriorate. It retains its sense from *Being and Time*. Thus, there is a sense of authenticity at work here as well as a requirement for "mortals" to *be* a certain way. To be open to death *as* death means to contemplate death as "shrine of the nought" and "refuge of being".

It is important to stress that Heidegger also argues that becoming mortal is tantamount to leaving behind the metaphysical representation of human beings as rational animals: "Rational living beings must first *become* mortals." (GA 7: 180/176) Heidegger's project of the "essential transformation" of the human being here undergoes a final alteration. Human beings are still to leave behind the metaphysical representation as rational animal. But now, instead of becoming authentic Dasein, human beings are to *become* "mortals." Mitchell thus rightly, I think, argues that Heidegger in his essays on the fourfold attempts a "reconception of existence" (Mitchell 2015: 231) with the demand of mortals to become properly mortal. But the thought of death as refuge and shrine is not restricted to the existential dimension of the human being, as death is of the dimension of beyng first.

Demske's (1970) and Scherer's (1979) readings of the passage in question both respectively rest on *Being and Time* as the default benchmark. Demske here sees a dialectical movement at work in Heidegger's thought. For Demske death is first shrine of the nought which is then sublated as refuge of being. Thus, Demske argues that death "moves quickly beyond the element of negativity to something positive." (Demske 1970: 164) More precisely, Demske claims that death quickly moves Dasein to the question of the meaning of being, in purely existential-ontological terms. In my view, this reading is problematic for two reasons. First, this is an existential-ontological perspective and thus this reading neglects the significance of being-historical thinking out of the event. For Demske Dasein and its understanding of being are still at the centre. Second, Demske assumes a dialectical movement which is not at all how Heidegger's thought moves. The fourfold, for example, does not sublate positionality. In fact, there can be no fourfold without positionality. As soon as positionality no longer is also the fourfold will have become impossible.

This will become clearer when I further explicate the fourfold at the end of this part and in Part IV. Heidegger's thinking is rather one of simultaneity, as most prominently exemplified in ἀλήθεια. Death is *at once* shrine and refuge. Death can only be beyng's hiding place, if death also safeguards the nothing and thereby makes sure there is *nothing* around beyng to support it. Scherer, in turn, argues along similar lines as my overall argument that death is not just subsidiary but in fact central to Heidegger's question: the question of being (cf. Scherer 1979: 194). Nonetheless, Scherer does not develop the genuine other approach of Heidegger's later philosophy and also makes recourse to *Being and Time*. Scherer argues that by running forth toward death as refuge, angst kicks in and this angst brings before being. Yet, Heidegger here has in mind something else entirely. I mention these older readings of this crucial passage precisely because they show the necessity to take seriously Heidegger's writings on the *Ereignis* in order to make sense of what is at stake in his thought "after" the turn. What, then, is at stake in the claim that mortals are to become mortals and that death is refuge and shrine?

It is one of the strengths of Mitchell's study of the fourfold to have considered Heidegger's late philosophy in its own right and from the perspective of the event. Nevertheless, I disagree when Mitchell claims that we are never really to become mortals, but that we are always only trying to be properly mortal. Death is, claims Mitchell, a medium and "[t]o be in a medium is to be always arriving, otherwise one would be trapped in a container" (Mitchell 2015: 230). Note that this is a rather representational account of "medium" and not on the level of thinking. Consequently, when Heidegger says that we must first *become* mortals, he does not mean, Mitchell claims, "a movement from one state into another. Rather this "movement" of becoming is no movement at all—it is instead a way of being, a being "not yet" mortal and "no longer" human, a way of being the between (*das Zwischen*). In this sense, no one dies in the sense of *sterben*, for no one is among the mortals." (Mitchell 2015: 231) First of all, Heidegger, especially in his post-war philosophy of technology, does not at all suggest that humans are not to be human any longer! The complete and utter opposite is the case. It is very important to stress that these attempts to read into Heidegger some sort of anti-human Derrideanism could not be further from Heidegger. As pointed out above, Heidegger fears that humans are about to lose their essence! Hence to be mortal means nothing but being human. I shall expand on this in Part IV when I turn to Heidegger's notion of the *homo humanus*, which he develops in the *Letter on Humanism*. For now it may suffice to point out that Heidegger sees the distinct possibility and even necessity for the human being to become *human* and leave behind entirely the metaphysical representations of man as rational *animal*. Note that Mitchell makes his claims in order to sanitise Heidegger's remarks on the Holocaust and in order to make Heidegger adhere to post-modern orthodoxy. In *The Danger* Heidegger appears to be saying that those who died in the death camps did not properly die. I shall address this issue below.

Mitchell also denies the possibility of becoming truly mortal because this would mean to move from the "state" of the rational animal to the "state" of mortals. Mitchell seems to understand the "not-yet" as a performative claim about the process-like dynamism of *becoming mortals*. Mortals are never quite what they are, they are *always* "not yet mortal," always striving to be mortals. Mitchell wants to avoid an understanding of "being mortal" as a state, which is a fair point. This is certainly not what Heidegger would have in mind. But if one is always "not-yet" something, is one not, even if always "arriving" whatever that may be, in the very "state" of "always arriving?" In the state of "the between", of a certain "twilight". But who says that "to *be*" automatically entails a represented state? Thus, I also understand Heidegger to make a performative claim about the being of mortals when he speaks of humans *becoming mortals*. Yet, I understand this radically differently insofar as I think that what this means is to welcome death into existence. This is Heidegger's way of saying that we welcome a mystery into our existence—the mystery of beyng's abyss. A mystery we cannot hope to solve, but which as such is a source of meaning. Understanding Heidegger here in this way also maintains a sense of arrival. Death as sanctuary points to the stance mortals take, a stance of thinking as I described in Part II, rather than a represented, reified state. Of course, this does not mean that once this has been achieved by a community of mortals that this community will once and for all have welcomed death into its existence *qua* state. Instead, this welcoming needs to take place *again and again* and it is this welcoming that lets humans become mortals.

In my view, becoming mortals in a practical sense means to become and appreciate who human beings *are*. This becoming is a task that every community of mortals has to accept in order to provide a good death. Hence there is a certain ethos in the fourfold, an ethos that also invites us to think after what world means for mortal beings. If mortals are properly mortals, then they encounter the fourfold: "When we say mortals, we are then thinking of the other three along with them by way of the simple oneness of the four [i.e. gods, sky, earth, mortals]." (GA 7: 180/177) "Mortals" is then not a represented state, but a way of being and it is a communal way of being that casts mortals into a profound interrelated web of meaning: the proper world of the fourfold where being is present in things. The task of mortals is not to establish a self-sustaining foundation for beings. But to find a ground that gives constancy to a community for a certain time. The fourfold comes about through mortal thinking and thinking articulates itself most prominently in poetry.

There is an important passage in *What is Called Thinking?* on the meaning of "mortal thinking." It reads:

> Wenn ein Denken es vermöchte, das, was *je und je* zu denken gibt, in sein eigenes Wesen zu verabschieden, dann wäre solches Denken der höchste Dank der Sterblichen. (GA 8: 151 *me*)
>
> If thinking could wish farewell and let go toward its own essence that which *again and again* gives pause and invites us to think, then such thinking would be the highest thanking of mortals.

This refers to what I argued in Part II on grounding. Grounding is a simultaneous welcoming and wishing farewell. Mortal thinking responds to beyng as the withdrawing ground that first unsettles us and so summons us to think. Heidegger here points out that mortal thinking is most grateful when it recognises and responds to the respective epoch of beyng. *Verabschieden*, wishing farewell, is a term of art for Heidegger. Parting, *Abschied* in German, does not mean loss for him (cf. GA 70:

24). Instead, "[i]n parting concealment itself begins and only now can unconceal-ment become a gift" (GA 70: 26).[2] In this sense the *Ab-schied*, is the beginning of the *Unter-schied*, of the differentiation of concealment and unconcealment, a move-ment gathered in death as shrine of the nought and refuge of being: "Thinking lives by an elective affinity with death." (GA 79: 114/107) Heidegger says this precisely in relation to "the leaps of thinking into its abyss." (GA 79: 114/106) Mortal think-ing can think inceptively, which means to think that differentiation to set forth another beginning. Mortal thinking is mindful of the darkness that makes it possible and always guides it: "Mortal thinking must let itself down into the dark depths of the well if it is to see the stars by day." (GA 79: 93/89) I understand this reference to Thales as saying that mortal thinking wishes farewell to the familiar, to beings, and lets itself fall into the unsupported abyss, not in order to lose itself, but in order to gain the perspective for the star, i.e., the essential, self-eliciting centre. Such a thinking also does not try to dominate or control the world.

The task of human beings, then, is to enter into a relationship with beyng's self-concealment. Contemplating death is necessary because, as Mitchell rightly points out, "[c]oncealment keeps disclosure from being concealed!" (Mitchell 2015: 238) In technology being conceals other ways of disclosure, it closes off other dimen-sions. But, as Mitchell says, if mortals think concealment then other dimensions of beyng come to light as other ways of disclosing world. Mitchell hence writes: "The secret of being is the announcement of concealment, an announcement that keeps concealment from falling into oblivion." (ibid.: 238) And via death mortals appreci-ate being in its withdrawal, they know that withdrawal and being-away from their death. Heidegger argues that "[d]eath, as the shrine of nothing, harbors in itself what essences of being." (GA 79:18/17) A shrine harbours what is holy. The nothing is the name Heidegger gives to the way in which being essentially occurs: "Death is the shrine of the nothing, namely of that which in all respects is never some mere being, but nonetheless essences namely as *being itself*." (GA 79:18/17 *me*) As Heidegger puts it elsewhere, "[b]eing itself nihilates insofar as it protects and keeps safe and conceals." (GA 70: 49)[3] To say that being occurs as nothingness is another way of saying that its fundamental process is self-concealment and death allows for being's self-concealing. Concealment is the way in which being discloses itself. Being is not something given that subsequently withdraws. Instead, being occurs and discloses itself as concealing *and* withdrawing (cf. GA 45: 210). Concealment and keeping safe is the process of giving things into the "Open" or the "clearing." In the other beginning being's self-concealment is specifically thought and this is mor-tal thinking. In fact, what Heidegger is saying here is that humans can distinguish between *what is* and *what is not* because they are touched by death which is at once "refuge of being" and "shrine of nothingness". Death as refuge or sanctuary of being is where being withdraws into. As shrine of nothingness death protects the nought against the overreaching of being. Hence the schism between being and nothing remains pure and foundational.

---

[2] "Im Abschied fängt die Verbergung selbst an und Entbergung kann jetzt erst ein Geschenk sein"

[3] "Das Sein selbst nichtet, indem es wahrt und verwahrt und verbirgt."

Death as shrine and sanctuary therefore regulate the clearing concealment, *lichtende Verbergung*, of beyng. Death here shows itself as the ultimate source of Heidegger's conception of beyng. Death is most fundamental to it, death is at the heart of the matter because death is the utterly inaccessible, that which *always already turns away*. Death is not mediator between nothingness and being, but death is as shrine and as refuge also the "*Ge-setz* [law]" (cf. GA 5: 304/228). That is, the law of the movement of concealment and unconcealment. Hence Heidegger says that death *is* beyng in *Über den Anfang*. Death is the ultimate law of the truth of beyng and all that that entails. Human beings must hence get profoundly involved with their mortality and take it seriously, if they are to delve into the history of beyng. As Heidegger says in *The Principle of Reason*:

> we dwell in proximity to death, which as the most radical possibility of existence is open to [*vermag*] bringing what is most elevated to the clearing and lighting of being and its truth. Death is the as yet unthought standard of measure [*Maßgabe*] of the unfathomable [*Unermeßlichen*; literally the immeasurable], which means, of the most elevated play, in which humans are engaged in on earth, a play in which they are at stake. (GA 10: 167/112[4] *ta*)

One cannot underestimate what Heidegger is saying here. Taking into account what I have argued on the "un-pre-thinkable" or the "immemorial" in Part II, and how Heidegger asks the few and rare to carry out being-toward-death in such a manner that the "un-pre-thinkable" becomes thinkable, Heidegger here says that death is the measure of that which cannot be measured, death is the measure of the cosmic play in which human beings are suffering participants. He also says that death has remained unthought as that very measure. This is to say that up until the thought of the event, which brings into focus the history of being and the history of loss, death has remained unthought. But once death as "being-away", as "*Ge-Birg*", as echo of non-availability, as the other side of being, as "*Ge-setz*" comes into view the play can be thought, where the play is another name for the "un-pre-thinkable" to which human beings belong. Heidegger here thus says that up until the thinking of the event had not come into view, that play was only ever covered over—*un-pre-thinkable*. But now, in the other beginning, concealment and hence that very realm called *Ereignis* come into focus thanks to which this "elevated play" becomes transparent. Therefore, the other beginning would no longer be a history of loss of concealment. The fourfold, as I shall aim to show in the last chapter of this part, is the way in which mortals enter into that play knowing that they are stake. The fourfold is the thoughtful response to that play.

In sum, becoming truly mortal is the task Heidegger sees for humans of the current epoch of *Gestell*, which is also an epoch of transition. Note that this is not an absolute historical claim. Heidegger, in my view, does not claim that up until his writings "becoming mortal" had been forfeited. Nor does Heidegger argue for humans to become "mortals" for all future. Rather, this is a call for humans now in the epoch of the disappearance of the divine and of the extreme powers of *Gestell*. For it is in being mindful of our mortal finitude that we are mindful also of our

---

[4] Lilly translation.

limitations and incapacity to control everything that is. Becoming mortal, of course, does not mean to "actualise" or make accessible the utterly inaccessible that is death. Instead, becoming mortals means just this: to accept that death is utterly inaccessible, that there is something that does remain utterly inaccessible and uncontrollable in the first place. Becoming mortal means to accept that not all can be controlled precisely because it is death as the "immeasurable, unfathomable"—in the age which assumes that only what is measurable is real—is the only true measure for mortals. That is to say, mortals *cannot* measure with absolute certainty what is supposed to be real. Instead, mortals are always already faced only with one certainty: the uncertainty of the hour of their death.

2   On the Holocaust

What I try to say here is not to defend Heidegger's politics. It is simply the attempt to read significant passages on death and the Holocaust, which Heidegger undeniably and publicly engaged with in a manner that is thought from within the *Ereignis*. Perhaps this may allow us to see what it is that we can learn from the thought rather than the thinker himself. None of what I say here claims to be a full account of the problem of Heidegger's alleged anti-semitism, his involvement with the NSDAP or his politics and I cannot do this problem justice here. It is an attempt to show the historical relationship of *Gestell*, *Geviert*, and the Holocaust. What this episode in Heidegger's life reveals is also that there is something uncanny and strange about this age, and about a thinker who delves into the abyss, death and meontology as deeply as Heidegger did.[5]

As just outlined, Heidegger says we are to become mortals. We are proper mortals, "when our essence is endeared [*mag* from *mögen*] to the essence of death." (GA 79: 56/53) One could hence understand the formula *Den Tod als Tod vermögen* as a loving relationship with one's mortality, a more profound reformulation of the *memento mori*. More profound because it does not just stress our mortal finitude, but reaches down into the depths of an as yet unseen history, which, nevertheless, is the route we are on. Note, however, that Heidegger makes this remark in context of addressing the horror of Auschwitz. Heidegger even says that we are not yet properly mortal, despite the "innumerable and measureless suffering." (GA 79: 57/54)

---

[5]Elliot R. Wolfson's (2018) recent book on Heidegger's Nazism is a welcome addition to Heidegger's engagement with the Nazi movement. Wolfson shows that Heidegger's anti-semitism is not biological, that Heidegger is even critical of the Nazi movement for its racism. But Wolfson also stresses that Heidegger's thought in this period is strange and uncanny, as uncanny as our very epoch and its signs. Moreover, if I understand Wolfson correctly, then Heidegger not only suspects Jewish people to be extremely organised in the sense of *Ge-stell*, but, and this is the crux, that Heidegger's anti-semitism is also mostly coined by his forgetting of the Jewish people. This, Wolfson points out, is the striking aspect of Heidegger's anti-semitism, as Heidegger's thought is centred around forgetting and concealment, but he himself forgets those who are forgotten by history.

Heidegger also apparently says that the victims of the camps did not die properly because they do not "carry out [*austragen*] death in its essence." (GA 79: 56/53) Does he deny the mortality of the victims? Does he even say that they were *essentially* incapable of dying a proper death?

There seems to be an unsettling echo of the authenticity-inauthenticity distinction here. If that were the case, then would indeed be saying that the Jewish prisoners of the camps are, at best, inauthentically towards their death. A sympathetic reading should, however, point out that that there can hardly be a good death in the death camps. The death in the camps is manufactured. In the language of *Being and Time* this would mean that the ownmost was taken away from them. But manufactured death also implies something else. Note that Heidegger in *The Danger* also says that there are "horribly undying [*ungestorben*] deaths all about" (GA 79: 56/54 *ta*) in the camps. This seems to imply that death is already of τέχνη and no longer their own death. That this is done "inconspicuously," as Heidegger strangely puts it, then means that we can hardly see how the unspeakable happens in the epoch technology: death, the ownmost, can now be taken away from human beings so that humans can be produced as dead bodies. This is the most fundamental shift that occurs and the reason we now need to appreciate our mortality in a more profound way than, e.g., Christianity did. When Faye argues that Heidegger allegedly says the victims of the Holocaust were *essentially*—understood in the metaphysical sense— *incapable* of dying, then he rather distorts what Heidegger means by *Wesen* and *vermögen* (cf. Faye 2009: 304ff). Faye reads Heidegger's threefold repetition of the question "Are they dying?" as a clear indication that Heidegger means to say that Jews were not properly dying because they are incapable of doing so according to their *essentia*. Note, however that Heidegger does not at all make a claim about the *essentia* of the victims. Note, moreover, that Heidegger does not answer his threefold repetition of the question whether they die with a definite yes. Instead, Heidegger here seems to tell us that we should not confuse the current demise of the masses with the *good* death he has in mind and which is possible in the fourfold.[6] Nevertheless, the talk of the oblivion and abandonment of beyng can all too easily be understood, and with some justification, as denying the responsibility of the perpetrators of the Holocaust. But the *responses* of human beings to the current "sendings" of beyng are crucial and thus there is room for responsibility because the way in which mortals respond is fundamental.

One of Heidegger's strangest claims is admittedly his talk of the essential sameness of agriculture food production and the production of dead bodies in the death camps. He writes that what enables that gruesome production of dead bodies is the same realm that makes possible industrial food production.[7] This does not deny the uniqueness of the Holocaust but points out its cruelty precisely by trying to show how it is of its age. Pattison hence argues that Heidegger sees a common horizon for

---

[6]Trawny (cf. 2003: 167ff) argues along similar lines and has also pointed out the vicinity of Heidegger's and Arendt's account of the holocaust.

[7] See also Weston (2016: 282).

industrial agriculture and the Holocaust (cf. Pattison 2016: 12). Thus, Pattison, with reference to Safranski, points out that Heidegger is not too far from Adorno's position. This is not to say that there are not different human motivations at work in agriculture and the Holocaust respectively. Nor is this to say that agricultural food production and the Holocaust are perfectly identical. But what *first* enables the machines of the former is also what enables the machines and calculation and rationalisation of the latter. However, one could level the criticism against Heidegger that the bodies of the victims are hardly *produced*. They are not part of an economy of production and consumption. Nor are these bodies sacrificed on the altar of a symbolic economy. They were exterminated like pathogen, stripped from their dignity. Then again this was done to them precisely for the sake of *producing* the fantasised perfect and pure body of the German "*Volk*." True, the bodies of the victims were not produced for consumption. But for Heidegger *herstellen* does not only mean "to produce" in that economic sense, but also to position and set something up—even if that setting up goes against the unique way of being of the beings in question. In the case of the Holocaust, production worked against the victims' mortality which, for Heidegger, is what makes them human in the first place.

In *Building Dwelling Thinking* Heidegger points out what is necessary in our epoch of technological production and the takeover of technology in all areas of existence: "To guide mortals into the essence of death in no way means to make death, as empty nothing, the goal." (GA 7: 152f/148f *ta*) Rather, the goal is, for there to be "a good death." (ibid.) In the fourfold an ethos emerges, an ethos of providing places and dwelling grounds that allow for there to be a good death. The machinic destruction of humans in extermination camps cannot by any stretch of the imagination be considered a good death. Heidegger (cf. GA 79: 56/54) explicitly speaks of these deaths as "undying" and "horrible." In positionality, there can be no good death because there is no sheltering-harbouring. Still, this means that the victims of the Holocaust did not die a proper death. Yet, this is the worst crime that could have been done to them and has nothing whatsoever to do with their supposed metaphysical "essence," as Faye insinuates. Thus, we see that Heidegger at the time of working on the fourfold wishes to provide a basis for there to be a good death. The fourfold, then, is Heidegger's response to the all-pervasive claim of positionality.

Chapter 15
The Fourfold

The fourfold, that peculiar gathering of gods and mortals, earth and sky, is Heidegger's response to positionality.[1] More precisely, the fourfold is his articulation of a possibility of world that is outside of the demands of positionality. The question is how positionality and the fourfold relate to each other. In what follows I shall provide an interpretation of the fourfold as response to the currently prevalent fate of being as positionality. The fourfold is crucial not just as a response to the dimensionality of technology, but as the world fit for humans and as such the fourfold is intimately related to Heidegger's understanding of language. I introduce the fourfold as a bridge that leads from the dimension of machines to the world of humans. Death, as we shall see, or rather "a good death", is central to the fourfold precisely because in the fourfold mortals are mindful of concealment in all disclosure. Where though does the fourfold stand with regards to positionality?

One might be inclined to assume the fourfold stands in opposition to positionality. Amongst others Markus Porsche-Ludwig argues that positionality is "the opponent of the fourfold." (Porsche-Ludwig 2009: 238).[2] Yet, Heidegger does not think in opposites or in any way dialectically. There is not a dichotomy of the two, the one does not stand against the other as diametrically opposed. Nor are they perfectly separated. Holger Schmid hence argues that positionality is the self-obstruction of the world as *fourfold* (cf. Schmid 2014: 214). Instead of asking how to get rid of positionality, as a reading such as that of Porsche-Ludwig implies, the question rather is, how we can get over positionality from within so that the fourfold shows itself and mortals can encounter can the fourfold. "World [*fourfold*] and *Ge-Stell* are the same," Heidegger says (GA 79: 52/49 *ta*). While they are not identical, their

---

[1] I would like to show my gratitude to the organiser of the *Collegium Phenomenologicum* 2017, Bret Davis, who put together a tremendous curriculum that treated Heidegger's writings on the fourfold in great detail. I remain grateful not only to him and all participants of the Collegium that year, but also and especially to Daniela Vallega-Neu and Alejandro Vallega who taught a course on the fourfold that helped me understand these pivotal texts by Heidegger.

[2] My translation.

© Springer Nature Switzerland AG 2021
J. A. Niederhauser, *Heidegger on Death and Being*,
https://doi.org/10.1007/978-3-030-51375-7_15

sameness, i.e., their relatedness, is precisely what allows for an exit from positionality, put differently, their sameness allows for overturning the prevalence of positionality in favour of the fourfold. They are the "same", for they are both of sendings of being. It is important also to note that the essays on the fourfold do not call for how the world should be nor for a return to some idealised past. In my view, they are rather remembrances of what has been and hence of a future that could be. Hence the stance of "waiting" is so crucial for Heidegger in these texts. Waiting for the return of the divine, waiting for grace. But this waiting occurs out of the deep memory of who we are.

As outlined in Chap. 11, Heidegger does not argue for luddism. He rather asks us to confront technology. Hans Ruin therefore points out that this confrontation serves "to develop an experience of technological modernity as "destiny", that is, as a "sending" (*Schicksal, Schickung*) of being within which we stand." (Ruin 2010: 190) Such an experience of confrontation might let us see another possibility of world, which Heidegger calls fourfold. In the fourfold human beings are not in every capacity functionaries of a manipulative technology that seeks to organise and order the planet in such a way that everything and everyone becomes a predictably secured standing reserve turning aimlessly around itself. In the fourfold humans are, instead, *mortals*. That is to say, they cherish their death as the refuge and sanctuary of beyng, as the inaccessible origin of beyng's abundance, that is, of meaning beyond calculation, meaning that arises and occurs only out of what cannot be and is not controlled or manipulated. Why the fourfold is the gathering of earth and sky, mortals and gods is Heidegger's term for proper world at the time of his preoccupation with technology is the question I shall answer here. The world as fourfold is not a static receptacle. Hence Heidegger speaks of the "world's worlding [*Welten*]" (GA 7: 91/177). The fourfold *worlds* (*weltet*) and we can always only encounter the fourfold, but we can never possess or control it. In this chapter and concluding in Part IV, I explicate in more detail why Heidegger sees death at the heart of bringing about the fourfold and thus at the heart of encountering a world not ruled by positionality. In my view there are at least three interrelated ways for encountering the fourfold. First, by a thinking through of death as described in Part II and III. Second, in more practical terms the fourfold comes about by a thoughtful welcoming of death. The latter is a communal effort. A third way is by language itself and poetry. I shall describe that possibility in Part IV.

Heidegger underlines the importance of death for the fourfold when he ends the essay *The Thing* as follows: "Men alone, as mortals, by dwelling attain [*erlangen*] to the world as world" (GA 7: 184/180). As mortals they are mindful of their limitations, they do not seek total control and dominion over the earth, and as such mortals attain, *erlangen*, the fourfold where they find a dwelling ground. Still, the fourfold does not annihilate positionality, but lets us encounter world in a different way in the age of positionality. In what follows I shall, first, explicate the meaning of "the thing" in the fourfold and in how far being lights up in the thing. Second, I look at divinities in the fourfold, as they are present in a withdrawn sense and point to the limitation of mortals. I have already begun to describe the role of mortals and will further explicate their role in Part IV. I will mention the regions of sky and earth where this helps determine the worlding of the fourfold better. I shall complete my reading of the fourfold in Part IV. As we shall see, language for its essential relation with death plays a pivotal role for the constitution of the fourfold.

I understand the later essays on the fourfold as critical extensions of the *Artwork* essay and his Heidegger's mentioning of a previous fourfold-structure in *Contributions*. In the former Heidegger argues that the artwork spans open a historical world for a people, for the artwork embodies the strife of earth (as that which self-conceals as it gives) and world (the self-opening openness). In the latter Heidegger places the event at the centre and as the centre of the four regions of human being, gods, world, and earth (cf. GA 65: 310/246). This indicates precisely that the sheer abundance and true diversity of the world does not emerge out of the event, but that through a thinking of the self-eliciting centre that abundance arises of its *own* accord. This tells us that and how beings come into their own. The later fourfold is, however, not restricted to the high and fine arts or the thinking leap into the abyss. There is a distinct practical ethos involved that not only lets mortals encounter the fourfold, but also requires them to form and sustain a community of mortals.

1   The Fourfold and the Thing

Heidegger describes the fourfold as a mirror-play of its four regions complementing each other. Each of the four regions takes part in all other regions, yet all retain their ownness and so preserve difference. Each region, nevertheless, requires all other regions and mirrors each region in its own way. Once we say mortals, we also say divinities or gods, because mortals require gods, the immortals, for their guidance. Gods flee when mortals forget their mortality and fall for the hubris to plan and organise the planet. The four are not poles because this would mean they are opposites. The sky is not the limitless and ever-expanding universe of modern astronomy and physics, but the unavailable limit that keeps mortals in check. The sky also sends mortals the inconspicuous hints of the weather that show mortals their belonging to the world and earth. Once we say mortals, we also say sky because mortals live underneath the sky. Once we say sky, we also say earth, because the sky *qua* Open only makes sense in relation to the earth as that which conceals—and the earth is where mortals dwell underneath the sky. The earth is that which gives by concealing and sheltering, the sky opens this up. The sky receives that which the earth gives. The divinities are those who enable the encounter with the divine. The divinities remind mortals of their finitude. Mortals protect the fourfold, when they are thoughtful of death as the gathering of concealment.

Not only do the regions partake in one another, they also enrich one another. Mirror-play does not refer to reflection. It is rather to indicate that no region can be without the other four regions. Heidegger writes: "By a *primal* oneness the four—earth and sky, divinities and mortals—belong together in one." (GA 7: 151/147) This primal oneness is not an ultimate foundation from which the fourfold emerges. Instead, this primal oneness is the inherent interrelation of the four regions. There is in the fourfold a balance, an equilibrium of all four poles. It is up to mortals to uphold that balance. Mortals do not attempt to become gods. Mortals dwell on the earth as that which gives because it self-withdraws, and they dwell under the sky as that which is a natural limit and gives orientation. The equilibrium is certainly reminiscent of a passage from Hölderlin's hymn *The Rhine* that reads: "Then gods and mortals celebrate their nuptials, / All the living celebrate, / And Fate for a while / Is levelled out, suspended [*ausgeglichen*]." (Hölderlin 1994: 441) Just as for Hölderlin, also for Heidegger the fragility of the fourfold holds true. The fourfold only ever stays or lights up for a while. The fourfold is neither a receptacle we enter into nor is it a state that we can reach and maintain. Instead, the fourfold is the other, forgotten possibility that appears when positionality fractures. That very fracture happens when its illusion of perfect disclosure and presence wanes. Hence again when mortals respond to their death as the source of all non-availability and non-controllability. All of a sudden then are there again distance, irritation, unplanned and unforeseen events. Where positionality is unbound in its will to dominate and control, the fourfold is the limit to that will to domination, but for that very limit and simplicity the fourfold is all the richer. Hence the simplest thing right before us, like a tree, a jug, a well, a simple stone bridge, invite us to be gathered in a different manner. Mitchell therefore argues that the fourfold is first and foremost "a thinking of things." (Mitchell 2010: 208) This is because what gathers us in the first place to consider the possibility of the fourfold is a simple thing like a jug or a stone bridge. Not something of the standing reserve, not something that is entirely dedistanced and available on flat digital screens or the Internet. Or to use Heidegger's own examples of the TV and the radio and their programmes, which seem to be closer to us than what is straight in front of us and where we actually are.

The thing is not something exchangeable and interchangeable, something to use and consume. Nor is the thing something de-distanced and indifferently available as is the standing reserve. Things in the fourfold are, as Mitchell puts it, "gathering points" (Mitchell 2010: 208) of the world and its four regions. Even though all kinds of "things" seem to be nearer to us than ever before, there is no true closeness left with them, as Heidegger writes in *The Thing*. He gives the example of the "germination and growth of plants which remained hidden throughout the seasons" (GA 7: 167/163). Today we can watch the plant grow in fast motion, regardless of the seasons, we can watch the plant grow at any place, but none of that means that we understand the plant any better in the sense of what it means to be a plant, how to heed plants and the earth so that they are not destroyed. Nor are we any closer to the plant itself. It might well be, as Heidegger implies, that we are further removed from the earth than before. Just as we are further removed from history, even though we can watch just about anything from any previous civilisation and today we can even by the use of CGI let arise all imagined worlds of the past as if they stood right in front of us. Thus, here we learn something else that is crucial about the workings of positionality. By using time and space as parameters, positionality works to discover and bring us closer to everything that was so distant it seemed impossible to reach. But a genuine nearness, which also always requires a strangeness, distance and mystery is lost. How we find a genuine nearness again, is the question of the fourfold essays.

As strange as it seems, what is at stake in order to find genuine nearness is precisely concealment. We need to appreciate concealment, non-availability, withdrawal, and closure in order to see again what is right in front of us. By scientific disclosure, by further moving down into the dimensions of subatomic or neuronal structures we discover more and more data that support the relevant posited hypothesis. By having instant access not just to what happens somewhere far removed, but now also to what other worlds might have looked like, we seem to learn what is important. But we drown in information and lose a sense of where we are. There is also a certain historylessness about an epoch that can at will reproduce imagined worlds of the past, if history is that which moves by self-concealments and withdrawals and if history is that which is directed towards the future, not the past. What CGI and its products reveal is not so much made possible by them, but rather CGI reveals that our epoch as the epoch of technology is precisely what Heidegger calls the "steadily rotating recurrence of the same" (GA 8: 112/109). The future, if anything, is a dystopia. But those imagined dystopian futures very often have nostalgic touches of the 1980s. Think, for example, of the latest sequel of the film *Blade Runner*. The future no longer appears to be the possibility of open horizons, mysterious at least, but frozen in a rotating repetition of the ever-same that is heralded every few months as "new" and "improved" and "optimised". Everything seems close to us, readily available, even black holes now flicker on the screens in our living rooms, but not a simple thing lights up in its essence and gathers us. Still, the rotating repetition already stands revealed and as it is no longer concealed, another dimensionality, another time of a space becomes possible. That other time of a space, that *place*, is the fourfold where concealment and limitations are cherished. Note that the fourfold is not utopia and that positionality is not a dystopia. There is in both utopias and dystopias a fear of limitations and finitude. Dystopias imagine the future to be either total and absolute destruction of everything or of a near-perfect unavoidable surveillance state. Utopias imagine futures that know no boundaries regarding energy and availability of resources. With Heidegger we are reminded of our limitations, our finitude, and hence also of the fragility of our worlds.

In the fourfold mortals do not deal with the appearances and representations of positionality. Rather, the thing *in itself* is salvaged and appreciated in the encounter of the fourfold precisely because a thinking of self-concealment, a thinking that is *of* death, sets into motion the mirror-play. The thing is not wilfully positioned to stand ready as standing reserve. Rather, the thing is left alone and this *letting* is based on appreciating self-concealment. However, the thing in the fourfold, for example a bridge, is not present *in itself* understood in a metaphysical sense. The bridge is not accessible in its substance. There is no substance at all. Rather, the bridge is a tempo-spatial occurrence of its own accord that is not cut off from its surroundings but entirely embedded in them, *eingelassen*. The nearness that occurs with an encounter of a proper thing is different from representation. In *What is called Thinking?* Heidegger gives the simple example of a tree that stands before and that we introduce ourselves to. We relate to the tree radically differently than both modern metaphysics, psychology and neurology assume. Heidegger also and crucially points out that we can wrest free from these now ordinary abstractions of representational, mental content, which we have become so accustomed to. So accustomed in fact that neurology with its machines only repeats what Schopenhauer wrote two-hundred years ago on the first page of his magnum opus: "the world is my representation." If we wrest ourselves free from those abstractions that interfere with our relationship with the world, we do make a leap, Heidegger says, but we do not leap into an utter abyss! Rather we leap "onto some firm soil. Some? No! But on that soil upon which we live and die, if we are honest with ourselves." (GA 8: 44/41) What Heidegger argues for here is not some naïve realism or any realism at all for that matter, if realism simply means that all that exists is what it means to exist. The proper things Heidegger has in mind do not just fall from the heavens as (new) realism assumes. Instead, in Heidegger's example here we encounter the tree insofar as the tree and we are always already in a relationship with each other. In this sense, Heidegger says, "the tree and we *are*." (GA 8: 44/41) That is to say, the tree stands there and it is insofar as it grows from the earth as that which gives by sheltering and withdrawing. The tree is left alone but also the tree only *is* insofar as we *are*. The tree is not just given, but fully comes to be when we are introduced to the tree and when the tree introduces itself to us. We disclose the tree, but this disclosure is only taking place insofar as the tree "be-things" us, *uns be-Dingt*, as Heidegger strangely puts it in *The Thing* (GA 7: 182/179). Only in a relationship that is characterised by a released stance on our behalf and where we realise that we are "conditioned" by the tree, i.e., that our existence is possible only on the earth and the very soil we stand and die on, can there be *being*. Hence the concealment that needs to be thought is not just the concealment that positionality brings with it, but also the concealment that comes from the abstractions of modern theory. Naïve or new realism is one of them, as it abstracts things as just being there, as simply existing. But the thing is not without us and we are not without the thing. Most importantly though, Heidegger calls for us to be honest to ourselves about something very specific. That despite all the wonders and achievements of technology, we are mortal beings, we will die— inevitably. This simple, but tragic insight into the unresolvable tension at the heart of existence, Heidegger thinks, could free us from the abstractions of modernity, the boredom and silliness that come with it (and that Hegel speaks of in the introduction to the *Phenomenology of Spirit*), and bring us into a relationship with things in such a manner that simplicity and releasement release us into the experience of another possibility of world, a world proper for humans. We persist or stand through, *durch-stehen*, spaces rather than representing something in our minds.

Dreyfus hence rightly points out that mortals are in fact free to change their relationship with things "whenever we find ourselves gathered by things rather than controlling them." (Dreyfus 2009: 57) Thus, mortals must first receive this possibility. Mortals are receivers rather than enforcers. In this receivership mortals are open to the Holy, to ceremony and festivity. To be gathered by the thing in its exuberant simplicity—where a jug lets us encounter the earth thanks to which we live and the gods that help guide our ways—means to be gathered by being's simplicity itself. Death as sanctuary and shrine retains the self-concealment for the clearing of the fourfold where things light up and gather us. The opposite is the case in positionality: "Ordering the standing reserve, positionality allows unconcealment and its essence to lapse into full forgetting." (GA 79: 52/50) In positionality things are dilapidated, and in that sense there is a certain worldlessness about positionality (cf. GA 79: 52/50). As I have noted above, Heidegger asks for the thing in itself in the fourfold. What Heidegger attempts here in the fourfold, as he asks for the thing in itself, is then also the disempowerment of transcendental logic and that also means the disempowerment of Newtonian physics. With Kant there is no access to things in themselves, only to appearances. Hence our world becomes deprived of the "real", the genuine, as all we perceive are shadows. With the thinking of the fourfold, a thinking of things, Heidegger asks us to return to simple things as they *are*, that they *are* as they appear—without falling for a (naïve) realism that has as its dogma that things just so exist and that sheer existence just is what it means to exist. This, of course, means that realism takes things as the *ratio essendi*, i.e., realism reifies things to serve as their own ground. Rather than falling for any realism, for Heidegger the thing *is* the original gathering of the four regions of the fourfold. Hence also a poem, a song, can be a proper thing that gathers mortals to be mindful of their death; to be mindful of the finitude and gift of the earth which self-withdraws from the demands and abstractions of the sciences; to be mindful of the openness of the sky, which invites the earth to give while as the Open the sky gifts itself and grants guidance, limit, horizon and orientation to mortals; and to be mindful of the possibility of the divine. The sky, however, can only be that Open, for the sky is also inaccessible for mortals. Sure, we can fly and send satellites into the atmosphere, fly to the moon and perhaps soon to Mars. Yet, in so doing we destroy the stability, sincerity, and freedom mortals find in their orientation along the sky. Only in this region between sky and earth, Heidegger reminds us, is there Μνημοσύνη, who is the daughter of the two and the gathered memory of our origin. This is why Heidegger is so worried about space travel. For him, this means the eradication, the utter desertification of our shared memory. Our being is inextricably and fatefully interwoven with the earth. Going beyond the earth would mean to catapult ourselves not into outer space, but into sheer nihilism; purposeless floating about as so forcefully portrayed in Stanley Kubrick's *2001: A Space Odyssey* in the scene where a crew member flies to the moon station and falls asleep during this incredible journey away from the earth and cutting through the sovereignty of the blue sky, turning into but a dark gloom, an abyss unfathomable for the mortal being. Hence Heidegger writes on the sky:

> "The sky is the vaulting path of the sun, the course of the changing moon, the wandering glitter of the stars, the year's seasons and their changes, the light and dusk of day, the gloom and glow of night, the clemency and inclemency of the weather, the drifting clouds and blue depth of the ether." (GA 7: 151/147)

A simple tempo-spatial occurrence, a thing like a stone bridge, can remind us of those regions—one of the regions we are ourselves as mortals and we only are this very region in virtue of the other regions.

In the fourfold the dilapidation of the thing is reversed. The *thing in itself* stands before mortals and gathers them. Demske puts it as follows: "The thing as such, insofar as it gathers and brings the [fourfold] to presence, is thus an appearing of being itself." (Demske 1970:151) With being at its centre the fourfold is nothing short of an answer of the question of being and the fourfold sets itself forth when mortals are open to their death! The insight into the workings of the event and the history of being remain crucial, for they let see positionality for what it is and how it originates from the responses of metaphysics to being (beyng). But now it is time for a response to the event from a distinctly non-metaphysical perspective. This response is the fourfold.

In the fourfold, there is room for creativity and spirited community. There is no room for organisation, bureaucratisation, and technocracy. A warning from the *Gay Science* comes to mind where Nietzsche argues that the modern haste covers life "with a most odd mindlessness. Already one is ashamed of keeping still; long reflection almost gives people a bad conscience." (Nietzsche 2003: 183) Moreover, "one no longer has time and energy for ceremony, for civility with detours, for *esprit* in conversation, and in general for any *otium*." (ibid.: 184) There is no sense of gathering, but an absentmindedness about the modern age. Letting oneself be gathered for Heidegger begins with bethinking death. Letting oneself be gathered for *another* beginning, which now means to encounter world in a different fashion than the prevalent and dominating ways of positionality. There is in the fourfold room for *otium* or rather *scholé*, which in the over-efficient ways of positionality has no place. With reference to Lao-Tse Heidegger speaks of the joyful leisure a thing like a useless tree can bring, if only we let ourselves be gathered by the tree rather than trying to make the tree comply to our fantasies about how useful it should be (cf. Heidegger 1989: 7ff). What lets or releases things into their essence is a thinking that resonates with the fourfold. Thinking is a form of dwelling, and it is mortal thinking at its core.

In *Building Dwelling Thinking* Heidegger gives an example of how simple things in a practical sense welcome death and birth into the midst of a community and its world. He speaks of the thing "treetrunk coffin" (*Totenbaum*) for those who have died and of the thing "childbed" for new-born children. These things are only meaningful for the relationship that mortals have with them and mortals only find their place in the world for their relationship with these things. One cannot be without the other. Both the coffin and the childbed have their place in the homes of families and are not outsourced to hospitals. This honours the dead and welcomes new-born children (cf. GA 7: 162/158). As such these things gather the community. Heidegger here explicitly places birth on the same level as death. Birth *and* death both gather and form the community. The treetrunk coffin and the childbed make for sacred places where a community gathers. These things grant the place so that there can be a good death *and* good communal life. The childbed and the treetrunk coffin are proper things *in themselves*. The death that in a practical sense gathers the community is the bodily death of loved ones. It is here, in my view, that the death of others becomes significant in Heidegger. This experience of the dying of others, which in *Being and Time* does not yield any insight into existential-ontological death, now brings mortals closer to their community. This also tells us that mortals build, craft, and cultivate things that last and gather a family, a community most properly when mortals contemplate their death. When mortals meditate in the sense of caring for beings. Thus, when mortals are in tune with their finitude and do not aim to become gods, when they do not fall for technology's Promethean promises, the worlding of the fourfold comes about.

Heidegger speaks of the "good death" in *Building Dwelling Thinking*. Heidegger here mentions the *"Brauch"* of the capacity of being mortal. Hence a certain "custom" and "tradition" is required for there to be a good death. Heidegger does not really explicate this any further directly, but one can distil what the good death would entail. A good death can be in the presence of a genuine community, for example an extended family. To arrive at the custom of providing the grounds on which a good death is possible mortals need to learn how to dwell first. Dwelling does not mean to search cheap comfort; proper dwelling means to safeguard and protect the earth and its inhabitants. Death, as Heidegger writes, does not become the goal or end of the community. Rather, in their responsible dwelling on the earth underneath the sky where gods reside, mortals develop a sense again for the need to protect what is not and never was theirs to possess. The responding to being's call here takes on the distinct practical sense. Mortals respond to their own finitude and limitations. Mortals respond to the finitude of being in this sense. They become responsible when they accept their limitations and their place in the order of things. This is to say the community of mortals is not centred around death, not some sort of death-cult. Quite the opposite, it is only when humans dwell in a way that is protective of the earth and of their community, when mortals appreciate the divine, and recognise their own limitations—then and only then can there be a good death. In such a world there is appreciation of one's ancestors for they have helped build the world thanks to which mortals dwell. In this essay Heidegger continuously speaks of the "keep", of protection, of care, of tending and nurturing, of waiting, of recognising signs of the gods. These are all outside the spectre of the will to will and yonder of *stellen*. I shall show in Part IV that it is precisely the poets as few and rare who have the most profound task in this re-orientation and remembering of what it means to be human. Then, when mortals remember their ways on the earth that protect and safe, that keep and nurture, rather than destroy and destruct, then can there be again a good death. And there is something distinct practical about this, where mortals find again a stance, a way of holding themselves in the midst of beings, so that they are not destroyers but guardians due to their unique responsibility and duty on the earth. As Heidegger points out in his *Freiburg Lectures* with reference to Periander, humans are to meditate for the whole of beings, i.e., care for the whole of beings. Heidegger explicitly says that he does not wish to return to an older, simpler time. Instead, by remembering and so coming in touch again with what has been—after all another name for being, as Aristotle says, is "the Old"—human beings can begin to see dwelling as safeguarding again as the trait of being which is theirs, which is where they can return home to. It is then that a good death can be, where death is not the focus or centre of attention but the "good death" can then come about for the human being is here entrenched in the good order of things and in touch with ancestry and descendants—no longer an isolated subject.

The dwelling ground of mortals is earth. "Earth" is not a Heideggerian abstraction, but it is the literal earth on which we stand and die, and out of which we grow.

The earth bears us, it fructifies and nourishes (cf. GA 79: 17/176). The earth can do so only because it withdraws. The earth is not a fixed, stable, ever-available and self-sufficient substantial ground and therefore reducible to an abstract mass of resources. Instead, the earth irreducibly withholds itself as it withdraws into itself. Earth is never fully available and this is the secret of its abundance and riches. Earth and death are thus in vicinity and precisely for that vicinity earth is the dwelling *ground* of mortals. Earth is that which gives and takes and death is that which always reminds mortals that they are never to become gods.

2   The Divinities

Who are the divinities of the fourfold? The gods are and remain unnamed. In a recent, extensive and impressive study on Heidegger and Hölderlin, Martin Bojda (2016) therefore argues that Heidegger demythologises Hölderlin's gods. Hölderlin takes Greek gods as a model, as Bojda points out. Heidegger, in turn, takes Hölderlin's notion of the last god and the possibility of a return of gods seriously but, argues Bojda, Heidegger deprives them of their mythological origin and depth. The fourfold is hence a reductive theology, concludes Bojda (cf. Bojda 2016: 307 and 370f). True, Heidegger does not appear to have a historical model for his gods. Nor does he take Hölderlin's idealised "Greek" gods as models. *Divinities* is but a name. But there are structural and argumentative reasons for this. Heidegger—the thinker as opposed to the poet Hölderlin—does not wish to write a mythology with the fourfold. Far from it. The other beginning is not something given, but the open possibility of a futural encounter with the divine and this future is what already plays into the presence. As the writings on the fourfold do not aim to provide a fixed mythology, and here I go well beyond Heidegger, we can rather understand the gods and the fourfold as a basis for a possible future mythology where the gods will indeed be named. But the fourfold speaks of possible encounters with the divine already in the age of positionality. Thus, even the unnamed gods are not abstract precisely because they are the name for possible encounters with the divine. Moreover, the gods cannot be named in this current age, because, and staying true to Hölderlin himself, this is an epoch where gods have departed. Hence, they cannot be named. Their return is possible if and only if mortals become mortals. These future encounters are of an immanent transcendence, so to speak. This is also why Heidegger in *The Thing* stresses that the disappearance of the divine in the dire age means the gods' impending arrival. This is precisely the sense of ethos (and pathos) in the fourfold, on how to dwell on the earth as mortals, in order for there to be the possibility of that arrival. Even as yet unnamed the gods of the fourfold are guarantors of meaning and of the possibility to reconnect with the Holy. In the fourfold Heidegger, therefore, maintains Hölderlin's notion of a "bridal festival between men and gods" as "the balance of fate." The bridal fest points to the equilibrium of the fourfold.

The earth is the obscure self-withholding dwelling ground of mortals. The sky, however, is not the heavens where divinities reside. Heidegger gives up on the metaphysical distinction between the earth as the earthly, the visible and the sensible, and the sky as locus of the intelligible and supersensible. The sky is rather the dimension of the Open which can be that Open only for its tension-filled relationship with earth as that which self-obscures. The equilibrium and the reciprocally enriching participation of each region in all others only comes about if mortals become mortals and accept again that they are not all powerful.

In a commemorative address in honour of the centenary of Conradin Kreutzer's death Heidegger determines the stance we are to take "in order to remain open for the concealed sense of the technical world [as]: *openness for the secret.*" (GA 16: 528) A proper mortal stance respects releasement and the secret: "The releasement toward things and the openness for the secret belong together." (ibid.) As indicated above, the secret refers to death as shrine, sanctuary, and law. Together releasement and the secret form "a new foundation and ground" (ibid.) for the world. The encounter of the fourfold opens a path toward the Holy, that which is wholesome. This possibility is articulated by the poets, for "[the gods] need the word of the poet for their appearance," (GA 4: 191/218) as Heidegger says in his lecture course on *Hölderlin.* The poets can properly respond to the call of beyng because they are open to their death in a distinct way. There is nothing heroic, tragic, optimistic or pessimistic about this. There are profound structural reasons for why Heidegger sees a relation between beyng, death and language—and explicating this relation shows why poets have an affinity for death. The last part will come back to the fourfold again and in more detail. For language, as Heidegger will come to argue, is what moves the world.

Part IV
Death and the Poetry of the World

Death is the sanctuary of beyng in the poem of the world
– Heidegger

To speak means to be forever on the path
– Ossip Mandelstam

Abstract In an important later essay entitled *The Essence of Language* (*das Wesen der Sprache*) Heidegger briefly mentions what he refers to as the "essential relation between death and language". Heidegger neither here nor elsewhere directly and explicitly further develops this relation. Hence in this last part I attempt to give an account of this "essential relation" from within the thinking path. In order to gain an access to Heidegger's claim of this relationship between death and language, it is important to understand what Heidegger means by language. For an understanding of Heidegger on language I introduce Heidegger's engagement with poets such as Rilke, George, and Hölderlin. Language for Heidegger is not the sounds or words we utter in order to communicate some subjective contents. Rather, language is *qua* house of being, the realm in which humans dwell and thanks to which the world is accessible at all. The relationship of language and death, then, turns out to be such that language, similar as is the case for being, finds rest and shelter in death as *Gebirg*. It is, therefore, the task of humans to heed their languages by being mindful of their mortality.

Keywords Thinking path · Language and death · Sprache und Tod · Poetic thinking · Heidegger and Rilke · Heidegger and George · Fourfold · Geviert · Essence of language

Introduction

Heidegger's thinking responds to the challenge of technology in that he articulates the essence of technology as positionality. To be more precise I should say that *something* addresses and claims him, in the sense of *Anspruch* (being called upon), which prompts Heidegger to attempt to correspond, in the sense of *Entsprechen*, to this claim by naming that essential occurrence "positionality:" the gathering and concentration of all forceful and volitional positioning. Together with *Ge-Stell* Heidegger speaks of two further gatherings. Those are the aforementioned *Geviert* and *Ge-Birg*. As I have argued in Part III, the fourfold does not abolish positionality. Rather, we are to understand the fourfold as unfolding out of the same realm in a heterological way and simultaneously with positionality. Wherever the fourfold is brought forth as the mirror-play of its regions, wherever in the proper, crafted thing being itself lights up, positionality is momentarily "sublated", insofar as another dimensionality lights up. As there is no progressive, teleological dialectics at work, but as what is at work eventuates itself simultaneously and heterologically, encounters with the fourfold are momentary and fragile. This says nothing about the measured length of the encounter. It could last the lifetime of a community of mortals or only for the brief moment when someone senses another dimension.

That which addresses Heidegger is, however, not some object that comes earlier and that speaks to him. Nor is there per se a givenness. The claim properly and essentially occurs only in the performance of mortal correspondence. That is to say, that which claims us only takes place *in* the act of a sheltering and listening correspondence. Yet, there is always a response, even if only the response of not being concerned by the call of being. This is reminiscent of the hermeneutic circle insofar as *I* can only say and interpret what *I* already understand, but that which *I* always already understand, *I* fully and properly understand only through interpreting and laying bare. For Heidegger's diagnosis of the technological world and of its meaning and origin that which we ordinarily call language seems to be fundamental. After all what Heidegger already stresses in *Being and Time* and even more so with the thinking of the event is the call and the response. *How* we respond, is crucial. In language there then seems to be the possibility, not to effectuate, but to bring forth the getting over of positionality. Hence it is not surprising that Heidegger also significantly devotes his thinking to language during his engagement with technology. Heidegger approaches language in its own right, as it were. That is to say that there is an essential relation between language and the event. The German *ent-sprechen* literally means to speak out of and against something. The English translation of *entsprechen* is "to correspond". I think of this as *co-responding* which is to indicate that human beings are required to respond to the claim of being in a collaborative manner. Co-responding is a finite occurring because it means to respond to something and to engage with a claim in order to pass on a message. Once the message has been carried on, the correspondent needs to wait for the next message. The one who corresponds is in each case a mortal, finite being. The silent call of conscience of *Being and Time* is now the claim or call of beyng. Hence the call is no longer of the fundamental care-structure of Dasein, but rather *of* being itself addressing the human being. In his later essays and talks on language anthologised in *On the Way to Language* Heidegger begins to say that it is language itself that addresses human beings and to which human beings respond, insofar as language is always first the language of being. As such it is language that opens the path for mortals to enter the fourfold and leave behind positionality, for language is that which lets see another dimension and possibility of being.

Yet, this does not simply take place by itself. Heidegger points out in *The Essence of Language* that mortals need to be able and open to experience death as death in order for language to bring forth the fourfold. Again, death appears to be crucial for the question of being. In *The Essence of Language* Heidegger hence explicitly speaks of an "essential relation [*Wesensverhältnis*] between death and language [which] flashes up before us." (GA 12: 203/107[1]) Yet, notes Heidegger, this crucial relation "remains still unthought" (GA 12: 203/107) and Heidegger does not explicitly develop it. I shall refer to this passage as "key passage" in this part. The implications of the key passage for Heidegger's later philosophy are the central question of this part. In my view, the notion of "flashing" indicates that any pursuit of the key passage and its claim cannot lie in an attempt to finalise and perfectly fixate the essential relation. Perhaps, the relation will continue to be present ever only as a flash. We shall see that the key passage is a crucial moment of the thinking path because it brings into dialogue death, the essential transformation, the fourfold, and language. The key passage indicates that death and language are related in terms of their *dimensionality* or *Wesensbereich*, insofar as both are interests of beyng first. They are to be thought out of that realm where dimensionalities prevail, *walten*, and come into their own, i.e., out of the event. As Heidegger says at the beginning of his essay *Language*: "To discuss language, to locate it [*erörtern*], means to bring to its place of being not so much language as ourselves: our own gathering into the event." (GA 12: 10/188[2] *ta*) Thus this essay and the other essays of the anthology *On the Way to Language* invite us to think language out of the essential event.

From the analytical camp Oberst (2009) has recently written a study on the key passage. Agamben (2006) on the continental side gave a seminar on the matter, which is now published as a book entitled *Language and Death: The Place of Negativity*. Agamben attended Heidegger's Le Thor Seminars in 1968. Agamben reports that Heidegger there said the following about the essential relation between death and language: "You can see it, I cannot." (Agamben 2006: xi) Thus, Heidegger gives his readers the task to think through the essential relation. However, Agamben does not take Heidegger's remark as an invitation to reflect on the key passage systematically from within the thinking path. Agamben instead turns to what he takes to be "decisive moments in Western philosophy" (Agamben 2006: xii) in order to explain the essential relation of death and language that Heidegger sees. In my view it is also problematic that Agamben understands "death" here as a marker for

---

[1] Hertz translation.

[2] Hofstadter translation.

negativity. His reading of Heidegger then appears to be too steeped in some sort of dialectics and fails to provide a genuine access to Heidegger's thought. The gist of Oberst's argument, in turn, is that human beings invented language as a reaction to their mortality and out of their longing for immortality. Such a claim is rather foreign to Heidegger's thought. Oberst's argument is some sort of evolutionary psychology or theology married with psychoanalysis. Oberst must, therefore, implicitly presuppose that language is primarily a human faculty and an expression of human fear of demise. For Heidegger, however, language is primarily not at all expression. Oberst thus, in my view, reduces the relation between death and language to a survival mechanism. Human beings' contingent reaction leads them to "invent" language by using their physical capacity to make sounds in order to cope with unfavourable living conditions. Not only does this place the human subject at the centre. This also seriously distorts what Heidegger means by language, the human being, which is not at all an animal organism, being, and death and mortality. Yet, as extraordinary as it may sound, Heidegger argues that human beings speak because language addresses them.

My reading of the key passage is different. Heidegger here explicitly thinks in the context of the fourfold and the event. In my view, the key passage is thus also to be understood in relation to positionality and sanctuary. In my approach to the key passage I follow Dastur who concludes her paper on the essence of language as follows: "What remains to be thought is the fact that death as the shelter of being and the nocturnal source of all light is what grants to world its realm and to the human being its existence." (Dastur 2013: 237) One must not underestimate here what Dastur is saying here. Death as *Ge-birg* is what grants the fourfold its openness and dimension as well as the possibility to exist for mortals. But mortals are insofar as they properly say something. I take it to be most promising to approach the essential relation between death and language by considering their respective "essences". At the time Heidegger writes the key passage death is the shelter of beyng and shrine of nothingness. The essence of language is a more complicated story. Heidegger provides several seemingly disparate "essences" of language. He describes language as originating out of silence, as the "house of being," and as "saying." Nevertheless, I shall argue that it is possible to unite these "essences" or rather dimensions, when we understand language as occurring out of the event. This will allow me to provide a reading of the key passage that speaks from within the thinking path. The last part of this book is then an attempt at an original reading of how Heidegger understands the dimension of language and how this dimension can be the home for mortals, while positionality is increasingly the place for machines. The main claim is that we can fully appreciate what Heidegger means by language, if we consider it from the perspective of death as refuge, *Ge-birg*.

There is a vicinity between my reading and Werner Marx's approach in his book *Is there a Measure on Earth?* (cf. Marx 1983: 118ff). Marx appreciates the turn in Heidegger's thought and it is a strength of his interpretation that he reads the key passage in context of the event. Marx understands the essence of language to be "saying" and the essence of death as shrine and refuge. Six years before the official publication of Heidegger's *Contributions* Marx is able to show convincingly that "[d]eath belongs together with the event of appropriation, to which ... saying also belongs." (Marx 1983: 124) Marx also indicates that death is the mystery Heidegger continuously refers to and that death is the window for mortals to think groundless being (cf. Marx 1983: 124). However, Marx criticises Heidegger's notion that human beings are no longer to be understood as the rational animal. For Marx this creates the problem that the "poetic dwelling" of mortals boils down to an "irrational" community guided by contingent moods (cf. Marx 1983: 125). I disagree with that reading. "Overcoming" the encrusted metaphysical definition of the rational animal means that the "irrational" is overcome, too. The irrational only makes sense in relation to the rational. But this is not a key theme of the thesis I am pursuing here, and thus I shall not further pursue this here either. In fact, as I point out in the Epilogue to this book the question of the relationship between the rational and the irrational, and the expectations that have been placed in the powers of reason, are to some degree what drives the transhumanist or posthumanist project. What matters more for the present project is that Marx neglects Heidegger's other determinations of the essences of language in his interpretation of the key passage.

To approach Heidegger's thought from within the thinking path does not mean that there are no influences on Heidegger's thought on language. I think there are at least three significant influences. The first is his reading of Parmenides which I shall return to in more detail below. Second, Heidegger's thought of language is influenced by Herder, Hamann, and Humboldt. Heidegger learns from them that the instrumental representation of language is inadequate because language is primarily not a means of communication and humans are not just bearers of the capacity to speak. Instead, beings are insofar as they are *in* language (cf. Gottschlich 2017: 262f). Heidegger, however, is also critical of Humboldt's theory of language precisely because Humboldt fails to think language in its own right and instead approaches language as the workings of the spirit (cf. GA 12: 236f). Third, Heidegger's focus on the importance of silence for language draws inspiration from a tradition that dates back at least to Augustine and extends to Pascal and Kierkegaard. They value silence, for silence can bring us closer to God. Heidegger's silence rather refers to the human's relationship[3] with beyng. Furthermore, I shall introduce Ossip Mandelstam's musings on language, as they can help us gain a clearer understanding of what Heidegger means by language. Heidegger's understanding of language is, of course, furthest removed from how we would ordinarily think of the matter.

Heidegger's work on language is not motivated by an interest to increase our knowledge of language. Nevertheless, there is a profound project in Heidegger's pursuit of language since he wishes to provide us with the possibility of making an experience with language that is at once entirely out of the ordinary, but also an

---

[3] Heidegger understands the German word *Bezug*, which is usually translated as relation, not as *relatio* but as *postulatio*. That is to say, "relation" is not meant in the logical sense but in the sense of something pulling human beings toward itself and addressing them. This is also how we are to understand the pair *Bezug - Entzug*. These two words then can be translated as *addressing - refusal to address* (cf. GA 12: 119/32).

experience with language in its simplicity and force. He attempts to show that language is precisely not something humans operate with in the world in order to express and communite, e.g., our desires. Rather, humans *dwell* in language. As a dimension language is a possibility for a home in the age of technology (cf. GA 12: 255/ 134). In his conversation with a Japanese scholar on language (henceforth *Conversation*) Heidegger says that our ordinary opinions regarding language fail to grasp what he means when he speaks of *Sprache* (cf. GA 12: 136f/47). On my reading, with the thinking of the history of beyng language belongs to beyng and therefore also to death as *Ge-Birg*. The basic event of beyng is *bergen*, which self-differentiates simultaneously as *entbergen* and *verbergen*. It remains to be shown that language *qua* poetry is a primary mode of *Bergung* and thus *of* beyng's basic event. This will also explain language's proximity with death. Still, the declared focus of Heidegger's concern with language in *On the Way to Language* is the question after the essence and place of the human being. In this regard, as Heidegger points out, he follows Humboldt (cf. GA 12: 9/187).

The structure of this part is as follows: First, I situate the later Heidegger's stance on language by introducing some of his readings of his preferred poets. Second, I explicate the essence of language in view of death. In the third chapter I look at the role of language in the fourfold and bring the key passage into focus. In the fourth and last chapter I explicate language in relation to the transformation of the human being. The anthology *On the Way to Language* serves as the foundation for this part. The anthology is a synthesis of Heidegger's thinking of the event, poetry, technology, transition, the fourfold, and the essential transformation of human beings. I shall also work in other relevant texts and passages of Heidegger's sustained pursuit of the role of language. This also allows me to show that there is a certain unity of the thinking path.

Chapter 16
The Later Heidegger on Language

It might be helpful to situate Heidegger's stance on language by turning to some of the most important poets he reads. In his later writings Sophocles, Rilke, Goethe, Trakl, George, and also the Alemannic poet Johann Peter Hebel are where Heidegger draws inspiration for his thought on language. Of course, Hölderlin also remains crucial. For the poet Hölderlin there is a "sovereignty of poetry over philosophy", as Beiser has argued (Beiser 2008: 378). Beiser also points out that for Hölderlin "poetry is the source of insights and ideas that philosophy presupposes but cannot express in its discursive language." (ibid.) Heidegger responds to this stance by Hölderlin with his poetic thought. With reference to George's *The Word* Heidegger puts it as follows in *The Essence of Language*: "in a poem of such rank thinking is going on, and indeed thinking without science, without philosophy." (GA 12: 154/61) Poetry can get behind the presupposition philosophy makes when it formulates its claims, for poetry speaks freely out of language itself. The freedom of poetry shows itself in the freedom it takes from grammar and by twisting free. In this chapter I first introduce these poets and show their influence on Heidegger's understanding of both poetry and death.

His turn to poetry may make it seem as though Heidegger romanticises language. But for Heidegger poetry is not at all something in which we take aesthetic pleasure. Instead, poetry is able to articulate profound thoughts, precisely for its nearness to the sheltering disclosing of ποίησις. Moreover, Heidegger follows Hölderlin who sees in language itself a great danger. Language's proximity with death indicates its inherent danger. In the second section of this chapter I thus address language as the "most dangerous good."

© Springer Nature Switzerland AG 2021
J. A. Niederhauser, *Heidegger on Death and Being*,
https://doi.org/10.1007/978-3-030-51375-7_16

1   Heidegger's Poets

In *Introduction to Metaphysics* Heidegger devotes a substantial chapter to Sophocles' *Antigone*. He learns from the play that death is what utterly defies the age-old human desire for perfect mastery of the world (cf. GA 40: 167/168). I cannot do justice here to any of the poets Heidegger reads intensely. But especially his reading of Sophocles seems to merit further investigation especially in light of Heidegger's understanding of the tragic. In Sophocles Heidegger sees a poetic articulation of the Heraclitean principle that war is the father of all things. In fact, this war is the war within being itself which gods and men carry out and where their respective being begins to show itself. In this battle the fate of men is decided, i.e., in the way in which humans respond and find their stance in the midst of beings. It is also in this lecture course that Heidegger begins to investigate the essential relation between thinking and poetising. He sees a connection, in fact an identity, between Parmenides's "thinking and being" and Sophocles' "τέχνη" and "δίκη", *art* and divine *justice*, or rather *measure* on the earth. For the poet τέχνη takes over δίκη just as thought takes over being, i.e., there is an early rebellion of the human being against being itself which is exemplified in thought and τέχνη. This primordial war has always already been ongoing. The art is, as it were, to find the right balance in every given epoch between the two battling forces. The tragedy is that human beings will always attempt to overpower being (and nature) but will ultimately fail—for their very mortal finitude. And the epoch of *Gestell* is the momentary overpowering of τέχνη against δίκη, a fundamental unbalancing, but not a total victory against measure. Rather, a momentary unsettling of the measure on the earth which will give its response and retaliate.

Heidegger's work on Rilke is decisive for his stance on death. In *What are Poets for?* an essay written in the immediate aftermath of the war Heidegger introduces Rilke as a poet *in desolate times*, a phrase Heidegger borrows from Hölderlin. In *Contributions*, as I have argued in Part II, Heidegger views Hölderlin together with Nietzsche and Kierkegaard as a thinker-poet who sees the desolateness of an age to come. In *What are Poets for?* Heidegger says: "The age is desolate because it lacks the unconcealedness of the essence of pain, death, and love." (GA 5: 275/205 ta) In what sense is death hidden? The technological age knows as true only what is actual and measurable. Put differently, positionality only knows what is positive and posited: "The self-assertion of technological objectification is the constant negation of death." (GA 5: 303/227) Technology denies and utterly negates death. Death is the natural enemy of positionality, because death is, with Rilke, "the side of life turned away from us, unlit by us" (GA 5: 302/227). As such death cannot be controlled by technology. Technology must work against death (good death) and pain because they impede technology's will to functionality. Technology works to negate death—for example, by trying to solve death as if it were a techno-logical problem. But to both Heidegger and Rilke, death is the "other relation" and as that other relation death has more stake in *what is* than technology can even begin to appreciate. Heidegger recognises in Rilke a kindred spirit because to Rilke death is also integral to being itself: "Death and the kingdom of the dead belong, as the other side, to beings in the whole." (GA 5: 302/227 *ta*)[1] As that other side, which belongs to being, death is not the negation of life or of the actual, but death is rather that which posits all that is. Death is, as Heidegger says and as I have already mentioned in Parts II & III, the *Ge-setz*, the law: "death gathers into the entirety of what has already been placed, into the *positum* of the whole attraction." (GA 5: 304/228) Death is that which "posits" into the Open precisely because death is the utterly non-available and that which withdraws. Death does not logically posit. Its positing is rather a literal setting and placing out of concealment. More precisely, death is the concealment surrounding appearance. As law death "touches mortals in their essence and so places them … into the entirety of the pure relation [*Bezug*]." (GA 5: 304/228 *ta*) Death pulls mortals into the pure relation with beyng, death binds mortals with the event. Thus, Heidegger learns from the poet Rilke that the Holy can only be experienced when mortals are open to their death and *love* it, rather than deny or fear their own death. Heidegger understands the Holy, *das Heile*, as related to the whole and wholesome. Already in *Being and Time* Dasein can only be whole by running forth toward its death. In Heidegger's later thought, where death belongs to beyng itself, there cannot be wholeness without death either. Positionality is thus essentially un-whole, for it entirely ignores death. This is why positionality strives for a totalitarian totality which positionality wants to achieve through an all-encompassing manipulation of all that is. But positionality does not even begin to see all that is, since positionality is ignorant of death. As argued in Part III, the subject *qua* ground of beings is attracted to the sphere of τέχνη precisely because that sphere promises the subject perfect control over beings. But with reference to Trakl Heidegger points out that the subject is "the decomposed form [*verweste Gestalt*] of man." (GA 12: 46/170).

Heidegger views Trakl as the poet who most vividly provides a possible path out of subjectivity. The subject is the decomposed gestalt of man because it is encrusted but also because the subject is estranged from its world and has to posit the objects it controls. The subject "has been removed from its kind of essential being, and this is why it is the "unsettled" kind." (GA 12: 46/170) The subject is the free-floating, transcendental ego trying to get back into the world by any means necessary. The *post*-modern subject, which is not only the ground of all beings, but also assumes that it can entirely make itself, is the utmost maximum of this decomposed gestalt of man. A mere semblance of who the human being is. The decomposed form is "unholy", removed from the Holy, insofar as wholeness is not possible for the subject. Thus, Heidegger finds in Trakl a companion for the essential transformation of the human being. Moreover, Trakl determines spirit, *Geist*, not as reason or *spiritus* first but as flame. This makes him a Heraclitean poet. Heidegger recognises Trakl as the poet who moves beyond a blind faith in reason. But most importantly, Trakl also poetises on death. The poem "Seven-song of Death" speaks of the holy number seven. For Heidegger the poem thus "sings of the holiness of death." (GA 12: 42/167) It is crucial to note that the poem speaks of a "going-down" to "something

---

[1] See also (Demske 1970: 139) on this.

strange" and that death summons us to do so. Death is here thus not "the conclusion to of earthly life," (ibid.), notes Heidegger. This going down into the abyss, into the unsupported, which death allows, "leaves behind the form of man which has decayed [i.e., the subject]." (ibid.: 42/168) I shall expand on Heidegger's reading of death in Trakl below and how death allows for the going-down that is a transformational experience. Heidegger writes this in the essay *Language in the Poem*. It is upon those who are "mad" to see other possibilities of being, but those must be strangers on the earth, able to *die* their death in life, go under and leave behind the current fades in order to throw open other ways of being for a genuine future connected to what has been, but not the fake future of the myth of progress which calculates a utopian fantasy using the "data" it has available at present. Such are the calculations of transhumanism, which of necessity must get rid of the decomposed form of the human being as well, for the human (or at least its representation of the human) fails to be able to belong to this fanciful science fiction sphere of machines. The coldness of the evangelists of post- or transhumanism is the coldness of dead formal rationality, which is itself the most prominent characteristic of subjectivity at its utmost maximum. Of this cold rationality Stefan George poetises.

Hence George is another poet close to Heidegger. Heidegger already notes in a lecture course on phenomenology in 1919/20 that George is dear to him because George has the capacity to see and describe phenomena directly and vividly (cf. GA 58: 69). According to the later Heidegger what George sees and what his poetry articulates is that there is a calculative, maximising, cold rationality at work in modernity. This cold rationality "is itself already the explosion of a power that could blast everything to nothingness." (GA 12: 179/84) George is the poet who most clearly captures the madness, *Wahn-sinn*, i.e., meaninglessness, of the age. Listening to George, to his sacrifice and renunciation in a simple poem such as *The Word*, could, Heidegger is sure, spark the move out of the sphere of machines: "The step back into the sphere of human being demands other things than does the progress into the machine world." (ibid.: 179/85) The move out of the world of machines means a return to earth also *via* a renaissance of regional vernacular.

Vernacular and dialect also become increasingly important to the later Heidegger, for he begins to understand them as rooted in the earth of the fourfold. Heidegger's appreciation of Hebel is especially important in this regard. Hebel is a poet of the Alemannic German dialect. Heidegger sees earth itself at work in vernacular: "The landscape, and that means the earth, speaks in dialects, [*Mundarten*], differently each time." (GA 12: 194/98 *ta*) The mouth is shaped in consonance with the shape of the earth and how the earth gives and shelters in a particular region. For the mirror-play of the fourfold all other three regions take part in earth. Thus, through speaking vernacular world and home arise. Mortals dwell in vernacular. In *Hebel—The Friend of the House* Heidegger emphasises that "vernacular is the mysterious well of each grown language. From this well all of what the spirit of language harbours flows toward us." (GA 13: 134) Dialects are not disfigurements or derivations of some assumed primary, standardised and nationalised language. There could be no such standardised language without the many grown vernaculars that are its

constitutive components: "Language is dialect according to its essential origin."
(GA 13: 156[2]) Heidegger writes this in *Language and Home*. As long as there is
vernacular—*Mundart* which literally means the manner of the mouth—there is the
wellspring of language. The word *Mundart* indicates that the mouth is shaped in
accordance with the landscape of where a community dwells. Thus, it remains the
task also of proper mortal speaking to cherish and care for vernaculars. This means
at once also to care for the earth on which a vernacular grows. In this sense Hebel is
the friend of the house, i.e., of language as the house of being. Hebel shows that
language is not an instrument, but that which gives rise to a communal world.

What Heidegger sees in his reading of these poets is the immanent and imminent
threat of technology to human beings precisely in the form of a threat to language itself.
Yet, these poets also provide us with possible ways out of the current epoch precisely
because of their ποίησις, their sheltering ways of bringing-forth of something that is
covered over in the worldless (in the sense that the interplay of the fourfold is absent)
sphere of machines, logistics, calculation, and manipulation. Also, the poets' proximity
to earth and death, i.e., to concealment, explains how their poetry point to other ways
of being. Today, positionality's manipulation increasingly takes place, if not exclusively so, in the manipulation of information, and language is represented as a tool of
information and communication. The genomic code, for example, is information as is
the content of a book. In *The Friend of the House* Heidegger warns that "[t]he representation of language as a tool of information today is pushed toward the outermost." (GA
13: 148[3]) This representation of language is an imminent threat to language and the
main problem, argues Heidegger, is that this "takes place in utmost silence." (GA 13:
149[4]) It is essential that Heidegger here speaks of a *representation*, of a mere *Vorstellung*
of language. Heidegger uses the term *Vorstellung* on purpose to indicate that here
Ge-Stell is *operative*. Language is reduced to a transmitter of information as language
is represented to be nothing but a tool for the wilful positioning and control of entities.
Language is here but an accidental property of the bearer of the faculty to speak: the
accidentally speaking and calculating animal. Heidegger reverses the metaphysical
definition of the human, which has become superficial and external. For Heidegger
language is not some accidental faculty attached to a biped creature. Rather, and I shall
develop this further in the next chapter, language is the realm where human beings find
a home and come into their own. In my view, this is how we should understand the
crucial notion of *Anspruch*. Humans are *claimed* and *called upon* to be human, but not
destroyers of the earth. That there is a mere "representation" of language also indicates
the flatness and one-dimensionality language has to assume in positionality. *Qua* transmitter of information language is not primarily of the mode of *sheltering recovery*
(*Bergung*), but of a deprived mode of making stand and available for manipulation.

Yet, the problem runs deeper than what we can see in technological manipulation. In
fact, for Heidegger the trouble begins with everyday speech. This is because everyday

---

[2] "Sprache ist nach ihrer Wesensherkunft Dialekt."

[3] "Die Vorstellung von der Sprache als einem Instrument der Information drängt heute ins
Äußerste."

[4] "Es geht überdies in der größten Stille vor sich."

speech is automated. Such speech poses a threat to language and our access to the world because it continuously covers over deeper relations. And this means that everyday speech relies on simplistic, one-dimensional representations. Those representations, in turn, reduce the dimensions of being. Following Goethe, who knew the Faustian spirit of Occidental man, Heidegger sees in poetic language a possibility to free us from the one-dimensionality of the everyday: "*Goethe* calls those other relations deeper relations [*Verhältnis*] and says of language: "In everyday [*gemeinen*] life we barely [*notdürftig*] get by with language because we only describe superficial relations. As soon as deeper relations are at stake, another language speaks: poetic language"." (GA 13: 149[5]). Poetry is not exclusive to what is generally considered poetry. For Heidegger poetry includes dialect and vernacular. Poetry or poetic language is that which brings forth without objectification and without instrumentalization and as such poetry is the foundation of all other arts. The path to language is a path back home, out of the world of machines towards the fourfold. The fourfold is a crucial continuation of Heidegger's early project to situate human beings in the midst of beings rather than in opposition to the world as object. There is hence something more profound at stake for Heidegger in his turn to poetry. Poetry is not only the language that can *describe* deeper relations. Rather poetry is the path toward the *Menschenwesen*, i.e., toward the essence as *home* of the human, insofar as language is poetry before anything else. The question of home becomes most pressing for Heidegger at the end of his life. His last written words ask whether *Heimat* is still possible in "the engineered homogeneous world civilisation." (GA 13: 243[6]) Far from sentimentalising poetry Heidegger's turn to poetry depicts the profound question whether human beings can regain their essence *qua* home or whether machines and technology take over and subdue and replace human beings by depriving them of their home: their mother-tongues which ground in poetry. If language is the house of being, then as such language can be a home, but *qua* house language can also turn into the utter opposite of a home. Note, viz., that the process of positionality's silent takeover takes place in language and that language, as we shall see below, has its origin in silence. Thus, language itself is dangerous.

2   The Danger *of* Language

The danger of positionality is *Nachstellen*, the resentful chasing and imitating of beings. By chasing and imitating beyng sets itself into its unessence. The same pertains to language. The threat to and of language comes from language itself. Recognising the danger of language does not do away with that danger either. There is no essence without unessence, there is no fourfold without positionality, there is

---

[5] "*Goethe* nennt diese anderen Verhältnisse die "tieferen" und sagt von der Sprache: "Im gemeinen Leben kommen wir mit der Sprache notdürftig fort, weil wir nur oberflächliche Verhältnisse bezeichnen. Sobald von tiefern Verhältnissen die Rede ist, tritt sogleich eine andere Sprache ein, die poetische." (Werke. 2. Abt. Bd. 11. Weimar 1893, S. 167)."

[6] "Denn es bedarf Besinnung, ob und wie im Zeitalter der technisierten gleichförmigen Weltzivilisation noch Heimat sein kann."

no language without danger. The danger *of* language is to indicate that this danger comes from language. Yet, how is language a danger to us and itself? I shall argue that it is precisely death as refuge and shrine that structures and permeates the danger of language.

In his lecture course on *Hölderlin* Heidegger explicates the poet's insight that language "is the most dangerous of goods ... given to man [who is the] destroying and perishing, and recurring [creature]." (GA 4: 35/54) Heidegger reads this as saying that language "is the danger of all dangers because it first creates the possibility of danger." (GA 4: 36/55) He continues: "Danger is the threat that beings pose to being itself." (GA 4: 36/55) Danger thus means that we forget being because of the prevalence of beings. Language is the most dangerous good because language appears to address beings and beings only. The problem is precisely that language discloses beings as beings and we, of course, need that disclosure as we necessarily are in the world. But at the same time this disclosure of beings covers over beyng. Heidegger, however, sees another possibility to disclose beings through language so that beings do not block beyng. For Heidegger the thinking of the essential event depicts a possibility to say out of beyng directly because, as exemplified by the very word *Er-eignis* in the unfolding passage, this saying is a non-propositional and non-representational saying. This saying and thinking of the simplicity of beyng discloses at once the true richness of beings. Yet, also beyng itself, for its very abyss, essentially occurs as danger. For Heidegger (cf. GA 11: 79) the word "is" harbours the entire fate of beyng. In any saying of the tiny word "is" there sway the fissures of beyng—and thus the abyss. The self-differentiation of beyng, where being means that beings are, at once opens an abyss because beings are unfounded. But meaning can also collapse. Meaning is fragile. Even where speaking lets something appear of itself as that which this something is, this letting-appear always at once covers over. Death as refuge and shrine structures these occurrences. Language is its own greatest danger precisely for its relationship with death, which as *Ge-Birg* is also the locus of all concealing concealment and thus of the breakdown of meaning. Language then exposes itself to danger because "[t]he word as word never offers any immediate guarantee as to whether it is an essential word or a deception." (GA 4: 37/55).

Yet, this is not primarily due to human erring, for language itself speaks. Language is, as Demske puts it, "not primarily a human instrument ... but rather ... a mode of the self-revelation of being." (Demske 1970: 130) That language speaks us shows itself in the automated speech of the everyday, for example, in the idiomatic expressions we use without having to think. To a certain degree language must be automated because this is how language can structure the everyday world in a reliable and therefore meaningful way. Yet, this is also precisely where language can at once also be harmful because in so doing language covers over deeper goings-on. "[L]anguage must constantly place itself into the illusion which it engenders by itself, and so endanger what is most its own, genuine utterance." (GA 4: 37/55) In everyday communication language necessarily places itself into a illusion. What seeming? The illusion that language is first and foremost expression of the contents of the soul or today of personal will and one's psychology. The illusion that language addresses beings and only beings. The illusion that language is but communication and transmitter of information. The illusion, as Heidegger puts it in *Traditional Language and Technical Language*, that language is first and foremost a system of signs and ciphers. The illusion that language is instrumental.

Heidegger, however, determines primordial language as a saying that lets something appear and that lets something show *itself from itself* (cf. Heidegger 1989: 23ff). I will explicate this further in the next chapter. The German word for showing is *zeigen*. A derivative mode of showing is the sign, *Zeichen*, a marker or cipher which signifies something, but which does so in such a way that what the sign points to, is predetermined and precisely does not show itself from itself. There is no original *saying* here. Thanks to the Boolean variable computers and informational technology precisely work by reducing the fundamental question of what *is* and what *is not* to the signs "Yes/No," or simply "1/0." The *Seinsfrage* is reduced to the simple but far-reaching answers, "Everything exists" and "Nothing exists." Their constant interplay now drives the codes of the algorithms that are the make-up of the technological world. The reduction of language in the information age, as Heidegger points out in *Traditional Language and Technical Language*, is caused by positionality but also by the way in which human beings co-respond to the challenges of technology (cf. Heidegger 1989: 23). Heidegger's examples are news, reporting, and journalism. Information is supposed to be clear, unambiguous, and fast. Hence the technological age must work to disambiguate the meaning of words so that information can instantly and ever faster reach human beings everywhere. In this way information allows the subject to be everywhere at the same time, scattered all over the world, with the world reduced to the subject's representation. Technical language is a reduction of language and therefore of human existence and nature. But technical language is a self-reduction of language and its aim is "[t]o relegate the animated, vigorous word to the immobility of a univocal, mechanically programmed sequence of signs. [This] would mean the death of language and the petrifaction [*Vereisung*] and devastation of Dasein." (GA 6.1: 145/144[7]) A way out of that is *poetic* language.

Ossip Mandelstam is a kindred spirit of Heidegger in this regard. There is a crucial passage in Mandelstam's *Conversations about Dante* that helps us better understand Heidegger's insight into the threat language posits to itself:

> Any given word is a bundle [of rays], and meaning sticks out of it in various directions, not aspiring toward any single official point. In pronouncing the word "sun," we are, as it were, undertaking an enormous journey to which we are so accustomed that we travel in our sleep. What distinguishes poetry from automatic speech is that it rouses us and shakes us into wakefulness in the middle of a word. Then it turns out that the word is much longer than we thought, and we remember that to speak means to be forever on the road. (Mandelstam 2001: 52f)

Mandelstam understands the word as a bundle of rays, not as a sign. To say the word "sun", a word we might "use" daily, is not a linear process. There is no word-object that simply means or directly refers to some concrete object out there that is

---

[7] Krell translation.

already given as that very object. To Mandelstam saying "sun" always takes us on a journey *to* the sun, on a long yet now ordinary and concealed path. The fundamental motion is not one of correspondence (in the ordinary, non-Heideggerian sense of correspondence) exclusively between the word-object or signifier "sun" and the object-object or signified "sun." "Sun" is hence not some contingent sign for some object we arbitrarily refer to as sun. When we say "sun," we travel to the sun itself and the sun travels towards us. Saying the word is not an isolated event, but through our saying the history of the word and the very mother-tongue to which it belongs is moved and moves through the word. In *The Essence of Language* Heidegger quotes a line from Hölderlin that is similar to Mandelstam. Hölderlin says, "words [are] like flowers." (GA 12: 196/100) Heidegger argues that this constitutes the bringing forth of the word "from its inception." (GA 12: 196/100) In the *Conversation* Heidegger and his interlocutor determine words, based on the Japanese term for language "*koto ba*," as "petals" (GA 12: 136/47). If words are flowers and petals, then words blossom and flourish, they spring from an opening bud, and are at once under threat of death. Words are finite as is any occurrence of language, any *Sprachgeschehen*.

Mandelstam also points out that everyday speech is "automatic." This means that everyday speech makes itself. It is not the activity of subjects as bearers of a set of capacities that make speech. Speech is automatic and repetitive in the everyday precisely because language speaks us. Speech is also automatic in the sense that it operates with a prefixed set of meanings. Speech is deaf to the very words that make speech possible. Everyday speech is communication, *Mitteilung*, i.e., the sharing of what is new and what is known. As Heidegger writes in *Being and Time*: "One means *the same thing* because it is in the same *averageness*." (SZ: 168/162) Everyday communication, as *Being and Time* points out, works by "*gossiping* and *passing the word along*." (SZ: 168/163) This repetition works by a certain sign-character of words, which words do have as they become reified. What is said, is always already and on average understood by everyone. Communication thus does not need to consider the unity of the manifold of the word. In everyday speech, language can automate itself to a degree that it becomes a sheer automatism. In *Being and Time* that automatism is interrupted by angst, facing death, and the call of conscience. The call of conscience calls on Dasein, yet there is no propositional message. Still, the call calls Dasein to become itself by running forth toward death, i.e., by facing its ownmost possibility, the possibility of its impossibility. The call of conscience calls upon Dasein in silence. There is a similarity between the silent call of conscience and the call of being. But while Dasein is called upon to arrive at its highest authenticity, the call of being calls upon the human being and the responses of humans co-determine the epochs to come.

The "claim" of being itself is precisely what is not yet fully developed in *Being and Time*. With the thought of the interdependent *Zuspruch—Entspruch* being and its tidings call upon the human being to co-respond.

For Mandelstam it also takes poetry as well as the poet and his experience with language to mediate the primordial relationship with language. Mandelstam says that poetry galvanises its readers. Poetry shakes us "in the middle of the word." That is, in the middle, the centre, which is the word. This very middle, however, itself a manifold, unfolds and breaks open as a "bundle of rays." Hence words can be "ambiguous", can have multiple meanings and shelter their history as does the word *Ereignis*. Poetry or rather poetic thinking breaks with the ordinary, it discloses what is literally there, hidden in the word. Poetry breaks open the word and frees its rays. Poetry shows that words are longer, deeper, wider, less clear than communication can allow for, since poetry is original language. Both Mandelstam and Heidegger see language as threatening itself in automated speech and they take the poet to be responsible for the heeding and safeguarding of language.

In the *Conversation* Heidegger mentions a further way in which language is a danger to itself—and to human beings. Heidegger recounts his conversations with Count Kuki and notes that "[t]he danger of our dialogues was hidden in language itself, not in what we discussed, nor in the way in which we tried to do so." (GA 12: 85/4) The danger here is translation. Count Kuki knew German, Heidegger spoke no Japanese. In an attempt to make himself intelligible to the European Heidegger, Kuki *applied* European concepts to Japanese thinking and art. The topic of the conversation, however, was not Schiller's aesthetic or Kant's *Third Critique*, but the Japanese notion of *Iki*. Heidegger admits that "it was *I* to whom the spirit of the Japanese language remained closed — as it is to this day." (GA 12: 85/4) But Heidegger here also implies something else. That is to say that translation is dangerous, especially in the age of instant communication, because translation works by means of the correspondence theory of truth and hence must assume that everything can easily and unambiguously be translated into another language. However, European categories of *aesthetics* do not easily and flatly correspond to the Japanese way of thinking about art. The reason for this is precisely that language is not the sum total of word-things belonging to a specific "language", say German or French. Language is not a tool like a hammer. Instead, language is the dwelling place of a people and as such translation must respect the otherness of the ways of dwelling of a specific people whose language is to be translated. Communication necessarily operates under the assumption that all languages say the same and that they can all be perfectly translated. This leads to a homogenisation of world-access and world-understanding. As outlined in Part III, Heidegger understands the Latinization of several ground-words of Greek thought to be highly problematic; first and foremost the word subject, a first simulacra, a translation blind to the original experience grasped in the Greek ὑποκείμενον. "The language of the dialogue [between Count Kuki and Heidegger]" Heidegger bemoans, "constantly destroyed the possibility of saying what the dialogue was about." (GA 12: 85/5) The language of the dialogue was the language that developed with and out of European spirit and history. That philosophical language of that particular tradition threatens to distort Japanese thinking, if we blindly apply the European concepts to Japanese thought. This is a prime example of how any disclosure simultaneously occurs with concealment. The conversation discloses something to the interlocutors, but the conversation also covers over something crucial. In this case the *Iki*, which was supposed to be the focus of the conversation, was actually concealed. There is hence a cleavage between European thinking and Japanese thinking and this cleavage cannot be translated or communicated away. We must rather specifically think this abyss, this schism, not in order to remain in an abyss, but in order to find common ground. Heidegger reminds his interlocutor of his notion of language as "the house of being." If language is indeed the house of being, then the Japanese live in a different house than Europeans. "[A] dialogue from house to house remains nearly impossible." (GA 12: 85/5) Yet, only "nearly impossible" because the different houses of language are neighbours. Thus, acknowledging this impossibility is the invitation to a proper dialogue between the neighbouring houses, where one always needs to be wary whether one still *says* something at all. Speaking is easy. But *saying*, in the sense of letting something show itself of its own accord, that is the art and that is where language comes into its own. Poetic saying is not preferable on some mere aesthetic grounds. This is not about preference at all. Poetic saying is what sparks a true community among mortals and genuine relationship with things, earth, divnities and sky because it is out of saying that a world proper for mortals can occur. A poem is not a representation of some objective world. Instead, the proper poem casts a proper world into the open and lets shine forth the sheer *occurring* of world and things, rather than violently reifying and trying to control beings.

As death is the concentration of *bergen*, death is at stake in all philosophical dialogues. Death as *Ge-birg* grants the possibility of a conversation to disclose something. But death at once also threatens total concealment and withdrawal because as shrine of the nought death also means the possibility of an utter breakdown of meaning. It is upon mortals to heed death precisely as refuge and shrine, as in this way they properly participate in occurring of clearing, the clearing for self-concealment—yonder of substantialisation and reification. *Letting* something *be* and shining forth in its own accord is precisely the mortal stance, rather than wanting to exercise control over something.

When Heidegger speaks of a danger or threat to language, we must again be mindful that *danger* is a term of art for Heidegger. There is always danger in beyng. Heidegger does not long for some imagined better earlier Golden Age when "Being" was—or will be—without danger. As long as humans are and as long as beyng *is*, there will be danger. Danger is how beyng discloses itself. But where there is danger, there also salvation is possible. Of course, one has to read this also in the other direction: where the saving grace grows, there is danger also. What comes to rescue is, by the law of equiprimordiality, *language* itself. Yet, this is only the case, if mortals properly say out of language itself, say poetically, i.e., in a heeding and safe-guarding manner. For the word "is" *is* the fate of being. The tremendous danger of language is its power to say ontologically and determine what is. Such is the task of mortals in the fourfold. More precisely, the task is to respond to the gift of tradition (*Überlieferung*), for example, by cherishing and reading again foundational texts. *Überlieferung* is the delivery and dedication of the gift that comes over us. Tradition is handed down *in* language. Since this gift is in excess of itself, it opens up a genuine future.

The threat to language is thus both imminent and immanent, external and internal, and language is under threat as long as it is, for language is primarily a threat to itself. This is precisely because language initially speaks itself. Language is a monologue. This introduces an element of self-relationality. In that language speaks itself, it opens the realm within which things and world are present. But as such language is also a threat to itself and to the world. As danger to itself language can hence close itself off from its sheltering mode. This is possible because of language's relation to death. Death is as refuge of beyng also the utterly inaccessible and that means that death is the realm where language can lose itself. Sheltering-harbouring is by its very locus, death, always under threat to self-conceal itself from itself. Human beings are responsible for cherishing language precisely as the realm thanks to which beings at all appear. Mortals must properly *say* and that means, as we shall see, to learn how to be properly silent, especially in an age of constant and instant communication. For stillness is what lingers in the essence of language.

Chapter 17
The Essence of Language in View of Death

In his later work Heidegger provides several, seemingly disparate determinations of the *essence* of language. In the *Letter on Humanism*, henceforth *Letter*, he calls language the "house of being" (GA 9: 313/239). In the *Conversation*, Heidegger bemoans this notion as clumsy (cf. GA 12: 85/5). He also points out that the house of being is not a philosophical concept that subsumes other definitions of language (cf. GA 12: 108). In the same conversation Heidegger thinks after the Japanese word for language, *koto ba*, in order to determine the essence of language. Heidegger translates *koto* as "*waltendes Ereignen*", as "happening holding sway." (GA 12: 136/47) *Ba* means "petals". Thus, language as *koto ba* is essentially nothing linguistic in the ordinary sense, but language is rather petals or leaves that prevail and eventuate, i.e., occur and self-withdraw. In other places, like *The Essence of Language* and the *Way to Language* Heidegger, however, determines the essence of language as *die Sage*, *saying* (cf. GA 12: 202; 224). Moreover, silence continues to play an important role for the determination of the *essence* of language as *Sage*. Silence, of course, is also already important in *Being and Time*. In this chapter I shall provide a synthesis of Heidegger's apparently disparate determinations of the "essence" of language. In Part III I have argued that Heidegger understands essence in the context of technology as a realm or dimensionality within and thanks to which beings unfold in a certain manner. This is also how Heidegger understands essence in *On the Way to Language*. Essence is not the timeless whatness of language. Heidegger understands essence, as Dastur notes, "in the sense of the old verb *wesen*, as the temporal unfolding of the being of something." (Dastur 2013: 224) Essence refers to the ways in which something essentially occurs rather than what something is. The mentioned "essences" of language are thus not metaphysical quiddities at odds with one another. In my view, we are to think these "essences" of language as unfolding out of the thinking of the event. The question is how, or if at all, it is possible to unify these ways of unfolding. This possibility shall be the focus of this chapter.

As language is of being first, we need to think language's unfoldings also in light of death, since death is where being takes refuge, comes into its own and where it rests. The *Letter's* proposal to free language from grammar (cf. GA 9: 313/239) is

© Springer Nature Switzerland AG 2021
J. A. Niederhauser, *Heidegger on Death and Being*,
https://doi.org/10.1007/978-3-030-51375-7_17

in the background of Heidegger's endeavours to say out of the essence of language. Or rather to say the language of essence, *die Sprache des Wesens*, which is to say of being itself and its inherent withdrawal, allowing to think sheer occurring without reification. It is precisely this attempt at non-reifying poetic language which brings language here in the vicinity with death, for the sheer swaying of language, and its silence, is related to concealment, withdrawal and to the nought.

1 On Silence

In *Being and Time* Heidegger argues that Dasein ordinarily understands language as made up of "word-things," (SZ: 161/156) which are found in dictionaries. Thus, Dasein tends to reduce language to something present-at-hand that Dasein operates with in the world. Dasein reifies words. There is a naïve realism at work here that attributes a *ratio essendi* to language, as if it were some object readily available in the world. This naïve realism goes together with an instrumental representation of language. Heidegger wishes to refrain from such a reductive understanding of language. This also means that language is not an accidental capacity attached to the human being *qua* calculating animal. For Heidegger, language, or ontological discourse, as he calls it in *Being and Time*, is co-constitutive of Dasein's existentiality and being-in-the-world. Dasein goes about its world *through* discourse, i.e., through its hermeneutic circles that by that very circular movement disclose world. Dasein's ontic language, for example, Dasein's automated speech, is only possible on the ground of ontological discourse. Ontological discourse, in turn, does not consist of "word-things." Instead, silence and listening co-constitute discourse. These are not deficient modes of discourse but are essential to it (cf. SZ: 161/156). As early as *Being and Time* silence is thus fundamental to Heidegger's thought of language.[1] There would be no ontic speech without the silence of ontological discourse. Ontological silence structures the world insofar as the primary structure of the world is non-propositional. Thus, a certain withdrawal takes place in silence. This withdrawal of words co-enables the disclosure of world and meaning.

Heidegger also points out that by keeping silent in the ontic sense one may be able to say more than someone who is eloquent and continuously talks. Speaking too much can even impair understanding because what is essentially at stake gets covered over (cf. SZ: 164/158). This is again an example of how a thinking of

---

[1] Among others, Polt makes the case that there must be a connection between the emphasis Heidegger places on silence and his support for the Hitler regime. Polt argues Heidegger emphasises silence so that he would not have to speak about his involvement with the Nazis (cf. Polt 2013: 63ff). Note, however, that Heidegger places emphasis on silence as early as 1925 (cf. GA 20: 368ff/267ff). Derrida (cf. 1990: 148) argues that a sympathetic reading of Heidegger's silence on the Holocaust should consider his silence as underlining the monstrosity of the crime. There is nothing to say about the Holocaust because anything that could be said would be a distortion of the horror.

presence that is forgetful of concealment and withdrawal brings about a concealment of its own. Keeping silent can, in turn, be an authentic way of *saying*, for
example, in the sense of showing someone that one understands and cares. When
someone dies or when someone tells us of something tragic, listening and keeping
silent might often more profoundly understand what is at stake. Saying too much
can cover over an authentic understanding. In some situations, we can *say* more by
not speaking. This is why *saying* is a showing. Dasein is properly able to be silent,
when it is authentically disclosed to itself, i.e., when it knows itself (cf. SZ: 165/159).
Dasein knows itself best when it is authentically towards its ownmost possibility,
death. Thus, when Dasein is properly mortal, Dasein is able to bear silence in a
proper way and so carry and support others.

Furthermore, the call of conscience, which calls on Dasein to be itself, is silent
and has no propositional message. Dasein needs to be able to keep silent so that it
can hear the call: "*Conscience speaks solely and constantly in the mode of silence.*"
(SZ: 273/263) Heidegger will later speak of a "saying nonsaying" (GA 11: 78) as
co-constitutive of language. Even though no proposition is uttered by the call of
conscience, there is a message. The message is a claim to Dasein to leave behind the
they-self. The message of the call of conscience is, "[s]trictly speaking — nothing."
(SZ: 273/263) In other words, the "not" that always already constitutes Dasein,
sways in the nothing of the call. The silent call is not indeterminate or aimless, but
it incites Dasein to accept its ownmost being-able-to-be. The call calls upon Dasein
to run forth toward its ownmost possibility, to take over its finite self and to accept
its authentic possibilities to be. This early nearness of death, silence, and the call
would guide Heidegger toward his thinking of beyng as the essential event, i.e., as
that which withdraws as it approaches; that which is abysmal and unsupported; that
which has literally nothing around itself and hence ordinary language finds nothing
to address beyng with.

In his Nietzsche lectures from the late 1930s on the eternal recurrence of the
same Heidegger thus says that the essence of language has "its origin in silence"
(GA 6.1: 423/208). Heidegger already says this from the perspective of the event. In
the 1930s Heidegger begins to call *Sprache*, language, an interest of beyng itself:
"every saying [*Sage*] arises from beyng and speaks out of the truth of beyng." (GA
65: 79/63) That is, language is *of* beyng and human beings are thrown into a language. Put differently, language speaks us insofar as language speaks. In the 1930s
language takes on another meaning than it did in *Being and Time*. Nevertheless, the
place language now occupies emerges from Heidegger's early focus on silence. In
Contributions silence, or rather Heidegger's notion of *Erschweigen*, bearing silence,
plays a crucial role. Contrary to *Being and Time*, silence as bearing silence is not a
mode *co*-constitutive of discourse. Silence now takes the upper hand. This is why
the fundamental attunement of the other beginning is reticence. The just quoted passage from the Nietzsche lecture continues: "wherever the matters of death and the
nothing are treated, being and being alone is thought most deeply" (GA 6.1: 423/206
ta). Thus, bearing silence means to think beyng abysmally, as outlined in Part II, and
this is possible for human beings because of death. Bearing silence, however, does
not mean to be mute. Rather, and this is how Heidegger understands a proper

speaking *out of* beyng in a thinking manner, bearing silence means to say of beyng through a non-saying. That is, a saying that shows beyng but that does not try to fixate and hence does not reify beyng. A saying non-saying is an elusive, non-reifying, non-propositional saying that articulates beyng's self-withdrawal as exemplified in the unfolding passage explicated in Part II.

Vallega-Neu thus argues: "The necessity to bear silence in speaking derives from Heidegger's experience that beyng itself occurs as withdrawal, that truth occurs as self-concealment." (Vallega-Neu 2013: 128) As I pointed out in Part II, Heidegger makes the experience of withdrawal in the analytic of Dasein's being toward its ownmost possibility that is at once Dasein's impossibility. Bearing silence is, the way in which we can speak *of* beyng without ever saying too much. Beyng's claim comes over the human being as the attunement of reticence. It is by *bearing* silence that mortals can think the abyss of beyng as the "unsupported unsafeguarded." Thus, here a realm opens up where mortals renounce beings so that mortals become open again for the true abundance of beings. Mortals can bear silence, and therefore most profoundly think beyng and only beyng, if mortals grant death and nothingness their claim over them. This call, then, is what lets human beings *stand in* or *inabide in* beyng's history, in beyng's traceless draft. To not reify beyng, for Heidegger, means to think beyng not *in*, but *as* its tidings and that means to think beyng itself as ebbing and evolving in a heterological way as its history. Beyng refuses itself, but through this refusal *it* gives. It is for beyng's inherent withdrawal that anything *is*, i.e., that anything at all can occur. Beings are because beyng withdraws itself. Mortals correspond to withdrawal through bearing silence.

In *Contributions* §§ 37 & 38, Heidegger says that any genuine experience with beyng as history and refusal is such that it leaves humans speechless. Therefore, humans do not need to invent a new language in order to speak out of beyng (cf. GA 65: 78/63f). This may seem odd because Heidegger is, on the face of it, notorious for his neologisms. With the beginning of the thinking of the history of being, Heidegger, however, noticeably returns to simple words of the vernacular like *Ereignis* and carves out their richness. For Heidegger this also includes the rather strange term *Ge-Birg*, as he assumes to free the word by hyphenating it and thereby letting the word itself unfold as a bundle of rays, as Mandelstam would say. According to Heidegger the German vernacular calls a mountain range *Gebirg* precisely because mountains are a tempo-spatial occurring that is never entirely accessible, i.e., always to a certain degree concealed. By hyphenating the word *Gebirg* all of a sudden the word breaks free from our ordinary associations and we can begin to hear the moments of *bergen* in it. The *Contributions* are in turn a prime example of a poetic language that tries to articulate beyng in its withdrawal and that, therefore, speaks in an elusive manner. For its very elusiveness this language, however, brings forth the truth of beyng. Wrathall points out that the silence of being points to absence, an absence that can, in fact, *be* (cf. Wrathall 2010: 150). Yet, this is not quite it. Note that Heidegger precisely does not want to understand silence or withdrawal or concealment as absence! That would be the ordinary metaphysical interpretation of these phenomena which have led to the abandonment of being in the first place. Concealment, silence, withdrawal are not at all absences or privations.

Instead, they are how beyng itself always already occurs. They *are* beyng. Which is also why, as I quoted in Part II, death is beyng. We have now already come closer to an understanding why Heidegger sees an essential relationship between being and language. Heidegger's language, for example in *Contributions* and *Über den Anfang*, is one that attempts to speak carefully and in a sheltering manner of beyng without fixating or reifying it. This is how in any saying of beyng death as beyng's refuge is at work.

Mortals correspond to beyng's silence through bearing silence. Bearing silence also safeguards beyng insofar as bearing silence is also a timid, non-representational approach to the history of beyng. The call of beyng is silent insofar as the message is still strictly speaking nothing, but now in the sense of the refusal of beyng. Human beings are receivers as well as messengers of the call. In the *Conversation* Heidegger redefines the meaning of hermeneutics as close not only to the Greek verb ἑρμενεύειν, "to explain, to interpret", but also to the Greek god *Hermes* who is the messenger of the gods (cf. GA 12: 115/29). But Hermes is also *the* god of hiding and concealing. Properly responding to the call also includes responsibility for tradition and origin. By the proper response human beings enact their *"being* human" (GA 12: 115/41), i.e., humans become responsible. The proper response to beyng's silent call is renunciation, *Verzicht*. As Davis shows, renunciation is the negation of the will to sheer self-affirmation, which is the driving force of machination. But renunciation is not resignation or world-denial. Renunciation is affirmative, insofar renunciation calls mortals to summon up the courage to refrain from the prevalent will to mastery (cf. Davis 2007: 95f). In the talks *The Essence of Language* and *The Word* Heidegger ties renunciation to the essence of language as saying. Heidegger argues that the German *Verzicht* comes from the verb *zeihen*, which means *zeigen*, to show, and which he understands as related to the Latin *dicere*, to say. Heidegger understands *zeigen* in the sense of "to allow to be seen" (GA 12: 210/142) and this, he claims, is the meaning of the old German word *sagan*. In renunciation hence "[s]aying dominates" (GA 12: 210/142). But not a saying of propositional claims or even human speaking. This saying is more fundamental and occurs consonant with the tidings of ἀλήθεια. This saying is a saying that knows it has to refrain from something. Heidegger says this with reference to his interpretation of George's poem *The Word*. George writes: *"So lernt ich traurig den verzicht: Kein Ding sei wo das Wort gebricht."* "So I renounced and sadly see: Where word breaks off no thing may be." (GA 12: 208/140) The poem speaks of a renunciation. But the poem does not, on Heidegger's reading, depict a pessimistic sentiment by George. The poem rather speaks of a successful, *geglückt*, grounding which the poet at once releases, *loslässt*. This includes the renunciation of the will to command over beings: "The poet must renounce having words under his control as the portraying names for what is posited." (GA 12: 215/147)

By his renunciation of control over words George properly *says*—in an intransitive sense—out of beyng in a reticent way. A poem as George's *The Word* is proper mortal correspondence, and it lets encounter the world precisely through the very renunciation of control. Such a poem is a grounding aware of its mortal finitude and of concealment in any disclosure. Thus poems, too, are *things* in the old sense, where "thing" meant gathering (cf. GA 7: 155/151) and nothing reified. Poems gather the world as fourfold. Poetry is *poietic* because it brings forth that other possibility of world, i.e., of a disclosure mindful of the inherent self-concealment in its midst, and poetry can do so precisely because poems do not objectify and do not want to control what they speak of. For Heidegger, poems *say* something, i.e., they let something show of its own accord. For example, how a winter evening occurs. Still, such a poem does not represent something in particular. The poem rather allows for the proper occurring of a winter evening. Here Heidegger's strange claim in *The Danger* can begin to show its meaning. There Heidegger says that "[d]eath is the refuge of beyng in the poem of the world." (GA 79: 56/53) The poem of the world is the "thing" that gathers the fourfold originally. The fourfold itself is a poem in the sense that the fourfold cannot be controlled by the mechanism of objectifying and reifying positionality. This world, however, can only open up, if mortals are open to experience death as the utter concealment of beyng. Then, the objectifying, reifying, making-present forces of positionality are denied their power, are renounced. Heidegger here says that this only comes about, if beyng itself appropriates the essence of the human being. This is, however, neither fatalism nor passivity. Again, this means that how mortals respond to their death, whether they welcome their death into their existence, as inextricably interwoven with who they are; that at the heart of existence, there is an unresolvable tension called death. If mortals welcome this concealment into the midst of who they are—rather than asking what they are and giving the same answer over and over again (rational animal)—then is there a possibility for salvation. Why? Precisely because "to save" means to free something to its essence and the "essence" of the human being is their death. Released or saved in this way there can be a good death. But the thought of death also allows to go down into abysmal beyng, and by renouncing the prevalence of the will, a genuine world for mortals emerges. Wrathall hence puts it as follows: "[Poetry] can attune us to that which does not belong in presence in our world." (Wrathall 2010: 152) As Rilke says, poetry can let us glimpse at the echoes of the utterly nonavailable that however co-constitutes this world: death. Poetic language in that sense thus lets us glimpse at death and only then do beings in the whole come into view: the Holy as Wholesome is achieved.

2   The House of Being

Silence and bearing silence are not to be understood as passivity or quietism. They rather indicate a sheltering. Saying less sometimes safeguards what is at stake, for example, when one keeps silent in moments of tragedy or joy rather than commenting the situation to bits. Such a *saying* non-saying is hence a showing of what presently occurs. The notion of language as the house of being speaks of a sheltering of being through language. Even though Heidegger calls the notion "clumsy" in the *Conversation*, he does not give up on it and rather tries to explain better what it is he means when he calls language the house of being. The problem with the term is that calling language the house of being inspires representation. Furthermore, house of being can all-too easily be understood as a philosophical concept subsuming essential features of language. Nor is the house an actual receptacle for being. It is crucial that Heidegger introduces the "house of being" in the *Letter on Humanism* where he also further develops his notion of being (or beyng) as the possible, *das Mögliche*. In the *Letter* Heidegger critiques the will to actualisation and effectuation, as *Wirkung* and *Verwirklichung*, of our epoch. The will to actualisation at work in positionality is on the one hand a manifestation of the metaphysical schema of potentiality-actuality. Heidegger begins the letter by pointing out that our age is predominantly characterised by a drive to produce and dominate the actual. This amounts to a production for the sake of dominance over beings without allowing for their respective being to unfold on its own. Exactly this kind of a will to dominance is what Heidegger also considers to be prevalent in Sartre's existentialism. Sartre notoriously turned the metaphysical schema of the prevalence of *essentia* over *existentia* on its head. By his privileging of *existentia* Sartre privileges the actual, the sheer thatness of *my* existence. Sartre thereby also makes the subject sovereign over its essence, for the Sartrian subject can freely choose its essence (cf. GA 9: 328ff/246ff). The Sartrian subject makes itself, i.e., it posits itself. On some level, that is the necessary consequence of Descartes' dictum and German idealism's subsequent determination of the subject as that which posits. The subject must ultimately also posit its own objectivity totally and absolutely and will and effectuate also its own essence. This is what I have been referring to as the post-modern subject in this book. Heidegger's philosophical project from *Being and Time* onwards can be understood as the struggle against objectifying subjectivism that makes the human subject the foundation of all that is. In the *Letter* Heidegger points to language as a way out of that subjectivism. We should hence not ignore the fact that language and a call to heed language is prominent in the *Letter* in which Heidegger clearly describes how his thought differs from Sartre's. What Sartre ignores in his reading of *Being and Time* is that *Being and Time* understands *existence* in a non-metaphysical but rather literal sense as *standing out*. Sartre's failure to heed language does not only cover over how Heidegger understands *ek-sistence*, but also reinforces the paradigm of the age, which is the metaphysical paradigm of actuality above possibility, of wilful production for the sake of dominance. That is the forgetting of being in a nutshell. Thus, it seems to be the case that we can get over the forgetting of being and think being as the possible by heeding language. There is, I argue, a vicinity of language as the house and death as the refuge of being.

In a footnote to the *Letter* from 1949 Heidegger mentions that the essential event is still held back and therefore the talk of being in the text must necessarily lead to confusion (cf. GA 9: 321/245 *n*a). This is a hint to us today that, after the publication of such texts as *Contributions* and *The Event*, we are to think "being" and "language" in the *Letter* out of the essential event. Moreover, being is here already fully articulated as realm of the *possible*. Thus, language as the house of being must be understood out of the tidings of the event and in terms of being as the possible. This is why Heidegger says in the *Letter* that "[l]anguage is the clearing-concealing advent [*Ankunft*] of being itself." (GA 9: 326/249) This claim points to the essential relation between beyng and death as sanctuary. Yet, the way in which we increasingly interact with language impedes this understanding of language. The threat to language is the same as Heidegger already identifies in *Being and Time*, namely the instrumental representation of language as a tool of information. Language is the instrument by which technology not only reports its operations, but, and this is crucial, reified language is also the instrument by which these operations function. Technical language is the *ratio essendi* of the technological constellation, of the planetary control-grid. We naturally speak of programming and coding language and also of neuro-linguistic programming, a means by which human beings, purely in their cognitive behaviour, can seemingly be reprogrammed at will. A thinking of language in terms of clearing-concealing denies the predominance of language as instrumentality. Heidegger here says that in language, properly understood, being itself *arrives*. But that means, of course, also that being here at once self-conceals. The "house of being" then, as Heidegger notes in the *Conversation*, is not a receptacle, which the object "being" is safely stored in (cf. GA 12: 112/26). Instead, the connotations of dwelling and shelter the notion of the "house" inspires are crucial. Being *dwells* in language, which occurs out of abysmal silence. Being is not without proper language and language is not without being. Human beings also dwell in language. Language is not a random human capacity to make sounds that we happen to agree are meaningful. Nor is language a random collection of words. Nor is language a transmitter of information. Rather, language is the realm where human beings dwell and where human beings get in touch with being. This is because being always *says*, where saying means to let show, the *Zwiespalt*, the schism between being and beings, to which human beings respond. As Heidegger writes in the *Onto-Theo-Logy Essay*: "Being which is *beings* … This is what the fairy tale of hedgehog and rabbit of the Brothers Grimm tells us: *"Ick bünn all hier"*—"*I am here already.*"" (GA 11: 69/62) Being always already *is* being, *says* beings in their being. A simple statement such as "I am here" is an ontological statement that speaks out of the schism between being and beings. "Difference" is not some mental model applied in order to make sense of the world. The *Unter-Schied*, the schism, always already sways. That is to say, the schism occurs as being eventuates and since mortals dwell in language. Humans are always in language and always address something as determined, insofar as something has always showed itself to them as distinguished from something else, as differentiated. What shows itself, shows itself because of this original schism, which, however also means that beings and being belong together, In this sense language is the "clearing-concealing advent of being itself"! As that very differentiating of what something is, what something is not, and how that something is different from something else. Of course, where *concealment* sways there death partakes in the occurring.

The much bemoaned "devastation of language" (GA 9: 318/243), which began to be a trope at the time when Heidegger wrote the *Letter*, is not a moral problem, but, according to Heidegger, stems out of being itself insofar as human beings forget being. In our age one of the most pressing question is how we respond to nihilism. That now says that nihilism means that we cannot make proper distinctions, that we exist in in-difference and hence nothing makes sense. But nihilism also means that we are cut off from being, from origin. Existentialism co-responds to this problem by reinforcing metaphysics' forgetting of being and by making the subject sovereign over its existence and essence. Heidegger's suggestion is to think out of the silent call of beyng itself, mindful of the fact that human beings do not make themselves, and this addresses the history of being. Language as house of being then denotes a dwelling place for human beings and is a place where they correspond to the history of being. The latter is, Heidegger says in the *Letter* "never past but stands ever before us; it sustains and defines every *condition et situation humaine*." (GA 9: 314/240) A house, of course, is not automatically a home. It is upon human beings to co-respond in such a way that language becomes a home (cf. GA 9: 333/247).

Thus, what Heidegger calls language belongs to the event and its movement. Heidegger says this explicitly in *The Essence of Language*: "Language belongs to this essential occurring, is ownmost to what moves all things because that is its most distinctive property. What moves all things [*All-Bewëgende bewëgt*] moves in that it speaks." (GA 12: 190/95 *ta*) Language *west*, essentially occurs, as moving and this occurrence self-differentiates as presencing, *Anwesen*, and withholding, *Abwesen*. Movement for Heidegger does not mean the measurable representation of something changing its position from A to B. Instead, Heidegger understands movement as opening a path (cf. GA 12: 186/129). Language is that which at all opens the possibility for human beings to be on the way. Mandelstam's dictum, that "to speak means to be forever on the road," now says that language is what lets human beings enter the history of being. The devastation of language diminishes those paths and enforces the forgetfulness and abandonment of being because language is *qua* house of being "the keeper [*Hut*] of being present [*Anwesen*]" (GA 12: 255/135). Heidegger places language notably close to death as refuge by calling language "keeper". Death and language are not identical, but they are essentially related, and we can now more clearly see why. Both of them grant shelter to beyng. Equally both can turn against beyng. Death is always the possibility of both beyng's self-appropriation and its utter abandonment. A house need not be a home. It is always upon mortals to co-respond appropriately to the silent call of beyng, and that means with reticence and releasement precisely in an epoch that revels in the fancy of supposed human omnipotence. Death is the constant reminder that we are only ever on the way and language is that which opens up finite, but immeasurable, uncountable paths (possibilities) for mortals to be on the way! This is why we need to cherish our languages. The house of being is the shelter of the openness of being. Not only poets and thinkers safeguard this house, but also those communities of mortals that cherish their dialects and vernacular. Death, in turn, as refuge is the turning place of beyng's self-concealing, self-refusal and self-withdrawal. Language *is* the arrival of beyng and death *is* beyng's departure. The house of being then is not an image or a metaphor. The house of being is the way in which language unfolds as a place of dwelling for mortals and beyng alike:

> Thinking builds upon the house of being, the house in which the jointure of being, in its destinal *unfolding*, enjoins the essence of the human being in each case to dwell in the truth of being. This dwelling is the essence of "being-in-the-world." (GA 9: 358/272 *me*)

3   Language as Saying

From what I have argued so far, a certain hierarchy of the dimensions and tidings of language emerges. Silence is the origin of language. As such silence guides language. Beyng's self-refusal and self-withdrawal, which occurs thanks to death, is what gives rise to language and to beyng's silent calls to human beings, beyng's echoes through its history. The silent call means that human beings as thrown always already find themselves in an epoch which is not of their choosing and which they have no full control over but which they, nonetheless, have to respond to. For they are shepherds of being, but not the lord of beings. The call is "silent" because there is no set of propositions by which beyng, this realm of the possible in excess of itself, communicates its demands to human beings. *In* silence, language paves the ways of beyng's history. Language is, as that which moves the world, the house, or the realm, of beyng. As such language and for its essential relation with death language gives rise to the historical dwelling grounds of mortals; in our epoch that dwelling ground is called fourfold.

What seems to be lacking in all of this, is how we ordinarily understand language. The ordinary representation of language is that language is a means of expression of subjective contents, that language is an instrument which we have created and which we use to communicate. Yet, Heidegger claims, "language is never *primarily* the expression of thinking, feeling, and willing." (GA 11: 118/41 *me*). Nevertheless, "saying", *die Sage*, which I take to be Heidegger's ultimate determination of the occurring of language, on the face of it seems to be rather close to expression. Saying is the ultimate determination of the essence of language since saying guides and encompasses the other ways language essentially occurs and eventuates. In how far? Insofar as silence needs saying because silence cannot rest with itself. Furthermore, insofar as saying, which Heidegger understands as a showing, is that which sets in motion the world and lets appear and insofar language as saying is the house of being, for being simply means withdrawing *presence*, i.e., *An-wesen* and *Ab-wesen*.

But how are we to understand *die Sage*, *saying*, as different from expression? Who is it here who does the *saying*? Adding to what I have outlined above I shall in the following further explicate the crucial notion of saying also in relation to death as refuge and why the essence of language ultimately is captured for Heidegger in saying.

In *Moira*, an essay devoted to Parmenides, Heidegger claims that the representation of language prevalent today as a means to transmit information stems from the Greek representation of language as φωνή, meaning voice and sound. This early reduction of language, i.e., this early forgetting of the true scope of language, has evolved into the representation of language, argues Heidegger, "as a system of signs and significations, and ultimately of data and information." (GA 7: 250/91) Φωνή is a derivative mode of what Heidegger means by *saying*. As φωνή language itself conceals itself since φωνή is directed at beings first. Language, after all, is the most dangerous good and as such language self-withdraws and self-conceals. It is the task of mortals always to return to quest after their understanding of language. Heidegger, however, believes that Parmenides articulates another possibility of language, a possibility Heidegger wishes to remind us of: "We have to learn to think the essence of language from the saying, and to think saying as the letting-lie-before [*vorliegen-Lassen*] (λόγος) and as bringing-forward-into-view [*zum-Vorschein-Bringen*] (φάσις)." (ibid.) Thus, λόγος, in the way that Heidegger understands it, and φάσις constitute *saying*. Λόγος is gathering for Heidegger. As such λόγος is the primary moment of saying and is what releases into *presence*. Λόγος constitutes the primary presence thanks to which beings appear and has primarily nothing to do with a statement or proposition. Λόγος *is* the free play of *letting*, releasing into presence, allowing preliminarily for something to appear of its *own* accord. This is the first moment of language as saying and it cannot stay on its own but needs φάσις. Φάσις, viz., is that which brings forth and thus fully releases phenomena into appearance. Thus, if the essence of language is saying, then this does not mean that language expresses subjective contents. Instead, language as saying is primarily the simultaneous occurring of λόγος and φάσις, of gathering and appearance and bringing-forth. In this sense saying is more primordial than human speaking as φωνή. Without saying, without that first opening of appearance, human φωνή would not be possible. Hence for Heidegger human speaking is not a mere "psycho-physical" reaction to, say, their mortal finitude. Instead, human saying is a correspondence to language as saying, to the dimensionality (realm) of language thanks to which, *qua* presence and appearance, the world is there. Hence how mortals respond to language is ultimately how the world appears. Releasing into presence and bringing forth are not presence *of* something or appearance *of* something. Instead, both are of a "*for…* -structure," which is to say that they allow *for* something to appear and be present. In the third part of the essay *The Essence of Language* Heidegger understands *Sage* in terms of its Indo-Germanic root s*agan*. Heidegger translates *sagan* as releasing into presence but also as "clearing-concealing releasing [*freigeben*]" (GA 12: 188). Heidegger here explicitly emphasises concealment as prevailing in saying. Hence death is here also silently mentioned.

Thus, the movement of language as saying is the same as the movement of the event. The concealing of saying is not only reminiscent of death as refuge. Death is where language, like being, finds rest and self-withdraws into. It is hence important to note that in the essay on the "essence" of language Heidegger turns the formula "*das Wesen der Sprache*" ("the essence of language") into "*die Sprache des Wesens*" ("the language of essence"). What he means by this is that language as saying addresses the way in which the event unfolds (cf. GA 12: 190/95).[2] The event is that which comes into its own *as* it withdraws. As saying, Heidegger suggests in the *Conversation*, language addresses the human being (cf. GA 12: 143/142). Language is the movement that brings forth a presence thanks to which beings appear. In this sense language discloses world and *speaks* us. Language then is what constitutes the human being as that being that discloses (cf. GA 12: 12/190). Poets are in a favoured receivership of language as that which constitutes the world. This is why their words properly disclose world to us.

---

[2] See also (Dastur 2013: 237) on this.

Language as saying brings forth a *presencing* which for its simultaneous withholding is in excess of itself and allows for an intelligible presence of beings. Understanding language in this way prohibits one to consider poems as aesthetic representations of objects. Instead, poems grant *being* to beings, i.e., poetry for Heidegger is that which casts something into its proper presence so that the world lights up and stands revealed. In *On the Origin of the Artwork* Heidegger argues that C.F. Meyer's poem "The Roman Fountain" does not represent some present-at-hand fountain. Instead, Heidegger argues, truth is set forth in the poem (cf. GA 5: 25/17). That is, the poem sets forth the temporal being of beings as the clearing-concealing thanks to which beings are intelligible and meaningful. There is not some contingent object "Roman Fountain" Meyer tries to describe and represent as accurately as possible. The poem rather gives meaning and access to a thing that is of a past historical world and people and epoch whose being lingers on through the ages. This is why the poem is meaningful. If it were a mere representation, an *Abbild* or copy, then the poem would not speak to us. With Hölderlin's hymn *The Rhine* this is even more obvious. Hölderlin does not at all attempt to give a representation of the river Rhine. Instead, the poem discloses and grants meaning to the river so that the Rhine first becomes the Rhine in the epoch of Hölderlin. The poem is a discovery of the river as the river that it is. The poem *is* the river, its history and fate. When we understand language as *saying*, poems release things into appearance in a different light. This light, however, always arises out of darkness, from out of what utterly cannot be mastered and tamed, from out of the unintelligible and thus from out of the shelter and limit of any clearing: from out of death.

We must bear in mind that Heidegger's determinations of the dimensions of language also aim at freeing language from positionality. Positionality perfects the reduction of language to information and this reduction devastates language as well as human beings' relationship with being and the world. Heidegger's determinations of language as *saying*, as house of being and silent call, depict a possibility of experiencing language in a non-technical, non-instrumental way. These ways of occurring of language cannot be formalised. They cannot be made operational. Positionality must of necessity operate with a formalised, non-ambiguous language, which positionality treats as a material. Heidegger writes: positionality "commandeers for its purposes a formalized language, the kind of communication which "informs" [*eingeformt*] man uniformly, that is, gives him the form in which he is fitted in to the technological-calculative universe, and gradually abandons "natural language."" (GA 12: 252/132) This in-forming of human beings is such that they, too, stand ready as a resource for the demands of positionality. Interpreting language originally as saying entirely eludes, even renders powerless the demands of positionality. One cannot formalise language as saying, one cannot build a computer programme that lets the world light up in the way that Hölderlin's or Rilke's poems do; this world, the fourfold, is as inconspicuous as the weather, as the blue of the sky. The programming languages of positionality want to achieve something else entirely. By means of these technical languages entire "worlds" of the past can be reconstructed on screens and reproduced over and over again, haunting the present epoch. Yet, do these "worlds" light up anything about that which *is today*? Or do they rather freeze us in a positive feedback loop of the production and consumption of "experiences"? Language as saying cannot at all become a means, for saying eludes objectification. Heidegger's work on language is not readily available for any kind of production, as are, for example, the results of linguistics for coding. Of course, today the issue is that, as Müller argues, that anything which cannot be formalised for immediate production "is degraded as "unclear" and "untrue"." (Müller 1964: 83) This is even more relevant today than when Müller originally wrote this. Müller also points out that universal objectification is not just a symptom of the forgetting of being. Objectification *is* the forgetting of being. Language as silence, as saying, and as the shelter of being is an exit out of technology since positionality cannot gain anything from *saying*.[3] This exit, though, is not somewhere else, is not some door we need to look for. Rather, this exit lies in the way in which mortals respond.

With the help of mortals, language as saying safeguards itself against self-reduction. In that saying shelters, saying is in harmony with language as the house of being and silence. Death is what gives rest to language as saying, for death is the refuge. Silence remains the origin of language, when Heidegger begins to refer to language as that which gives presence because any presence only occurs consonant and simultaneously with refusal and withdrawal, which metaphysics interpreted as privative absence and lack. Thanks to refusal and withdrawal, which function as shelter, language as saying does not exploit and exhaust itself as an object of use. Rather, language as saying is in excess of itself precisely because there is an essential relation between death and language. I can now focus on this unthought relation. Death as that which always withdraws, as that which utterly defies the self-aggrandising subject's will to mastery—which is why the transhumanist subject must act against death—will prove to be the realm where language finds rest. From that tension-filled relation a path towards the fourfold opens up.

---

[3] See also Iain Thomson's crucial work on how positionality affects and transforms education and how it does so by reducing language to a transmitter of information (cf. Thomson 2005: 156ff).

Chapter 18
Language and Death in the Fourfold

The key passage speaks of the essential relation between language and death. As I have tried to show in this part so far, this does not mean that this relation is at stake only in the key passage. Nevertheless, I now turn to an in-depth interpretation of the passage in question and read it against the background of the tension between the fourfold and positionality. I first explicate the key passage and combine this with my findings so far. This will allow me to elaborate on the role death plays in the constitution of the world as fourfold.

1   The Essential Relation in Focus

The passage where the essential relation is mentioned reads as follows:

> Reserving itself in this way, as Saying of the world's fourfold, language concerns us, us who as mortals belong within this fourfold world, us who can speak only as we respond to language. Mortals are they who can experience death as death. Animals cannot do so. But animals cannot speak either. The essential relation between death and language flashes up before us but remains still unthought. It can, however, beckon us toward the way in which the nature of language draws us into its concern and so relates us to itself, in case death belongs together with what reaches out for us, touches us. (GA 12: 203/107f)

As noted in the introduction to this part, Agamben reports Heidegger's apparent inability to justify the claim that there is an essential relation between death and language. Heidegger is here, argues Agamben, at "a crucial outer limit ... perhaps the very limit" of his thought (Agamben 2006: xi). This limit is death itself and concealment, which Heidegger does bring into focus, but which nonetheless is barely articulable.

The notion of "flashing up" is crucial here. In *The Turning* Heidegger says that beyng itself *flashes* in technology every time when positionality shows its true danger (cf. GA 11: 122/44). Just as a flash is a sudden burst of light that immediately disappears, those moments of greatest technological danger erupt suddenly but

© Springer Nature Switzerland AG 2021
J. A. Niederhauser, *Heidegger on Death and Being*,
https://doi.org/10.1007/978-3-030-51375-7_18

instantly fall prey to forgetting. This may be most obvious with the explosion of the Atomic bomb. In such lethal moments beyng as abyss itself flashes and human beings, if they are awake to that danger, realise just how powerless they are in the face of the history of beyng. The task of humans is to respond to these flashings. Hence Heidegger follows Hölderlin and says that in danger salvation is enshrined. Beyng only ever reveals itself in flashing up. But beyng does not always or only flash that visibly. The outburst of the Atomic bomb is a symptom of earlier, deeper goings-on that occur silently. Thus, the flashing of beyng is more originally related to beyng's silent call. This is what makes beyng dangerous and the responsibility of mortals so tremendous. To hear those silent shifts in beyng is precisely what mortals "walking the boundary" and "seeking mystery" have to do. For Heidegger only a released stance can hear those silent shifts in the fissures of beyng. It is worth noting here that the "*Gelassenheit*", which Heidegger speaks of in later years, is hence nothing to do with some "mindful relaxation" or attempts to find inner peace. Quite to the contrary, *eingelassen* into the world as it is and into the tidings of beyng, released still from the immediate demands of positionality, the *gelassene,* released thinker begins to harken the mystery: the shifts of the fissures of beyng, this dark mountain range mortals stride through. Only rarely do mortals see beyng as flashing. For the most part beyng tides in concealment.

In an essay on Heraclitus Fragment B50[1] Heidegger maintains that "the essence of language flashed in the light of being" (GA 7: 233/78) when Heraclitus thought after the key word λόγος. More precisely, when Heraclitus explicated the λόγος he thought after the schismatic presence thanks to which beings appear. This, in turn, means that Heraclitus thought the "difference" between being and beings. In his first fragment Heraclitus understands λόγος as that which attunes human beings even if they do not listen to the λόγος (cf. Hahn 1987: 30). With Heidegger we can translate Heraclitus' fragment as saying that the λόγος gathers human beings precisely by self-withdrawing from presence. The world appears as meaningful for the very self-withdrawal of λόγος. Heraclitus thus understood language as *saying*, maintains Heidegger. Among other things it was the reduction of language to phonetic expression, which begot the history of the first beginning as history of loss. With the flashing up of the essential relation between language and death Heidegger appears to suggest that there is again a historical chance to achieve a nearness with language and being and this happens precisely by accepting mortality. Thus, I understand the flashing in the key passage as a literal being-historical flashing, which is, as Agamben rightly puts it then, at the limit of Heidegger's thought. In *The Essence of Language* Heidegger says that the essential relation gives us a hint at "the way in which the essence of language draws us into its concern and so relates us to itself, in case death belongs together with what reaches out for us, touches us" (GA 12: 203/107f *ta*). This means that human beings can think the simultaneity of

---

[1] By no means do I claim to do justice to Heidegger's reading of Heraclitus and λόγος. This is just to give an idea where Heidegger draws inspiration for the essential relation between death and language. For an in-depth account of Heidegger on λόγος in Heraclitus see, for example Ivo De Gennaro's study (2001).

presencing and withdrawing, clearing and concealing because humans are touched by language and death alike. What I have argued so far in this book must hence be read against this claim that language is always already at work wherever death is, too.

It is also crucial that Heidegger introduces the essential relation with a reference to animals. Animals neither speak nor die, claims Heidegger. Rather, the animal is numb and perishes. What the animal lacks is access not to beings but to beings *as* beings, to beings in their unique presence, i.e., animals have no access to being itself. There is no world for the animal, only a circle around it thanks to which the animal can orientate (cf. GA 29/30: 274ff/186ff; 344ff/236ff). This is why language as an interest of beyng first, language as that which clears and conceals, does not concern and address the animal. I shall here not focus on the contested issue of the animal in Heidegger scholarship.[2] What is important for my endeavours is to stress that Heidegger does not understand the animal to be addressed by being, language and death in the way human beings are. That is to say that the animal is not responsible for being in the same way as mortals are. None of this is to reduce the animal in its being. Instead, Heidegger's claim about the difference between animals and humans wishes to free human beings from metaphysics. The metaphysical encrustation of human beings as rational animals, as bipeds that happen to speak and to calculate instead of, say, being feathered, is what Heidegger declaredly wishes to get over. But freeing human beings from metaphysics is tantamount to freeing nature from anthropomorphisms. I should also point out that transhumanism, for all its supposed scientific justification and longing for a non-human future, operates with the traditional metaphysical definition of the human being as *rational animal*. It is either the rational part that is supposed to be free from the prison of the flesh, the animal part. Or the animal part needs to be "advanced" and "enhanced" as bio-hackers propagate. But the question who the human being is entirely disappears behind these encrusted representations.

In the *Letter*, Heidegger thus says, "[m]etaphysics thinks of the human being on the basis of *animalitas* and does not think in the direction of *humanitas*." (GA 9: 323/246f) The motivation here is to free the human being radically from classifications in terms of species and genus. According to Heidegger, these classifications are responsible for the objectification of the human being and ultimately for the fact that even the human being is reduced to standing reserve, for these classifications are timeless and transtemporal reifications of what it means to be human. Furthermore, the human being represented as the supposed highest developed form of animal and organic life becomes the measure for all things in nature. This is why Heidegger warns that "[i]t could even be that nature, in the face it turns toward the human being's technical mastery, is simply concealing its essence." (GA 9: 324/247)

---

[2] See for example Wild (2013) and Calarco (2008). Problems surround the question whether Heidegger turns animals into something present-at-hand, and whether he anthropomorphises the animal. Note that Heidegger refers to the animal a *be-fähigt*, capable or competent to *be* in its own way (cf. GA 29/30: 342/234). However, the animal does not ask for the being of beings precisely because its own being is not an issue for it.

In an age in which the human being assumes to be the driving and all-determining force of the history of the planet—if something like the history of the planet even exists—what masks as total human control might be just the opposite: self-delusion and hence a loss of origin and genuine access to the world. The very last section of *Contributions*, which bears the title *Language (its origin)*, addresses the problem. Heidegger there says that language seems to be the "primary and farthest human-izing [*Vermenschung*] of beings." (GA 65: 510/401) However, Heidegger suggests that in language the "dehumanizing [*Entmenschung*] of the human being as *objectively present living being* and "subject" and everything hitherto" (ibid.) is possible. This sounds cruel at first, yet this is not a moral but rather an "ontological" claim. What Heidegger means by this is that there is in language the possibility to de-anthropomorphise nature *and* free the human being from the norms of metaphysics. In context of the *Contributions* this means the grounding of Da-sein as the adverbial site of beyng. In the context of the later writings the human being is to become "mortals." I reserve the question of the transformation of human beings in terms of language and death for the last chapter of this part. For now, it may suffice to point out that in the last section of *Contributions* Heidegger implicitly refers to the *Artwork* essay where he asks in how far the propositional sentence structure "subject-predicate-object" interferes with beings in their being (cf. GA 5: 8/6). To assume the human being as *subject* above all is primarily a result of the process of language's structuring of the world. Similar to the propositional sentence structure "subject-predicate-object," the human subject commands over the object. However, there is a possibility to step out of the assumption that language must always be propositional in order to be intelligible and meaningful. This is true, for example, for one of Heidegger's favourite poets, Rilke. The "dehumanising" of nature Heidegger speaks of would then mean both a renunciation of the reification of lan-guage and a return to the genuine occurring *of* language. There is also a reversal in and of language which Heidegger attempts. To a certain degree Heidegger attempts this with his language in the *Contributions*. Heidegger there reverses words like *Machenschaft* so that they no longer speak of a human activity but of an activity of beyng itself. Heidegger sees in this the possibility to free nature from human cate-gorisation, objectification, and hierarchizing because it revokes the subject's pow-ers. Nature would no longer be represented and produced as something present-at-hand available for use and consumption, if a change in thinking and thus language were to set in. Such a change in thinking would include abandoning the will, but it must begin with language. By surrendering language to beyng the subject realises its limited powers. In the last section of *Contributions* Heidegger thus writes, "[l]anguage is grounded in silence." (GA 65: 510/401) To answer Hölderlin's question, whether there is a measure on the earth, Heidegger in the last paragraph of *Contributions* also says that keeping silent "is the most concealed holding to mea-sure" and that language is "the positing of measures" (GA 65: 510/401). As I have argued in Part III, death is the standard of measure. Death and language together, if heeded by mortals, provide a measure on the earth. If heeded, they both bring about the equilibrium of the fourfold. It is the task of mortal saying to uphold that measure and ground other possibilities of human and non-human existence. Those other, wholesome groundings leave no room for subjectivistic fantasies of human omnipotence, but, as Heidegger writes in the last sentence of the *Contributions*, they only leave room for "moderation" (ibid.). Moderation matters because even what makes us human, language and death, are not our possession, our capacities, but are gifts.

Hence in the "flashing up" of the essential relation between death and language Heidegger sees a distinct possibility to get over the encrustations of metaphysics. This is not, however, a privileging of the human being but rather a warning to human beings that they must heed language because the measure of the world lies in language. Language can only have that role because it is essentially related with death, i.e., with the concentration of all concealing, sheltering, and withdrawing and thus of giving but also of abysmal destruction. Human beings then speak insofar as they are mortal, that is, insofar as they are touched by death and pulled into the realm of language by death. Mortals speak by responding to language as that which gives presence because language is related to that which withholds presence: death. This tension between language and death is what sets the worlding of the fourfold in motion.

2 Language and the Movement of the Fourfold

As I have indicated above, Heidegger argues that language as saying moves the world (cf. GA 12: 195/108). This must seem rather a strange claim by Heidegger. Yet, Heidegger does not mean by this that language moves the world represented as the planet. Language rather moves the four regions of the fourfold. Still, Heidegger speaks of the satellite "Sputnik" several times in *On the Way to Language*. Sputnik was launched in 1957 and was the first satellite that flew around planet earth. By means of the parameters "time" and "space" satellites allow the subject to surveil the planet. Heidegger sees in satellite technology evidence for "the battle for the dominion of the earth [which] has now entered its decisive phase." (GA 12: 201/105) By this Heidegger does not mean a battle between nation states for political domination. Note that Heidegger says this in the essay on the *essence* or dimension of language. Who or what is fighting over the dominion of the earth? What does language have to do with this battle? What is the endgame of that battle?

The battle is the battle between the world of humans and the dimension of machines, which humans are increasingly adapting to. Humans are adapting to the demands of machines by using time and space as parameters to generate a matrix within which total control over beings deprived of their being, i.e., over illusions and simulacra can be executed. The destructive machinery of the world wars is only the most visible display of the nihilism at work. Heidegger quotes George's ode "The War" from 1917 on the war machines: "These are the fiery signs – not the tidings [*Kunde*]." (GA 12: 179/84) The destruction of the war machines is that which is most visible about a deeper event that shapes the world. That deeper event is, for Heidegger, the battle over the earth *as* earth. That is to say over the earth as that which grants and gives because it conceals and harbours and shelters. For this earth now is challenged to stand ready as the measured and quantified planet that is to serve as a sustainable source of energy—by whatever means—for the sustained functioning of machines and their circuits and positive feedback loops. The drive to control and to dominate the earth represented and surveilled—and hence seemingly perfectly present and revealed—as a planet by satellite photographs is the endgame of that battle. This is the case precisely because, as Heidegger puts it, the "all-out challenge to secure dominion over the earth can be met only by occupying an ulti-mate position beyond the earth from which to establish control over the earth." (GA 12: 201/105). While the human subject assumes that it is at the centre of this drive and will to power, there is something else at work. For Heidegger that is being as *Gestell, Machenschaft*, or beyng in its "un-essence". The human subject is merely the functionary and executes demands the human subject has no control over. Nevertheless, the self-aggrandising subject fools itself to assume that it is really itself which is establishing its unchecked rule over the earth *as* planet. Perhaps this is but a hasty attempt to cover up the loss of meaning and direction. By establishing a perfect organisation of the planet the subject then might want to give itself direc-tion again. For Heidegger, this clearly means, however, that the human being must leave the earth.

Here Heidegger's reference to Thales, which I mentioned in Part III, shows a further implication. Leaving the earth behind does not take us to the stars, i.e., to that which grants orientation and destiny, but takes us away from them. Mortals can only see and walk towards the stars and hence find direction and orientation, when they are truly part of the earth and know their place. That a mortal being, a being that once knew of the *memento mori* and of the ephemerality of existence—the traceless draft of being—would attempt to assume godlike powers reminds us of Nietzsche's warning in *The Mad Man* that the human subject has killed God. Far from proclaiming a triumph Nietzsche warns that the time is not ripe for humans to become God or even understand the mad man's message. For Nietzsche the murder of God means that we have wiped "away the entire horizon" and have unchained "this earth from its sun" (Nietzsche 2003: 120). Thus gluttony, measurelessness, and disequilibrium, and even, depending on how we understand the word "horizon," a certain worldlessness all announce themselves in modernity. Nihilism and absur-dity are the consequence. This nihilism is countered with the hubris of the subject believing to be at the centre of the universe, the sun around which the planet revolves.

The total control over the planet is executed by time and space as parameters, but also by reducing language to a transmitter of information. Information is the unam-biguous formatting and hence storing of everything that once had to experienced, researched, investigated, discovered. Information stands ready and available and seems to make everything available—even the most distanced in terms of time and space. The seeming nearness of the world and history represented on the screen eradicates distance. This works by language as transmitter of these informational values. Language itself becomes information, an instrument, a system of formalised signs and signifiers standing ready to make everything that is and everything that was. Formalised informational language forms the "world" of machines. Thus, as I pointed out above, Heidegger presents the possibility to think language as *saying* as a way out of the dimension of machines. There is no control in saying, only a letting and seeing off, which, however, move the world as the gathering of the four regions. The fourfold is a world, rather a worlding, that cannot in any way be represented as the planet of surveillance satellites and "self-" flying drones. The fourfold shows itself as inconspicuous to representation. The fourfold withdraws from representation.

In *The Essence of Language* Heidegger writes on saying: "Saying, as the way-making movement of the world's fourfold, gathers all things up into the nearness of face-to-face encounter, and does so soundlessly, as quietly as time times, space spaces, as quietly as the play of time-space is enacted." (GA 12: 203/108) A focus on silence is necessary to see how language as saying moves the regions of the four-fold. Heidegger writes this right after he mentions the essential relation between death and language. Silence is the origin, the wellspring of saying and hence the origin of language. The essential relation of death and language, of concealment and opening, lies in that original silence. A return to silence is necessary *again and again*. Yet, the "world" of modern technology is one of permanent noise. As Heidegger writes in *The Turn*, "we do not yet hear, we whose hearing and seeing are perishing … under the rule of technology." (GA 11: 123/48) This is one of the clear-est ways Heidegger articulates the threat of technology. Namely that we lose our senses of proper hearing and seeing and hence access to origin. Hearing is not just the physical mechanism of processing soundwaves. Our ears are not simply ontic receivers of soundwaves. The ear is the locus of equilibrium, of the sense of orienta-tion and stability. The ear is the locus of the receivership of λόγος. The noises of household machines, cars, airplanes, helicopters, trains, air conditioning, back-ground music that serves to drown out stillness, the permanent buzzing, humming and purring that make up the backdrop of our daily lives—what are those but attempts to mute the silence necessary to begin to hear again. Outside the spectacle of the modern planetary entertainment and surveillance grid operating on sheer presence and a fake lack of distance without any ultimate goal but self-preservation—there is the possibility of the fourfold. There, in silence, gods and mortals, sky and earth gather around simplest things like a childbed. The fourfold provides the pos-sibility to understand the world in a radically different way than we do in positional-ity. Saying enacts in silence the self-concealing openness of the fourfold, where human beings are neither centre nor ground, but mortals who are fragile and vulner-able and who are because "[s]ong still lingers over their desolate land." (GA 5: 274/204).

This silent lingering is an invitation to enter the history of beyng. Heidegger ends the paragraph on the essential relation between death and language as follows: "only saying confers what we call by the tiny word "is," and thus we say after saying [*ihr—der Sage—nachsagen*]. Saying releases the word "is" into cleared freedom and therewith into the sheltered [*Geborgene*] of its thinkability." (GA 12: 203/108 ta). The tiny word "is" harbours the history of beyng because "*what is*" is deter-mined by how being currently occurs and our subsequent understanding of what it means to be. There are, however, always several dimensions at stake and at work. This is what Heidegger calls "vibrating". In these dimensions there are also the responses of metaphysics to the question of being at stake and as such these continue to have bearing on our future and our presence. Put differently: the responses to the questions "what is" and "what it means to be" are possible because of what announces itself in a self-concealing presencing. This self-concealing presencing now has the name "saying", which prevails, for its relationship with death—and death is the "goad" of the history of beyng. This is how language as saying, for its relationship with death, silently moves the world through an unheard history. This is also why the co-response of *mortals* is crucial. The vast dimensions of beyng set forth ways of presencing consonant with how mortals respond. Mortals respond all the more carefully and mindfully, the more they are aware of their death and hence of concealment at work in history. Thus, it remains to say that, yes, there is to some extent something vast and unfathomable at stake in history for mortals, something that cannot always be recovered by thought and response. Nevertheless, in order to gain the being-historical perspective, the perspective of *Ereignis*, i.e., the full insight into the thought of concealment-unconcealment is necessary.

Chapter 19
Language and the Essential Transformation

The question of the last chapter addresses what exactly it is Heidegger means by "mortals" and how language and its relationship with death plays into Heidegger's ultimate articulation of the transformation of the human being. The transformation of the human being means to cast the free-floating subject back into its world, onto the ground on which we stand and dwell and die. One could, of course, argue that it is rather reductive to name the human being primarily, if not exclusively, "mortals". Is this not even a retrograde step for Heidegger's philosophy? After all, one of Heidegger's most formidable, genuine accomplishments of *Being and Time* was to have thought Dasein holistically and deeply involved with its world. On the face of it, the notion of "mortals" seems to suggest that death and nothing else is what determines human beings. In what follows I show that this final step in the transformation of the human being is not a reductive account of what it means to be human. In order to do so one has to include what Heidegger says on *humanitas* in the *Letter on Humanism* but also who mortals are in his essays on language.

1 Homo Humanus

As argued in Part III, Heidegger sees human beings at a crossroads. Either human beings become "human material" artificially produced in factories (cf. GA 7: 93). Or they become what Heidegger in the *Letter* refers to as the *homo humanus*. This is Heidegger's response to metaphysics which has thought of the human being according to his animality but not according to his humanity. The sciences as the heirs of metaphysics, continue to imagine the human being as an animal. In *The Essence of Language*, hence in an essay where we might least expect such a claim, Heidegger warns that technological progress is about to turn humans into "monstrous creatures of technology, assimilated to machines." (GA 12: 179/85) He continues: "The step back into the sphere of human being demands other things than does the progress into the machine world." (GA 12: 179/85) This step back is a step

© Springer Nature Switzerland AG 2021
J. A. Niederhauser, *Heidegger on Death and Being*,
https://doi.org/10.1007/978-3-030-51375-7_19

into the realm of language as saying because language is what releases the human being towards his path of becoming the *homo humanus* (cf. GA 9: 345/262). The *homo humanus*, I aim to show, are human beings who fully embrace and appreciate their mortality.

For Heidegger the problem with metaphysical humanism is first of all that the metaphysical representation of the human as animal is prevalent in it. Furthermore, humanism is an "-ism" (GA 9: 345/262). That is to say, humanism does not begin to think, humanism does not think after the essence of the human being. Humanism rather operates with available schematic representations of the human being. The prevalent metaphysical representation of what it means to be human is that of the rational animal. Yet, the question where that representation comes from is not asked (GA 9: 345/262). Heidegger's critique of humanism, however, does not mean that Heidegger wants to do away with the human being. In the *Letter* Heidegger returns to his notion of *ek-sistence* to address the essence of the human being. *Eksistence* is still the multi-layered tripartite temporality where all three temporal *ecstasies* flow into each other. Yet, now *eksistence* is introduced into the history of beyng and thought of as touching and determining the human being from out of the event. In a crucial passage in the *Letter* Heidegger says: "This means that the human being, as the *ek-sisting* counterthrow [*Gegenwurf*] of being, is more than *animal rationale* precisely to the extent that he is less bound up with the human being conceived from subjectivity." (GA 9: 342/260) In footnote *c* added to the word "being" Heidegger adds: "Better: within being *qua Ereignis*." (GA 9: 342/260 *ta*) The human being ecstatically exists as the counterthrow of being means precisely to say that the human being is always already responding to being and that those responses return *to* the event and recur again *from* the event. Thus, the human being is dependent on the disclosures and withdrawals of beyng. As the counterthrow the human being is neither a present-at-hand living organism nor subject nor rational animal. Thus, the essence of the human being becomes *geschicklich*, destinal (cf. GA 9: 345/263). Human essence is now being-historical: "In his essential unfolding within the history of being, the human being is the being whose being as *ek-sistence* consists in his dwelling in the nearness of being." (GA 9: 342/261) This is also why Heidegger speaks of the poverty of human *ek-sistence* (cf. GA 9: 342/261). The poverty of human beings and their role as the shepherd of being have as a consequence that human beings are at the mercy of beyng's call. But they are equally at the mercy of their responses to that call. One could argue that due to human mortal finitude those responses are never fully transparent and therefore there is always something "un-pre-thinkable" or immemorial prevailing in history. This is however true only to a certain degree. With the thinking of the *Ereignis*, of inherent withdrawal, that which appeared as "immemorial" to metaphysics has now been brought into perspective. The finite responses are still finite. Nevertheless, the fact that Heidegger sees the importance of the response now means that there is a possibility to respond properly to the call and let those responses take their time, where these responses are spoken from out of the *Ereignis*, the realm of simultaneous withdrawal and arrival. The *Ereignis* is what metaphysics calls the "immemorial".

In this mortal poverty lies human dignity, argues Heidegger (cf. GA 9: 342/261). Accepting poverty denies the omnipotence which the subject assumes for itself and which the subject secures by organising all beings according to its desires. To accept that poverty is to accept mortality, is to let go of the assumption that human beings are the agents of history. To accept that poverty means to accept limitations and finitude. Hence the *homo humanus* is the mortal human being, the human being who is open to death as death—*den Tod als vermögen*. This thinking is what lets us see the richness of things as they are of their own accord. The *homo humanus* is the human being who does not forget the question of being and that means that the *homo humanus* does not revolt against being by assuming power over that which determines what it means to be. The insight that the human being as counterthrow of being does not determine what it means to be comes precisely from the human being as the mortal being. The way of mortals is a *letting* rather than a forceful production for the sake of increased production. Mortal thinking is mindful of concealment and hence it brings that which once was called "un-pre-thinkable" into focus while still being mindful of the fact that this, *beyng*, cannot be controlled. For there is a play, in which humans are at stake, and humans co-write this play as they respond. The less humans *will* something to happen, the less power the will has. This denial of will comes about from accepting death and being mindful of concealment.

On this reading the *homo humanus* is thus the mortal human being who is intimately related with beyng for his relationship with death. As we know from *Being and Time* and the *Contributions* the transformation of the human being begins with being-towards-death. In the *Contributions* it is the task of a few to initiate the transformation. This does not change with the later writings on language, as I shall show next. Yet, now in *On the Way to Language* there is a stronger focus on a community of mortals than there is in the *Contributions*.

2 Rare Mortals and the Community of Mortals

Running forth toward in *Being and Time* reveals death as Dasein's ownmost and non-relational possibility. These are the moments where Dasein is most authentic. Heidegger says that in this radical individuation "any being-with others fails." (SZ: 263/252) Heidegger even speaks of Dasein's *solipsism* in this context. Dasein is thus apparently cut off from others when Dasein becomes authentic. It seems as though there is no room for community in *Being and Time*. In the texts on the fourfold Heidegger, however, explicitly speaks of mortals in the plural which suggests a community of mortals. But also in Being and Time, even in the most radical individuation of Dasein its modes of taking care and being concerned "are not cut off from its authentic being a self." (SZ: 263/252) That is to say, Dasein is most authentic when Dasein runs forth towards its ownmost possibility and accepts this possibility on its own because this full self-responsibility is what first opens Dasein to be with others authentically. In fact, to say Dasein means to say being-with-others. Dasein then no longer "lives according to the mode of the empty majority" (de

Beistegui 2003b: 35) but can participate in forming genuine communities. Such communities are then ultimately formed by Dasein's ownmost possibility. Still, I would like to stress again that Dasein in *Being and Time* is an attuned structure, the being of the human being, not some individual. Hence the proclaimed "solipsism" of Dasein is not the solipsism of some subject, but rather shows the radical singularity and finitude of Dasein as the being of the human being.

This sense of community, which death sparks, resurfaces again along the thinking path in essays like *The Thing*, *Building Dwelling Thinking*, and also in *Language* and *The Way to Language*. Heidegger there expands on the relation between death and community and he explicitly does so in terms of dwelling. In a nutshell, the ultimate transformation of the human being Heidegger works towards, means to leave behind the atomised and nihilistic existence of the atomised, post-modern, rational animal maximising its utility by reducing itself to its desires, in order to enter into a community of mortals. Heidegger learns from Hölderlin the right kind of language that can articulate the fourfold and poetic dwelling. From Hölderlin Heidegger also learns the proximity between thinking and poetry and this marks the most significant alteration of Heidegger's own philosophical language. Heidegger's experimental language becomes *poietical*, a saying non-saying, an elusive language that still says the abyss and self-concealment of beyng clearer than any metaphysical language before.

In a crucial passage in *Language* Heidegger writes with reference to Trakl's poem *A Winter Evening*:

> Not all mortals are called, not the many ..., but only "more than a few"— those who wander on dark courses. These mortals are open [*vermögen*] to their dying as the wandering toward death. In death the supreme concealedness of being crystallizes. Death has already overtaken every dying. Those "wayfarers" must first wander their way to house and table through the darkness of their courses; they must do so not only and not even primarily for themselves, but for the many, because the many think that if they only install themselves in houses and sit at tables, they are already bethinged [*be-dingt*], conditioned, by things and have arrived at dwelling. (GA 12: 20/198 *ta*)

This passage has strong echoes from the *Contributions*. As argued in Part II, only a few, who are called by beyng, have to carry out being-toward-death, and their responses, for example, in poetry and art and the sciences, disclose possible ways of existence. The few mediate possibilities of being. Here Heidegger now tells us almost the same. A few hermits have to wander toward death. What Heidegger calls running forth in *Being and Time*, he here refers to as wandering toward death. Yet, death is now to be understood as refuge of beyng and shrine of the nothing. That is, what has disclosed itself to some remote and lonely few, is that beyng self-conceals and self-withdraws *as* its history. The few do not span open a realm for the many, they rather safeguard the world of the many. The fact that this arises out of "wandering toward death" also means that this is a finite event and that this has to be performed *again and again*. There will be an end to this, either when the last death will have been died or if machines should take over—an outcome Heidegger apparently assumes to be quite possible. Even though those who wander toward death, are remote from the many, they spark a community of mortals insofar as they selflessly think the concealment which any wholesome community of mortals requires. In my view, Heidegger thus understands Hölderlin's notion that "man dwells poetically" as follows. Poetic dwelling comes about when a few think concealment, when they go down into the abyss by carrying out death, and so help bring forth the rich simplicity of the fourfold and in this find a ground again. This takes place, for example, through the successful grounding and seeing off[1] of a world-forming artwork, that opens the realm for a community. That is to say, "ordinary" mortals are also responsible for their world. The ethos of the fourfold is to reflect in a communal way on what it means to be in the world and what it means to be mortal—for there to be a good death. Thus, Heidegger in these later writings on the fourfold no longer understands the everyday as inauthentic as *Being and Time* does. The poet's words are invitations to reflect on the community.

Note also that it is again the human being's relationship with his death that lets world arise. In *Being and Time* death as Dasein's ultimate limit co-constitutes world as the horizon of significance against which Dasein continuously projects its possibilities. The world begins where Dasein *ends*. In *Language* the world *worlds* as fourfold. The fourfold is in balance. Mortals can dwell there as mortals and the fourfold *worlds* because a remote few wander toward death as the refuge of beyng. This means to say that the few begin to think the concealment of beyng.

This takes place in the dialogue between thinking and poetising, as Heidegger himself undertakes it in his writings. Heidegger understands the German verb *dichten*, to poetise, as related to the Greek τίκτοσα, to bring forth. In poetry, or at least the poetry Heidegger considers, he sees the distinct possibility to bring about a disclosure of being. Being means that beings are. The poet is the one who can properly articulate this difference insofar as the poet calls upon, *heißen*, things, for there to be world (cf. GA 12: 23/199). That is, the poet is the one who can articulate the meaningful inter-relationality that makes up our world. This is the reason why language is essentially saying, i.e., a disclosure mindful of concealment, which provides the presence for all things.

The few are then those who can hear the call of beyng. They respond sooner to openings in history, yet they are and remain mortally finite and so is their response to history. Their existence is not described as privileged or elitist. Rather, their existence is a burden. With reference to Trakl Heidegger even speaks of them as *abgeschieden* meaning secluded and lonely (cf. GA 12: 48/170). Heidegger warns that we should not understand his remarks regarding the few as "dreamy romanticism, at the fringe of the technically-economically oriented world of modern mass existence." (GA 12: 76/196). Such dreamy romanticism would fail to accomplish anything precisely because romanticism only ever achieves escapist fantasies. Instead, there is a certain ecstatic dis-placedness, *Ver-rücktkeit*, about the few which allows them to face the world as it is and then see different possibilities of being. They have

---

[1] As Heidegger notes in the *Conversation*, departure, seeing off, *Abschied*, is not meant as simple negation, but as "the coming of what has been [*Gewesen*]" (GA 12: 146/54). We see here again the ecstatic movement of the history of beyng. What has been, will come toward us and out of this oscillation the presence forms.

to see something else that is possible *from within* where they are and where history is, for that is how proper responses to beyng are formulated. Escapist fantasies are just that: fantasies. The few and rare are literally dis-placed from the pieties of the current age, but for that very displacedness they are inserted into the arrival of beyng and its fate. For their displacedness they are able to think and articulate possible ways to get over the homogeneity of the technological world. They show us that despite the threat of the machine-world there is the possibility to come into one's own. Heidegger does not give an indication who exactly they might be in our age. Presumably his poets are among them. Yet, given the importance placed on concealedness, their emergence is not utterly contingent, but predicated on and necessitated by the movement and call of beyng. The call calls on humans to return home. Heidegger's thinking path is a remote path, but, as he writes on the *Holzwege*, his thinking does "walk in errancy, but [it] does not get lost." (GA 13: 91) Thinking always tries to find a way back home, for there to be a possibility of *poetic* dwelling: a dwelling in harmony with self-concealment. Language as saying is that home for Heidegger.

In a talk from 1960 entitled *Language and Home* Heidegger suggests that language is that which "gifts and brings forth home" "thanks to its poetic essence" (GA 13: 180). This is an echo of his earlier talk *Language* I have referred to at the beginning of Part IV. In the essay entitled *Language* Heidegger says that it is through language that we enter the essential event and come into our own, i.e., find a home. As mentioned above Heidegger's last written words ask whether being-at-home is at all still possible in the technological age. This must mean that language itself is under severe threat, for language is the home of the human being. Language can be a home precisely for its essential relation with death, i.e., with that which utterly defies technology's will at mastering and in this way provides shelter and possibility of withdrawal. Hence as long as mortals are mortal, song will linger in their lands. Withdrawal and letting-go are precisely what is needed in order to step out of the homogenising and flattening forces of positionality. Language is a home, when we heed our languages and our mortality. In 1969 Heidegger says to Wisser that what we require is "a new diligence of language. No invention of new terms as I once believed, but a return to the original contents [*ursprünglicher Gehalt*] of our own language. Language is, however, always under threat of decay." (Wisser 1970: 77) For language not to decay, but for language to flourish goes hand in hand with thinking concealment and the refuge of being: death.

Epilogue: A Response to the Question

In December 1975 Heidegger wrote a short poem in memory of his friend Erhart Kästner. Kästner had died in February of 1974. Heidegger himself died in May 1976. In the original German the first verse of the poem reads:

Wo aber sind wir, wenn wir uns mühen,
Rilkes Zuruf zu vollziehen:
 "*Sei* allem Abschied voran …"?
 Wohnend im Tod?
  Unbetretenes Gelände,
  das – Ende nicht, nicht Wende.
  Ungehörter Klang
  von An-Fang in die reine Nichtung:
  Urfigur des Seyns,
  unzugangbar der Vernichtung;
  im Selbander Eins:
  Fernste Gegend
  nächster Nahnis. (cf. GA 13: 241)

Heidegger here once more comes back to Rilke, the poet he had first become acquainted with during his time in Marburg. He asks where humans are when they try to carry out Rilke's call to be ahead of death. Heidegger asks once more, whether it is indeed likely for humans to dwell *in* death as he had argued in his writings on the fourfold. Death again is brought in touch with beyng. Heidegger refers to nihilating as the "*Urfigur*", the original gestalt of beyng, to which mortals belong insofar as they are in death. It is crucial to note that only if they belong to death, then *Vernichtung*, i.e., total destruction, does not occur.

The second verse of the poem addresses once more the gratitude mortals are to have for thinking, for being, and for their existence. Being grateful for thinking is necessary especially in an epoch that understands thinking as a mere neuronal function and which according to its functioning can also be mimicked for maximising effectivity. It is a strange gratitude, perhaps. For it requires one to be mindful of the presence of that which always already withdraws, but which as such gives. This

© Springer Nature Switzerland AG 2021   243
J. A. Niederhauser, *Heidegger on Death and Being*,
https://doi.org/10.1007/978-3-030-51375-7

withdrawal Heidegger calls beyng, this draft withdraws for its relationship with death. This draft itself, as Heidegger writes in *Über den Anfang, is* death. In a short text Heidegger wrote in honour of his student and friend Fridolin Wiplinger, Heidegger also speaks of a profound gratitude for their friendship in thinking. Heidegger recounts Wiplinger's last visit to him in Messkirch. The text tells us that Heidegger was shocked when he heard of Wiplinger's sudden death soon after his last visit to Heidegger. Heidegger notes the shock and "nearly insurmountable pain" (GA 13: 239)[1] his family and friends must have felt, when Wiplinger died. Yet, Heidegger also writes that the pain "slowly but surely transforms and relieves itself" (ibid.).[2] In this way the pain gradually turns into gratitude for the deceased. It is important that Heidegger does not speak of Wiplinger as "*Verschiedener*" (deceased) in the German, but as "*Abgeschiedener*". That is, Heidegger speaks of his student and friend as someone who has parted but who is on the other side of being, i.e., on the side of utter concealment called death. A "*Verschiedener*", someone deceased, would be someone who merely disappeared. But as an "*Abgeschiedener*" there remains an echo in the draft of being that can transform the pain into gratitude as long as mortals still dwell on the earth, as long as they are bound by the earth and cherish their ancestors. The thanking for thinking Heidegger speaks of is then on some level not just the profound act of thinking through the history of being. It is also the simple, but solemn gratitude of mortals to have met and existed, to have walked together with other mortals some parts of the tightrope walk that we call history and existence—more often than not on the edge. Without death there would be no thinking, for mortal thinking always needs darkness first in order to "see the stars", i.e., to find direction and orientation. A sheer presence and availability, limitless as they may seem, blind and numb human thought, for they capture us in the immediate and cut us off from being, which never stands ready in a sheer, immediate availability. A sheer givenness stifles thought as much as it stifles gratitude for the simple fact that there is something and that *I* am too: *sum moribundus*. If everything is simply available all the time and anywhere, then there is no poverty that we need in order to appreciate the richness of simple things—and that means of being itself.

"*Sei* allem Abschied voran ..." is a quote from Rilke in the poem Heidegger writes for Kästner. A quote that Heidegger seems to ponder at the end of his life. How can we be "ahead" of all departure, asks Heidegger. Rilke is the poet who calls death his friend and who speaks of death as the other side of being. There is in being always an echo of death. Heidegger's tentative response to Rilke is that mortals might dwell in death when they strive to perform Rilke's word of being ahead of departure. Can we dwell in death? What would that entail? Perhaps it is necessary to ask for the opposite: What would it mean to dwell with-out death, outside its realm, in a deathless sphere? Rilke gives an answer in his Tenth Elegy (cf. Rilke

---

[1] "Für seine Nächsten und die Freunde brachte der jähe Abschied einen kaum verwindbaren Schmerz."

[2] "Indes – langsam wandelt und mildert der Schmerz sich zum Dank an den Abgeschiedenen."

2013: 779). He describes the screeching sounds and noises of modernity as they cover over what Heidegger would refer to as *Geläut der Stille*, the ringing of silence. For it is primordial silence that first lets us hear of other possibilities of being—outside the power of positionality and its eradicating forces. For Rilke the modern world is "deathless". Advertisements of the beer brand "*Todlos*" indicate this to Rilke. Is it not strange that a beer is called "Deathless"? These billboards keep modern man endlessly distracted. Only behind the boards can the world be genuine, *wirklich*, Rilke writes. There are clearly echoes here of Plato's Cave. Note especially that for Rilke the world is not genuine when there is no death. There is no death in a world of distractions, commodification and objectification, for such a world knows only functionality and availability. Perhaps such a world as Rilke describes can only come about when mortals have already begun to forget their death. *If forgetting death comes first, then remembering death is necessary to return to being.* The ringing of silence together with simple gratitude for thinking could open another side of being. Dwelling in death then for Heidegger might mean the following: Being on the way, on the path in "untrodden terrain", in "pure nihilation" which means that there is nothing to hold on to for this thinking. "Pure nihilation", as Heidegger writes in his poem for Kästner, is the "original figure of beyng". For mortals in their concrete existence this means to let go of or to disempower the operational will at work when mortals attempt to control all beings. Letting go of this "Will to Will" takes place precisely when mortals are *as* mortals. Letting go of this Will frees for that which Heidegger calls *Stiften*, founding or instituting, because a profound gratefulness for being sets in when mortals begin to appreciate that they are and that something is at all. What is it that *founding* brings about? Founding brings about sense, meaning, grounding, and orientation. Not because mortals of their own accord emanate sense or are the origin of meaning. Rather, because by taking a mortal stance humans begin to see another beginning, where they are not at the centre of history, but from where humans receive meaning from history—if they respond properly. To be in this receivership means to be ahead of the schism of departure, for in this departure another historical beginning shows itself. The profoundest schismatic parting, *Ab-schied*—"threefold separation" as Goethe poetises—known to humans is death. This, then, is the response to the question of being: thinking ahead out of the schism of what has been, appreciating the necessity to depart from encrusted and reified representations of the human being and of the world toward another beginning in which beyng is thought always already as withdrawing and as such refusing reification. This means to twist free from the decisionless[3] and endless "and-so-on" which Heidegger speaks of in *Contributions* and which the "completion" of metaphysics brings with itself. In this *state* of completion "life" appears as a set of technical problems waiting to be solved once and for all. But this would mean never to depart from the Cave and to reify and encrust being further.

---

[3] Note that in German "to decide" means "*ent-scheiden*" where the *Schied* of *Unter-Schied*, of the schism, sways.

For Heidegger, the human being is always on a ridge walk between light and dark, hiking through the fissures of the mountain range of the history of beyng: through death. At any moment they can fall of the edge and become great destroyers. To provide so that there can be a good death is thus the task of mortals; for there to be a good death rather than a destructive all-eradicating death on a planetary scale or a lonely death of those isolated and without community, going to a lonely grave. There is thus also a practical response to the question of being: we are to become mortal, capable of death *as* death, open to death. That also means to be forever mindful of the darkness at work in history and an inherent danger, from which at once the saving grace arises. Becoming mindful of this is possible not only for those few and rare who think through the unsupported, unsafeguarded or the concentration of concealment. But for all those who *dwell* in the sense of keeping, protecting, and caring, where this sense of dwelling becomes attainable precisely because of one's mindfulness of the inherent withdrawal of being, the impossibility to make available and reify all that is. If the response to being means to become mortal, then this also means to reconnect with being itself, for being is *the Old*, that which was, as Aristotle says. To become mortal means to begin to remember what was, for that which was, lays concealed and waits to be discovered.

Still, the response to the question of being cannot lie in an isolated proposition, as Heidegger makes clear in *Being and Time*. The response arises from reading Heidegger's texts in view of the tradition he is part of and in view of the tidings of being. Heidegger makes the decisive experience with being in the analytic of Dasein's being-toward-death in *Being and Time*. Being-toward-death brings Dasein most radically and before the intensity of being. During its transcendental self-investigation Dasein realises that its ownmost possibility, that which simultaneously limits *and* releases all of Dasein's other possibilities, is *at once* Dasein's utmost impossibility of being. Being withdraws in the moment Dasein gets closest to it. Being, *beyng*, is that which self-withdraws. But this is precisely what continues to draw us toward being and to the question of being.

This experience of withdrawal together with the movement of ἀλήθεια and of ecstatic time explain why Heidegger speaks of the "turning" of beyng and of beyng as essentially occurring. I have argued that truth as ἀλήθεια is pivotal for the "turn" in Heidegger's thought. By way of ἀλήθεια Heidegger can more radically approach the basic occurrence of beyng he saw taking place in Dasein's being-toward-death—namely, that beyng self-conceals. With this thought Heidegger is already beyond the metaphysics of availability and actuality; he is already beyond the attempt to provide an ultimate foundation of beings. That is to say, Heidegger can begin to think being as the possible precisely because his thinking finds a path early on towards an understanding of death as ownmost possibility *and* impossibility. The sameness of being and nothing, their belonging-together is at the heart of Heidegger's thought. To think being as the possible, a path Heidegger embarks on in *Being and Time*, also allows him to see the history of being as a realm of possibilities from within which new horizons tear open thanks to the responses of mortals.

This is why death remains crucial throughout the thinking path—until, as we just saw, the very last of Heidegger's writings—and this is also why death is perhaps the most important way one can appreciate the very unity of that path. Death is the "highest testimony to beyng" precisely because death brings Heidegger's thinking close to being from the very beginning of the thinking path. Death even *is* beyng on the most fundamental level, for death is this utter withdrawal and sheer non-availability. Death as *Ge-Birg*, as the concentration of all *bergen* (sheltering, harbouring, concealing), is also most intimately related to time as that which ecstatically regulates the clearing of beyng's self-concealment. As *Ge-Birg* death is fundamentally related to the most fundamental figure of Heidegger's thought: ἀλήθεια. Hence death is also connected with time. Death is also what provides a window unto thinking the abyss of beyng, to think beyng as the utterly "unsupported and unprotected". This thinking of the utterly unsupported first fully brings the difference between beyng and beings to the fore. Which is precisely what metaphysics has forgotten and which is what, on Heidegger's understanding, metaphysics sees, but must work against in order to establish a permanent foundation. In other words, metaphysics, for it flees from the schismatic abyss, must establish a permanent foundation in form of the beingness of beings. The drive to establish a foundation, in turn, is what constitutes and drives positionality. This is why positionality must work against death, for death is that which continuously reminds of the non-available. Death reminds the human being of his limitations. It is likely that the inflated post-modern subject hence feels the urge to eradicate death. This, in turn, could be why Heidegger wishes to welcome death into the midst of being, especially so in the writings of the fourfold. The fourfold as another possibility of world, as another dimension mortals can poetically dwell in—dwelling in the sense of being mindful of concealment and therefore appreciative of the richness of things—is possible *now* and as long as positionality is the prevalent fate of beyng. As death is at work in the worlding of world as fourfold, the presence of being in the thing is a good presence, a presence mindful of concealment and finitude, of singularity and uniqueness.

In an age in which the human subject assumes to be almighty; in which the solutions to all the world's problems, be they hunger, disease, ageing, health, the planet's climate and future; in which even birth, life, and death seem at the mercy of human will and manipulation—or even of human making; in a world that purportedly becomes ever more complex; in such a world Heidegger's voice sounds like an anomaly. Not only does he tell us that there is just one question that matters, the simple question of being. He also tells us that we can only ask this question because we are mortal and that we have to accept our mortal finitude as our most fundamental way of being. For any attempt at dominance and manipulation must ultimately accept the uncontrollable, the unmasterable and the inaccessible. The unmasterable and the inaccessible belong to the concentration of all concealment, death, where death is a dimension mortals always already also take part in—whether they properly dwell in that dimension or whether they deny it. Those who believe that death is now a problem waiting to be solved once and for all by the wonders of technology might find it surprising that their urge to solve this "problem" is driven by the very source of unclarity and mystery they wish to eradicate: death.

Death, as I have tried to show here, is always *present*, for death is a dimension which mortals participate in. For Heidegger death is not a transition to an afterlife.

Death is not the end of a finite timeline. Death is for its inaccessibility the source of the exuberance of the abundance of beyng's possibilities. Death is in that sense what goads on history and human creativity.

A decisive passage in the note *Das Sein (Ereignis)* says that when we allow death into our existence, then death releases the gods into appearance: "The gods do not appear *after* death but *through* death." (Heidegger 1999: 9).[4] Heidegger's notorious remark in the *SPIEGEL* interview comes to mind where he says that only a god can save us now. Here in just quoted passage we learn what he means by this. Heidegger tells us that the divine appears through death which I read as saying that human beings have the distinct duty to appreciate their mortality in order to come in touch again with the divine and that also means with limitation and finitude. In this sense the *memento mori* is simultaneous with the appearance of the divine and this could spark another beginning. There is a certain solemnity about the passage just quoted. The gods appear through death and this allows for the "bridal festival" to take place, for a measure to be found again on the earth. This equilibrium, however, only ever lasts for a while, for the question of being has to be asked and responded to *again and again*.

Addendum: Death and Transhumanism

The present book is in part also a response to the question of what it means to be human today—and for the ages to come. Post-humanism and trans-humanism are just two of the possible names for the project to retire human beings and replace them one way or another with the digital and machinic. The programme of these extensions of metaphysical humanism seems to imply that it is ironically human-ism, i.e., the assumption that the human being is the maker of his own destiny and of all of history, which is at the heart of the drive to get rid of the human. For the human is no longer deemed good enough to fulfil the promises of *Reason*. It is not here the place to show how what calls itself transhumanism or posthuman-ism is deeply entrenched in and originating from within what Heidegger calls metaphysics. Posthumanism and transhumanism are born from the spirit of post-modernism broadly construed, if it is indeed the post-modern subject that assumes that it can makes itself and transform *itself* at will. Still, what post- and transhumanism operate with are the reified metaphysical interpretations of the human being, as if the "problem" *what* the human being is, has already been solved for good and we are now at best only waiting for optimisation of this *whatness* or, at worst, once and for all retire this corroborated whatness of the human being. Hence there is a need to depart towards another beginning, as Heidegger stated also in his public writings on cybernetics. Yet, the question for

---

[4] My translation. "Nicht *nach* dem Tod, sondern *durch* den Tod erscheinen die Götter."

the other beginning is not "what" the human being is. Instead, for the other beginning to occur the question of the "who" of the human being is pivotal, for here the human being is addressed in his essence.

Heidegger understood the catastrophe of modernity—this explosion of power and accumulation of abstract intelligence—as the human being's revolt against being. The human being began to take itself as the subject, the underlying ground of all beings in their objectivity. The revolt against being is epitomised for Heidegger in Descartes's notorious dictum of the *ego cogito*. The *"sum"* is here simply posited, not questioned further. Heidegger's early response was to bring the human being radically before death and mortality. *"Sum moribundus"* is a reformulation of the *memento mori*. There are places where Heidegger sees that the human being will begin to make itself and will begin to work actively against death. As quoted in Part III Heidegger mentions that in *Ge-Stell* humans will begin to produce humanoids just as *Ge-Stell* requires them. *Ge-Stell* need not even produce humans in factories, as Heidegger sometimes provocatively remarks. *Ge-Stell* produces humanoids inconspicuously as its functionaries, as simulacra of replaceable types. It is from within *Ge-Stell* that the desire for the retirement of the human in exchange for the mere fantasy of a future that never was and never will be human. Where Heidegger sees self-aggrandisement of the subject inflating itself and its power further, I see something else. The subject is beginning actively to get rid of itself, or rather of the residue human dimension of which it was born. Heidegger sees the possibility of the end of the human. But perhaps not the wilful working towards that goal.

The idolisation of man that takes hold in modernity, expressed for example by Francis Bacon, comes into full force in transhumanism. At the same time, and not coincidentally, the late-modern subject begins to be doubtful and suspicious of its capacities. And this is crucial. Where for Heidegger subjectivity is still for the most part in a place where it is about inflating human capacity and willpower, subjectivity now, in post-modernity or late modernity, resentfully seems to want to rid itself of its human origin. Whether the technological side is actually achievable or rather a total pipe dream I cannot answer here. Yet, the will to retire the human body *and* the human being is there and is reinforced by the fantasy that death is now optional, that death is now something that can be eradicated. Post-humanism's resentment against death mirrors its deep resentment against human limitation and finitude.

To argue against this is futile. One cannot argue *against* a linear process, one cannot argue *against* resentment. Nevertheless, one can point to other ways of being human, one can formulate a different break-away civilisation than the one proposed by the functionaries of technics. A civilisation that alters the ways of *Ge-Stell* and its self-exhausting modes. An access to another way of being lies in the tragic truth of history and a new appreciation of what Plato meant with the word σχολή. It is here, I believe, that the two trajectories part ways. To this I shall return when the time is right.

Bibliography

Adkins, Brent. 2007. *Death and Desire in Hegel, Heidegger and Deleuze*. Edinburgh: Edinburgh University Press.

Agamben, Giorgio. 2006. *Language and Death: The Place of Negativity*. Trans. K.E. Pinkus and M.Hardt. Minneapolis: University of Minnesota Press.

Arendt, Hannah, and Martin Heidegger. 1994. *Briefe 1925–1975 und andere Zeugnisse*. Frankfurt am Main: Vittorio Klostermann.

Beiser, Frederick C. 2008. *German Idealism: The Struggle Against Subjectivism, 1781-1801*. Cambridge, MA: Harvard University Press.

Blattner, William. 1994. The Concept of Death in *Being and Time*. *Man and World* 27: 49–70.

———. 1999. *Heidegger's Temporal Idealism*. Cambridge: Cambridge University Press.

Bojda, Martin. 2016. *Hölderlin und Heidegger*. Freiburg: Karl Alber Verlag.

Buhr, Manfred, and Robert Steigerwald. 1981. *Verzicht auf Fortschritt, Geschichte, Erkenntnis und Wahrheit: Zu den Grundtendenzen der gegenwärtigen bürgerlichen Philosophie*. Frankfurt am Main: Verlag Marxistische Blätter.

Calarco, Matthew. 2008. *Zoographies: The Question of the Animal from Heidegger to Derrida*. New York: Columbia University Press.

Carel, Havi. 2006. *Life and Death in Freud and Heidegger*. Amsterdam: Rodopi Publisher.

Chanter, Tina. 2002. *Time, Death, and the Feminine: Levinas with Heidegger*. Palo Alto: Stanford University Press.

Cohen, Hermann. 1922. *Logik der reinen Erkenntnis*. Berlin: Bruno Cassirer Verlag.

Coxon, A.H. 2009. *The Fragments of Parmenides*. Las Vegas: Parmenides Publishing.

Dahlstrom, Daniel. 2005. Heidegger's Transcendentalism. *Research in Phenomenology* 35: 29–54.

———. 2009. *Heidegger's Concept of Truth*. Cambridge: Cambridge University Press.

———. 2011. Being at the Beginning: Heidegger's Interpretation of Heraclitus. In *Interpreting Heidegger: Critical Essays*, ed. D. Dahlstrom, 135–155. Cambridge: Cambridge University Press.

Dastur, Françoise. 1996. *Death: An Essay on Finitude*. Trans. John Llewelyn. London: Athlone.

———. 2013. Heidegger and the Question of the "Essence" of Language. In *Heidegger and Language*, ed. Jeffrey Powell, 224–239. Bloomington: Indiana University Press.

Davis, Bret. 2007. *Heidegger and the Will: On the Way to Gelassenheit*. Evanston: Northwestern University Press.

de Beistegui, Miguel. 2003a. The Transformation of the Sense of Dasein in Heidegger's *Beiträge zur Philosophie*. *Research in Phenomenology* 33: 221–246.

———. 2003b. *Thinking with Heidegger: Displacements*. Bloomington and Indianapolis: Indiana University Press.

© Springer Nature Switzerland AG 2021

J. A. Niederhauser, *Heidegger on Death and Being*,

https://doi.org/10.1007/978-3-030-51375-7

———. 2004. *Truth and Genesis: Philosophy as Differential Ontology*. Bloomington: Indiana University Press.

De Gennaro, Ivo. 2001. *Logos: Heidegger liest Heraklit*. Berlin: Duncker & Humblot.

———. 2012. Nietzsche: Value and the Economy of the Will to Power. In *Values Sources and Readings on a Key Concept of the Globalized World*, ed. Ivo De Gennaro, 201–234. Leiden: Brill Publishing.

———. 2013. *The Weirdness of Being: Heidegger's Unheard Answer to the Seinsfrage*. Durham: Acumen.

Demske, James. 1970. *Being, Man, and Death: A Key to Heidegger*. Lexington: University Press of Kentucky.

Derrida, Jacques. 1990. Heidegger's Silence. In *Martin Heidegger and National Socialism: Questions and Answers*, ed. G. Neske and E. Kettering. Trans. L. Harries and J. Neugroschel. New York: Paragon House.

Dreyfus, Hubert L. 2009. Heidegger on Gaining a Free Relation to Technology. In *Readings in the Philosophy of Technology*, ed. D. Kaplan, 53–62. Lanham: Rowman & Littlefield.

Faye, Emmanuel. 2009. *Heidegger: The Introduction of Nazism into Philosophy in Light of the Unpublished Seminars of 1933-1935*. New Haven: Yale University Press.

Figal, Günter. 2013. *Martin Heidegger: Phänomenologie der Freiheit*. Tübingen: Mohr Siebeck.

Gadamer, Hans-Georg. 1986. *Gesammelte Werke Band 2: Hermeneutik II: Wahrheit und Methode*. Tübingen: Mohr Siebeck Verlag.

Givsan, Hassan. 2011. *Zu Heidegger: ein Nachtrag zu "Heidegger - das Denken der Inhumanität"*. Würzburg: Königshausen & Neumann.

Goethe, J.W. 1874. *The Poems of Goethe*, 1874. Trans. E.A. Bowring. London: George Bell and Sons.

Golob, Sacha. 2014. *Heidegger on Concepts, Freedom and Normativity*. Cambridge: Cambridge University Press.

Gonzalez, Francisco J. 2008. And the Rest Is *Sigetik*: Silencing Logic and Dialectic in Heidegger's *Beiträge zur Philosophie*. *Research in Phenomenology* 38: 358–391.

Gottschlich, Max. 2017. Das Problem von Sprache und Weltansicht bei Hamann, Herder und Humboldt. *Allgemeine Zeitschrift für Philosophie* 42 (3): 261–278.

Gourdain, Sylvaine. 2017. *L'éthos de l'im-possible Dans le sillage de Heidegger et Schelling*. Paris: Hermann Editions.

Guignon, Charles. 2005. The History of Being. In *A Companion to Heidegger*, ed. H.L. Dreyfus and M.A. Wrathall, 392–406. Oxford: Blackwell Publishing.

Gumbrecht, Hans Ulrich. 2003. *1926: Ein Jahr am Rand der Zeit*. Berlin: Suhrkamp.

Haar, Michel. 1993. *Heidegger and the Essence of Man*. Trans. W. McNeill. Albany: Suny Press.

Hahn, Charles H. 1987. *The Art and Thought of Heraclitus: An Edition of the Fragments with Translation and Commentary*. Cambridge: Cambridge University Press.

Harari, Yuval Noah, and Daniel Kahnemann. 2015. Death is Optional. In *Edge*. https://www.edge.org/conversation/yuval_noah_harari-daniel_kahneman-death-is-optional (accessed 10th June 2019).

Hegel, G.W.F. 2010. *Science of Logic*. Trans. George Di Giovanni. Cambridge: Cambridge University Press.

———. 2018. *The Phenomenology of Spirit*. Trans. Michael Inwood. Oxford: Oxford University Press.

Hoffman, Piotr. 2005. Dasein and "Its" Time. In *A Companion to Heidegger*, ed. H.L. Dreyfus and M.A. Wrathall, 325–334. Oxford: Blackwell Publishing.

Hölderlin, Friedrich. 1994. *Poems and Fragments*. Trans. Michael Hamburger. Oxford: Anvil Press Poetry.

———. 2008. In *Gesammelte Werke*, ed. H.J. Balmes. Berlin: Fischer Verlag.

Houlgate, Stephen. 2006. *The Opening of Hegel's Logic: From Being to Infinity*. West Lafayette: Purdue University Press.

————. 2009. *An Introduction to Hegel: Freedom, Truth and History.* Oxford: Blackwell Publishing.

Husserl, Edmund. 1985. *Einleitung in die Logik und Erkenntnistheorie. Vorlesungen 1906/07. Husserliana 24.* The Hague: Martinus Nijhoff.

————. 1989. *Ideas Pertaining to a Pure Phenomenology and to a Phenomenological Philosophy: Second Book Studies in the Phenomenology of Constitution.* Dordrecht: Kluwer Academic Publishers.

Hutter, Axel. 2003. Das Unvordenkliche der menschlichen Freiheit: Zur Deutung der Angst bei Schelling und Kierkegaard. In *Kierkegaard und Schelling: Freiheit, Angst und Wirklichkeit,* ed. J. Hennigfeld and J. Stewart, 117–132. Berlin: Walter de Gruyter Verlag.

Ionel, Lucian. 2017. Sinn und Verbergung. Heideggers Theorie über die Konstitution von Bedeutsamkeit. In *Perspektiven mit Heidegger: Zugänge, Pfade, Anknüpfungen,* ed. G. Thonhauser, 207–223. Freiburg: Alber Verlag.

Keiling, Tobias. 2015. *Seinsgeschichte und phänomenologischer Realismus: Eine Interpretation und Kritik der Spätphilosophie Heideggers.* Tübingen: Mohr Siebeck.

Koch, Dietmar. 2007. "Das erbringende Eignen". Zu Heideggers Konzeption des Eigenwesens im Ereignis-Denken. In *Das Spätwerk Heideggers. Ereignis – Sage – Geviert,* ed. D. Barbaric, 98–107. Würzburg: Königshausen & Neumann.

————. 2012. Negativität und Geschichte. Zu Heideggers Auseinandersetzung mit Hegels Negativitätsbegriff im Kontext des "Anderen Anfangs". In *Zblizavanja. Zbornik povodom sezdesete obljetnice zivota Damira Barbarica,* ed. O. Zunec and P. Segedin. Zagreb: Matica Hrvatska.

Lehmann, Karl. 2003. *Vom Ursprung und Sinn der Seinsfrage im Denken Martin Heideggers.* http://www.freidok.uni-freiburg.de/volltexte/7/ (accessed 12th September 2013. Written in 1961/62).

Leibniz, G.W. 1991. *Leibniz's Monadology.* Trans. Nicolas Rescher. Pittsburgh: University of Pittsburgh Press.

Magnus, Bernd. 1970. *Heidegger's Metahistory of Philosophy: Amor Fati, Being and Truth.* Heidelberg: Springer.

Mandelstam, Ossip. 2001. In *The Poet's Dante,* ed. P.S. Hawkins and R. Jacoff. New York: Farrar, Straus and Giroux.

Marinopoulou, Anastasia. 2017. *Critical Theory and Epistemology: The Politics of Modern Thought and Science.* Manchester: Manchester University Press.

Marx, Werner. 1983. *Is There a Measure on Earth? Foundations for a Nonmetaphysical Ethics.* Trans. T.J. Nenon and R. Lilly. Chicago: University of Chicago Press.

Megill, Allan. 1985. *Prophets of Extremity: Nietzsche, Heidegger, Foucault, Derrida.* Berkeley: University of California Press.

Mitchell, Andrew. 2010. The Fourfold. In *Martin Heidegger: Key Concepts,* ed. B. Davis, 208–218. Durham: Acumen Publishing.

————. 2015. *Fourfold: Reading the Late Heidegger.* Evanston: Northwestern University Press.

Müller, Max. 1964. *Existenzphilosophie im Geistigen Leben der Gegenwart.* Heidelberg: F.H. Kerle Verlag.

Müller-Lauter, Wolfgang. 1960. *Möglichkeit und Wirklichkeit bei Martin Heidegger.* Berlin: De Gruyter.

Natorp, Paul. 2004. *Philosophische Systematik.* Hamburg: Meiner Verlag.

Nelson, Eric S. 2011. Individuation, Responsiveness, Translation: Heidegger's Ethics. In *Heidegger, Translation, and the Task of Thinking: Essays in Honor of Parvis Emad,* ed. Frank Schalow. New York: Springer Science and Business.

Niederhauser, Johannes Achill. 2017a. Death as World Collapse or Death as World Enabling Condition? A Response to Iain Thomson. In *Perspektiven mit Heidegger: Zugänge, Pfade, Anknüpfungen,* ed. G. Thonhauser, 177–190. Freiburg: Alber Verlag.

————. 2017b. Das Sein zum Tode als Weg aus der Seinsvergessenheit? *Perspektiven der Philosophie* 43: 114–136.

Nietzsche, Friedrich. 2003. *The Gay Science*. Trans. J. Nauckhoff, ed. B. Williams. Cambridge: Cambridge University Press.

Oberst, Joachim. 2009. *Heidegger on Language and Death: The Intrinsic Connection in Human Existence*. London: Continuum.

Pattison, George. 2016. *Heidegger on Death: A Critical Theological Essay*. London: Routledge.

Pöggeler, Otto. 1983. *Heidegger und die hermeneutische Philosophie*. Freiburg: Alber-Broschur.

Polt, Richard. 2006. *The Emergency of Being: On Heidegger's "Contributions to Philosophy"*. Ithaca: Cornell University Press.

———. 2013. The Secret Homeland of Speech: Heidegger on Language, 1933–1934. In *Heidegger and Language*, ed. J. Powell, 63–85. Bloomington: Indiana University Press.

Porsche-Ludwig, Markus. 2009. *Wegmarken normativer Poltik (wissenschaft)*. Zürich: Lit-Verlag.

Richardson, William J. 1963. *Heidegger: Through Phenomenology to Thought*. Heidelberg: Springer.

Rilke, Rainer Maria. 2013. *Gesammelte Werke*. Köln: Anaconda Verlag.

Robson, David. 2017. The Birth of Half-human, Half-animal Chimeras. *BBC*. http://www.bbc.com/earth/story/20170104-the-birth-of-the-human-animal-chimeras (accessed 2nd April 2018).

Römer, Inga. 2010. *Das Zeitdenken bei Husserl, Heidegger und Ricoeur*. Heidelberg: Springer.

Ruin, Hans. 2010. *Ge-stell*: Enframing as the Essence of Technology. In *Martin Heidegger: Key Concepts*, ed. B. Davis, 183–194. Durham: Acumen Publishing.

Sallis, John. 1990. *Echoes: After Heidegger*. Indianapolis: Indiana University Press.

Schalow, Frank. 2001. *Heidegger and the Quest for the Sacred: From Thought to the Sanctuary of Faith*. New York: Springer Science and Business.

Schelling, F.W.J. 1979. Über die Natur der Philosophie als Wissenschaft. In *Schellings Werke: Fünfter Hauptband. Schriften zur geschichtlichen Philosophie 1821 – 1854*, ed. M. Schröter. München: C.H. Beck Verlag.

Scherer, Georg. 1979. *Das Problem des Todes in der Philosophie*. Darmstadt: Wissenschaftliche Buchgesellschaft.

Schmid, Holger. 2014. Logos and the Essence of Technology. In *The Multidimensionality of Hermeneutic Phenomenology*, ed. B. Babich and D. Ginev, 207–223. Heidelberg: Springer.

Schmidt, Dennis J. 1988. *The Ubiquity of the Finite: Hegel, Heidegger, and the Entitlements of Philosophy*. Cambridge, MA: MIT Press.

———. 2013. Truth Be Told: Homer, Plato, and Heidegger. In *Heidegger and Language*, ed. J. Powell, 163–179. Bloomington: Indiana University Press.

Sheehan, Thomas. 2010. The Turn. In *Martin Heidegger: Key Concepts*, ed. Bret Davis, 82–97. Durham: Acumen Publishing.

Singh, R. Raj. 2013. *Heidegger, World, and Death*. Lanham: Rowman & Lexington Publishing.

Sommer, Konstanze. 2015. *Zwischen Metaphysik und Metaphysikkritik: Heidegger, Schelling und Jacobi*. Hamburg: Felix Meiner Verlag.

Staehler, Tanja. 2016. *Hegel, Husserl and the Phenomenology of Historical Worlds*. London: Policy Network.

Thomson, Iain. 2000. Ontotheology? Understanding Heidegger's *Destruktion* of Metaphysics. *International Journal of Philosophical Studies* 8 (3): 297–327.

———. 2005. *Heidegger on Ontotheology: Technology and the Politics of Education*. Cambridge: Cambridge University Press.

———. 2011. *Heidegger, Art, and Postmodernity*. Cambridge: Cambridge University Press.

———. 2013. Death and Demise in *Being and Time*. In *The Cambridge Companion to Heidegger's Being and Time*, ed. M. Wrathall, 260–290. Cambridge: Cambridge University Press.

Trawny, Peter. 2003. *Heidegger Einführung*. Frankfurt am Main: Campus Verlag.

———. 2016. Heidegger and The Shoah. In *Reading Heidegger's Black Notebooks 1931–1941*, ed. I. Farin and J. Malpas, 169–180. Cambridge, MA: MIT Press.

Vallega, Alejandro. 2003. *Heidegger and the Issue of Space. Thinking on Exilic Grounds*. University Park: Penn State University Press.

Vallega-Neu, Daniela. 2003. *Heidegger's Contributions to Philosophy: An Introduction*. Bloomington and Indianapolis: Indiana University Press.

———. 2010. *Ereignis*: The Event of Appropriation. In *Martin Heidegger: Key Concepts*, ed. Bret Davis, 140–154. Durham: Acumen Publishing.

———. 2013. Heidegger's Poietic Writings: From *Contributions to Philosophy* to *Das Ereignis*. In *Heidegger and Language*, ed. J. Powell, 119–145. Bloomington: Indiana University Press.

———. 2015. Heidegger's Reticence: From *Contributions* to *Das Ereignis* and Toward *Gelassenheit*. *Research in Phenomenology* 45: 1–32.

von Herrmann, Friedrich-Wilhelm. 1987. *Hermeneutische Phänomenologie des Daseins. Ein Kommentar zu Sein und Zeit: Bd. 1 (§ 1-8)*. Frankfurt am Main: Vittorio Klostermann.

Weston, Nancy. 2016. Thinking the Oblivion of Thinking: The Unfolding of *Machenschaft* and *Rechnung* in the Time of the *Black Notebooks*. In *Reading Heidegger's Black Notebooks 1931–1941*, ed. I. Farin and J. Malpas, 269–288. Cambridge, MA: MIT Press.

Wild, Markus. 2013. Tierphilosophie bei Heidegger, Agamben, Derrida. *Journal Phänomenologie* 40: 23–35.

Wisser, Richard. 1970. *Martin Heidegger im Gespräch*. Freiburg: Alber Verlag.

Wolfson, Elliot R. 2018. *The Duplicity of Philosophy's Shadow: Heidegger, Nazism, and the Jewish Other*. New York: Columbia University Press.

Wrathall, Mark. 2010. *Heidegger and Unconcealment: Truth, Language, and History*. Cambridge: Cambridge University Press.

Works by Heidegger

GA 3 Gesamtausgabe, Vol. 3: *Kant und das Problem der Metaphysik*. F.-W. von Herrmann, ed. Frankfurt am Main: Vittorio Klostermann, 1991.

GA 4 *Gesamtausgabe*, Vol. 4: *Erläuterungen zu Hölderlins Dichtung*. F.-W. von Herrmann, ed. Frankfurt am Main: Vittorio Klostermann, 1981.

GA 5 *Gesamtausgabe*, Vol. 5: *Holzwege*. F.-W. von Herrmann, ed. Frankfurt am Main: Vittorio Klostermann, 1977.

GA 6.1 *Gesamtausgabe*, Vol. 6.1: *Nietzsche I (1936 - 1939)*. B. Schillbach, ed. Frankfurt am Main: Vittorio Klostermann, 1996.

GA 7 *Gesamtausgabe*, Vol. 7: *Vorträge und Aufsätze*. F.-W. von Herrmann, ed. Frankfurt am Main: Vittorio Klostermann, 2000.

GA 8 *Gesamtausgabe*, Vol. 8: *Was heißt Denken?* P.-L. Coriando, ed. Frankfurt am Main: Vittorio Klostermann, 2002.

GA 9 *Gesamtausgabe*, Vol. 9: *Wegmarken*. F.-W. von Herrmann, ed. Frankfurt am Main: Vittorio Klostermann, 1976.

GA 10 *Gesamtausgabe*, Vol. 10: *Der Satz vom Grund*. P. Jaeger, ed. Frankfurt am Main: Vittorio Klostermann, 1997.

GA 11 *Gesamtausgabe*, Vol. 11: *Identität und Differenz*. F.-W. von Herrmann, ed. Frankfurt am Main: Vittorio Klostermann, 2006.

GA 12 *Gesamtausgabe*, Vol. 12: *Unterwegs zur Sprache*. F.-W. von Herrmann, ed. Frankfurt am Main: Vittorio Klostermann, 1985.

GA 13 *Gesamtausgabe*, Vol. 13: *Aus der Erfahrung des Denkens*. H. Heidegger, ed. Frankfurt am Main: Vittorio Klostermann, 1983.

GA 14 *Gesamtausgabe*, Vol. 14: *Zur Sache des Denkens*. F.-W. von Herrmann, ed. Frankfurt am Main: Vittorio Klostermann, 2007.

GA 15 *Gesamtausgabe*, Vol. 15: *Seminare*. C. Ochwadt, ed. Frankfurt am Main: Vittorio Klostermann, 1986.

GA 16 *Gesamtausgabe*, Vol. 16: *Reden und andere Zeugnisse eines Lebensweges*. H. Heidegger, ed. Frankfurt am Main: Vittorio Klostermann, 2000.

GA 20 *Gesamtausgabe*, Vol. 20: *Prolegomena zur Geschichte des Zeitbegriffs*. P. Jaeger, ed. Frankfurt am Main: Vittorio Klostermann, 1979.

GA 22 *Gesamtausgabe*, Vol. 22: *Die Grundbegriffe der antiken Philosophie*. Blust, F.-K., ed. Frankfurt am Main: Vittorio Klostermann, 2004.

GA 25 *Gesamtausgabe*, Vol. 25: *Phänomenologische Interpretation von Kants Kritik der reinen Vernunft*. I. Görland, Frankfurt am Main: Vittorio Klostermann, 1995.

GA 26 *Gesamtausgabe*, Vol. 26: *Metaphysische Anfangsgründe der Logik im Ausgang von Leibniz*. K. Held, ed. Frankfurt am Main: Vittorio Klostermann, 2007.

GA 29/30 *Gesamtausgabe*, Vol. 29-30: *Die Grundbegriffe der Metaphysik: Welt - Endlichkeit - Einsamkeit*. F.-W. von Herrmann, ed. Frankfurt am Main: Vittorio Klostermann, 1983.

GA 32 *Gesamtausgabe*, Vol. 32: *Hegels Phänomenologie des Geistes*. I. Görland, ed. Frankfurt am Main: Vittorio Klostermann, 1997.

GA 33 *Gesamtausgabe*, Vol. 33: *Aristoteles: Metaphysik IX, 1-3*. H. Hüni, ed. Frankfurt am Main: Vittorio Klostermann, 2006.

GA 34 *Gesamtausgabe*, Vol. 34: *Vom Wesen der Wahrheit: Zu Platons Höhlengleichnis und Theätet*. H. Mörchen, ed. Frankfurt am Main: Vittorio Klostermann, 1988.

GA 40 *Gesamtausgabe*, Vol. 40: *Einführung in die Metaphysik*. P. Jaeger, ed. Frankfurt am Main: Vittorio Klostermann, 1983.

GA 45 *Gesamtausgabe*, Vol. 45: *Grundfragen der Philosophie: Ausgewählte "Probleme" der "Logik"*. F.-W. von Herrmann, ed. Frankfurt am Main: Vittorio Klostermann, 1984.

GA 54 *Gesamtausgabe*, Vol. 54: *Parmenides*. M. Frings, ed. Frankfurt am Main: Vittorio Klostermann, 1992.

GA 58 *Gesamtausgabe*, Vol. 58: *Grundprobleme der Phänomenologie*. H.-H. Gander, ed. Frankfurt am Main: Vittorio Klostermann, 1993.

GA 65 *Gesamtausgabe*, Vol. 65: *Beiträge zur Philosophie (Vom Ereignis)*. F.-W. von Herrmann, ed. Frankfurt am Main: Vittorio Klostermann, 1989.

GA 67 *Gesamtausgabe*, Vol. 67: *Metaphysik und Nihilismus*. H.-J. Friedrich, ed. Frankfurt am Main: Vittorio Klostermann, 1999.

GA 68 *Gesamtausgabe*, Vol. 68: *Hegel*. I. Schüssler, ed. Frankfurt am Main: Vittorio Klostermann, 1993.

GA 70 *Gesamtausgabe*, Vol. 70: *Über den Anfang*. P.-L. Coriando, ed. Frankfurt am Main: Vittorio Klostermann, 2005.

GA 71 *Gesamtausgabe*, Vol. 71: *Das Ereignis*. F.-W. von Herrmann, ed. Frankfurt am Main: Vittorio Klostermann, 2009.

GA 76 *Gesamtausgabe*, Vol. 76: *Leitgedanken zur Entstehung der Metaphysik, der neuzeitlichen Wissenschaft und der modernen Technik*. C. Strube, ed. Frankfurt am Main: Vittorio Klostermann, 2009.

GA 79 *Gesamtausgabe*, Vol. 79: *Bremer und Freiburger Vorträge*. P. Jaeger, ed. Frankfurt am Main: Vittorio Klostermann, 1994.

GA 81 *Gesamtausgabe*, Vol. 81: *Gedachtes*. P.-L. Coriando, ed. Frankfurt am Main: Vittorio Klostermann, 2007.

GA 89 *Gesamtausgabe*, Vol. 89: *Zollikoner Seminare*. P. Trawny, ed. Frankfurt am Main: Vittorio Klostermann, 2017.

GA 90 *Gesamtausgabe*, Vol. 90: *Zu Ernst Jünger*. P. Trawny, ed. Frankfurt am Main: Vittorio Klostermann, 2004.

GA 97 *Gesamtausgabe*, Vol. 97: *Anmerkungen I-V (Schwarze Hefte 1942-1948)*. Peter Trawny, ed. Frankfurt am Main: Vittorio Klostermann, 2015.

Heidegger, Martin. 1989. *Überlieferte Sprache und Technische Sprache*. St. Gallen: Erker Verlag.

———. 1999. Das Sein (Ereignis). In *Heidegger Studies, Vol. 15, Renewal of Philosophy, Questions of Theology, and Being-historical Thinking*, 9–15. Berlin: Duncker & Humblot GmbH.

Translations of Heidegger

Heidegger, Martin. 1968. *What is Called Thinking?* Trans. F.D. Wieck and J. Glenn Gray. New York: Harper & Row.

———. 1971a. *On the Way to Language.* Trans. Peter D. Hertz. New York: Harper & Row.

———. 1971b. *Poetry, Language, Thought.* Trans. Albert Hofstadter. New York: Harper & Row.

———. 1974. *Identity and Difference.* Trans. Joan Stambaugh. New York: Harper Torchbooks.

———. 1975. *Early Greek Thinking.* Trans. D.F. Krell and F.A. Capuzzi. New York: Harper & Row.

———. 1977. *The Question Concerning Technology and Other Essays.* Trans. William Lovitt. New York: Harper & Row.

———. 1985. *History of the Concept of Time: Prolegomena.* Trans. Theodore Kisiel. Bloomington: Indiana University Press.

———. 1988. *Hegel's Phenomenology of Spirit.* Trans. P. Emad and K. May. Bloomington: Indiana University Press.

———. 1990. *Kant and the Problem of Metaphysics.* Trans. Richard Taft. Bloomington: Indiana University Press.

———. 1991. *Nietzsche, Volume I: The Will to Power and Art.* Trans. D.F. Krell. New York: Harper & Row.

———. 1992. *Parmenides.* Trans. A. Schuwer and R. Rojcewicz. Bloomington and Indianapolis: Indiana University Press.

———. 1995a. *Aristotle's Metaphysics Θ 1-3: On the Essence and Actuality of Force.* Trans. W. Brogan and P. Warnek. Bloomington: Indiana University Press.

———. 1995b. *The Fundamental Concepts of Metaphysics: World, Finitude, Solitude.* Trans. W. McNeill and N. Walke. Bloomington: Indiana University Press.

———. 1996a. *Being and Time.* Trans. Joan Stambaugh. Albany: New York State University Press.

———. 1996b. *The Principle of Reason.* Trans. Reginald Lilly. Bloomington: Indiana University Press.

———. 1998. In *Pathmarks,* ed. William McNeill. Cambridge: Cambridge University Press.

———. 2000a. *Elucidations of Hölderlin's Poetry.* Trans. Keith Hoeller. New York: Humanity Books.

———. 2000b. *Introduction to Metaphysics.* Trans. G. Fried and R. Polt. New Haven: Yale University Press.

———. 2001. *Zollikon Seminars: Protocolls – Conversations – Letters.* Trans. Franz Mayr and Richard Askay. Evanston: Northwestern University Press.

———. 2002. *Off the Beaten Track.* Trans. J. Young and K. Haynes. Cambridge: Cambridge University Press.

———. 2009. *The Event.* Trans. Richard Rojcewicz. Bloomington and Indianapolis: Indiana University Press.

———. 2012a. *Bremen and Freiburg Lectures: Insight into that Which Is and Basic Principles of Thinking.* Trans. A.J. Mitchell. Bloomington: Indiana University Press.

———. 2012b. *Contributions to Philosophy.* Trans. Richard Rojcewicz and Daniela Vallega-Neu. Bloomington: Indiana University Press.

———. 2015. *Hegel.* Trans. J. Arel and N. Feuerhahn. Bloomington: Indiana University Press.

Index

A
Abgeschiedener, 244
Abstraction, 31
Abysmal, 116
Accepting death, 52
Actualisation, 35, 56, 58
Agriculture, 183
Agriculture food production, 182
Aletheiatic turning, 89
Aletheiological thinking, 80–81
Analogy, 69
Analogy of the Cave, 75, 78–82
Analytic of temporality, 61
Angst, 30, 36
Animals, 231
Anspruch, 198
Anthropology, 24, 62
Antiquarian, 65
Anwesen, 13
Ap-propriation, 36
A priori, 29
Aristotelian, 58
Atomic bomb, 230
Attunement, 30
Authentic being a self, 41
Authentic future, 45
Authenticity, 39, 44
Authentic repetition, 65

B
Bearing silence, 218
Being
  meaning, 15
  temporal disclosure, 14

traditional assumption, 14
transcendens, 25–31
universal concept, 14
Being-able-to-be-whole, 49–51
Being-ahead-of-itself, 35
Being and Time, 73, 74, 162, 198, 221, 239–241, 246
  analysis of death, 19
  analytic of death, 11, 56
  automatism, 211
  being-toward-death, 135
  "claim" of being itself, 211
  communication, 211
  Dasein, 2, 4
  death and demise, 9
  death brings, 6
  demise, 10
  ecstatic temporality, 6
  Ereignis, 5
  existential-ontological, 56
  Heidegger's thinking path, 5
  Iain Thomson's interpretation of death, 10
  Jakob Böhme, 10
  language, 182
  later Heidegger, 177
  limitations, 29
  mortality, 10
  ontology, 5–7
  possibility, 12, 58
  radical *futurity*, 6
  Seinsgeschichte, 5
  technological tools, 140
  thinking, 5
  understanding, 17
  ur-possibility, 55

Printed in Great Britain
by Amazon

79726615R00169